# HISTORY

## OF THE

# AMERICAN THEATRE:

## BEFORE THE REVOLUTION.

BY

GEORGE O. SEILHAMER.

---

GREENWOOD PRESS, PUBLISHERS
NEW YORK

#22893

TO

# AUGUSTIN DALY,

This Work is Inscribed by

## THE AUTHOR,

in Recognition of

His Rare Earnestness as a Student of Dramatic Literature,
Evinced by Revivals of the Works of the Masters;

His Faithful Adherence Throughout his Career as a Manager and
Dramatist to the Methods Which Make the Drama
an Art as well as a Business;

AND

His Enthusiasm in Gathering the Scattered Records of the
Stage, so that the Achievements of the Past may
do Honor to the Present, and Delight
and Instruct Posterity.

# CONTENTS.

1749-1774

# A History of the American Theatre:

## BEFORE THE REVOLUTION,

---

## CHAPTER I.

---

### THOMAS KEAN.

DAWN OF THE AMERICAN DRAMA—THE FIRST ACTOR WHO PLAYED
RICHARD III, AND CAPTAIN MACHEATH, IN AMERICA—WERE HE
AND HIS ASSOCIATES AMATEURS OR PROFESSIONAL PLAYERS?

THE dawn of the drama in America is unfortunately without a historian. This is the less to be regretted, however, because it was a dawn that emitted only a feeble light. It is known, for instance, that a regularly organized theatrical company played in New York as early as 1732. Whether the company was made up wholly of amateurs or whether it numbered among its members professional players from England makes little difference, because, as an attempt to transplant the drama to the Colonies, it had no effect upon the development of the American stage. Neither is it necessary to investigate the reputed theatrical visit of John Moody, afterwards a celebrated London comedian, to Jamaica, in 1745, as it in no way contributed to the introduction of the drama to this continent. Nor is the performance of Otway's "Orphan" at a coffee-house in King Street, in Boston, in 1750, by two young Englishmen, assisted by some young men of the town, to be looked upon as in itself a part of American dramatic history. The performance with which that history may be said to begin, was the production of Addison's "Cato" in Philadelphia, in August, 1749. The only direct information on this point is derived from a MS. journal left by John Smith, Esq.,[1] who was a son-in-law of James Logan. His testimony is important, because, brief as it is, his entry treats the theatre, as it then existed, from the standpoint of its possible development as a permanent force in society. That the Philadelphia season began with "Cato" is probable, but it is likely that other pieces were presented, and that a regular series of theatrical entertainments followed, since early in 1750 the Recorder, William Allen, afterwards Chief Justice of the Province, reported to the Common Council that certain persons had lately taken upon them to act plays in the city, and, as he was informed, they intended to make frequent practice thereof, he expressed the fear that their performances would be attended with mischievous effects. Among these evils he named the encouragement of idleness and the possibility of the performers "drawing great sums of money from weak and inconsiderate persons who are apt to be fond of such entertainment, though the performance

[1] ENTRY IN JOHN SMITH'S MS. JOURNAL.—Sixth Month (August) 22d, 1749.—Joseph Morris and I happened in at Peacock Bigger's, and drank tea there, and his daughter, being one of the company who were going to hear the tragedy of "Cato" acted, it occasioned some conversation, in which I expressed my sorrow that anything of the kind was encouraged.

be ever so mean and contemptible." In consequence of this present-ment, the board unanimously requested the Magistrates to take the most effectual measures for suppressing the "disorder," by sending for the actors and binding them to their good behavior.

Were these players professional actors or only amateurs?

In Watson's "Annals of Philadelphia" it is assumed that they "were Thespians of home-made production, of such untutored genius as had never trod the stage," while Dunlap in his "History of the American Theatre" declares that "as early as 1749 it is on record that the Magistracy of the city had been disturbed by some idle young men perpetrating the murder of sundry plays in the skirts of the town, but the culprits had been arrested and bound over to their good behavior after confessing their crime and promising to spare the poor poets for the future."

Neither the implied condemnation of the Recorder nor Dun-lap's snap judgment is to be taken as conclusive either that the per-formances were "mean and contemptible," or that the actors were "idle young men perpetrating the murder of sundry plays." A Recorder, who had probably never seen a play in his life, was not a competent critic, and Dunlap was only asserting what he knew nothing about. The historian of the American theatre had made up his mind that the drama in America should begin with the Hallam company, and so he contemptuously ignored all previous theatrical efforts.

The probabilities in the case of the Philadelphia performers of 1749 are that the company was made up in part of actors who had had some experience in England, and in part of amateurs who were desir-ous of adopting the stage as a profession. An aged colored man, Robert Venable, who was born in Philadelphia in 1736 and died in

1844, told John F. Watson that he "went to the first play at Plumstead's store;" that "the company there was genteel," and that many persons "fell out with Nancy Gouge because she went there to play." Mr. Watson throws doubt on Venable's statement in regard to seeing the first play at Plumstead's, but if Nancy Gouge, or George, played there at all, it was with Murray and Kean's Company, and not with Hallam's. That this company was to all intents a professional one is apparent from the fact that Nancy, although she may have been an amateur, went with it to New York, where she had a regular benefit in the spring of 1751 as a member of the same company that had previously played in Philadelphia.

It is worthy of remark that at the time the theatre was so earnestly opposed because of its evil influences, crime was common in Philadelphia. Highway robberies were of frequent occurrence, though the penalty was death, and by an odd coincidence, while Kean is supposed to have been playing in Plumstead's store, in September, 1749, a Mr. Garrick was stopped by a highwayman in Walnut Street, but gave the fellow a blow with his stick and managed to get away without being robbed.

There is no reason to doubt that "the company of comedians" from Philadelphia which appeared in New York for the first time on the 5th of March, in 1750, was substantially the same that Dunlap described as "some idle young men perpetrating the murder of sundry plays in the skirts of the town." The managers were the same, Messrs. Murray and Kean, and in both cities Thomas Kean played the leading roles, both in tragedy and comedy. Subsequently Mr. Kean described himself as a writer by profession, and John Tremain, another member of the company, was by trade a cabinet-maker. That Tremain, as an actor, was next in importance to Kean is apparent from the fact that his benefit in New York followed immediately after those of Murray and Kean. To assume that Tremain was no actor because he was a cabinet-maker, would be as unfair as to deny to John McCullough his character as a tragedian because he was a chairmaker, and because Thomas Kean spoke of resuming his employment of writing, no more proves that he had not learned the business of acting than the fact that William E. Burton edited the *Gentleman's Magazine* proves that he was not a comedian of distinguished merit. Indeed, it must be conceded that Robert Venable would not have been likely to remember the Philadelphia company of 1749 as a "genteel" one if it had been composed of amateurs, and it is not likely that a mere collection of barn-stormers, without any knowledge of stage business, would have been able to gather "a very numerous audience" in New York a year later to witness such a play as "Cato," in whose opinion, according to the *Weekly Postboy*, "it was pretty well performed." It seldom happens that a company of professionals in these later years is able to extort any higher praise from the press.

It is scarcely surprising that we should know little of the merits of Thomas Kean as an actor, in 1749–51, when the primitive state of the journalism of that epoch is considered. But that Kean was the first actor to attempt *Richard III* on the American stage is certain, and it is equally certain that he was the original *Captain Macheath* in the "Beggars' Opera" in America. On the 26th of February, 1750, the New York *Gazette*, revived in the *Weekly Postboy*, announced that a company of comedians had arrived the previous week from Philadelphia, and taken a room in Nassau Street, that formerly belonged to Rip Van Dam, as a playhouse. This announcement was afterwards copied by the *Pennsylvania Gazette*,[1] which is in itself a proof of the claim to regularity of the company. Had the performers been only some idle young men and women perpetrating the murder of sundry plays, it is not likely that their appearance in New York would have been regarded as legitimate news in Philadelphia, where they were well known.

The opening play was "King Richard III," with Kean as the crook-backed tyrant. Because the play was actually produced in that city March 5th, 1750, New York claims the honor of the first Shaksperean production in this country, but it is by no means certain that "Richard III" was not among the plays that caused the actors belonging to this company to be bound over to their good behavior in Philadelphia two months before. Whatever the fact in regard to the pieces that so scandalized the Philadelphians in 1749–50, "King Richard III" was the only one of Shakspere's plays given by Murray and Kean's company in New York during their first season in 1750. It was repeated on the 12th of March, together with the farce of "Beau in the Suds," and was followed by the "Spanish Fryar," Otway's "Orphan," and the "Beaux' Stratagem." "Richard III" was repeated on the 30th of

ADVERTISEMENT FOR MARCH 5, 1750.

———

By his EXCELLENCY'S Permission.
At the Theatre in Nassau Street,
This Evening will be presented
The Historical Tragedy of King Richard III.
Wrote originally by Shakespeare and altered by Colley Cibber, Esq.
Tickets to be had of the Printer hereof.
Pitt, 5s. Gallery, 3s.
To begin precisely at Half an Hour after 6 o'clock, and no person to be admitted behind the scenes.

---

[1] PENNSYLVANIA GAZETTE, MARCH 6TH, 1750.— New York, February 26th. — Last week arrived here a company of comedians from Philadelphia, who, we hear, have taken a convenient room for their purpose in one of the buildings lately belonging to the Hon. Rip Van Dam, deceased, in Nassau Street, where they intend to perform as long the season lasts, provided they meet with suitable encouragement.

April, with the "Mock Doctor," and the season closed July 23d with "Love for Love" and the "Stage Coach." The second season opened September 13th, 1750, with the "Recruiting Officer," and "Cato" was first produced a week later. According to the *Postboy* of September 24th, "Cato" attracted the largest houses ever seen in New York, whereupon that journal rejoiced that this fact showed that "the taste of the place was not so much vitiated or lost to a sense of liberty as not to prefer a representation of virtue to one of a loose character." But when "Cato" was repeated, a pantomime was added. During October, November and December, 1750, the plays that were new to New York were "Amphitryon," "George Barn-

MURRAY AND KEAN'S REPERTOIRE.

*Plays.*

| | |
|---|---|
| A Bold Stroke for a Wife, . . | Centlivre |
| Amphitryon, . . . . | Dryden |
| Beaux' Stratagem, . . . | Farquhar |
| Beggars' Opera, . . . | Gay |
| Busybody, . . . . | Centlivre |
| Cato, . . . . . | Addison |
| Distressed Mother, . . . | Philips |
| Fair Penitent, . . . . | Rowe |
| George Barnwell, . . . | Lillo |
| Love for Love, . . . | Congreve |
| Orphan, . . . . | Otway |
| Recruiting Officer, . . | Farquhar |
| Richard III, . . . | Shakspere |
| Sir Harry Wildair, . . . | Farquhar |
| Spanish Fryar, . . . | Dryden |

*Farces.*

| | |
|---|---|
| Beau in the Suds, . . | Anonymous |
| Damon and Phillida, . . | Cibber |
| Devil in the Wine-Cellar, . . | Coffey |
| Devil to Pay, . . . . | Hill |
| Hob in the Well, . . . | Cibber |
| Miss in her Teens, . . . | Garrick |
| Mock Doctor, . . . . | Fielding |
| Stage Coach, . . . . | Farquhar |
| Virgin Unmasked, . . | Fielding |

well," "A Bold Stroke for a Wife," the "Beggars' Opera" and the "Fair Penitent," with the farce of the "Lying Valet." Additional pieces were offered at the benefits, which began January 7th, 1751, although it is probable that most, if not all, of these had been previously presented during the regular season. Our knowledge of the work actually performed is necessarily incomplete, because the sources of information are confined to the few advertisements that have been preserved in the newspapers of the time. In Philadelphia Murray and

Kean did not advertise at all, and in New York but seldom.  A fair specimen of their announcements, when any were made, was the advertisement of Otway's "Orphan" in the *Weekly Postboy* of the 2d of April, 1750.  As the list stands, however, it must be looked upon as a formidable undertaking for mere amateurs, without professional training, or a knowledge of stage business, pretending to be a company of comedians from Philadelphia.

By his Excellency's Permission:
At the Theatre in *Nassau-street*, This evening will be presented
A TRAGEDY *called*
The ORPHAN, or the Unhappy Marriage.
To which will be added
A FARCE called, The
BEAU in the SUDS
Tickets to be had at the Theatre in Nassau-street and of the Printer hereof:
PITT, 5s.   GALLERY, 3s.
To begin precisely at half an Hour after 6 o'clock.

The benefits taken by the performers who seem to have held the highest rank in the company were those of Mr. Kean, Mr. Murray, Mr. Tremain, Mr. Scott, Mr. Woodham, Mrs. Taylor, Miss Osborne and Miss Nancy George.  Mrs. Taylor, who evidently was the leading lady, first announced her benefit in the *Weekly Postboy* of the 28th of January, 1750–51, but on the 18th of February she printed another announcement that is a model of theatrical frankness and simplicity.  Among the pieces played at the benefits were the "Recruiting Officer" and "Miss in Her Teens" for Tremain's, and "Cato" and the "Devil to Pay" for Scott's.  Murray's bill comprised "A Bold Stroke for a Wife," the "Devil to Pay" and

MRS. TAYLOR'S FIRST BENEFIT.

By his Excellency's Permission,
At the Theatre in *Nassau-street*
(For the Benefit of MRS. TAYLOR,)
ON Monday Evening next, will be presented
A Comedy called LOVE *for* LOVE, with entertainments of Singing and Dancing between the Acts.  To which will be added an Opera, called, The Devil to Pay; or, the Wives metamorphosed; . . . . . Those Gentlemen and Ladies who please to favor this Benefit are desired to send for Tickets either to the Theatre, or to the Printer's hereof.
Box, 5s.   Pitt, 4s.   Gallery, 2s.

"Colin and Phœbe," the sketch being "sung by Mr. Woodham and Mrs. Taylor in pastoral dresses." The pieces for Kean's benefit were the "Beggars' Opera," "Miss in Her Teens," and "an Oratorio to be sung by Mr. Kean." As an additional attraction "a Harlequin Dance, a Pierot Dance and the Drunken Peasant, all by a gentleman recently from London," were done between the acts. Whether it was that Kean was a very great favorite, or that the taste of New York had become so vitiated in a few months as to prefer

MRS. TAYLOR'S SECOND BENEFIT.

By his Excellency's Permission,
At the Theatre in Nassau-street,
(For the Benefit of Mrs. Taylor;)
On Monday the 25th Instant will be presented the tragical history of King Richard III. To which will be added a Ballad Opera called Dæmon and Philida and a favourite Dialogue called Jockey and Jenny to be sung by Mr. Woodham and Mrs. Taylor. As there wasn't much company at Love for Love, the Managers took the Profit arising by that Night to themselves and gave Mrs. Taylor another Benefit; who hopes that the Ladies and Gentlemen that favour'd the other Benefit will be so kind as to favour hers with their Company.

a play of loose character to one of virtue, the pernicious "Beggars' Opera" drew a larger house than that which had assembled to witness Addison's dull but virtuous "Cato." Kean had a bumper, but unfortunately not all to whom tickets had been sold were able to gain admittance. This occasioned great dissatisfaction, and to allay the storm Kean induced James Parker, the publisher of the *Postboy*, by whom the tickets were printed, to certify that, in all, the tickets printed were as follows:

161 Pit tickets,

10 Boxes,

121 Gallery.

Mr. Kean evidently was as keen as Mr. Boucicault in using the press to hoodwink the public; but as money was taken at the door, it is not difficult to understand how some of the ticket-holders came to be excluded. The principles taught on the stage that night seem to have been practiced in the front of the house for the benefit of the *Macheath* of the evening. But Kean's troubles did not stop with the dissatisfaction of the outsiders; the insiders also had a grievance. It was asserted that Mrs. Taylor "endeavored to perform her part in a worse manner than she was capable" in consequence of a falling out with Kean, whereupon he was again compelled to resort to the friendly columns of the *Postboy*, by means of a card in which he said: "There was no falling out between her and me, and I believe her being out so much in her part was owing to her not getting the part in time."

In those early days of the drama in America the theatrical business could not have been a very profitable one at best. Taking Mr. Parker's figures as the capacity of the New York Theatre in 1751, and the shillings in the scale of prices as New York shillings, the following would have been the result of Mr. Kean's benefit had no money been taken at the door:

| | |
|---|---|
| Boxes—10 at 5 shillings—50 . . . . | $6 25 |
| Pit—161 at 4 shillings—644, . . . . | 90 50 |
| Gallery—121 at 2 shillings—242, . . . | 30 00 |
| Total, . . . . . . . | $126 75 |

Even in shillings sterling a clear benefit would have amounted to only $253.50. It is not surprising, therefore, that before the close of the season Mr. Kean should announce that "by the advice of several gentlemen in town who are his friends" he had "resolved to quit the stage and follow his employment of writing, wherein he hopes for encouragement." Of course he took another benefit, and his announcement, taken in connection with the foregoing figures, will give an idea of the value of the theatrical properties of the New York Theatre at that time. The benefit was announced for April 29th, "Mr. Murray having agreed to give him a clear night of all his expenses for his half of the cloaths, scenes, etc.," of the playhouse. Kean announced "Richard III" for this occasion, "the part of *Richard* to be performed by Mr. Kean, being the last time of his appearing on the stage." Instead, however, he gave the "Busybody" and "Virgin Unmasked," and Mr. Woodham sang "Briton's Charter."

After Kean's retirement a number of benefit performances took place, including one for Master Dickey Murray; one for Mr. Moore and Mr. Marks, when "a comedy called 'Sir Harry Wildair,' being the sequel to 'The Trip to the Jubilee,' with a farce called 'Hob in the Well, or the Country Wake,'" was given; one for Mr. Jago, "as he has never had a benefit before and is just out of prison," and one for Mrs. Davis, "granted to enable her to buy off her time." The "Distressed Mother" was played for Mr. Jago's benefit, and Mrs. Davis' bill comprised "George Barnwell" and the "Devil in the Wine Cellar." Besides the Widow Osborne, whose advertisement

WIDOW OSBORNE'S ADVERTISEMENT.

On Monday next will be presented for the Benefit of the Widow *Osborne*, the *Distrest Mother* with several Entertainments to which will be added the *Beau in the Suds*. As 'tis the first Time this poor Widow has had a benefit, and having met with divers late Hardships and Misfortunes, 'tis hoped all Charitable Benevolent Ladies and others will favour her with their Company.

was a curiosity in its way, Mrs. Leigh and Mr. Smith were each accorded a benefit. Smith's was the last on the list. It took place July 8th, 1751, and then the house closed, and the company, of which Thomas Kean had been the bright and particular star, disbanded.

# CHAPTER II.

---

## ROBERT UPTON.

THE FIRST ADVANCE AGENT AND BUSINESS MANAGER IN AMERICA—
INITIAL PERFORMANCE OF "OTHELLO" IN THE AMERICAN COLO-
NIES—ARRAIGNMENT OF UPTON BY HALLAM.

THE first man in advance of a theatrical company in America
was Robert Upton. Upton's merits as an actor are not celebrated in the picturesque chapters of Doran's "Annals of the Stage,"
nor is his skill as a manager on record in the known pages of English
dramatic history. Such fame as is his—and it must be confessed it is
not creditable either to his integrity or his histrionic abilities—is
entirely confined to America. That he was an Englishman is to be
assumed, for he was sent from London to New York in 1751 to prepare the way for the Hallam company, which followed the next year.
In those days the most influential class in the community, especially
in Philadelphia, New York and Boston, was opposed to the theatre.
Puritan and Quaker and worthy Dutch burgher alike looked upon
the stage as the devil's workshop. In Philadelphia the first attempt
to give theatrical representations had been summarily crushed. Even
in New York there had been pronounced opposition to Murray and
Kean's company in 1750–51, and besides, it was necessary to obtain
the permission of the Governor of the Province in which it was
intended to perform. To obtain such permission for his principals
was Mr. Upton's first duty after his arrival in America. To build a

theatre, at least in New York, was also a part of the duty with which this advance agent was charged, as it was a fact well known in England that in America there were no buildings suited to the production of plays. The Philadelphia company in 1749 had performed in Plumstead's store. The same company, when it went to New York in 1750, was content with a room in Nassau Street. It is probable that only a temporary structure was intended by the projectors of the enterprise in behalf of which Upton was sent out from England, and it is on record that he was supplied with the funds necessary for the purpose. From all this it is plain that Robert Upton, the first advance agent and business manager in America, was charged with duties not less arduous than those that have devolved upon his successors.

There was no announcement of Robert Upton's arrival in New York in the newspapers of the time, which is a proof that the business manager of the period had not yet acquired all the arts of a press agent. Either the man in advance was more modest then than he is now or the newspapers were not so obliging. Whatever the time of Upton's departure from England or the indifference of the press to his arrival in America, it is known that he was in New York in December, 1751, where he made the acquaintance of John Tremain, actor and cabinet-maker. Mr. Upton, according to a card published by Lewis Hallam, in 1753, upon his arrival in New York "quite neglected the business he was sent about from England," but instead he joined his fortunes with "that sett of pretenders," the "company of comedians from Philadelphia," which had afforded the Knickerbockers "a taste of their quality" at intervals between March 5th, 1750, and July 8th, 1751. Upton's conduct after his arrival in America does not show him to have been a man of the strictest integrity, especially if, as was charged,

William Hallam[1] had supplied him with a sum of money with which to erect a theatre in New York. But the Hallam fling at the "sett of

[1] The Case of the *London* Company of COMEDIANS, lately arrived from *Virginia*:

As our Expedition to *New York* seems likely to be attended with a very fatal Consequence, and our selves haply censur'd for undertaking it, without Assurance of Success; we beg leave, humbly to lay a true State of our Case before the worthy Inhabitants of this City; if possible, endeavour to remove those great Obstacles which at present lie before us, and give very sufficient Reasons for our Appearance in this part of the World, where we all had the most sanguine Hopes of meeting a very different Reception; little imagining, that in a City, to all Appearance so polite as this, the Muses would be banished, the Works of the immortal *Shakespear*, and others the greatest Geniuses *England* ever produc'd, deny'd Admittance among them, and the instructive and elegant Entertainment of the Stage utterly protested against: When, without Boasting, we may venture to affirm, That we are capable of supporting its Dignity with proper Decorum and Regularity.

In the Infancy of this Scheme, it was proposed to Mr. *William Hallam*, now of *London*, to collect a Company of Comedians, and send them to *New York*, and the other Colonies in America. Accordingly he assented, and was at a vast expense to procure Scenes, Cloathes, People, &c. &c. And in *October* 1750, sent over to this Place, Mr. *Robert Upton*, in order to obtain Permission to perform, erect a Building, and settle every Thing against our Arrival; for which Service, Mr. *Hallam* advanc'd no inconsiderable Sum. But Mr. *Upton* on his Arrival found here that Sett of Pretenders, with whom he joined, and unhappily for us, quite neglected the Business he was sent about from *England*; for we never heard from him after.

Being thus deceived by him the Company was at a Stand, 'till *April* 1752, when by the Persuasion of several gentlemen in *London*, and *Virginia* Captains, we set sail on Board of Mr. *William Lee*, and arrived after a very expensive and tiresome Voyage, at *York* River, on the 28th of *June* following: Where we obtained Leave of his Excellency the Governor, and performed with universal Applause, and met with the greatest Encouragement; for which we are bound by the strongest Obligations, to acknowledge the many and repeated Instances of their Spirit and Generosity. We were there eleven Months before we thought of removing; and then asking Advice, we were again persuaded to come to *New York*, by several Gentlemen, &c. whose Names we can mention, but do not think proper to publish: They told us, that we should not fail of a genteel and favourable Reception; that the Inhabitants were generous and polite, naturally fond of Diversions rational, particularly those of the Theatre: Nay, they even told us, there was a very fine Play-house Building, and that we were really expected. This was Encouragement sufficient for us, as we thought, and we came firmly assured of Success; but how far our Expectations are answered, we shall leave to the Candid to determine, and only beg leave to add, That as we are People of no Estates, it cannot be supposed that we have a Fund sufficient to bear up against such unexpected Repulses. A Journey by Sea and Land Five Hundred Miles, is not undertaken without Money. Therefore, if the worthy Magistrates would consider this in our Favour, that it must rather turn out a publick Advantage and Pleasure, than a private Injury, They would, we make no Doubt, grant Permission, and give an Opportunity to convince them we were not cast in the same Mould with our Theatrical Predecessors; or that in private Life or publick Occupation, we have the Affinity to them.

pretenders" Upton found there, and with whom he joined, proves nothing. There never yet was a theatrical manager who did not look with disdain upon the pretensions of a rival company, but in every age the public has found that their depreciation of each other was nothing more than the pot calling the kettle black.

Mr. Hallam's manifesto shows the perfidy of Upton beyond all question, but it shows also that his defection was known in London before the Hallam company left England. Its importance, however, as a historical document is in the light it sheds upon the difficulties that beset the drama in its early days in America. There seems to be no doubt, from the tone of Hallam's card, that Upton's conduct had tended to bring the stage into disrepute in New York. It is not likely that this disfavor was purely professional. A want of integrity in Upton does not excuse Hallam's bitterness toward his predecessors, although his claims to superiority for his own company were probably effective in removing the prejudices that Upton had excited against all play-actors. But apart from these considerations, this card is interesting in being the first contribution toward the voluminous literature for and against the theatre that was written during the infancy of the American drama.

The outcome of Upton's desertion of the cause of his principals, in whose behalf he had been sent to pave the way in America, was a dramatic season in New York in the winter of 1751–52, with Upton himself as the star. These representations began December 26th, 1751, in the same room that had been occupied by Murray and Kean's company. The opening piece was "Othello," with Upton as the Moor. This was the second of Shakspere's plays produced on the American stage, and thus Robert Upton achieved the distinction of being the original *Othello* in America. It is probable that Tremain played *Iago* and that Mrs. Upton was the *Desdemona*. "Othello" was repeated on the 30th of December, and on the 6th of January, 1752, the "Provoked Husband" was produced, together with the farce of "Lethe." A week later there was another performance, the bill comprising the "Fair Penitent" and the "Miller of Mansfield." On the 23d of January Tremain had a benefit, when "Richard III" was given, with Upton as *Richard*. This play was repeated on the 17th of February for the benefit of Widow Osborne. Thus it will be seen that Upton was not only the first *Othello*, but the second *Richard* to tread the American boards. Such a repertoire demands better material than was likely to be at Upton's command, and so, unworthy as the manager's *Othello* and *Richard* must have been, it is not unlikely the other parts were even less acceptable.

UPTON'S REPERTOIRE.

*Plays.*

| | |
|---|---|
| Fair Penitent . . . . . . . . . . . | Rowe |
| Othello . . . . . . . . . . . | Shakspere |
| Provoked Husband . . . . . . | Vanbrugh |
| Richard III . . . . . . . . . | Shakspere |
| Venice Preserved . . . . . . . . | Otway |

*Farces.*

| | |
|---|---|
| Lethe . . . . . . . . . . . . . | Garrick |
| Miller of Mansfield . . . . . . . | Dodsley |

Upton did not meet with much encouragement in New York. His want of success, and not improbably a fear that Lewis Hallam would arrive and compel him to give an account of his stewardship, led him to determine upon a return to England early in 1752. Previous to his departure, on the 20th of February, Mrs. Upton took a benefit, "Venice Preserved" being the play. This performance was intended as the last night of the season, and was so announced, but as the vessel in which Mr. and Mrs. Upton were to make their return voyage was delayed, the "Fair Penitent" was repeated, with Mrs. Tremain in the part of *Lavinia*. It is to be assumed that this lady was the wife of John Tremain, and this was apparently her *debut*, as it was announced that she would "attempt" the part. At this performance "a farewell epilogue adapted to the occasion by Mr. Upton" was recited. From this it appears that Upton was not only the first business manager and the first *Othello* in America, but also the first "adapter" who had the courage to spoil the work of another for the American public.

It is a noteworthy fact that of the twenty plays and their attendant farces which comprised the repertoire of the Hallam company that was forming in England, while Murray and Kean's and Upton's companies were playing in New York, not fewer than five—"Richard III," "Beaux' Stratagem," the "Recruiting Officer," "George Barnwell" and the "Fair Penitent"—among the plays, and three—"Mock Doctor," "Lying Valet" and "Miss in her Teens"—among the farces, had been performed by Murray and Kean's company, while of the Hallam repertoire Upton added to the plays and farces produced before the arrival of the Hallams, "Othello," "Provoked Husband" and "Lethe." Besides, Murray and Kean had presented Otway's "Orphan," the "Spanish Fryar," "Love for Love," "Cato," "Amphitryon," "A Bold Stroke for a Wife" and the "Beggars' Opera," and the farces of "Beau in the Suds" and "Stage Coach," and Upton "Venice Preserved," and the farce, "Miller of Mansfield," which were not included in the Hallam repertoire. There is something exceedingly suggestive in this anticipation of seven out of twenty plays and four out of eight farces provided by the Hallams for their American campaign. Even when the Hallam company went outside of its original repertoire it was apt to find that it had been anticipated. Considering how determined Lewis Hallam was to ignore "that sett of pretenders" that had preceded him, it must have annoyed him to hear complaints about the production of "old pieces," or to receive requests for "something new," while the leading actors of his company no doubt had the mortification of being compared with their predecessors, whom they affected to despise.

Altogether fourteen plays and eight farces are known to have been produced in New York before the arrival of the Hallams, in 1752. Most of them were played more than once, and contemporary criticism shows that they were acceptably played. All this was done between the 5th of March, 1750, and the 4th of March, 1752— exactly two years. That mere amateurs should have accomplished so much in a city containing only seven thousand inhabitants, that they should have been "able to keep the house open" month after month, is contrary to all theatrical experience. Audiences in those days were at least as critical as they are now, as Mrs. Taylor discovered when she was believed to have played " her part in a worse manner than she was capable." Besides, the plays selected by Murray and Kean, and afterwards by Upton, were beyond the reach of mere amateurs. It is thus seen that argument as well as history is in favor of the professional claims of these early players.

It is to be regretted that so little is known in regard to these early actors. It is barely possible that Thomas was a brother or other relative of Aaron, the reputed father of Edmund Kean. It would be interesting to know something of the fortune that befell Robert Upton after his return to England. But the newspapers of those days were not much given to personal and especially theatrical journalism, and we may never hope to know even whether Mrs. Tremain's first night was her last.

# CHAPTER III.

____

## WILLIAM HALLAM.

THE FIRST "BACKER" WHO SENT A COMPANY ON THE ROAD IN AMERICA — WHO WERE THE HALLAMS? — HOW THE COMPANY WAS ORGANIZED, AND ITS REPERTOIRE.

THE first "backer" of an American theatrical enterprise, to use a modern phrase, was William Hallam. Dunlap calls this man "the father of the American stage," a title that he does not deserve. He was at most only a projector who sent a company of poor players to the New World to retrieve his own fortunes at home. It is an old story, believed to be true because it has been often repeated, that when Giffard retired from the management of the theatre in Goodman's Fields, where Garrick made his *debut* in 1741, William Hallam succeeded him. There does not seem to be any foundation for the story. After Giffard's retirement, in 1742, the Goodman's Fields' Theatre was closed, and there is no record in Genest's remarkably full history of the London stage of Hallam's management between that time and 1750, when Dunlap says he failed and was compelled to relinquish the undertaking. It is not unlikely, however, that Mr. Hallam was in some sense the manager of another theatre in Goodman's Fields, described as "at the Wells in Lemon Street." Giffard's was in Ayliffe Street. Adam Hallam, the father of William and Lewis Hallam, had a benefit at the Wells Theatre, in March, 1746. Subsequently this Lemon Street Theatre was "altered in a more theatrical manner, is made warm, and front boxes made at the upper end of the pit." Previously it had been used for rope dancing and performances of a low grade, but a Mrs. Hallam played there in legitimate roles in the autumn and winter of 1746, appearing on the 29th of October as *Lady Percy* in "Henry IV," on the 6th of November as *Angelica* in "Love for Love," and on the 22d of December as *Lady Outside* in "Woman's a Riddle." Genest notes that at this time there were three Hallams engaged at the theatre in Goodman's Fields, which was not the Goodman's Fields' Theatre—Hallam, Sr., L. Hallam and G. Hallam. There is no mention of W. Hallam, but he may

WILLIAM HALLAM'S BENEFIT.

1756.—William Hallam had a benefit at Sadler's Wells, Islington, on account, he said, of being turned out of his house, G. F. Wells.

have been the manager then, as he certainly was ten years later, as appears from a scrap record of the old Sadler's Wells Theatre, now in possession of Charles N. Mann, of Philadelphia. This is all the more probable since on the 5th of September, 1751, exactly one year before the first appearance of the Hallam company in America, at Williamsburg, Va., Mrs. Hallam had a benefit at the Lemon Street house, appearing as *Desdemona*, while Lewis Hallam played *Roderigo*. This is clearly the Lewis Hallam who was soon to sail for America, and the *Desdemona*, it may be assumed with safety, was his wife. It may also be assumed that the Mrs. Hallam who played *Lady Percy*, *Angelica* and *Lady Outside* at the Wells, in 1746, was the Mrs. Hallam who was the *Desdemona* there in 1751.

Little is known of William Hallam's personal history beyond the fact that he was a Whitechapel victualer, who was gazetted a bankrupt in 1745, but the accounts of him printed in Brown's "History of the American Stage" and "Dunlap's History of the American

Theatre" are amusing, if not instructive. In the former it is said that he "was an actor of great reputation at Goodman's Fields' Theatre, England," and then it is gravely asserted that "he was manager, but not actor." There is evidence that he played *Mother Coupler* in "Marina," a play taken from Shakspere's "Pericles," at Covent Garden for three nights, in 1738, and the *Poet* in the puppet-show called "The Pleasures of the Town," in Fielding's "Author's Farce," when it was acted at the Haymarket, in 1729, but beyond this there is no reason to suppose that William Hallam ever was an actor. If he was it is strange that nobody except Colonel Brown knows anything of his great reputation. That he was the successor of "the great Garrick" in any sense is simply preposterous. The last clause, "he was man-ager, but not actor," probably refers to his relations to the American Company, but of that his brother, Lewis Hallam, was manager, while he was only the backer. Dunlap is equally absurd. On winding up the business of the Goodman's Fields' Theatre, that acute historian says, "Hallam's debt proved five thousand pounds, a trifling sum as the amount of loss in such a complicated and hazardous speculation." If money had been worth only as much as now, instead of twice as much, $25,000 was rather large for a "trifling sum." Dunlap adds that "the accounts and conduct of Mr. Hallam were so fair and satis-factory to his creditors that they presented him with the wardrobe and other theatrical property of the establishment, thus discharging him from debt and leaving him in possession of a capital to commence business anew." These large-hearted creditors no doubt knew the exact value of the wardrobe and other theatrical properties of an old barn of a theatre at the Wells in Lemon Street, on the outskirts of London.

The Hallams, William and Lewis, were brothers of Admiral Hallam, of whom the cyclopædias do not condescend to give any account, and another brother, George Hallam, was the actor mentioned by Genest.  There was still another Hallam on the English stage, Thomas, who was killed by accident by the celebrated Charles Macklin, in the green-room at Drury Lane Theatre.  Thomas Hallam and Macklin were friends.  They were together at the Haymarket, in 1734, where Hallam played *Dr. Wrench* and Macklin *Squire Badger* in " Don Quixote in England," and together they went to Drury Lane.  There, on the 10th of May, 1735, they played the two servants in a farce called " Trick for Trick."  The farce was acted but once, in consequence of the fatal quarrel between Macklin and Hallam about a wig that Macklin had worn the night before in " Love Makes a Man." In his excitement Macklin ran a stick into Hallam's eye, as the result of which Hallam died the next day.  Macklin was tried at the Old Bailey and convicted of manslaughter.  His punishment was not severe, however, for in 1741, the year of Garrick's *debut*, he established his fame by playing *Shylock* for the first time as a serious part.  It is generally assumed that Thomas was an uncle of William and Lewis Hallam, but Mrs. Mattocks, who was a daughter of Lewis Hallam, is quoted as saying that he was a relation, but she did not know in what degree.  Dunlap, with the capacity for blundering for which he was remarkable, says this Hallam was a brother of Lewis and William.

According to Dunlap, Lewis Hallam was a member of his brother William's company at Goodman's Fields, and "sustained the first line of low comedian," while his wife, who was related to Mr. Rich, the manager of Covent, played the first line of tragedy and comedy.  "To have been the first low comedian and the first tragic and comic actress in a company which had to strive against Covent Garden and vie with Drury Lane, having Garrick for its leader," says that marvelous chronicler, "gives us reason to believe that Mr. and Mrs. Hallam were far above mediocrity in their profession, and tradition fully supports the belief." If the Hallams had been in Ayliffe Street, Goodman's Fields, instead of at the Wells in Lemon Street, it would have been up-hill work to strive against Covent Garden and vie with Drury Lane having Garrick for its leader, but in an old barn that had been "altered in a more theatrical manner," there could be no chance either to strive or to vie.

There is nothing in the annals of the English stage to indicate that either Lewis Hallam or his wife ever played at Covent Garden. It was his mother-in-law, Mrs. Anne Hallam, who was a relation of Rich, and his father, Adam Hallam, who was with his wife in Rich's company. This Mrs. Hallam was a large, unwieldly person, utterly unsuited to comedy parts or light tragedy roles long before the second Mrs. Hallam appeared at the Wells in Lemon Street, Goodman's Fields. Before she became Mrs. Hallam she was Mrs. Berriman, and before she became Mrs. Berriman she was known on the stage, both in London and the Provinces, as Mrs. Parker. Davies says that as Mrs. Parker she distinguished herself in the Norwich Theatre before she joined Rich in London, and she was with Rich as early as 1723 when he was still at the Theatre in Lincoln's Inn Fields. Even at this early period—thirty years before the appearance of the Hallams in New York and Philadelphia—she was an actress of mature powers, commanding the best of everything. When Rich went to Covent Garden she went with him, appearing as *Mrs. Marwood* in the "Way of the World" on his opening night, December

7th, 1732. She was then Mrs. Berriman, having changed her name in 1726. It is believed she married Berriman, an actor who played a small part in "Philip of Macedon," in 1727. On the 20th of September, 1731, she played *Isabella* in the "Conscious Lovers" as Mrs. Berriman, and on the 14th of December following she appeared in the same part as Mrs. Hallam. So quietly was her marriage with Mr. Hallam conducted that the celebrated Dr. Burney, who kept the cast-book at Covent Garden, wrote after the name of Mrs. Hallam on this occasion, "her first appearance on the stage," but he afterward scratched it out again. As an actress, Mrs. Hallam was a great favorite with the public in spite of her bulk, and even in parts for which her size made her unsuitable. How unsuited her appearance often was to her parts is illustrated by an anecdote that Davies relates of Quin. Seeing a barrel on the stage, the actor asked what it was. "Ah, I see,"

ANNE HALLAM'S PARTS.

———

*As Mrs. Parker—Lincoln's Inn Fields.*

**1723.**

Nov.  2.—Island Princess  . . . . Quisara
      4.—Tamerlane  . . . . . . Arpasia
   26.—Rival Queens  . . . . . Statira
Dec.  2.—Spanish Fryar  . . . . . Queen
    7.—Mariamne  . . . . . Mariamne

**1724.**

Feb. 24.—Edwin, King of Britain . Adeliza
Mar. 16.—Beaux' Stratagem  . Mrs. Sullen
   26.—King and No King  . . Spaconia
April 9.—Measure for Measure . . Isabella
   14.—Belisarius . . . . . . . Valeria
   28.—Merry Wives of Windsor
                 Mrs. Page
   29.—Don Sebastian  . . . . Almeyda
Sept. 23.—Œdipus  . . . . . . Jacasta
Oct. 22.—Richard III . . . . . . Queen

**1725.**

Jan. 27.—Bath Unmasked  . . . . Cleora
April 5.—Rover . . . . . . . . Angellica
Sept. 24.—Lear . . . . . . . . Cordelia
Oct.  4.—Country Wife . . . . . Alithea
   15.—Rival Queens . . . . . Roxana
   23.—Love's Last Shift . . . Amanda
   28.—Hamlet . . . . . . . . Queen
Nov.  2.—Double Dealer . Lady Touchwood
   11.—Rover . . . . . . Florinda
Dec.  2.—Macbeth . . . . Lady Macbeth
    7.—Æsop . . . . . . . Hortensia
    8.—Capricious Lovers . Mrs. Fading
   16.—Confederacy . . . . . Clarissa

**1726.**

Jan.  7.—Female Fortune Teller . Astræa
Mar. 19.—Provoked Wife . . . Lady Brute
   21.—She Would if She Could
               Lady Cockwood
April 22.—Henry VIII . . . . . . Queen

he said; "Mrs. Hallam's stays in which she played *Monimia* last night." In "Hamlet" Mrs. Hallam was the *Queen Mother* of Ryan, as Mrs. Porter was of Wilks. Davies says she died about 1738, but unless there were two Mrs. Hallam's at Covent Garden, the one succeeding to the other's professional rank and parts, her demise could not have occurred before 1740—in fact, June 6th, 1740.

Is it possible that such a startling hypothesis can be true?

There is only one thing that would suggest such a possibility, and that is an examination of the parts attributed to Mrs. Anne Hallam. In her earlier years at the theatre in Lincoln's Inn Fields she was seen in many new parts, sometimes as many as four in a month, but from the close of 1730 to the beginning of 1738 she seldom created a new role. During this period her best year was 1734, when she is set

1726.    *As Mrs. Berriman.*
Oct. 24.—Mistake . . . . . . . Isabella
Nov. 14.—Orphan . . . . . . . . Monimia
    30.—Fond Husband . . . . . Maria

1727.
Jan. 16.—Fall of Saguntum . . . Candace
Feb. 7.—Venice Preserved . . . Belvidera
April 17.—Jew of Venice . . . . . Portia
    29.—Philip of Macedon . . . Isteria
May 19.—Caradoc the Great . Cartismanda

1728.
Jan. 17.—Sesostris . . . . . . . Nitocris
Mar. 9.—Fortune Hunters . . . Mrs. Sly
    28.—Love Makes a Man . . . Elvira

1729.
Feb. 10.—Themistocles . . . . Artemisia
Mar. 4.—Frederick, Duke of Brunswick-
        Leinenberg . . . . Adelaide
Sept. 17.—Sir Walter Raleigh. Lady Raleigh
Nov. 8.—Maid's Tragedy . . . . Evadne
    25.—Rape . . . . . . . . . Queen

1730.
May 9.—False Friend . . . . . Isabella
    23.—Don Quixote . . . . . Duchess
Oct. 27.—Unhappy Favorite. . . . Queen
Nov. 23.—Conscious Lovers . . . Isabella

1731.
April 3.—Orestes. . . . . . . . . Circe

*As Mrs. Hallam—Covent Garden.*
1732.
Dec. 7.—Way of the World. Mrs. Marwood

1733.
April 4.—Fatal Secret . . Duchess of Malfy

1734.
Jan. 9.—Lady's Revenge . . Lady Traffic
Feb. 14.—Careless Husband . . Lady Easy
Sept. 30.—Albion Queens . . . . Elizabeth

1735.
Feb. 22.—Rival Widows . . Lady Lurcher

1737.
Feb. 26.—King John . . . . . Constance

1738.
Jan. 12.—Distrest Mother . . . Hermione
14.—All for Love . . . . . Octavia
28.—Jane Shore . . . . . . . Alicia
Feb. 6.—Richard II . . Duchess of York
Mar. 13.—Henry VI . . . Joan la Pucelle
16.—Theodosius . . . . . Pulcheria
20.—Cymbeline . . . . . . . Queen
April 19.—Mourning Bride . . . . . Zara
28.—Relpase . . . . . . . Amanda

1739.
Jan. 3.—Parricide . . . . . . . . Eliza
Mar. 25.—Married Philosopher . . Melissa
April 26.—Lady's Last Stake
Lady Wronghead
29.—Philotas . . . . . . Antigona

down for *Lady Traffic* in "Lady's Revenge," *Lady Easy* in the "Careless Husband," and *Elizabeth* in the "Albion Queens." But in January, 1738, she again came to the front, and from that time until April, 1739, she was accorded a number of parts that, perhaps, ought to have gone to a younger and less robust actress. These later parts were in the younger Mrs. Hallam's line of business ten years after. It is not easy to conceive such a transfer of parts, if at all, without the fact being on record, but without such a transfer the American Mrs. Hallam could not have been at Covent Garden at all, as it is certain Lewis Hallam never was. After Anne Hallam's death there were no longer any Hallam's under Rich's management, and so the American print collectors, who fondly hoped they had found in the frontispiece to Thomson's suppressed play, "Edward and Eleanora," a portrait in character of Mrs. Hallam-Douglass, will be compelled to concede it was intended for the elder Mrs. Hallam. Thus is not only the hypothesis shattered, but the apparent discrepancy may be accounted for by a remark of Davies to the effect that Rich always manifested a spirit of hostility to her progress, probably because of her bulk, notwithstanding she was a relative, that may have been overcome by the exigencies of the theatre and the favor in which she was held by the public. When Mrs. Hallam died in 1740 she was recorded in the *Gentleman's Magazine* as "an excellent actress," a tribute that would not likely have been paid to her if she had failed to retain her place and rank in the theatre until her death.

There was a Mr. Hallam at Smock Alley in Dublin playing such parts as the *Bookseller* in the "Committee," and the *Musician* in "Timon of Athens," as early as 1715. In 1733 there was a Hallam booth at Bartholomew Fair, and the next year, 1734, Adam Hallam is first noticed at Covent Garden as *Gregory* in the "Plain Dealer." It would be impossible to say whether the Mr. Hallam of Smock Alley and Adam Hallam of Covent Garden are identical, but it is likely that Adam was the father of the American adventurers, with Mrs. Anne Hallam as his second wife. The history of Adam Hallam, the father, is important, as showing why William projected the American company and Lewis conducted it across the Atlantic. Adam Hallam succeeded in making a seven years' engagement with Rich, at Covent Garden, probably through his wife's influence, but as an actor his best parts were *Worthy*, in the "Recruiting Officer;" *Malcolm*, in "Macbeth;" *Lærtes*, in "Hamlet;" *Careless*, in the "Double Gallant," and *Altamont*, in the "Fair Penitent." He was an imitator of Wilks, especially in his way of pulling down his ruffles and rolling his stockings. He was useful, however, in the mechanical department, and when "Richard II" was revived at Covent Garden in 1738, after being shelved for forty years, he invented the armor and decorations for the scene in the lists. He was at Drury Lane in 1742–43, and translated the "Beggars' Opera" into French for the Haymarket, where it met with some success. Subsequently he became an itinerant player and a pensioner on the managers, taking a benefit in 1746, as has been shown, at the rope-dancing establishment at the Wells. These facts not only show the financial condition of the Hallams about the year 1750, but indicate the estimation in which they were held in England as actors after the family ceased to enjoy the favor of their relative, Rich, at Covent Garden. They organized the company that crossed the Atlantic because the wilds of America could not well be worse than the barns of England. Curiously enough Adam Hallam created the part of *Severn* in a play called the "Prodigal Reformed," at Covent Garden in 1738, young Severn being sent as a boy to America to be educated, where he was reduced by pecuniary difficulties and deserted by supposed friends. Young Hallam crossed the ocean expecting better luck than befell young Severn.

In regard to the organization of the American Company, Dunlap is the only guide. It was formed on the sharing plan. The number of shares was fixed at eighteen. There were twelve adult performers, including the manager, and each performer was allowed a share. Lewis Hallam had another share as manager and a share was allowed to his three children. The remaining four shares were for the profit of the backer for the use of his money. As the amount invested was necessarily small, coming as it did from a man situated as William Hallam was, the capi-

ORIGINAL HALLAM REPERTOIRE.

*Plays.*

| | |
|---|---|
| Beaux' Stratagem | Farquhar |
| Careless Husband | Cibber |
| Committee | Howard |
| Conscious Lovers | Steele |
| Constant Couple | Farquhar |
| Fair Penitent | Rowe |
| George Barnwell | Lillo |
| Hamlet | Shakspere |
| Inconstant | Farquhar |
| Jane Shore | Rowe |
| Merchant of Venice | Shakspere |
| Othello | Shakspere |
| Provoked Husband | Vanbrugh |
| Recruiting Officer | Farquhar |
| Richard the Third | Shakspere |
| Suspicious Husband | Hoadly |
| Tamerlane | Farquhar |
| Theodosius | Lee |
| Twin Rivals | Farquhar |
| Woman's a Riddle | Bullock |

*Farces.*

| | |
|---|---|
| Anatomist | Ravenscroft |
| Damon and Phillida | Cibber |
| Devil to Pay | Coffey |
| Hob in the Well | Cibber |
| Lethe | Garrick |
| Lying Valet | Garrick |
| Miss in Her Teens | Garrick |
| Mock Doctor | Fielding |

talist, in case of success, could not fail to have the best of it. The scheme being arranged, a company willing to agree to the terms was enlisted, the plays were selected and the parts assigned. The pieces chosen were those that were most popular on the London stage at the time, and many of them continued to be played by the American Company from 1752 down to the Revolution. With this repertoire and one pantomime, "Harlequin Collector; or, the Miller Deceived," the adventurers set sail in the Charming Sally, Captain Lee, early in May, 1752.

# CHAPTER IV.

---

## THE VIRGINIA COMEDIANS.

CONTINUED EXISTENCE OF THE PHILADELPHIA COMPANY—IT PLAYS AT
ANNAPOLIS, IN 1752—RE-INFORCED BY TWO OF HALLAM'S
PLAYERS—THE ANNAPOLIS THEATRE.

ALTHOUGH the Company of Comedians from Philadelphia disbanded at the close of the New York season of 1751, it was soon re-organized, and was playing in Virginia in the spring of 1752. Unfortunately the journalism of the period gives few traces of the travels in the Old Dominion of these wandering thespians.

Within a fortnight of Lewis Hallam's arrival at Yorktown, the "Company of Comedians from Virginia" reached Annapolis. This company had some kind of existence for more than twenty years. In Virginia it was generally known as the Virginia Company of Comedians, but it did not always retain its distinctively Virginia character, for when it appeared at Upper Marlborough, in the autumn of 1752, it was billed as the Company of Comedians from Annapolis. As this history proceeds it will be found showing itself in unexpected places, and on one occasion, it will be seen, it ventured to assert itself as the New American Company. These facts not only prove that the Hallam Company was not the first regularly organized theatrical company in this country, but that the American Company, so-called, was never without a rival south of the Chesapeake.

When the Company of Comedians arrived at Annapolis, it

(30)

announced its presence through the advertising columns of the *Maryland Gazette.* There was no editorial mention of their arrival previous to their appearance and no remark upon the performances afterward. As a consequence the only source of information is that afforded by the advertisements. These, however, tell their story with such simplicity and directness, that it is surprising that the writers on early American theatrical history never thought it worth while to consult them in the pages where they were first printed. It is easier, perhaps, to take supposed facts at second hand, but in thus avoiding the duties of verifica

MARYLAND GAZETTE, June 18, 1752.

By Permission of his Honor, the PRESIDENT, At the New Theatre in Annapolis by the Company of Comedians from Virginia, on Monday, being the 22nd of this instant, will be performed
THE BEGGARS' OPERA,
likewise a Farce called
THE LYING VALET.
To begin precisely at 7 o'clock.
Tickets to be had at the printing office.
Box, 10s. Pit, 7s. 6d.
No person to be admitted behind the scenes.
N.B.—The Company immediately intend to *Upper Marlborough*, as soon as they have done performing here, where they intend to play as long as they meet with encouragement and so on to *Piscataway* and *Port Tobacco.* And hope to give Satisfaction to the Gentlemen and Ladies in each Place, that will favor them with their Company.

tion the blunders of an incompetent historian become consecrated as historical truth. No better example of such perpetuation of error can be cited than Dunlap's treatment of this season at the Annapolis theatre. In 1828, a writer in the *Maryland Gazette* claimed for Annapolis the first theatre, in point of time, erected in the United States. This writer quoted the advertisement of the 18th of June, 1752, ignoring that of June 13th, and as printed by Dunlap, omitting the words "from Virginia" in the name of the company. Ridgely, in his "Annals of Annapolis," prints the advertisement of June 13th, but omits the note concerning the company, which was the concluding and most interesting part of it. The article assumes that the descrip-

tion, "new theatre," was employed in contradistinction to the temporary theatres, generally commercial warehouses, previously used. Had
this writer taken the trouble to examine the files of the *Gazette* he
would have found an announcement of the 7th of December[1] that
shows the Annapolis theatre of 1752 to have been little better
than a commercial warehouse, instead of a theatre that he describes
as "a neat brick building, tastefully arranged and competent to contain
between five and six hundred persons." Dunlap, without further inquiry, cites this as proof that the claim for Annapolis of having
erected the first theatre appears fully made out, when the truth is that
the brick building described in the *Maryland Gazette*, in 1828, was
not built until 1771.

If the writer in the *Maryland Gazette*, in 1828, had examined
the files of that journal for 1752, he would have known that the Company of Comedians from Virginia played two engagements at Annapolis in that year, and that the appearance of the Company at
Upper Marlborough[2] was an important part of their programme.
Besides, he would have had no occasion to bewail his inability to
ascertain anything in regard to the identity of the company, "as no
*dramatis personæ* are given," the advertisement of the "Beggars'
Opera" at that place being in itself a clue. Mr. Woodham, who
sang the "Mason's Song," was a member of the Company of Comedians from Philadelphia, when they played in New York. Had
he looked further he would have found also that Kean and Miss

---

[1] MARYLAND GAZETTE, December 7, 1752.
—N.B.—The House is entirely lined throughout for the reception of Ladies and Gentlemen; and they have also raised a Porch at
the Door that will keep out the inclemency
of the weather.

[2] MARYLAND GAZETTE, July 2, 1752.—
N.B.—As the Company have now got their
Hands, Cloaths &c. compleat, they now con-
firm their Resolution of going to *Upper Marlborough*, as soon as ever encouragement fails
here.

Osborne, who were New York favorites, were the leading members of the Company of Comedians from Virginia.

So far as the *Maryland Gazette* shows, the same bill was twice given at Upper Marlborough, the first time on the 20th of August, and the second time on the 14th of September, but the Annapolis repertoire was more complete, and extended over a period embracing the months of June and December. If the names of the performers and the dates of the performances had been considered, much oracular but irrelevant discussion would have been avoided, and erroneous conclusions would not have been made to pass for history. Dunlap, for instance, argues that as Hallam's company did not appear at Williamsburg until the 5th of September, there was ample time for Wynell and Herbert, who were inferior members of the company, to have gone to Annapolis and "performed with a Mr. Eyanson," and he thought the fact of their performing the parts of *Richard* and *Richmond* accords with this supposition. As

MARYLAND GAZETTE, August 13, 1752.

———

By Permission of his Honor, the
PRESIDENT
At the New Theatre
in Upper Marlborough by the Company of Comedians from Annapolis, on Thursday next being the 14th of September, (at the request of the Ancient and Honorable Society of FREE and ACCEPTED MASONS) will be performed
The
BEGGARS' OPERA
with instrumental to each air given by a set of Private Gentlemen;
And
"A Solo on the French Horn:"
also
A Mason's Song by Mr. Woodham; with a Grand Chorus.
To which will be added a Farce call'd
THE LYING VALET.
Tickets to be had at Mr. Benjamin Barry's.
Pit, 7s. 6d. Gallery, 5s.

ANNAPOLIS REPERTOIRE.

———

1752.
June 22.—Beggars' Opera . . . . . . Gay
  Lying Valet . . . . . . Garrick
July 6.—Busybody . . . . . . Centlivre
  Lying Valet.
  13.—Beaux' Stratagem . . . Farquhar
  Virgin Unmasked . . . Fielding
  21.—Recruiting Officer . . . Farquhar
  Mock Doctor . . . . . Fielding

July 27.—George Barnwell . . . . . Lillo  
    Damon and Phillida . . . Cibber  
   31.—Bold Stroke for a Wife. Centlivre  
    Beau in the Suds.  
Aug. 3.—Drummer . . . . . . Addison  
    Devil to Pay . . . . . . Coffey  
Oct. 2.—Constant Couple . . . Farquhar  
    Lying Valet.  
   21.—Cato . . . . . . . . Addison  
    Miss in her Teens . . . Garrick  
    (Benefit of Mr. Eyanson.)  
Dec. 11.—Richard III . . . . . Shakspere  
    Miss in her Teens.  
       *Richard* . . . . Mr. Wynell  
       *Richmond* . . . Mr. Herbert  
  (From the Theatre in Williamsburg.)  
   13.—Constant Couple.  
    Anatomist . . . . . Ravenscroft  
    Principal parts by Mr. Wynell,  
    Mr. Kean, Mr. Herbert and Miss  
    Osborne.  
   16.—Richard III.  
    Lying Valet.  
  (Benefit of Talbot Co. Charity School.)

they appeared in December instead of in July, and were distinctly announced as from the theatre at Williamsburg, speculative theory gives place to fact by showing that they were in Annapolis after and not before Hallam's engagement at the capital of the Old Dominion. The facts settle another problem that puzzled the ingenious Dunlap. While he concedes, erroneously, as was his habit, that Annapolis has the honor of having erected the first temple to the muses, he is surprised that this circumstance should have escaped Lewis Hallam, the second. The description contained in the advertisement in the *Maryland Gazette* of the 7th of December shows that the "new theatre" at Annapolis, in 1752, was like those that were previously erected at Williamsburg and New York, and so it was unworthy of mention as a "temple to the muses."

# CHAPTER V.

## HALLAM AT WILLIAMSBURG.

INITIAL PERFORMANCE OF THE HALLAM COMPANY IN VIRGINIA—A
NOVELIST'S ACCOUNT OF IT—THE MERCHANT OF VENICE—
INCIDENTS OF THE SEASON.

IT would be surprising had not the appearance of the Hallam
Company in the "Merchant of Venice" at Williamsburg, on
September 5th, 1752, been utilized in some of the novels it has long
been the ambition of Virginia novelists to write of the "Old Dominion"
in the colonial period. In itself the advent of the first theatrical company ever specially organized in England for America is an interesting
and important event. It not only possessed the charm of novelty at
the time, but it readily blended with the romance of a romantic epoch
when the obscuring mists of years had made it a mere tradition.
When it was announced, therefore, that the late John Esten Cooke
had seized upon the episode as the foundation of one of his stories
there was a tremor of delight among the students of American dramatic history. Unfortunately Mr. Cooke drew too largely upon his
imagination for his facts. In his "Virginia Comedians" he brings the
Hallams to Williamsburg eleven years later than the year of their
arrival—that is, in 1763 instead of 1752. He makes Mr. Hallam, whom
he describes as "a fat little man of fifty or fifty-five, with a rubicund
and somewhat sensual face," play *Bassanio* instead of *Launcelot*, and he
assigns the part of *Portia* to Miss Beatrice Hallam, Hallam's daughter,

instead of to his wife, Mrs. Hallam. For Mr. Malone, who was the *Shylock* on the occasion, he substitutes a fictitious Mr. Pugsby, but Mr. Hallam is introduced in his own name. Both are drawn as exceedingly repugnant characters. Hallam is represented as brutal, base and selfish, and the manager is made to say after the initial performance that "*Shylock* was too drunk" to play this great role acceptably. As compensation for this harsh treatment of the real Mr. Hallam, he makes the fictitious Miss Beatrice Hallam one of the most striking, truthful and lovable characters in modern fiction. All this, it must be confessed, is open to grave objection. In a historical novel in which dates are given some respect is due to chronology. Mr. Hallam was dead and buried when he is made to figure in Mr. Cooke's story. In a historical novel in which real men are introduced by name, it is incumbent on the novelist that the figures he draws shall be as nearly as possible truthful portraits. These laws Mr. Cooke boldly set aside, and so, instead of presenting a brilliant, if ideal, picture of the introduction of the drama into America, the "Virginia Comedians" is only a rude caricature of a party of barn-stormers, such as leave New York annually for a Thanksgiving or Christmas "snap."

While Mr. Cooke's treatment of Mr. Hallam is open to such serious objection, his description of the first night of the "Merchant of Venice" is in every way worthy of his subject. It is easy enough to imagine the interest that would be excited among the Virginia planters by the arrival of a company of comedians at Williamsburg from England.

"Ah, I see we are to have a theatrical performance in Williamsburg next week," says Mr. Lee, looking up from the latest number of the Williamsburg *Gazette* and then reading the announcement in the newspaper. "Mr. Hallam and his Virginia Company of Comedians in the 'Merchant of Venice,' by permission of his worship, the Mayor, at the Old Theatre near the Capitol." "Let us go to see the play, father," said Henrietta. "Oh, yes," said Clare. "Certainly, if you wish it," the father assents.

When the time comes for going to the theatre Miss Henrietta is radiant in a dress of surpassing elegance—flowered satin, yellow lace, jewels, powdered hair, pearl pendants and rich furbelows.

"You know I have never seen a play," says Clare on the way to the theatre to her cousin Champ Effingham, a Virginia exquisite, who has just returned from London and who is of the party. "But read a plenty," he answers. "Oh, yes," Clare replies; "and I like the 'Merchant of Venice' very much: the character of *Portia* is so delicate and so noble." "Who will act *Portia?*" Henrietta asks. "*Shylock*— Mr. Pugsby; *Portia*—Miss Beatrice Hallam," the fop answers, reading from a copy of the play-bill with which he had provided himself. "I have never seen or heard of her," Champ then says. "Which means," Henrietta interposes, laughing, "that Miss Beatrice Hallam cannot be well worth going to see."

In the boxes were Parson Tag, a Virginia fox-hunting clergyman, and 'Squire Effingham, the father of Champ, while a young reformer of the epoch, Charles Waters, was in the pit. "Not so bad as you predicted, eh Parson?" said the 'Squire to Tag, when the curtain fell on the first act. "I don't think that fellow, *Antonio*, acts so badly." "Oh, lovely, papa!" exclaimed Kate Effingham, clapping her hands. "I was never more pleased with anything," said Clare to Champ. "Much like Shuter at Covent Garden," the Anglo-American fop remarks of the *Shylock*. The scene between *Portia* and *Nerissa* in the first act was cut out, but Miss Beatrice Hallam played the scene with the Prince of Morocco for all it was worth in the second act. "Every word rang and told; there was no hurry, no slurring, no hesitation." Finally came the scene with the caskets. "It ended with great applause. The young woman had evidently produced a most favorable impression on the audience." Champ, after the London fashion, forced his way behind the scenes during the play and insisted on speaking to *Portia*, whereupon the gallery hissed and the young reformer in the pit frowned. "What were they hissing for?" Clare asked, when the curtain went down. "Some folly which deserved hissing, probably," Champ answered, without a blush. The play ended amid universal applause, but the next morning Champ Effingham told his father, the 'Squire, that all the parts were well acted except *Portia*—that was overacted. The 'Squire thought his son "too English."

In marked contrast with this imaginary description is the account given by Dunlap, which is probably the first theatrical interview printed in America. It was furnished by Lewis Hallam, the younger, forty years after the event—then, after another forty years it found its way into print. According to Dunlap's recollections of the recollections of the younger Hallam, Lewis Hallam, the elder, found a building in the suburbs of the town which he turned into a theatre. It was said to be so near the wood that the manager often stood in his door and shot pigeons for dinner. After its destruction by fire some years later, Dunlap says another theatre was built below the Old Capitol. It is, perhaps, too late to determine the exact locality of Hallam's theatre, but wherever it was situated it is certain that Williamsburg had a theatre many years before the arrival of the Hallam

Company, as appears from an advertisement in the *Virginia Gazette* of September 10th, 1736. In an early work entitled "The British Empire in America" it is said that near the market-place, or what perhaps was only an area for a market-place, there was a good bowling alley and a play-house, but doubt is expressed of the excellence of the performances on the Virginia stage at that early day.

ADVERTISEMENT.

This evening will be performed at the Theatre by the young Gentlemen of the College, the Tragedy of "Cato," and on Monday, Wednesday and Friday next will be acted the following Comedies by the young Gentlemen and Ladies of this country—The "Busybody," the "Recruiting Officer" and the "Beaux Stratagem."

Advertisements in the *Virginia Gazette* of 1768 accord with Mr. Cooke's description. If any credence is given to Dunlap's statement the London company occupied neither of these, but in his eagerness to prove that the company that landed at Yorktown, Virginia, in June, 1752, and appeared at Williamsburg in the "Merchant of Venice" on the 5th of September, was the first professional company of comedians in America, he was blinded to every fact that militated against his theory. In order to make the facts square with his theory, he is not only compelled to assert that the building occupied by Lewis Hallam at Williamsburg was "the first theatre opened in America by a company of regular comedians," but is led to assume that a theatre at Annapolis, Md., built before the arrival of the Hallams, "was used by boys or young men to enact plays after their fashion, as was the case and probably will be the case everywhere." The only thing that gives Dunlap's statement value is the fact that he received it from Lewis Hallam, the younger.

It is, of course, impossible to give any connected account of the Williamsburg season. There does not seem to be extant a file of the

*Virginia Gazette* for 1752, although it was revived in 1751, and so it is necessary to accept for the opening night the statement that Dunlap derived from the younger Lewis Hallam forty years afterward. The play of the evening was the "Merchant of Venice," which was followed by the farce of "Lethe." That these were the pieces is probable, but whether the casts as printed by Dunlap are absolutely accurate it is impossible to say. Although "Mr. Hallam seemed to remember every transaction of that period, every circumstance attending these first histrionic adventures, as though they were of yesterday," experience teaches that nothing is more untrustworthy than such recollection. The bill comprised the entire strength of the company, except Mrs. Clarkson,

DUNLAP'S WILLIAMSBURG CASTS.

*Merchant of Venice.*

| | |
|---|---|
| Shylock . . . . . . . . . . | Mr. Malone |
| Bassanio . . . . . . . . . | Mr. Rigby |
| Antonio . . . . . . . . . . | Mr. Clarkson |
| Gratiano . . . . . . . . | Mr. Singleton |
| Salanio ⎱ Duke ⎰ . . . . . . . . | Mr. Herbert |
| Salarino ⎱ Gobbo ⎰ . . . . . . . . | Mr. Wynell |
| Launcelot ⎱ Tubal . ⎰ . . . . . . . | Mr. Hallam |
| Servant to Portia . . | Master Lewis Hallam |
| (His first appearance on any stage.) | |
| Nerissa . . . . . . . . . . | Miss Palmer |
| Jessica . . . . . . . . . | Miss Hallam |
| (Her first appearance on any stage.) | |
| Portia . . . . . . . . . | Mrs. Hallam |

*Lethe.*

| | |
|---|---|
| Æsop . . . . . . . . . | Mr. Clarkson |
| Old Man . . . . . . . . | Mr. Malone |
| Fine Gentleman . . . . . | Mr. Singleton |
| Frenchman . . . . . . . | Mr. Rigby |
| Charon . . . . . . . . . | Mr. Herbert |
| Mercury . . . . . . . . | Mr. Adcock |
| Drunken Man ⎱ Tattoo . . . ⎰ . . . . | Mr. Hallam |
| John . . . . . . . . . . | Mr. Wynell |
| Mrs. Tattoo . . . . . . | Miss Palmer |
| Fine Lady . . . . . . . | Mrs. Hallam |

Mrs. Rigby and Adam Hallam, a child. It will be observed that the *Tailor* was cut out of the farce. The absence of *Lord Chalkstone* is accounted for by the fact that the part was an afterthought of the author. Miss Hallam, who made her first appearance on the stage as *Jessica* in the play, was, Dunlap says, the daughter of Lewis Hallam. The surroundings must have been exceedingly primitive. There was no orchestra but Mr. Pelham, who taught the harpsichord in the town, was engaged with his instrument to supply the music. The performance began with a prologue, written for the occasion by Mr. Singleton. It was spoken by Mr. Rigby. As it was the first composition written for and addressed to an American audience that was preserved, it may be regarded as a curiosity. John Singleton, by whom it was written, was content with small parts as an actor, but he aspired to be a poet, and in 1767 he published at Barbadoes "A General Description of the West Indian Islands" in blank verse, and had his poem republished in London ten years later. As to the merits of the performance we know nothing except that Master Lewis Hallam, who had only one line to speak, stood speechless before the audience when his time came, and then bursting into tears rushed off the stage.

### PROLOGUE.

To this new world, from fam'd Britannia's shore,
Through boist'rous seas where foaming billows roar,
The Muse, who Britons charm'd for many an age,
Now sends her servants forth to tread the stage;
Britain's own race, though far removed, to show
Patterns of every virtue they should know.
Though gloomy minds through ignorance may rail,
Yet bold examples strike where languid precepts fail.

The world's a stage, where mankind act their parts;
The stage a world to show their various arts;
While th' soul, touch'd by Nature's tend'rest laws,
Has all her passions rous'd in Virtue's cause.
Reason we hear, and coolly will approve,
But all's inactive till the passions move.
Such is the human mind, so weak, so frail,
"Reason's her chart, but passion is her gale."
Then raise the gale to waft fair Virtue o'er
The sea of life where Reason points the shore.
But ah! let Reason guide the course along,
Lest Passion, list'ning to some siren's song,
Rush on the rocks of Vice, where all is lost,
And shipwreck'd Virtue renders up the ghost.

Too oft, we own, the stage with dangerous art,
In wanton scenes has played the siren's part.
Yet if the Muse, unfaithful to her trust,
Has sometimes strayed from what is pure and just,
Has she not oft, with awful, virtuous rage,
Struck home at vice and nobly trod the stage—
Made tyrants weep, the conscious murderer stand
And drop the dagger from his trembling hand?
Then, as you treat a favorite fair's mistake,
Pray spare her foibles for her virtue's sake
And while her chastest scenes are made appear—
For none but such will find admittance here—
The Muse's friends, we hope, will join our cause
And crown our best endeavors with applause.

The only subsequent performance of the Williamsburg engagement that I find anywhere is that of the 9th of November, 1752. This occurs in a Williamsburg letter to the *Maryland Gazette*,[1] but it is probable that even this performance would have been passed by without notice had not a lot of savages visited the theatre as the guests of the Governor. On this occasion "Othello" and "Harlequin Collector" comprised the bill. Malone probably played the *Moor*, Rigby *Iago* and Singleton *Cassio*. Mrs. Hallam certainly was the *Desdemona*. So far as is known these were the only performances in America of the "Merchant of Venice" and "Othello" by the original Hallam Company. It will be observed that the simplicity exhibited by "the Empress" at the play was more than equaled by the grotesque servility of the high-flown language in which the visit of savage royalty to the theatre is described.

Lewis Hallam remained in Virginia eleven months, and went directly from Williamsburg to New York. He was accompanied by his entire company, except Wynell and Herbert, who had seceded the previous December and joined "the Virginia Comedians" at Annapolis. It is evident from the assumption of such roles as *Richard* by Wynell and *Richmond* by Herbert, that parts like *Salanio* and *Salarino*, the *Duke of Venice* and old *Gobbo* could not satisfy their ambition. The Annapolis opportunity, therefore, was not to be lost, but it seems

[1] MARYLAND GAZETTE. Williamsburg, Nov. 17. — The Emperor of the Cherokee nation with his Empress and their son, the young Prince, attended by several of his Warriors and Great Men and their Ladies were received at the Palace by his Honour the Governor, attended by such of the Council as were in Town on Thursday the 9th instant with all the Marks of Courtesy and Friendship and were that Evening entertained at the Theatre with the Play (the Tragedy of "Othello") and a Pantomime Performance which gave them great surprise as did the fighting with naked swords on the Stage which occasioned the Empress to order some about her to go and prevent them killing one another.

to have brought them no permanent advantage, for neither of them was ever heard of afterward, unless indeed the Herbert of whom an anecdote is related in Bernard's " Retrospections of America " is the same. It is an account of an adventure in Jamaica with Three-fingered Jack, in which a member of the old American Company, Owen Morris, is made to say that Herbert, who had a sweet voice and was of respectable parentage, "had quitted England, owing to an unfortunate attachment." His melancholy led him to take long rambles in the country, in which he was occasionally joined by another actor. One sultry day, when they reached the shelter of an "umbrageous palm," Herbert proposed they should open their wallet and take some refreshment. Unfortunately they found the brandy, so necessary to a lover's melancholy, had been forgotten. Herbert remained under the " umbrageous palm " while his friend visited a neighboring plantation to obtain the required fluid. When his friend was gone, "the loneliness and stillness of the spot" brought back to Herbert "the thought of home, and he gave vent to his oppressed spirit in some vocal effusion, unconscious that the savage scourge of the island, driven by hunger from his hiding place on the hills, was ready to dispatch him " just as his " lips opened and the breathings of a broken heart" poured forth. It is unnecessary to add that the " breathings " so charmed the outlaw that Herbert's life was saved. The next day Three-fingered Jack was captured. As Herbert left Hallam's Company in 1752, and Three-fingered Jack was not captured until 1781, it will be noted that his broken heart had lasted him fully thirty years.

# CHAPTER VI.

## HALLAM IN NEW YORK.

THE FIRST SEASON OF WHICH THERE IS DEFINITE KNOWLEDGE—OPPOSITION TO THE THEATRE—A SKETCH OF THE PLAYS AND THE PLAYERS AND THEIR PARTS.

AN entire year elapsed between the initial performance of the Hallam Company in Virginia and their first appearance in New York. Where was the year spent, and how? Dunlap says that, after leaving Williamsburg, Lewis Hallam's Company performed at Upper Marlborough, Piscataway and Port Tobacco, then places of wealth and consequence in Maryland, but that the whole Company was not at Annapolis, he thinks, is proved by the silence of Lewis Hallam, the second. The fact is that no part of it was at Annapolis at any time, except the two seceding members, Wynell and Herbert, who joined the Company of Comedians from Virginia, the existence of which the historian ignores. Indeed, there is no reason to believe that the Company stopped at any of the places of wealth and consequence in Maryland on the journey from Williamsburg to New York. Proof of this is contained in Mr. Hallam's appeal to the New York public, printed in 1753. Dunlap's mistake was due to the fact that he confounded Hallam's Company with the comedians whose existence he so strenuously denied. There was good reason why Hallam should go direct to New York. The Maryland field had been pretty thoroughly tilled by the Virginia comedians, and in Philadelphia the opposition to the theatre was too violent to make a stop possible at that time. When the Company left the capital of the "Old Dominion" Governor Dinwiddie gave Mr. Hallam a certificate, recommending the comedians as actors and testifying to the correctness of their conduct as men. Such a testimonial was useful at that time, especially with the functionaries whose consent it was necessary to obtain before performances could be given. Armed with this "character," Hallam arrived in New York in June, 1753. But even in New York the welcome to the players was not very cordial, and permission to perform was at first denied. This difficulty was overcome, however, Hallam using the wrongs he had suffered at the hands of Upton as a means of softening the hearts of the authorities. There was still another difficulty. The old theatre in Nassau Street was not adapted to the use to which it had been put, and so it was demolished and another one erected in its place. Finally, Hallam announced in Gaine's *Mercury*, on the 17th of September, that he had built a fine, large theatre in the place where the old one stood, and "by his Excellency's authority" would that evening present a comedy, called the

HALLAM'S FIRST ADVERTISEMENT.

*By His Excellency's Authority*
By a Company of Comedians from *London*
At the New Theatre in *Nassau Street*,
This Evening will be presented, a Comedy, called,

THE CONSCIOUS LOVERS.

Young Bevil . . . . . . . . . Mr. Rigby
Mr. Sealand . . . . . . . . Mr. Malone
Sir John Bevil . . . . . . . . Mr. Bell
Myrtle . . . . . . . . . . Mr. Clarkson
Cimberton . . . . . . . . . Mr. Miller
Humphrey . . . . . . . . Mr. Adcock
Daniel . . . . . . . . Master L. Hallam
Tom . . . . . . . . . . . Mr. Singleton
Phillis . . . . . . . . . . Mrs. Beccely
Mrs. Sealand . . . . . . . Mrs. Clarkson
Lucinda . . . . . . . . . Miss Hallam
Isabella . . . . . . . . . Mrs. Rigby
Indiana . . . . . . . . . Mrs. Hallam

A new Occasional Prologue to be spoken by Mr. RIGBY.
An *Epilogue* (addressed to the Ladies) by Mrs. HALLAM.
*Prices:* Box, 8s. Pit, 6s. Gallery, 3s.
No Persons whatever to be admitted behind the Scenes.
N.B. Gentlemen and Ladies that chuse Tickets, may have them at the New Printing Office in Beaver Street. To begin at 6 o'clock.

"Conscious Lovers," and the ballad farce of "Damon and Phillida." The bill of the evening for the opening night, as it was
published in the *New York Gazette, or Weekly Postboy*, contained no
allusion to the farce. The bill has often been reprinted, but is
necessary here as part of the record. The new occasional prologue, spoken by Mr. Rigby, was the one given in Williamsburg
a year before, and the epilogue, unfortunately, was not printed.
The prices on the opening night: Box, 8 shillings; pit, 6 shillings;
gallery, 4 shillings; for the second night were reduced to: Box, 6
shillings; pit, 5 shillings; gallery, 3 shillings. A month later there
was a further reduction, the pit being put at 4 shillings and the gallery
at 2 shillings. The days of performance were Mondays, Wednesdays
and Fridays, the season lasting from the 17th of September, 1753, to
the 18th of March, 1754.

In those days the newspapers appeared only once a week, and
consequently it is not possible to list more than one-third of the performances of the season. Fortu-
nately the plays and farces comprised in the list are of a character
to give a very complete idea of
the entertainments afforded the
New York public by the company of comedians from London.
Here were twenty-one distinct
plays and twelve farces, comprising only one-third of the performances of a season of six months,
given under circumstances that

LIST OF PERFORMANCES.

1753.
Sept. 17—Conscious Lovers . . . . Steele
   Damon and Phillida . . . Cibber
  24—Tunbridge Walks . . . . Baker
Oct. 1—Constant Couple . . . Farquhar
   Anatomist . . . . . Ravenscroft
  8—Conscious Lovers.
   Virgin Unmasked . . . Fielding
  22—Love for Love . . . . Congreve
   Tom Thumb . . . . . Fielding
  29—George Barnwell . . . . . Lillo
   Lying Valet . . . . . . Garrick
Nov. 5—Distressed Mother . . . . Philips
   Hob in the Well . . . . Cibber
  12—Richard III . . . . . Shakspere
   Devil to Pay . . . . . . Coffey

must have rendered the representations doubly difficult, but always played with full casts, and, if tradition is to be believed, with all the parts acceptably filled.

To the modern play-goer the work of the Hallam Company must seem marvelous, but apart from the labor of presenting so many pieces in such rapid succession, both the plays and the farces comprised in the list are capable of an exceedingly interesting analysis. It comprises not only the best works in a dramatic sense, but the purest plays the English stage had produced up to that time. The dramatists were men with a few exceptions whose fame will form a part of the glory of English dramatic literature until the world ceases to prize English letters. As names these writers for the stage

Nov. 19—Beggars' Opera . . . . . . Gay
Lying Valet.
26—Committee . . . . . . . Howard
Dec. 3—Careless Husband . . . . Cibber
Lethe . . . . . . . . Garrick
10—Beaux' Stratagem . . . Farquhar
Harlequin Collector.
17—Committee.
Miss in her Teens . . . Garrick
26—Twin Rivals . . . . . Farquhar
Damon and Phillida.
1754.
Jan. 7—Drummer . . . . . . . Addison
14—King Lear . . . . . Shakspere
21—Woman is a Riddle . . . Bullock
Devil to Pay.
28—Romeo and Juliet . . Shakspere
(Mr. Clarkson's Benefit.)
Feb. 4—Gamester . . . . . . Moore
(Mr. Rigby's Benefit.)
11—Earl of Essex . . . . . Jones
Miller of Mansfield . . . Dodsley
(Mrs. Beccely's Benefit.)
18—Suspicious Husband . . Hoadley
Harlequin Skeleton.
(Mr. Miller's Benefit.)
25—Albion Queens . . . . Banks
Virgin Unmasked.
(Mrs. Hallam's Benefit.)
Mar. 4—Jane Shore . . . . . . Rowe
Harlequin Skeleton.
(Mrs. Rigby's Benefit.)
11—Romeo and Juliet.
Stage Coach . . . . . Farquhar
(Benefit of Miss Hallam and her two brothers.)
16—Beggars' Opera.
Devil to Pay.
(Mr. and Mrs. Love's Benefit.)

have a familiar sound, but, with the exception of Shakspere's, their plays have disappeared from the boards. None of the farces and none of the comedies survive, and only two of the tragedies—Moore's "Gamester" and a revamped version of Rowe's "Jane Shore"—have been seen by this generation.  That they should have been so completely forgotten is all the more remarkable because their authors are still acknowledged as the masters of English dramatic writing, and Mr. Hallam's list comprised only the masterpieces of the masters.  To begin with Hallam's initial production, the "Conscious Lovers," it was not only Steele's best play, but the most moral play produced since the Restoration, and in itself a protest against stage immorality.  In *Bevil* Steele portrayed a model gentleman, of whom Thomson sang in "The Seasons":—

—— whate'er can dec᠄ mankind
Or charm the hear᠄ in generous B᠄᠄l showed.

It will thus be seen that Mr. Rigby had an excellent part for his introduction to the favor of New York theatre-goers.  When the "Conscious Lovers" was originally presented at Drury Lane Mrs. Oldfield was the *Indiana,* and it is not improbable that Mrs. Hallam had seen that great actress in the part before she played it in America. Colley Cibber, who did not disdain to give Shakspere the benefit of his improving touch, had a hand in preparing the piece for the stage, but it is not likely that Singleton ever saw him as *Tom.*  Mrs. Beccely's part of *Phillis* had been created by Mrs. Younger, and was yet to become a favorite hoyden with Mrs. Abington and Peg Woffington.  Baker's play, "Tunbridge Walks," was the least meritorious piece in the list.  But even Baker's com-

HALLAM'S SECOND ADVERTISEMENT.
————
*By His Excellency's Authority.*
By a Company of Comedians from *London,*
At the New Theatre in Nassau Street,
This Evening will be presented a Comedy, called
TUNBRIDGE WALKS
Or,
THE YEOMAN OF KENT,
Woodcock . . . . . . . . . Mr. Malone
Reynard . . . . . . . . . . Mr. Rigby
Loveworth . . . . . . . . . Mr. Miller
Capt. Squib . . . . . . . . . Mr. Hallam
Maiden . . . . . . . . . . Mr. Singleton

edy was interesting and entertaining in its day, Singleton's part of *Maiden* being the original of all the *Fribbles* and *Foppingtons* of the first half of the last century. The part, it is said, was a portrait of the author of the comedy when he was a young man, and was written by him to enable others to avoid the rock of contempt on which he had himself been wrecked.

After William Congreve, George Farquhar, whom Pope sought to depreciate by calling him a farce-writer, was the most successful dramatist of his day. He excelled in the gay relation of sprightly incidents. His two comedies, the "Constant Couple" and the "Twin Rivals," and his farce, the "Stage Coach," were, after his "Beaux' Stratagem," his best pieces. In the "Constant Couple" Mr. Singleton as *Sir Harry Wildair* had by all odds the best part. *Sir Harry*, although a profligate, was as gay in manners as he was easy in morals, and he was not altogether selfish and abandoned. The character was

Hillaria . . . . . . . . . . Mrs. Hallam
Belinda . . . . . . . . . . Mrs. Beccely
Mrs. Goodfellow . . . . . . . Mrs. Rigby
Penelope . . . . . . . . . Mrs. Clarkson
Lucy . . . . . . . . . . . Miss Hallam

In Act II. Singing by Mrs. LOVE.
End of Act III. a Scotch Dance by Mr. HULETT.
End of Act IV. Song by Mrs. LOVE.
End of the Play, a Hornpipe by Mr. HULETT.

Prices: Box 6*s*.  Pitt 5*s*.  Gallery 3*s*.

No Persons whatever to be admitted behind the Scenes.

N.B. Gentlemen and Ladies that chuse Tickets, may have them at the New Printing Office in Beaver Street.

To begin at 6 o'clock.  Money will be likewise taken at the Door.

The Company intend to Play on Mondays, Wednesdays, and Fridays.

LEWIS HALLAM.

### CONSTANT COUPLE.

Sir Harry Wildair . . . . . Mr. Singleton
Colonel Standard . . . . . . Mr. Rigby
Vizard . . . . . . . . . . . Mr. Miller
Alderman Smuggler . . . . . Mr. Malone
Clincher, Sr. . . . . . . . . Mr. Hallam
Clincher, Jr. . . . . . . . . Mr. Clarkson
Dicky . . . . . . . . Master L. Hallam
Tom Errand . . . . . . . . . . Mr. Bell
Constable . . . . . . . . . Mr. Adcock
Lady Lurewell . . . . . . Mrs. Hallam
Lady Darling . . . . . . . . Mrs. Rigby
Angelica . . . . . . . . Mrs. Beccely
Parly . . . . . . . . . . . Miss Hallam
Porter's Wife . . . . . . . Mrs. Clarkson

created by Wilks, but it afterward became a favorite actress' role, Peg Woffington esteeming it as her greatest part, and Mrs. Jordan playing it long after Singleton played it in America. The second of Farquhar's pieces played by the Hallam Company in New York was the "Beaux' Stratagem." The two beaux, *Aimwell* and *Archer*, having run through their money, go to Lichfield as "master and man," fortune hunting. *Aimwell* is very fascinating and handsome, but altogether a man of the world.

### BEAUX' STRATAGEM.

| | |
|---|---|
| Aimwell | Mr. Adcock |
| Archer | Mr. Singleton |
| Sir Charles Freeman | Mr. Bell |
| Mr. Sullen | Mr. Rigby |
| Foigard | Mr. Hallam |
| Boniface | Mr. Miller |
| Gibbet | Mr. Clarkson |
| Scrub | Mr. Malone |
| Mrs. Sullen | Mrs. Hallam |
| Dorinda | Mrs. Beccely |
| Lady Bountiful | Mrs. Rigby |
| Cherry | Miss Hallam |
| Gipsy | Mrs. Clarkson |

He pretends to be ill, and as *Lady Bountiful s* hobby is playing the leech, she orders him to be removed to her house. There he falls in love with and marries *Dorinda*, her daughter. *Archer* is in every way a less satisfactory character than *Aimwell*, and his love affair with *Mrs. Sullen* is far from commendable. *Squire Sullen* is the son of *Lady Bountiful* by a former marriage—*Mrs. Sullen* is the sister of *Sir Charles Freeman*. Never was a pair, even in a play, worse mated. The Squire was sullen, she was sprightly; he would not drink tea with her, and she would not drink ale with him; he disliked ombre and picquet, and she hated cock-fighting and racing; he declined to dance, and she refused to hunt. It was natural enough that such a pair should be divorced, but not even Farquhar dared to make *Archer's* marriage to the real heroine of the comedy a part of the play. The third and last of Farquhar's full pieces given this season was the "Twin Rivals." It was the least successful of his comedies, although the one most praised by the critics. The *outre* qualities of the younger *Wouldbe, Teague* and *Mrs. Midnight,* however, served to make it a success, but it fell far below the "Beaux' Stratagem"and "Constant Couple" in popularity. It is a curious commentary on the soundness of American taste even at that early period, that this the least meritorious of Farquhar's works should have proved also the least acceptable, and consequently it was dropped from the Hallam repertoire. In addition to

### TWIN RIVALS.

| | |
|---|---|
| Elder Wouldbe | Mr. Rigby |
| Young Wouldbe | Mr. Clarkson |
| Richmore | Mr. Bell |
| Trueman | Mr. Singleton |
| Subtleman | Mr. Miller |
| Balderdash Alderman | Mr. Malone |
| Clear-account | Mr. Adcock |
| Teague | Mr. Hallam |
| Frizure | Master L. Hallam |
| Constance | Mrs. Hallam |
| Aurelia | Mrs. Beccely |
| Mrs. Midnight | Mrs. Adcock |
| Mrs. Clear-account | Mrs. Rigby |
| Maid | Mrs. Clarkson |

these three comedies, Mr. Hallam presented one of Farquhar's farces, the "Stage Coach," for the benefit of his children, as the afterpiece to "Romeo and Juliet." The scene is laid at an inn upon the arrival of

### STAGE COACH.

| | |
|---|---|
| Torlough Rawer Macahone | Mr. Hallam |
| Captain Basil | Mr. Bell |
| Sir Nicodemus Somebody | Mr. Miller |
| Uncle Michar | Mr. Clarkson |
| Filch | Mr. Rigby |
| Jolt | Mr. Adcock |
| Landlord | Mr. Singleton |
| Isabella | Mrs. Clarkson |
| Dolly | Miss Hallam |

the coach, but the plot and much of the dialogue were borrowed from a French piece called " Les Carosses d'Orleans." One entire scene between *Captain Basil* and *Sir Nicodemus* was transferred bodily from the French original. This diverting farce proved as popular in America when first produced in this country as it had been in England during the previous half century.

The next dramatist in Mr. Hallam's list was Congreve, of whom Voltaire said that he raised the glory of comedy to a greater height than any English writer before or since his time, but singularly enough he was represented by only one piece, but that his best, "Love for Love." In this play the part of *Angelica* was created by Mrs. Bracegirdle in her advanced age, but it was said of her that she showed the same melting tenderness and playful coquetry she had displayed as *Statira* and *Milla-ment.* *Valentine* was Betterton's great part. In *Sir Sampson Legend* Malone had one of those

### LOVE FOR LOVE.

| | |
|---|---|
| Sir Sampson Legend | Mr. Malone |
| Valentine | Mr. Rigby |
| Scandal | Mr. Bell |
| Tattle | Mr. Singleton |
| Ben, the Sailor | Mr. Hallam |
| Foresight | Mr. Clarkson |
| Jeremy | Mr. Miller |
| Angelica | Mrs. Hallam |
| Mrs. Foresight | Mrs. Rigby |
| Mrs. Frail | Mrs. Adcock |
| Miss Prue | Miss Hallam |
| Nurse | Mr. Adcock |

testy, prejudiced and obstinate old men to which he seems to have been adapted. Although Congreve never borrowed either his plots or his dialogue, and notwithstanding that his plays were exquisite in spite of the heartlessness and duplicity of many of the characters, it is not improbable that the controversy with Jeremy Collier operated toward his exclusion from the stage in America. Even "Love for Love" would not be tolerated at this day, when *Mrs. Foresight* and *Mrs. Frail* are played by actresses off but not on the stage.

Lillo's tragedy of "George Barnwell" was originally produced in 1730, with Theophilus Cibber as *George*, and Mrs. Cibber as *Maria*. In 1752, when Ross was playing *George Barnwell*, a merchant's apprentice in Great St. Helen's was so stricken by remorse upon

### GEORGE BARNWELL.

| | |
|---|---|
| Thorowgood | Mr. Malone |
| Uncle | Mr. Adcock |
| Barnwell | Mr. Bell |
| Trueman | Mr. Rigby |
| Blunt | Mr. Miller |
| Maria | Mrs. Beccely |
| Millwood | Mrs. Hallam |
| Lucy | Mrs. Adcock |

seeing the performance that he became ill, and narrowly escaped death in consequence of his own embezzlements.

Ambrose Philips' tragedy, the "Distressed Mother," was a translation of the "Andromache" of Racine. The heroine was a favorite part with Charlotte Charke, the wayward daughter of Colley Cibber, and afterward with Mrs. Yates. The epilogue to this tragedy was the most successful ever spoken on the stage, and it continued to be expected by audiences while the play held the boards.

### DISTRESSED MOTHER.

| | |
|---|---|
| Pyrrhus | Mr. Singleton |
| Orestes | Mr. Rigby |
| Pylades | Mr. Bell |
| Phœnix | Mr. Clarkson |
| Hermione | Mrs. Adcock |
| Cleone | Miss Hallam |
| Cephisa | Mrs. Rigby |
| Andromache | Mrs. Hallam |

It was printed in the name of Budger but is known to have been written by Addison.

Three of Shakspere's plays were produced during the New York season of 1753–4, all of which still hold the stage. These plays were "Richard III," the Colley Cibber version, of course, "King Lear" and "Romeo and Juliet." In the first mentioned Mr. Rigby played the title role. This was evidently a com-

### RICHARD III.

| | |
|---|---|
| Richard | Mr. Rigby |
| Henry VI | Mr. Hallam |
| Prince of Wales | Master L. Hallam |
| Duke of York | Master A. Hallam |
| Richmond | Mr. Clarkson |
| Buckingham | Mr. Malone |
| Norfolk | Mr. Miller |
| Stanley | Mr. Singleton |
| Catesby | Mr. Adcock |
| Lieutenant | Mr. Bell |
| Queen Elizabeth | Mrs. Hallam |
| Lady Anne | Mrs. Adcock |
| Duchess of Rutland | Mrs. Rigby |

### KING LEAR.

| | |
|---|---|
| Lear | Mr. Malone |
| Kent | Mr. Hallam |
| Gloster | Mr. Bell |
| Edgar | Mr. Singleton |
| Edmund | Mr. Clarkson |
| Cornwall | Mr. Miller |
| Albany | Mr. Adcock |
| Burgundy | Mr. Hulett |
| Usher | Mr. Rigby |
| Cordelia | Mrs. Hallam |
| Regan | Mrs. Adcock |
| Goneril | Mrs. Beccely |
| Aranthe | Mrs. Rigby |

promise with Malone, who, on this occasion, sank into the unimportant part of *Buckingham.* In "King Lear," however, Malone again had the commanding role, while Rigby was only the *Usher.* While

Malone has the honor of being the first *Shylock* and the first *Lear* on the American stage, to Rigby must be accorded the distinction of being the first *Romeo*. The original *Richard* on this continent, it will be remembered, was Thomas Kean, who played the part two years before the arrival of the Hallam Company at Yorktown. The representatives of these parts in America since 1754 comprise nearly all the great names on both the English and American stage, Edwin Booth being the latest.

ROMEO AND JULIET.

| | |
|---|---|
| Romeo . . . . . . . . . . . | Mr. Rigby |
| Mercutio . . . . . . . . . | Mr. Singleton |
| Paris . . . . . . . . . . | Mr. Adcock |
| Tybalt . . . . . . . . . . | Mr. Malone |
| Capulet . . . . . . . . . . | Mr. Bell |
| Montague . . . . . . . . . | Mr. Hallam |
| Friar Laurence . . . . . . . | Mr. Clarkson |
| Balthazar . . . . . . . | Master L. Hallam |
| Juliet . . . . . . . . . . | Mrs. Hallam |
| Lady Capulet . . . . . . . . | Mrs. Rigby |
| Nurse . . . . . . . . . . | Mrs. Adcock |

Gay's Newgate pastoral, the "Beggars' Opera," had been sung in New York by Murray and Kean's company, but it was presented at least twice during the season by Hallam. Miss Fenton, who afterward became Duchess of Bolton, was the original *Polly*, and Walker the first *Macheath*, but Charles Hulett, whose family was represented in the *Nimming Ned* of the American cast, was subsequently esteemed as his superior. The popularity of this work continued down to the Revolution, and among the many *Macheaths* of that period was the younger Lewis Hallam after he had long been pre-eminent in all the great parts of comedy and tragedy.

BEGGARS' OPERA.

| | |
|---|---|
| Peachum . . . . . . . . . | Mr. Hallam |
| Lockit . . . . . . . . . . . | Mr. Malone |
| Macheath . . . . . . . . . | Mr. Adcock |
| Filch . . . . . . . . . . . | Mr. Miller |
| Mat o' the Mint . . . . . . . | Mr. Bell |
| Wat Dreary . . . . . . . | Mr. Singleton |
| Nimming Ned . . . . . . . | Mr. Hulett |
| Mrs. Peachum . . . . . . | Mrs. Adcock |
| Polly . . . . . . . . . . | Mrs. Beccely |
| Lucy . . . . . . . . . . | Mrs. Clarkson |
| Mrs. Coaxer . . . . . . . | Miss Hallam |
| Diana Trapes . . . . . . | Mrs. Adcock |
| Mrs. Vixen . . . . . . . . | Mrs. Rigby |
| Jenny Diver . . . . . . . | Mrs. Love |
| Moll Brazen . . . . . . . | Mr. Clarkson |

Another comedy, presented apparently to give Mr. Malone a part, was the "Committee," which was originally produced as early as 1665, and long continued to hold the stage. It was written by Sir Robert Howard, who was not a great dramatist, but who was so dogmatic that he was ridiculed by Shadwell, in the "Sullen Lovers," as *Sir Positive At-all.* The low comedy parts in this play, *Obadiah*, a clerk to Justice Day, very dull, but very fond of drinking, and *Teague*, an Irish lad, always blundering, and always doing mischief with the best intentions, were very amusing. In a one-act version by T. Knight, "Honest Thieves," Munden was exquisite as *Obadiah*, and Jack Johnstone, the grandfather of Lester Wallack, was irresistible as *Teague*. One night the property-man supplied *Teague* with a bottle of lamp-oil instead of sherry and water, with which he dosed *Obadiah*. When the curtain fell, Johnstone asked Munden why he had not given a hint of the mistake. "There was such a glorious roar at the faces I made," Munden answered, "that I hadn't the heart to spoil it."

COMMITTEE.

| | |
|---|---|
| Mr. Day . . . . . . . . . . | Mr. Malone |
| Abel Day . . . . . . . . . | Mr. Clarkson |
| Colonel Careless . . . . . . | Mr. Singleton |
| Colonel Blunt . . . . . . . . | Mr. Bell |
| Obadiah . . . . . . . . . | Mr. Miller |
| Teague . . . . . . . . . | Mr. Hallam |
| Bailiff . . . . . . . . . . | Mr. Adcock |
| Mrs. Day . . . . . . . . | Mrs. Adcock |
| Ruth . . . . . . . . . . | Mrs. Hallam |
| Arabella . . . . . . . . | Mrs. Beccely |
| Mrs. Chat . . . . . . . | Mrs. Clarkson |

Colley Cibber, who was still alive to hear of the production of his pieces in America, was represented by two farces and his best comedy, the "Careless Husband." Singleton played Cibber's part of *Lord Foppington*, and Mrs. Hallam took Mrs. Oldfield's original

CARELESS HUSBAND.

| | |
|---|---|
| Sir Charles Easy . . . . . . | Mr. Miller |
| Lord Foppington . . . . . | Mr. Singleton |
| Lord Morelove . . . . . . . | Mr. Rigby |
| Lady Betty Modish . . . . . | Mrs. Hallam |
| Lady Easy . . . . . . . . . | Mrs. Adcock |
| Lady Graveairs . . . . . . | Mrs. Beccely |
| Edging . . . . . . . . . . | Miss Hallam |

role of *Lady Betty Modish*.   Macklin used to say that nature formed Cibber for a coxcomb.   It is no wonder, therefore, that he made *Foppington* the king of court fops.   After Mrs. Oldfield, *Lady Betty* was played by Mrs. Pritchard and Mrs. Abington.   *Sir Charles Easy* is the "careless husband," and he is so careless he even leaves his love-letters lying about.   Cibber's ballad farce, "Damon and Phillida,"

### DAMON AND PHILLIDA.

Arcas . . . . . . . . . . . . . Mr. Bell
Ægon . . . . . . . . . . . . . Mr. Rigby
Corydon . . . . . . . . . Mr. Clarkson
Cymon . . . . . . . . . . Mr. Miller
Mopsus . . . . . . . . . . Mr. Hallam
Damon . . . . . . . . . . Mr. Adcock
Phillida . . . . . . . . . Mrs. Beccely

was given as the afterpiece on the first night of the season.   It was followed a few weeks later by " Flora, or Hob in the Well," as the afterpiece to the tragedy of the " Distressed Mother."   The former of these farces has a curious history.   In 1729, Mr. Cibber produced his comedy, " Love in a Riddle," at the theatre in Lincoln's Inn Fields.   On the first night it

### HOB IN THE WELL.

Hob . . . . . . . . . . . Mr. Hallam
Sir Thomas Testy . . . . . Mr. Clarkson
Friendly . . . . . . . . . . Mr. Adcock
Dick . . . . . . . . . Master L. Hallam
Old Hob . . . . . . . . . . Mr. Miller
Flora . . . . . . . . . . Mrs. Beccely
Betty . . . . . . . . . . . Miss Hallam
Hob's Mother . . . . . . . Mrs. Clarkson

was received with so much clamor that only Miss Raftor (Mrs. Clive) was given a hearing.   The following evening Frederick, Prince of Wales, was present, but it was only allowed to proceed out of respect to his Royal Highness, upon a promise that it should be then withdrawn.   Cibber kept the agreement, but out of the comedy he selected the scenes of the farce, which, being produced without his name, met with instant success.   "Hob" was only an appropriation of Dogget's "Country Wake."

Addison was represented by his comedy, the "Drummer," and Rowe by his tragedy, "Jane Shore."   The "Drummer," although elegantly written, is slight in plot and deficient in action. Consequently whatever success it attained was almost wholly due to the popularity of its author. Addison's play will probably never be seen again, but *Jane Shore*, as Rowe paints her in her penitence, and suffering the agony of remorse in abject poverty, must be acknowledged to be one of the great heroines of the English stage, worthy of resuscitation. When the tragedy was originally produced, Mrs. Oldfield was *Mistress Shore*, with Barton Booth as *Hastings* and Cibber as *Gloster*. Later Miss O'Neil played the part, Genevieve Ward being its most recent representative, in England and America.

### DRUMMER.

Sir George Truman . . . . . . . Mr. Bell
Tinsel . . . . . . . . . . . . Mr. Miller
Fantome . . . . . . . . . . . Mr. Adcock
Vellum . . . . . . . . . . . Mr. Malone
Butler . . . . . . . . . . . Mr. Clarkson
Coachman . . . . . . . . . Mr. Singleton
Gardener . . . . . . . . . Mr. Hallam
Lady Truman . . . . . . . Mrs. Beccely
Abagail . . . . . . . . . . Mrs. Adcock

### JANE SHORE.

Jane Shore . . . . . . . . Mrs. Hallam
Gloster . . . . . . . . . . Mr. Hallam
Dumont . . . . . . . . . Mr. Singleton
Hastings . . . . . . . . . . Mr. Rigby
Belmour . . . . . . . . . . . Mr. Bell
Catesby . . . . . . . . . . Mr. Adcock
Ratcliffe . . . . . . . . . Mr. Miller
Alicia . . . . . . . . . . . Mrs. Adcock

The rest of the plays produced by Mr. Hallam during the season—five in all—were those by which the author of each made his reputation as a dramatist. The first of these, the "Gamester," in which Moore had the assistance of Garrick, was a very popular tragedy for many years. It was last presented in this country by Barry Sullivan. As showing the enterprise, as we should now call it, of the Hallams, it must be said of this piece that it was presented in New York within a year of its

### GAMESTER.

Beverly . . . . . . . . . . . Mr. Rigby
Stukely . . . . . . . . . . Mr. Singleton
Lewson . . . . . . . . . . . Mr. Miller
Jarvis . . . . . . . . . . . Mr. Hallam
Dawson . . . . . . . . . Mr. Clarkson
Bates . . . . . . . . . . . . Mr. Bell
Mrs. Beverly . . . . . . . Mrs. Hallam
Charlotte . . . . . . . . . Mrs. Beccely

original production in London, and the same is true of Henry Jones'
"Earl of Essex." The poetic interest in this tragedy turns upon
the assumption that Essex had married the Countess of Rutland,
thus provoking the jealousy both of the Queen and of the Countess
of Nottingham. Mrs. Melmoth, afterward a favorite actress in
this country, was one of the most noteworthy representatives of *Elizabeth* ever seen on the London
stage or on the American boards.

#### EARL OF ESSEX.

| | |
|---|---|
| Earl of Essex . . . . . . . | . Mr. Rigby |
| Earl of Southampton . . . . . | . Mr. Bell |
| Lord Burleigh . . . . . . | . Mr. Singleton |
| Sir Walter Raleigh . . . . . | . Mr. Miller |
| Lieutenant of the Tower . . . | Mr. Adcock |
| Queen Elizabeth . . . . . | . Mrs. Adcock |
| Countess of Rutland . . . . | Mrs. Hallam |
| Countess of Nottingham . . | Mrs. Beccely |

Dr. Hoadly's "Suspicious Husband" was originally produced
in 1747, but even of this it may be said, in the language of Dunlap,
that it "exhibits licentiousness that we turn from as unfit for representation." With a young and sprightly wife, an attractive ward,
and a gay young lady visitor in his house, *Mr. Strictland* could
not fail to see that he was sur- rounded by a great deal of in-
trigue. He is suspicious of every- body about him, including his
servants. George II was so well

#### SUSPICIOUS HUSBAND.

| | |
|---|---|
| Mr. Strictland . . . . . . . | . Mr. Rigby |
| Frankly . . . . . . . . | . Mr. Singleton |
| Bellamy . . . . . . . . . . | . Mr. Bell |
| Ranger . . . . . . . . . . | . Mr. Miller |
| Jack Meggot . . . . . . . . | Mr. Clarkson |
| Tester . . . . . . . . | Master L. Hallam |
| Simon . . . . . . . . . . . | . Mr. Hulett |
| Buckle . . . . . . . . . | . Mr. Adcock |
| Mrs. Strictland . . . . . . | Mrs. Beccely |
| Clarinda . . . . . . . . | . Mrs. Hallam |
| Jacintha . . . . . . . . . . | . Mrs. Adcock |
| Lucetta . . . . . . . . . . | . Miss Hallam |
| Landlady . . . . . . . . . | . Mrs. Rigby |
| Milliner . . . . . . . . . | Mrs. Clarkson |
| Maid . . . . . . . . . . . | . Mrs. Love |

pleased with this comedy that he sent the author £100, a liberal contribution for the German king who then ruled over England.

The comedy of "Woman is a Riddle" has a curious history.
It was a translation of a Spanish comedy, "La Dama Duenda," by

Mrs. Price, wife of Baron Price, one of the judges of the Court of Exchequer. She gave copies of it to three different persons, including the eccentric Richard Savage and Christopher Bullock, a performer at Lincoln's Inn Fields. Bullock was the first to have the piece produced, but while the authorship really belonged to neither, Savage laid claim to a share in it. Bullock has always been credited with it, because he made some changes in Mrs. Price's translation.

WOMAN IS A RIDDLE.

| | |
|---|---|
| Colonel Manly | Mr. Bell |
| Courtwell | Mr. Singleton |
| Sir Amorous Vainwit | Mr. Hallam |
| Vulture | Mr. Rigby |
| Aspen | Mr. Miller |
| Butler | Mr. Adcock |
| Lady Outside | Mrs. Hallam |
| Miranda | Mrs. Adcock |
| Clarinda | Mrs. Clarkson |
| Necessary | Miss Hallam |
| Betty | Mrs. Rigby |

The tragedy of the "Albion Queens" was, of course, based upon the misfortunes of Mary, Queen of Scots, made familiar to theatre-goers in recent years by Ristori's representation of *Marie Stuart*, in Schiller's tragedy. Both Bullock, the author of "Woman's a Riddle," and Banks, who wrote the "Albion Queens," are completely forgotten; but of the latter

ALBION QUEENS.

| | |
|---|---|
| Duke of Norfolk | Mr. Singleton |
| Davison | Mr. Rigby |
| Morton | Mr. Miller |
| Cecil | Mr. Bell |
| Gifford | Mr. Clarkson |
| Douglas, the Page | Master L. Hallam |
| Queen Elizabeth | Mrs. Adcock |
| Mary of Scotland | Mrs. Hallam |

it was said that his plays drew more tears and excited more terror, even from judicious audiences, than the works of better writers.

In the early days of the American stage the English rule of a farce or pantomime as an afterpiece to the play was rigidly followed. In England this custom is still observed, but in this country it has been so long disused that many theatre-goers are unaware that it ever existed. It is perhaps to be regretted that the custom has fallen into desuetude, for many of these pieces were in their day among the most perfect specimens of dramatic writing in the English language, and some of the most distinguished English dramatists had occasion to be proud of their exquisite little comedies.   Two of these were in this list.   Of the farces presented during Hallam's first season three were by Garrick and two by Fielding. Garrick's were the "Lying Valet," "Lethe" and "Miss in her Teens." *Sharp*, in the first mentioned, as the valet of *Gayless*, is the Mercury between his master and *Melissa*.   His lying consists in trying to make *Gayless*, who has not a sixpence in the world, pass for a man of fortune.   "Lethe," played by the Hallam Company at Williamsburg on the opening night, showed some changes in the cast when it was presented in New York.   In view of these changes it is impossible not to wonder where the new members of the company came from.   It is worthy of note, that although "Miss in her Teens" had been produced as early as 1747, it was played in New York the same year that it was published in London.   It is possible that Singleton as *Fribble*, and Clarkson as *Captain Flash*, had seen Garrick and Woodward in their respective parts at Drury Lane.

### LYING VALET.

| | |
|---|---|
| Sharp | Mr. Singleton |
| Gayless | Mr. Adcock |
| Justice Guttle | Mr. Malone |
| Beau Trippet | Mr. Bell |
| Dick | Mr. Miller |
| Melissa | Mrs. Adcock |
| Kitty Pry | Miss Hallam |
| Mrs. Gadabout | Mrs. Rigby |
| Mrs. Trippet | Mrs. Clarkson |

### LETHE.

| | |
|---|---|
| Tattoo | Mr. Miller |
| Charon | Mr. Bell |
| Fine Lady | Mrs. Beccely |
| Mrs. Tattoo | Mrs. Adcock |

### MISS IN HER TEENS.

| | |
|---|---|
| Captain Loveit | Mr. Adcock |
| Captain Flash | Mr. Clarkson |
| Fribble | Mr. Singleton |
| Jasper | Mr. Rigby |
| Puff | Mr. Miller |
| Miss Biddy Belair | Miss Hallam |
| Tag | Mrs. Adcock |

The present generation has not seen either of Fielding's two pieces, the "Virgin Unmasked" and "Tom Thumb," produced by Hallam during the season of 1753–4, but of the former it has been said that it was presented in its day oftener than it deserved, while the latter was not played in America, at least, often enough. The "Virgin Unmasked" was without plot, and it was laughable only because all the characters were *outré*. "Tom Thumb," on the contrary, which preceded Kane O'Hara's burletta by half a century, was an admirable burlesque on the tragedies of its time; the meeting between *Octavia* and *Cleopatra*, in Dryden's "All for Love," especially, being most effectively parodied.

### VIRGIN UNMASKED.

| | |
|---|---|
| Goodwill | Mr. Clarkson |
| Blister | Mr. Malone |
| Coupee | Mr. Singleton |
| Quaver | Mr. Adcock |
| Wormwood | Mr. Miller |
| Thomas | Mr. Bell |
| Miss Lucy | Miss Hallam |

### TOM THUMB.

| | |
|---|---|
| Tom Thumb | Master A. Hallam |
| King Arthur | Mr. Singleton |
| Lord Grizzle | Mr. Rigby |
| Noodle | Mr. Miller |
| Doodle | Mr. Bell |
| Bailiff | Mr. Clarkson |
| Follower | Mr. Malone |
| Queen Dollalolla | Mrs. Hallam |
| Princess Huncamunka | Mrs. Adcock |
| Cleora | Miss Hallam |

According to Dunlap, whose statements must always be accepted with caution, Ravenscroft's farce, the "Anatomist," stood first on the Hallam list for popularity and profit, because of the excellence of Rigby as the French doctor. A better one, and one that was oftener played, in spite of Rigby's excellence and popularity, was Coffey's "Devil to Pay." The cobbler's wife, *Nell*, had been reduced to obedience by

### ANATOMIST.

| | |
|---|---|
| M. le Medicin | Mr. Rigby |
| Old Gerald | Mr. Clarkson |
| Young Gerald | Mr. Adcock |
| Crispin | Mr. Hallam |
| Martin | Mr. Bell |
| Beatrice | Mrs. Hallam |
| Doctor's Wife | Mrs. Rigby |
| Angelica | Mrs. Clarkson |
| Waiting Maid | Miss Hallam |

the application of "strap-oil." By a device of the spirits, Nadir and Abishog, *Sir John Loverule*, whose wife was a termagant, and *Jobson* were made to exchange spouses. Before *Lady Loverule* is restored to her husband, the cobbler's strap had made her also one of the most amiable of women. It was as *Nell*, in this farce, that Mrs. Clive first showed her excellence. No cast of Dodsley's farce, the "King and the Miller of Mansfield," has been found. Speaking of the pantomime, Dunlap says that for a long time the company had only one, "Harlequin Collector," but if this was so it was sometimes played as "Harlequin Skeleton." The manner in which the principal parts in the pantomime were distributed has peculiar interest.

DEVIL TO PAY.

| | |
|---|---|
| Sir John Loverule | Mr. Adcock |
| Jobson | Mr. Malone |
| Butler | Mr. Miller |
| Footman | Mr. Singleton |
| Coachman | Mr. Rigby |
| Lady Loverule | Mrs. Adcock |
| Nell | Mrs. Beccely |
| Lettice | Mrs. Clarkson |
| Lucy | Mrs. Love |

HARLEQUIN COLLECTOR.

| | |
|---|---|
| Harlequin | Mr. Miller |
| Miller | Mr. Singleton |
| Clown | Mr. Hallam |
| Columbine | Mrs. Hallam |

It is noteworthy that Mrs. Clarkson and Mrs. Rigby come in for many of the smaller roles. Their parts, by their insignificance, determine the relation of the two ladies as the wives of the actors whose names they bear, and show beside that neither of them was identical with Miss Palmer, the *Nerissa* at Williamsburg, whose name has disappeared from the bills. But the *Regan* of "Lear" and the *Nurse* of "Romeo and Juliet" filled roles scarcely less ambitious than those of Mrs. Hallam, pointing to the probability that the *Nerissa* of the "Merchant of Venice" and the *Mercury* of "Lethe," in 1752, had in the meantime made the first theatrical marriage in America. Mrs. Adcock's New York *debut* was made as *Mrs. Frail* in "Love for

Love." She also played *Mrs. Tattoo* in " Lethe." *Mrs. Tattoo* was Miss Palmer's part at Williamsburg. If Miss Palmer and Mrs. Adcock are identical, her New York parts show that she must have developed into a capable actress.

It is apparent from the Shaksperean casts that Malone and Rigby were rivals, although apparently friendly ones, for when Malone played *Shylock* and *Lear*, Rigby was content with *Bassanio* and *Usher*, while when Rigby was *Richard* and *Romeo*, Malone sank into *Buckingham* and *Tybalt*. Of the two Rigby was clearly the better actor, for he was given most of the parts really worth having, except the juveniles that fell to Singleton. Between these two again there was the natural rivalry of the "lead" and "juvenile lead." These contrasts are important as showing the liberality in the distribution of parts that prevailed under Hallam's management. It is still further illustrated by the cases of Adcock and Clarkson. The former, as has been shown, had the satisfactory part of *Macheath* in the " Beggars' Opera," but for the rest was content with small parts. Mr. Clarkson had *Jack Meggot* in the " Suspicious Husband," a charming bit that many distinguished actors did not disdain, but in everything else he was simply useful.

While their parts determine the relative standing of the members of the company, it is, of course, impossible from them to gain any real knowledge of their merits as performers. That Rigby was the first in consequence there is no doubt, but the only direct testimony to his ability is Dunlap's record of the tradition that he was so excellent as the French doctor in the " Anatomist " that it was the most popular piece in the repertoire. This, however, had no influence on Dunlap's judgment, and he goes on to assure us that " Mr. and

Mrs. Hallam were first in consequence and in talents," and Mr. Rigby "only inferior to the leaders." This may or may not have been true of Mrs. Hallam, but it was certainly not true of the manager. The lady had the choice of parts, and that she took full advantage of her liberty is apparent from the fact that she disdained the farces, appearing only as *Beatrice* in the "Anatomist," but appropriating to herself everything that she considered best adapted to her powers, and yielding to others only those parts in which she would have made a sorry figure. Mr. Hallam, on the contrary, was quite content to be out of the bills altogether, and when he was in he was not always exacting as to the first low comedy roles, as the list of his parts will show.

The new members of the company were Mrs. Beccely and Messrs. Miller and Bell. Mrs. Beccely was the singing soubrette, her best part being *Polly*, in the "Beggars' Opera." Whether the lady was a member of the company at Williamsburg there is probably no means of ascertaining, nor is there any source of information in regard to the actors. Besides, Mr. and Mrs. Love and Mr. Hulett were engaged as dancers. Mrs. Love appeared twice in a "speaking part," as *Jenny Diver* in the "Beggars' Opera," and *Lucy* in the "Devil to Pay," and Mr. Hulett was the *Nimming Ned* in the "Beggars' Opera," and had one or two other small parts. The Loves were apparently resident in New York, where Mr. Love was a teacher of music. It is probable that Mr. Love was Mr. Hulett's assistant in the Hallam orchestra. Mr. Hulett afterward kept a dancing-school in New York, and spent the rest of his life in that city.

# CHAPTER VII.

## HALLAM IN PHILADELPHIA.

DETERMINED OPPOSITION TO THE THEATRE IN THE QUAKER CITY—
A SHORT BUT SUCCESSFUL SEASON—QUAINT CONTROVERSY OVER
A FAREWELL EPILOGUE.

L EWIS HALLAM, comedian, intending for Philadelphia, begs
the favor of those that have any demands upon him to bring
in their accounts and receive their money.

Such was an announcement contained in the bills for the closing
performance of the Hallam Company in New York, March 18th, 1754.
It is gratifying in a double sense, showing that the manager had money
enough to pay his bills and was willing to pay them. The invasion
of Philadelphia was not made without due consideration and preparation. Even while the company was playing in New York Malone was
detached and sent on in advance to prepare the ground. As a reward
for his exertions, if successful, he was to have the parts of *Falstaff* in
" Henry IV " and the " Merry Wives of Windsor " and *Don Lewis* in
" Love Makes a Man." As he was not accorded the parts it may be
assumed that his success was not considered satisfactory by the manager. Indeed, he seems himself to have considered his mission a
failure, for, finding the opposition more determined than he expected,
he wrote to Mr. Hallam to come to his assistance. The application to
Governor Hamilton for leave to open a theatre even for a limited
number of nights was vigorously resisted. A petition numerously

signed was presented to the Governor, protesting against profane stage-plays, and this was met by a counter-petition from the friends of the theatre. In the end the theatrical party prevailed, and permission was granted to Mr. Hallam to give twenty-four performances, on condition that nothing indecent or immoral should be presented. Mr. Hallam was also required to give one night for the benefit of the poor, and enter into security for all debts contracted on behalf of the company.

The theatre occupied by "the company of comedians from London" at that time was the same that had previously been used by Murray and Kean's Company in 1749–50. It was in a warehouse belonging to William Plumstead, in King or Water, between Pine and Lombard Streets. The building extended through to Front Street, from which there was an entrance by means of stairs placed on the outside of the warehouse. This building remained standing until 1849. It was used as a sail-loft for many years, and Dunlap said in 1832 that "the remains or traces of scenic decoration were to be seen in it within forty years." Among these decorations was a glittering motto over the stage: "*Totus mundus agit histrionem.*" The attitude of William Plumstead toward the theatre must be conceded to be a bold one, when his position and surroundings are considered. To let a building for theatrical purposes at that time in Philadelphia was something that required courage. For a Magistrate to become the lessor must have been in the nature of a scandal. William Plumstead was elected a Common Councilman in 1739, an Alderman in 1747, and became Mayor of Philadelphia in 1750. He was three times Mayor—first from October, 1750, to October, 1751, again for the unexpired term of Charles Willing, deceased, from December, 1754, to October, 1755, and finally by re-election from October, 1755, to Octo-

ber, 1756. He was four times commissioned a Justice of the Peace—
in 1752, 1757, 1761 and 1765, the date last named being the year of
his death. Mr. Plumstead besides represented Northampton County
in the General Assembly of the Province in 1757–8, and he was
Register-General of Pennsylvania from 1745 until his death. He was
one of the first contributors to the Pennsylvania Hospital, and for
many years a Trustee of the College and Academy of Philadelphia.
Originally a Quaker, he abandoned the principles of the Society of
Friends early in life and became a vestryman and warden of Christ
Church. As a sign of the liberality of sentiment that would lead him
to become the lessor of a theatre against the prejudices of a large part
of the community it may be noted that he was an original member of
the famous fishing club, "the Colony in Schuylkill," instituted in 1732,
and a subscriber to the first dancing assembly in Philadelphia, held in
1748. This biography is important in affording a glimpse of the powerful social and political influence that assisted in the introduction of the
drama into the city, in spite of a determined and active opposition.

How the good people of the Quaker City must have been
shocked when they found the London play-actors acting stage-plays.
The first performance of the
Hallam Company in Phila-
delphia, which occurred on
the 15th of April, 1754, is
especially memorable for the
epilogue spoken on the occasion by Mrs. Hallam.
The prologue was the one
attributed to Singleton, which

EPILOGUE.

Much has been said in this reforming age
To damn in gross the business of the stage;
Some for this end, in terms not quite so civil,
Have given both plays and players to the devil.
With red-hot zeal, in dreadful pomp they come,
And bring their flaming tenets warm from Rome—
Fathers and Councils, hermits from their cell,
Are brought to prove this is the road to hell.
To me, who am, I own, but a weak woman,
This way to reformation seems uncommon;
If these authorities are good, we hope
To gain a full indulgence from the Pope—

We, too, will fly to Holy Mother Church
And leave these sage reformers in the lurch.
But to be serious—now let's try the cause
By Truth and Reason's most impartial laws.
The play just finish'd, prejudice apart—
Let honest nature speak—how feels the heart?
Did it not throb, then tell it to our foes;
To mourn the parent, friend and husband's woes,
Whilst at the cause of all a noble indignation rose?
If, then, the soul in virtue's cause we move,
Why should the friends of virtue disapprove?
We trust they do not by this splendid sight
Of sparkling eyes that greet our scenes to-night.
Then smile, ye fair, propitious on the cause,
And every generous heart shall beat applause.

had been spoken originally in Williamsburg and repeated in New York, but the epilogue was written for the occasion and took special cognizance of the opposition that had been encountered by the company. In its nature it was an argument in behalf of the drama, but the lines relating to " flaming tenets warm from Rome," and to " Fathers and Councils," brought to prove that the play-house is the road to hell, would be unintelligible but for a note which accompanies the epilogue as printed in the *Pennsylvania Gazette.* It is there explained that the allusions are to "the Pamphlet lately published here, entitled *Extracts, &c.*, and given away gratis." What could be more grotesque than this attempt to discourage the stage in America by the reproduction of the opinions of a dissolute Bourbon prince, written at the close of a dissipated life? What could be more amusing in a city whose inhabitants had a horror of Rome, than a recommendation of " the sentiments of the Fathers " and the " Decrees of the Councils " to the

EXTRACTS
of
Several Treatises
wrote by the
Prince of Conti,
with the
Sentiments of the Fathers
and some of the
Decrees of the Councils
concerning
Stage Plays:
Recommended to the Perusal and Serious Consideration of the Professors of Christianity in the City of Philadelphia.

———

Philadelphia:
Printed by William Bradford at the sign of the Bible in Second Street.
MDCCLIV.

perusal of Quakers and Presbyterians? At best this was rather a heavy document to be hurled by the good people of Philadelphia at a company of strolling players, who had been required to give security that they would pay their debts. But the pamphlet was not the only resort to types to overcome the players. On the 19th of March, *A. B.* wrote to the *Pennsylvania Gazette,* asking for the publication of some extracts from " Britain's Remembrances " against profane plays, to which *Y. Z.* responded the following week. The opposition only served to attract attention to the theatre, and on the opening night the house was crowded. The play was Rowe's "Fair Penitent," with "Miss in her Teens " as the afterpiece. It is worthy of remark that on this night an incident occurred that shows how bitter the feeling was against the anti-theatrical party. One of the petitioners was found among the audience, but his presence created so much dissatisfaction that he was ejected from the theatre. He was looked upon not only as an enemy, but as a spy.

The only way by which it is possible to learn what plays were presented during the brief season of two months is from the advertisements in the *Pennsylvania Gazette,* all of which are included in the subjoined list. It is somewhere stated that the comedy of "Tunbridge Walks" and the farce of "Hob in the Well" were presented during the season. Besides these, it is likely that many of the pieces produced in New York were

GAZETTE LIST.

1754.
April 15—Fair Penitent . . . . . . Rowe
     Miss in her Teens . . . Garrick
June 10—Gamester . . . . . . . Moore
     Miss in her Teens.
(Benefit of Miss Hallam and her brothers.)
June 12—Tamerlane . . . . . . . Rowe
     A Wife Well Managed . Centlivre
     (Mr. Adcock's Benefit.)
   20—Careless Husband . . . . Cibber
     Harlequin Collector.
(Benefit of the Charity Children.)
   27—Provoked Husband . . . Cibber
     Miss in her Teens.

given in Philadelphia between the 15th of April and the 10th of June. Only two additional casts have been preserved—those of Rowe's tragedies, the "Fair Penitent" and "Tamerlane." The former was a mere *rechauffé* of Massinger's "Fatal Dowry." The part of *Calista* was a favorite role of Mrs. Barry, Mrs. Siddons and Mrs. Merry. Of the latter it is said that Louis XIV was Rowe's

FAIR PENITENT.

Sciolto . . . . . Mr. Malone
Altamont . . . Mr. Clarkson
Horatio . . . . . Mr. Rigby
Lothario . . . Mr. Singleton
Rossano . . . Mr. Adcock
Servant . Master L. Hallam
Calista . . . . Mrs. Hallam
Lavinia . . . . Mrs. Adcock
Lucilla . . . . . Mrs. Rigby

TAMERLANE.

Tamerlane . Mr. Singleton
Monesses . . . Mr. Rigby
Axalla . . . . . Mr. Bell
Prince . . . . . Mr. Adcock
Stratocles . . . Mr. Miller
Bajazet . . . Mr. Malone
Omar . . . . Mr. Clarkson
Deroise . . . Mr. Hallam
Haly . . Master L. Hallam
Selima . . . Mrs. Beccely
Arpasia . . . Mrs. Hallam

*Bajazet,* and William III his *Tamerlane.* While King William lived, and long afterward, it was the custom to produce the piece on the 5th of November, the king's birthday. A singularly interesting souvenir of this season is a play-bill of the benefit of the Hallam children on the 10th of June, in the possession of Mr. Charles R. Hildeburn, the compiler of a monumental record of the work of the early Pennsylvania printers. This, it is believed, is the earliest American play-bill in existence.

The Philadelphia Academy was opened the same month that the players of Murray and Kean's Company were held to their good behavior. In connection with the Academy was a charity school. In 1753 Dr. William Smith took charge of the Academy. Like most English divines of the

CHARITY PROLOGUE.

Our humble Prologue means not to engage
Candor for Scenes that long have grac'd the Stage;
Nor vainly strives to pay with words, at last,
For cheering smiles and kind protection past.
Weak is the power of language to explain
The sacred feelings, or th' ingenious pain
And silent strugglings of the virtuous breast,
Beneath the load of *Gratitude* opprest.

But tho' no words can picture what we feel,
Our aims may speak it and our actions tell.

Established Church, he was not opposed to a well regulated stage nor averse to drawing upon the theatre for aid to the church schools. When the agreement in regard to the charity performance was fulfilled on the 19th of June, with the "Careless Husband" and "Harlequin Collector" comprising the bill, the proceeds went "for the benefit of the charity children belonging to the Academy in this city," according to the *Pennsylvania Gazette*. The audience was a very crowded and polite one, in the language of the same authority. On this occasion a prologue suited to the character of the entertainment was spoken by Mr. Rigby. By whom it was

To-night we glory in the double view
Of pleasing soft-eyed Charity—and You.
For this our cheerful service we bestow—
'Tis all our slender fortunes will allow;
"And those who give the little in their power,"
The Skies acquit—and Earth can ask no more.

Thrice happy you, whom kinder fates have given,
With liberal hand to ease the care of Heaven;
To raise the drooping head of modest Worth;
From Fortune's blast to save the Orphan-birth,
To pierce the dark retreats where mis'ry sighs,
And wipe the trickling tear that dews her eyes;
If deeds like these can bid the bosom glow
With Joys sincere,—what bosom glows not now?
For sure, if aught be gen'rous, great or fair,
It must be Truth and public Worth to rear!

Where Virtue blooms in yonder hallow'd Ground,*
With each ennobling Science opening round;
How many † Maids and Youths, with kindling fires,
Now grow in all that living worth inspires.
Whom Fortune, in their dawn, neglected laid,
To pine untutor'd in the barren Shade,
Where Wisdom never did her page unroll,
And Want still froze the current of their soul;
Till, by your bounteous hand, redeem'd from fate,
You bade them rise to grace a rising State.

Thus pinch'd beneath stern winter's rigid reign,
The flowers lie mourning thro' the frozen plain,
Till Spring, soft issuing from her southern hall,
Sweeps o'er the dew-bright lawn, with breezy call,
And wakes them into life;—they straight unfold
To th' orient sun their vegetable gold;
And in return embalm the fost'ring air,
Or grace the lovely bosoms of the fair.

written is not known, but had Dunlap found it, he would have been sure to attribute the authorship to Singleton. Indeed, he did this with an epilogue delivered in New York in 1758, the original version of which was recited by Mrs. Hallam, in Philadelphia, June 27th, 1754,

* The Academy.            † The Charity Children.

when the Hallam Company took its farewell of that city and the continent. With that facility for guessing, for which he was re-

FAREWELL EPILOGUE.

Oft thankless slaves for favours humbly ask,
But to be grateful is a nobler task:
That task to-night be ours.—And thus to you,
Our generous friends, we pay the tribute due,
Accept our hearty thanks for favors past,
And for the present, should it prove the last;
Yet wou'd we fain presume some hopes remain,
Some distant hopes, that we may meet again;
Again to hear the virtuous fair complain
In Shakspere's, Lee's or Otway's moving strain,
And teach the heart another's grief to know
And melt the soul in tears of generous woe.
Who was not grieved to-night to see the strife
Betwixt a generous husband and a thoughtless wife?
And who from tears of joy could well refrain
To see them meet in mutual love again?
But when to humorous mirth you're more inclin'd
Sheer comic wit shall feast the cheerful mind,
Fools of all sorts, and fops, a brainless crew,
To raise your mirth we'll summon to your view;
Make each pert coxcomb merry with his brother,
Whilst knaves concealed shall grin at one another.
'Tis magic ground we tread, and at our call
Those knights appear that represent you all.
But, hold! methinks I hear some snarler cry,
"Pray, Madam, why so partial—rat me—why
Don't you do justice to your own sweet sex?
Are there no prudes, coquettes or jilts to vex?
Or must we be confined to female rules,
To laugh at none but brainless fops and fools?"
Be calm, kind sir, the satire's not at you—
You rob your coxcomb brethren of their due.
'Tis granted; vice and folly's not confined
To men alone, but spreads to womankind.
We frankly own—we may, indeed, as well—
For every fluttering beau we've an affected belle.
Nor has dramatic satire's candid page,
Failed to chastise them justly on the stage.
Thus human life's our theme—a spacious field,
Which nature's noblest entertainments yield,

markable, he not only attributed the New York epilogue to the author of the company's first prologue, but reprinted it as "marking the improvement of poet Singleton by transplantation." Curiously enough the original of this New York epilogue was printed in the *Pennsylvania Gazette* the eek following its delivery in the theatre on Water Street, where it was explained that the allusion to "our Latin motto" was to the inscription over the stage: *Totus Mundus agit Histrionem.* A recently established organization called the "Dunlap Society," has actually included this epilogue among its publications as Singleton's, thus perpetuating the mistaken assumption of the historian after whom the society was named by its founders. There probably never was a writer who was less deserving of such an honor than William Dunlap. As a theatrical manager he confessed himself a failure. As a dramatist his plays are deservedly forgotten; they were without merit either for stage representation or as literary productions. As a historian he was at once dull and inaccurate. That a society should have been named after him is perhaps not more remarkable than that it should perpetuate his blunders. The epilogue attracted so much attention in Philadelphia that it was parodied in the *Gazette* of August 15th, 1754. The parody was signed " Buckram " and purported to be the address of a journeyman tailor to his sweetheart. It was feeble enough, it must be confessed, but feeble as it was, there was somebody who was willing to pay for the privilege of answering it, as appears from a

By men of worth admired from ancient time
Who following nature never judged a crime.
Then bravely dare to assert the taste you've shown,
Nor be ashamed so just a cause to own;
And tell our foes what Shakspere said of old—
Our Latin motto speaks it I am told—
That here the world in miniature you see,
And all mankind are players as well as we.

### PARODY.

Let thankless slaves for favors humbly **ask**,
But to be grateful is a nobler task;
Accept my thanks then, Sue, for favors past
And for the last, if it should prove the last.
    Yet would I fain
    Presume some hopes remain,
Some distant hopes that we may meet again—
Again to hear your constant swain complain,
And whistle through his nose a dying strain.
From tears of grief I could not well refrain,
To think, dear Sue, we should not meet again.
But hark! methinks I hear some snarler cry,
Zounds, Buckram, 'tis vain—why, demme, why?
Kind Sue will never let a lover die.
Then, Snarler, peace, for rat me, but I'll try.
Forbid it, Sue, that I should ever see
Some dog stroll o'er thy sweets and drink them all from me.
This sight would drive me to some fatal tree
And, rat me, but I'd rather hang on thee.
Then trust me, Sue, my love is aimed at you—
To mend your gown I'll summon to your view
Patches of every hue, both old and new,
    Brown, yellow, black and blue,
Of velvet, worsted, silk, a motley crew.
And when to mirthful mirth you are inclin'd,
Sheer comic wit shall feast the cheerful mind.
For comic sheer wit was design'd, you'll find

Like sharpest shears to shape the humankind.
Thus shaping is my trade—a spacious field
Which nature's noblest entertainments yield.
By men of cloth admired from ancient time
Who fitting nature never thought a crime.
Then, dearest Sue, accept my whining rhyme,
And let your heart to mine in loving measure chime.

                              BUCKRAM.

quaintly worded notice in the *Gazette* of the 29th.[1]  In a note appended to the parody it was said that the author of the epilogue was also the author of " Julia Imitated " and of a play.  All this had the effect of bringing to the front the writer of the epilogue, Adam Thomson, a Scotchman, in an elaborate reply (September 12th), entitled " The humble remonstrance of the Journeyman Taylors against a certain Journeyman Schoolmaster for imperiously assuming the character of one of their fraternity in a late dull, pedantic and ill-natured performance subscribed Buckram."  Like most Scotchmen Thomson was impervious to a joke.  The result was that he not only took "Buckram's" burlesque to heart, but explained his personal allusions with great seriousness and sincerity.  " As this epilogue," he said, "was wrote by particular desire, on a short warning, the author could have no other view than to oblige and entertain."  Mr. Thomson's poem, to which allusion was made, was verse in praise of an American beauty, published in the *Gentleman's Magazine*, in June, 1752, with the title of "The Fifth Elegy in Joannes Secundus' First Book, intitled Julia, imitated."  His play was called the " Disappointed Gallant, or Buckram in Armour," and was acted at the New Theatre in Edinburgh, in 1738, when its author was only fifteen years old.  "Though full of puerilities," Mr. Thomson wrote, " a good and polite audience was pleased to applaud, as they knew

---

[1] The person that left the Piece at the New Printing-Office signed *Buckram in Armour* is desired to call for it, and the money therewith sent, as it will not be printed there being no name to it, and the publishers are well assured it was not wrote by the Author of the Epilogue lately burlesqued.

it to be the performance of a boy." But of all the liberties taken with his epilogue by the "Journeyman Critic," its author was most hurt with the lines in the burlesque,

> This sight would drive me to some fatal tree,
> And, rat me, but I'd rather hang on thee,

and in justification of the couplet he, quaintly enough, offered the following translation :—

> Yet let me die, my Julia, in thy arms,
> Around thy neck my dying arms to twine,
> Whilst you support my falling corpse with thine.
> Far happier thus suspended I should be
> Than through despair suspended on a tree.
>
> JOANNES SECUNDUS, EL. V.

An incident of the Philadelphia season was a visit from William Hallam, the projector of the company, who returned to England after a settlement of their accounts by the brothers. When the season closed the company went to Jamaica, in the West Indies, where Lewis Hallam died and the organization disbanded.

With the exception of Mrs. Hallam, when she became Mrs. Douglass, and her two sons, Masters Lewis and Adam Hallam, none of the regular members of the company were seen on the American stage again. In taking leave of them, therefore, the accompanying statement of the parts each of them was known to have played, will have a peculiar interest in showing the work accomplished by them, and as a basis for future comparison. It will be seen from this summary that during the Hallam campaign of two years, twenty-four distinct full pieces and eleven afterpieces were produced. These include only the productions of which the casts have been preserved. A glance at the tables will show how completely the strength of the company was utilized. Mr.

Singleton, for instance, had a part in all the plays except "George Barnwell." Mr. Rigby was in all except three—the "Beggars' Opera," the "Committee" and the "Drummer." Even Malone was only out of seven and Hallam out of eight of the twenty-four plays. Besides, Malone had parts in five, Hallam and Rigby in seven and Singleton in eight of the farces. Turning from the first to the second table, it will be found that the supporting actors, Messrs. Adcock, Clarkson, Bell

RETIRING ACTORS.—LEAD.—PARTS.

| PLAYS. | Hallam. | Rigby. | Malone. | Singleton. |
|---|---|---|---|---|
| Albion Queens . . . | . . . . . . . . . . | Davison . . . . . . | . . . . . . . . . . | Duke of Norfolk . . |
| Beaux' Stratagem . | Foigard . . . . . . | Sullen . . . . . . . | Scrub . . . . . . . | Archer . . . . . . |
| Beggars' Opera . . | Peachum . . . . . | . . . . . . . . . . | Lockit . . . . . . . | Wat Dreary . . . . |
| Careless Husband . | . . . . . . . . . . | Lord Morelove . . | . . . . . . . . . . | Lord Foppington . . |
| Committee . . . . | Teague . . . . . . | . . . . . . . . . . | Mr. Day . . . . . | Colonel Careless . . |
| Conscious Lovers . | . . . . . . . . . . | Young Bevil . . . | Sealand . . . . . . | Tom . . . . . . . |
| Constant Couple . . | Clincher, Sr. . . . . | Colonel Standard . | Alderman Smuggler | Sir Harry Wildair . |
| Distressed Mother . | . . . . . . . . . . | Orestes . . . . . . | . . . . . . . . . . | Pyrrhus . . . . . |
| Drummer . . . . . | Gardener . . . . . | . . . . . . . . . . | Vellum . . . . . . | Coachman . . . . . |
| Earl of Essex . . | . . . . . . . . . . | Earl of Essex . . . | . . . . . . . . . . | Lord Burleigh . . . |
| Fair Penitent . . . | . . . . . . . . . . | Horatio . . . . . . | Sciolto . . . . . . | Lothario . . . . . |
| Gamester . . . . . | Jarvis . . . . . . . | Beverly . . . . . | . . . . . . . . . . | Stukely . . . . . . |
| George Barnwell . . | . . . . . . . . . . | Trueman . . . . . | Thorowgood . . . | . . . . . . . . . . |
| Jane Shore . . . . | Gloster . . . . . . | Hastings . . . . . | . . . . . . . . . . | Dumont . . . . . |
| Lear . . . . . . . . | Kent . . . . . . . . | Usher . . . . . . | Lear . . . . . . . | Edgar . . . . . . |
| Love for Love . . . | Ben . . . . . . . . | Valentine . . . . . | Sir Sampson Legend | Tattle . . . . . . |
| Merchant of Venice | Launcelot, Tubal . . | Bassanio . . . . . | Shylock . . . . . . | Gratiano . . . . . |
| Richard III . . . . | Henry VI . . . . . | Richard . . . . . . | Buckingham . . . . | Stanley . . . . . |
| Romeo and Juliet . | Montague . . . . . | Romeo . . . . . . | Tybalt . . . . . . | Mercutio . . . . . |
| Suspicious Husband | . . . . . . . . . . | Mr. Strictland . . . | . . . . . . . . . . | Frankly . . . . . |
| Tamerlane . . . . | Dervise . . . . . . | Monesses . . . . . | Bajazet . . . . . . | Tamerlane . . . . |
| Tunbridge Walks . | Captain Squib . . . | Reynard . . . . . | Woodcock . . . . . | Maiden . . . . . . |
| Twin Rivals . . . . | Teague . . . . . . | Elder Wouldbe . . | Balderdash, Alderm'n | Trueman . . . . . |
| Woman is a Riddle | Sir Andrew Vainwit | Vulture . . . . . . | | Courtwell . . . . . |
| | | | | |
| FARCES. | | | | |
| Anatomist . . . . . | Crispin . . . . . . | M. le Medecin . . . | . . . . . . . . . . | . . . . . . . . . . |
| Damon and Phillida | Mopsus . . . . . . | Ægon . . . . . . . | . . . . . . . . . . | . . . . . . . . . . |
| Devil to Pay . . . . | . . . . . . . . . . | Coachman . . . . . | Jobson . . . . . . | Footman . . . . . |
| Harlequin Collector | Clown . . . . . . . | . . . . . . . . . . | . . . . . . . . . . | Miller . . . . . . |
| Hob in the Well . . | Hob . . . . . . . . | . . . . . . . . . . | . . . . . . . . . . | . . . . . . . . . . |
| Lethe . . . . . . . | Drunken Man, Tattoo | Frenchman . . . . | Old Man . . . . . | Fine Gentleman . . |
| Lying Valet . . . . | . . . . . . . . . . | . . . . . . . . . . | Justice Guttle . . . | Sharp . . . . . . |
| Miss in her Teens . | . . . . . . . . . . | Jasper . . . . . . | . . . . . . . . . . | Fribble . . . . . . |
| Stage Coach . . . . | Macahone . . . . . | Filch . . . . . . . | . . . . . . . . . . | Landlord . . . . . |
| Tom Thumb . . . | . . . . . . . . . . | Lord Grizzle . . . . | Follower . . . . . | King Arthur . . . . |
| Virgin Unmasked . | . . . . . . . . . . | . . . . . . . . . . | Blister . . . . . . | Coupee . . . . . . |

and Miller, were seldom without parts either in the plays or the after-pieces, and the same thing is true of the two ladies, Mrs. Adcock and Mrs. Beccely, in the list of the parts of the retiring actresses. All this is interesting in itself, but these lists must be looked upon simply as a record of the work actually performed by these early players, not as indicative of their professional merits. Like all pioneers they were hard workers, and they are to be honored for what they accomplished

RETIRING ACTORS.—SUPPORT.—PARTS.

| PLAYS. | *Adcock.* | *Clarkson.* | *Bell.* | *Miller.* |
|---|---|---|---|---|
| Albion Queens . . . | . . . . . . . . . . | Gifford . . . . . . | Cecil . . . . . . . | Morton . . . . . . |
| Beaux' Stratagem : | Aimwell . . . . . . | Gibbet . . . . . . | Sir Charles Freeman | Boniface . . . . . |
| Beggars' Opera . . | Macheath . . . . . | . . . . . . . . . . | Mat o' the Mint . . | Filch . . . . . . |
| Careless Husband . | . . . . . . . . . . | . . . . . . . . . . | . . . . . . . . . . | Sir Charles Easy . . |
| Committee . . . . | Bailiff . . . . . . . | Abel Day . . . . . | Colonel Blunt . . . | Obadiah . . . . . . |
| Conscious Lovers . | Humphrey . . . . | Myrtle . . . . . . | Sir John Bevil . . . | Cimberton . . . . . |
| Constant Couple . . | Constable . . . . . | Clincher, Jr. . . . . | Tom Errand . . . . | Vizard . . . . . . |
| Distressed Mother . | . . . . . . . . . . | Phœnix . . . . . . | Pylades . . . . . . | . . . . . . . . . |
| Drummer . . . . . | Fantome . . . . . | Butler . . . . . . . | Sir George Truman | Tinsel . . . . . . |
| Earl of Essex . . . | Lieut. of the Tower | . . . . . . . . . . | Southampton . . . | Raleigh . . . . . . |
| Fair Penitent . . . | Rossano . . . . . . | Altamont . . . . . | . . . . . . . . . | . . . . . . . . . |
| Gamester . . . . . | . . . . . . . . . . | Dawson . . . . . . | Bates . . . . . . . | Lewson . . . . . . |
| George Barnwell . . | Uncle . . . . . . . | . . . . . . . . . . | Barnwell . . . . . | Blunt . . . . . . . |
| Jane Shore . . . . | Catesby . . . . . . | . . . . . . . . . . | Belmour . . . . . . | Ratcliffe . . . . . |
| Lear . . . . . . . | Albany . . . . . | Edmund . . . . . . | Gloster . . . . . . | Cornwall . . . . . |
| Love for Love . . . | Nurse . . . . . . | Foresight . . . . . | Scandal . . . . . . | Jeremy . . . . . . |
| Merchant of Venice | . . . . . . . . . . | Antonio . . . . . . | . . . . . . . . . | . . . . . . . . . |
| Richard III . . . . | Catesby . . . . . . | Richmond . . . . . | Lieutenant . . . . | Norfolk . . . . . . |
| Romeo and Juliet . | Paris . . . . . . . | Friar Laurence . . | Capulet . . . . . . | . . . . . . . . . |
| Suspicious Husband | Buckle . . . . . . | Jack Meggot . . . | Bellamy . . . . . . | Ranger . . . . . . |
| Tamerlane . . . . | Prince of Tanais . | Omar . . . . . . . | Axalla . . . . . . | Stratocles . . . . |
| Tunbridge Walks . | . . . . . . . . . . | . . . . . . . . . . | . . . . . . . . . | Loveworth . . . . |
| Twin Rivals . . . . | Clear-account . . . | Young Wouldbe . . | Richmore . . . . . | Subtleman . . . . . |
| Woman is a Riddle | Butler . . . . . . . | . . . . . . . . . . | Colonel Manly . . . | Aspen . . . . . . . |
| FARCES. | | | | |
| Anatomist . . . . . | Young Gerald . . . | Old Gerald . . . . | Martin . . . . . . | . . . . . . . . . |
| Damon and Phillida | Damon . . . . . . | Corydon . . . . . | Arcas . . . . . . . | Cymon . . . . . . |
| Devil to Pay . . . | Sir John Loverule . | . . . . . . . . . . | . . . . . . . . . | Butler . . . . . . |
| Harlequin Collector | . . . . . . . . . . | . . . . . . . . . . | . . . . . . . . . | Harlequin . . . . . |
| Hob in the Well . . | Friendly . . . . . . | Sir Thomas Testy . | . . . . . . . . . | Old Hob . . . . . |
| Lethe . . . . . . . | Mercury . . . . . | Æsop . . . . . . . | Charon . . . . . . | Tattoo . . . . . . |
| Lying Valet . . . . | Gayless . . . . . . | . . . . . . . . . . | Beau Trippet . . . | Dick . . . . . . . |
| Miss in her Teens . | Captain Loveit . . . | Captain Flash . . . | . . . . . . . . . | Puff . . . . . . . |
| Stage Coach . . . . | Jolt . . . . . . . . | Uncle Michar . . . | Captain Basil . . . | Sir Nicodemus . . |
| Tom Thumb . . . | . . . . . . . . . . | Bailiff . . . . . . . | Doodle . . . . . . | Noodle . . . . . . |
| Virgin Unmasked . | Quaver . . . . . . | Goodwill . . . . . | Thomas . . . . . . | Wormwood . . . . |

in clearing the way for the drama in the New World, without regard to their artistic excellence. It is in the fact that these pioneers were able to hold their own that the subsequent existence of the American Company was due, and nothing can be clearer than the conclusion that they were able to hold their own only by the earnestness and sincerity with which they devoted themselves to their calling.

There was one result incident to this Hallam campaign of which

RETIRING ACTRESSES.—PARTS.

| PLAYS. | Mrs. Adcock. | Mrs. Beccely. | Mrs. Clarkson. | Mrs. Rigby. |
|---|---|---|---|---|
| Albion Queens . . . | Elizabeth . . . . . | . . . . . . . . . . | . . . . . . . . . . | . . . . . . . . . . |
| Beaux' Stratagem . | Mrs. Peachum . . . | Dorinda . . . . . . | Gipsy . . . . . . | Lady Bountiful . . |
| Beggars' Opera . . | Diana Trapes . . . | Polly . . . . . . . | Lucy . . . . . . . | Mrs. Vixen . . . . |
| Careless Husband . | Lady Easy . . . . | Lady Graveairs . . | . . . . . . . , . . | . . . . . . . . . . |
| Committee . . . . | Mrs. Day . . . . . | Arabella . . . . . | Mrs. Chat . . . . . | . . . . . . . . . . |
| Conscious Lovers . | . . . . . . . . . . | Phillis . . . . . . | Mrs. Sealand . . . | Isabella . . . . . . |
| Constant Couple . . | . . . . . . . . . . | Angelica . . . . . | Porter's Wife . . . | Lady Darling . . . |
| Distressed Mother . | Hermione . . . . . | . . . . . , . . . | . . . . . . . . . . | Cephisa . . . . . . |
| Drummer . . . . . | Abagail . . . . . | Lady Truman . . . | . . . . . . . . . . | . . . . . . . . . . |
| Earl of Essex . . . | Elizabeth . . . . . | C. of Nottingham . | . . . . . . . . . . | . . . . . . . . . . |
| Fair Penitent . . . | Lavinia . . . . . . | . . . . . . . . . . | . . . . . . . . . . | Lucilla . . . . . . |
| Gamester . . . . . | | Charlotte . . . . . | . . . . . . . . . . | . . . |
| George Barnwell . . | Lucy . . . . . . . | Maria . . . . . . . | . . . . . . . . . . | . . . . . . . . . . |
| Jane Shore . . . . | Alicia . . . . . . . | | . . . . . . . . . . | . . . . . . . . . . |
| Lear . . . . . . . | Regan . . . . . . | Goneril . . . . . | . . . . . . . . . . | Aranthe . . . . . . |
| Love for Love . . . | Mrs. Frail . . . . . | | . . . . . . . . . . | Mrs. Foresight . . . |
| Merchant of Venice | . . . . . . . . . . | . . . . . . . . . . | . . . . . . . . . . | . . . . . . . . . . |
| Richard III . . . . | Lady Anne . . . . | | . . . . . . . . . . | Duchess of Rutland |
| Romeo and Juliet . | Nurse . . . . . . . | | . . . . . . . . . . | Lady Capulet . . . |
| Suspicious Husband | Jacintha . . . . . . | Mrs. Strictland . . | Milliner . . . . . . | Landlady . . . . . |
| Tamerlane . . . . | | Selima . . . . . . | | |
| Tunbridge Walks . | . . . . . . . . . . | Belinda . . . . . . | Penelope . . . . . | Mrs. Goodfellow . . |
| Twin Rivals . . . . | Mrs. Midnight . . . | Aurelia . . . . . . | Maid . . . . . . . | Mrs. Clear-account |
| Woman is a Riddle . | Miranda . . . . . . | . . . . . . . . . . | Clarinda . . . . . | Betty . . . . . . . |
| FARCES. | | | | |
| Anatomist . . . . . | . . . . . . . . . . | . . . . . . . . . . | Angelica . . . . . | Doctor's Wife . . . |
| Damon and Phillida | . . . . . . . . . . | Phillida . . . . . . | . . . . . . . . . . | . . . . . . . . . . |
| Devil to Pay . . . . | Lady Loverule . . . | Nell . . . . . . . . | Lettice . . . . . . | . . . . . . . . . . |
| Harlequin Collector | . . . . . . . . . . | . . . . . . . . . . | . . . . . . . . . . | . . . . . . . . . . |
| Hob in the Well . . | . . . . . . . . . . | Flora . . . . . . . | Hob's Mother . . . | . . . . . . . . . . |
| Lethe . . . . . . . | Mrs. Tattoo . . . . | Fine Lady . . . . . | . . . . . . . . . . | . . . . . . . . . . |
| Lying Valet . . . . | Melissa . . . . . . | . . . . . . . . . . | Mrs. Trippet . . . | Mrs. Gadabout . . |
| Miss in her Teens . | Tag . . . . . . . . | | | |
| Stage Coach . . . . | . . . . . . . . . . | . . . . . . . . . . | Isabella . . . . . . | . . . . . . . . . . |
| Tom Thumb . . . | Princ's Huncamunka | . . . . . . . . . . | . . . . . . . . . . | . . . . . . . . . . |
| Virgin Unmasked . | . . . . . . . . . . | . . . . . . . . . . | . . . . . . . . . . | . . . . . . . . . . |

America has reason to be proud. The boy who made his first appearance on the stage at Williamsburg, in 1752, was destined, while still a youth, to redeem the failure with which he began, and to occupy the front rank on the American boards for half a century. Lewis Hallam the second was essentially an American actor. He came to this continent a boy. His *debut* was made here. He learned his art before American audiences. By the Americans he was esteemed as equal to the best English actors. He never became a really great actor, but in his prime, it is not to be denied, he was above mediocrity. What Lewis Hallam the elder attempted in vain, Lewis Hallam the younger accomplished. To his skill before the Revolution the American stage owed much of the credit it enjoyed—his reputation and example entitled him to be regarded as its father under the Republic.

# CHAPTER VIII.

## AMERICAN THEATRICAL TOWNS, 1750–58.

ADVERSE CONDITIONS OF THE DAWN OF THE DRAMA IN AMERICA—
VIRGINIA AND MARYLAND—NEW YORK—PHILADELPHIA—AMERI-
CAN SOCIETY AND MORALS AT THE MIDDLE OF THE EIGHTEENTH
CENTURY.

AS an example of the carelessness with which theatrical biography and history have been written, it may be mentioned that
the " Thespian Dictionary " and other publications of the epoch when
Mrs. Mattocks died (1808) unite in declaring that Mr. Hallam made
£10,000 by his American adventure, and notwithstanding the fact that
he died as early as 1755, it is added that he lost his money in the
American war. It is not likely that Hallam did much more than make
two ends meet between 1752 and 1754, and even had he lived until
1774, fifty thousand dollars in the English money of the period would
have been a large sum with which to measure the acquisitions of the
manager of a troupe of strolling players. His successor, who was his
superior both as a business-man and an actor, could not, it is certain,
boast of such good fortune. America, in the middle of the eighteenth
century, was not a land of gold like California in 1849. As a rule the
people were poor, and even those who were richest were not rich

according to modern standards.   America, in the Hallam period, was a rough land of earth and stone and tree, and even the theatrical towns—Williamsburg, Annapolis, New York and Philadelphia—were mere villages in comparison to what is called "a good show town" in the theatrical slang of this age.   In 1751, Dr. Franklin estimated the English population of the Colonies at only a million.   Scattered as it was from Maine to Georgia, but little of it was available as patrons of the theatre.

It is probable, Dunlap writes with that readiness of assumption to which he was so apt to resort in the absence of facts, that William Hallam was induced to send his company to Virginia, in preference to the other Colonies, from the knowledge that Episcopalians were more liberal in regard to the drama than most other denominations of Christians.   Much as the historian commends Hallam's wisdom in directing his brother Lewis to the genial South, the joyous welcome with which he claims the adventurers were received seems to have brought with it no substantial profit, and but little temptation for a return of "the Thespians in their manifold wanderings."   The truth is that Lewis Hallam found greater encouragement in the North than the South, as is proved by the fact that he did not return to Williamsburg after the Philadelphia season of 1754, and never played at Annapolis at all.   The capitals of Virginia and Maryland were both small towns in 1752–4, incapable of yielding a prolonged support to a theatrical company.   At Williamsburg much of the patronage came from the Virginia planters, who differed from the plain farmers in the neighborhood of Philadelphia, and the self-sufficient country gentlemen of the county of Westchester in New York, but the Virginians of that period were too busy with schemes of territorial aggrandizement to devote much time to the drama, and the comedians of Hallam's company found the columns of the *Virginia Gazette* devoted to negotiations with the Mingoes, Shawnees and Twightees, and accounts of Indian massacres instead of criticisms on plays and players. While the stage in Virginia was not retarded by the opposition of sectarian narrowness, it suffered from the neglect due to the hard conditions of life in a new land.

New York and Philadelphia, on the contrary, had some claims to be considered cities even then. Each, however, had disadvantages peculiar to itself. New York, originally a Dutch province, retained much of the language and manners of its first settlers. These were alike indifferent to English literature and the English stage. The Quakers of Philadelphia were of all people the most opposed to dramatic representations, while their Presbyterian neighbors surpassed them in active hostility to what were called in the cant of the time "profane stage-plays." With the non-theatrical elements in both cities eliminated, the possible patrons of the theatre in either were reduced to so small a number that the only wonder is that Mr. Hallam found his seasons as profitable as they proved.

New York, in 1753, was a little city clustered around Fort George and the Battery. The theatre in Nassau Street was near Maiden Lane and on the outskirts of the town. None of the buildings now standing had yet been erected. Even the famous old Federal Hall, as it was afterward called, where Washington was inaugurated the first President of the United States, was little more than half as old as the present City Hall is now. The population was about twelve thousand, of which one-sixth were negro slaves. The means of communication with the surrounding country was exceedingly primitive, and between

New York and Philadelphia there was only Andrew Ramsay's[1] promise of a " stage waggon " from Brunswick to Trenton, and of a " stage boat " from Philadelphia to Trenton, as indicated by his advertisement in Gaine's *Mercury*, in 1753. Indeed, it was not until 1756 that the first regular stage started between the two cities. In the winter, for many months at a time, New York was completely isolated from the rest of the world, except by sea. It was probably by sea that the Hallam Company went from Williamsburg to New York, in the summer of 1753. A city so situated could not be expected to support a theatre for many months year after year. Besides, Mr. Hallam was not entirely without opposition. Before his season began, in 1753, Dugee, a performer on the slack wire, had been giving entertainments at Van Denberg's Garden, as appears from his elaborate advertisement in the *Mercury*, August 13th, 1753. That Dugee seriously interfered with the patronage of the theatre is not to be doubted.

MR. DUGEE'S ADVERTISEMENT.

*By Permission,*

THIS is to inform the PUBLICK, That there is just arrived in this City, and to be seen at a new House built for that Purpose, in Mr. *Adam Van Denberg's Garden*, This EVENING, being Monday the 13th instant, The *Surprizing Performances* of the celebrated *Anthony Joseph Dugee,* Late an Apprentice to the Grand Turk *Mahomet Caratha,* On a *Slack Wire* scarcely perceptible, with and without a Balance. To give the Reader a just Idea of this Performance, by a meer Description, (which has given the highest Satisfaction to the King of *Great Britain,* and most of the great Personages and Virtuosoes in that Kingdom) would

[1] This is to give NOTICE, To all Travellers, who may have Occasion to travel between New York and Philadelphia, that the Trenton Ferry is now revived by Andrew Ramsay, late of Long Island Ferry; where all Travellers, who are pleased to put up at his House, may depend on having good Entertainment for themselves and Horses: Said Ramsay is providing a STAGE WAGGON to go from Brunswick to Trenton, and a STAGE BOAT from Philadelphia to Trenton. Such Passengers as are pleased to favour him with their Custom, may depend upon being forwarded on their Journey, with the utmost Expedition, from the latter to the former, or from the former to the latter.—N.B. Notice will be given, what Days in the Week the Boat and Waggon will proceed from Stage to Stage, per me.

ANDREW RAMSAY.

be too difficult a Task to undertake; however a faint Conception of it may be formed by these few following Particulars, *viz* I. He raises the Wire to a Swing, then rises on his feet, walking forwards and backwards in full Swing; and turns himself, and swings to Admiration on one Foot. II. He will balance a single Pipe on his Nose. III. He balances a Stone on his Nose also. IV. He plays with four Balls at once, in a surprising manner. V. He balances a Plate on the point of a Sword, turning it round at the same time. VI. He stands on his Head on the Wire at full Swing. ALSO, Several new Exercises on the Stiff Rope, by Mr. DUGEE, the *Indian*, and young *Negro Boy*. And a Hornpipe, and several curious Equilibres, on a Table, three Pins, and a Chair, by the young Negro Boy.

Doors open at six o'Clock, and to begin precisely at Seven.

TICKETS to be sold at the House of Mr. James Ackland, at the *Royal Exchange;* and at the Printing Office opposite the *Old Slip Market*. PITT, Four Shillings, GALLERY, Two Shillings.

N.B.—Mr. Dugee intends to perform every Monday, Wednesday and Friday (Weather permitting) in every Week during his residence here, which will be but short, as he proposes to exhibit eighteen Nights only.

There were other things that diverted money from Hallam's treasury, as the church lotteries and the Greenwich races, and finally the smallpox became epidemic and was raging with great virulence at the time the company left for Philadelphia. The prints of the period give us but few glimpses of the way in which the comedians lived in New York. We only know that tickets for the benefits could be had at "Scotch Johnnie's," probably the favorite theatrical tap-room in 1754; that Mrs. Beccely lodged at Mrs. Milliner's, and that the Hallams and Rigbys lived together as one family.

Philadelphia, in 1754, was the leading city on the American continent, its taxable inhabitants alone approaching the entire white population of New York. It was also the wealthiest and most enterprising city in America. Its people were more public-spirited than any of their fellow-countrymen. The Philadelphia Library had already been in existence nearly a quarter of a century. The famous structure on Chestnut Street, which is still standing and revered by the whole country as Independence Hall, had been erected, and its historic bell, that was to proclaim liberty throughout the land, had been hung the

year before.  The Philadelphia Academy, later on the Philadelphia
College and now the University of Pennsylvania, had just been established.  The ground had been purchased on which was erected and
where still stands the Pennsylvania Hospital.  But in spite of its size,
of the wealth of its inhabitants and their public spirit, Hallam encountered a stronger opposition to the drama in Philadelphia than would
have been possible anywhere in the Colonies, outside of New England.
The Quakers were not only hostile, but they exercised great influence
both in the municipality and the government of the Province.  The
Presbyterians had, if possible, a greater horror of "profane stage-
plays."  Then there was the German element, already a large one in
the city of Penn, which, if it was not opposed to the theatre, was
wholly indifferent to it.  As a consequence the play-goers were reduced
to a very small number, and like New York, Philadelphia was not yet
prepared to become the permanent home of the drama.  Paradoxical
as it may seem, another circumstance that militated against the immediate success of the stage was the fact that Philadelphia was proud
of its scientific and literary pre-eminence in the Colonies.  The golden
youth of the metropolis, emulating the solid attainments of Dr. Franklin, affected to regard the lectures of Professor Kinnersly on electricity
and his practical experiments at the Academy as more instructive and
entertaining than the exhibition of stage-plays by a company of strolling players.  Besides, politics at this period ran unusually high.  There
were constant disputes between the General Assembly and the Pro-
prietaries over the question of paper money, and Hallam's patrons
always paid him in a depreciated currency.  It was at a time, too,
when the campaign that ended in Braddock's defeat the next year was
impending, and enlistments for the forces designed to resist the

encroachments of the French on the Monongahela were going forward
with great activity.    Under conditions so unfavorable it is not surprising that Mr. Hallam resolved to abandon the continent for awhile.
This conclusion may have been accelerated by the fact that when his
season closed in Philadelphia a fever plague was raging in that city.

Of the domestic life of the comedians during their stay in Philadelphia there is no trace whatever.    When Miss Hallam and her two
brothers had their benefit on the 10th of June, tickets were on sale at
Mrs. Bridges', over against the Globe, in Front Street; at Mr. Nichol-
son's, sign of the Admiral Warren's Head, in Arch Street; and at
Mr. Mullen's, sign of the One Tun, in Water Street.    These are the
only names that have come down to us as taking even so slight an
interest in the personal fortunes of the players.

American society and morals at the middle of the eighteenth
century were not to be measured by the same standard that was
applied to the stage.    The rich were higher and the poor lower in the
social scale than they are to-day.    In Philadelphia there were many
showy equipages, but there was no provision for those unable to keep
their own carriages.    Wealth everywhere was a species of aristocracy.
The Virginia planter was a fox-hunting squire with the airs of an
English duke.    In the cities the first families were scarcely less
haughty than royalty itself.    The rich were too mighty to patronize
the theatre at home.    Among rich and poor wines or liquors were
in universal use.    Although the penalties were severe crime was
common.    The condition of the working population was little better
than that of the slaves.    It thus happened that at its dawn the
drama in America was encouraged almost wholly by the middle
class, through whose influence the Republic itself was established.

# CHAPTER IX.

———

## DAVID DOUGLASS.

HALLAM'S THEATRICAL SUCCESSOR ARRIVES—SPECULATIONS RELATING
TO THE HALLAM FAMILY—THE NEW MEMBERS OF MR. DOUG-
LASS' COMPANY—NAMES THAT BECAME HISTORIC ON THE
AMERICAN STAGE.

IT was four years after the dissolution of the Hallam Company, in 1754, when the Hallam family again bid for the
patronage of the American theatrical public. It is generally believed
the intervening years were spent in the West Indies. While the
family was sojourning on the island of Jamaica, Lewis Hallam, the
elder, died, and there his widow subsequently married David Douglass, who reorganized the company in 1758, and renewed the experiment of 1752, with Mrs. Hallam, now known as Mrs. Douglass,
as the star, and young Lewis Hallam, then only eighteen years
of age, as the leading man, except in the heavier roles, such as
*Richard III, Lear* and *Tamerlane.* Adam Hallam, who was younger
than Lewis, was with the company, and was occasionally entrusted
with a small part. His success, apparently, was not great, for
after a year or two his name disappears from the bills altogether.
Miss Helen Hallam was not with the company at this time, but
in her stead Miss Nancy Hallam occasionally was seen in children's
parts. Nancy Hallam is not mentioned by any of the historians

(87)

of the American stage, but it is fair to assume that she is not
the child referred to by Dunlap, who was left with her uncle
William six years before, and who afterward became famous in
English dramatic history as Mrs. Mattocks. Isabella Hallam, who
became Mrs. Mattocks, was younger than the Miss Hallam that
was in America from 1752 to 1754, and Nancy must have been
younger than Isabella. Who, then, was Nancy Hallam? Probably
the Miss Hallam of later years, and who was referred to in the
newspapers of 1773 as the niece of Mrs. Douglass. In 1761 the
name of Mrs. Hallam appears in the bills playing parts like those
previously filled by Miss Hallam. Mr. Ireland, in his " Record
of the New York Stage," assumes that this Mrs. Hallam was identical
with Miss Hallam of an earlier and a later period. A more probable
assumption would seem to be that the Mrs. Hallam of 1761 was,
in fact, Mrs. Hallam, wife of Lewis Hallam, the younger. It is
known that Mr. Hallam married early in life, but that he and his wife
soon separated and lived apart many years, until her death after
the Revolution enabled him to marry again. That his first wife
should at least try to be an actress would not be surprising. At the
time the name of Mrs. Hallam disappears from the bills Nancy
Hallam was old enough to take her place. It does not seem probable
that the *Jessica* of 1752 should be the *Juliet* of twenty years later,
having only attained the rank of leading lady. Such, however, would
be the natural progress of the *Fleance* of 1759 if she was the Miss
Hallam of 1766–74. If this reasoning is incorrect, it is singular that
Miss Hallam began as the daughter of Lewis Hallam, the elder,
and ended by becoming the niece of Mrs. Douglass.

David Douglass, by virtue of his marriage with the widow

Hallam, became not only the manager of the company, but an actor. At first he was content with small parts, the roles that Malone had previously filled falling to Mr. Harman, who had married a granddaughter of the celebrated Colley Cibber. Mrs. Catharine Maria Harman, who died in New York in 1773, was the successor of Mrs. Adcock. Mrs. Harman was an excellent actress and an exemplary woman, of whom it was said, at the time of her death, that she was sensible, humane and benevolent. Mrs. Beccely's parts were now taken by Mrs. Love, who was the only member of the old company, outside of the Hallam family, who had a place in the new. Mr. Douglass, the new manager, was a man of character and ability. He continued to control the theatrical destinies of this continent until the feeling against English players, consequent upon the stamp act and the impending war for independence, compelled him to relinquish the undertaking, when he returned to Jamaica, where he subsequently became one of His Majesty's printers, a master in chancery and a magistrate. Mr. Douglass died at Spanish-Town, in 1786, having, it is said, accumulated a fortune of £25,000.

Besides the performers already named, the company included Mr. Morris, Mr. and Mrs. Allyn, Mr. and Mrs. Tomlinson and Mr. Reed. Of these Owen Morris became the most distinguished. With the exception of Reed and the Allyns, they remained under Mr. Douglass' management down to the Revolutionary period. How they were recruited by Douglass, or whether they had any previous theatrical experience, is nowhere reported. Mr. Harman, whose name none of the historians mention at all, was at first the leading actor of the company in the heavy roles, Mr. Hallam succeeding to most of the parts that had previously been played by Mr. Rigby. Mr. Reed was

Singleton's successor, Allyn and Tomlinson sharing the lighter roles
with him.  Morris played the low comedy parts.  That the ladies,
with the exception of Mrs. Harman, were without experience is apparent from the fact that Mrs. Love was accorded better parts than those
filled by Mrs. Allyn and Mrs. Tomlinson.  It may be added, that
while Allyn and Tomlinson occupied a respectable professional standing before the American public for a number of years, their wives
never advanced to positions of consequence.

It is to be regretted that so little is known of the personal
history of these early players.  It is probable that all of them made
their American *debuts* at the beginning of the New York season of
1758–9, but neither the prints of the time nor the recollections of the
memoir-writers give any information respecting them, except as their
work is recorded in the play-bills of the period.  This is all the more
singular, because they were favorites as actors and thoroughly identi-
fied with American interests by long residence.  This is especially true
of Morris.  He was, after the elder Hallam, the first noteworthy
representative of comic old men on the American boards, and he continued on our stage until the close of the century.  Late in life Morris
was known both to John Bernard and William B. Wood.  In what
purports to be Bernard's " Retrospections of America " there are several
references to this old comedian, with an American experience of forty
years behind him, but not one that gives any information in regard to
him or that is accurate in matters of fact.  Wood refers to him only
incidentally as the husband of his second wife, and as looking " like
the wearer of the first cut of coat and vest, when the earliest approach
to modern dress was attempted," in a part that he played at Annapolis,
in 1798.  Dunlap only speaks of him as playing " the old men of

comedy and farce, when the shuffling gait and whistling treble which time had forced upon him were applauded as most exquisite imitations of old age." To the Harmans the newspapers and the annalists are equally indifferent. Their motives in coming to America, and the causes that led to their joining their fortunes with the players of Mr. Douglass' company, would make an interesting chapter in theatrical history could they be ascertained. Who were the Tomlinsons and the Allyns, and what finally became of them? These were the actors and actresses who took up the work of the pioneers and carried it forward. America became their home. With one or two exceptions their dust forms part of the mould in our graveyards. That they were enthusiasts in their work is certain, and yet how little do we know of these players whose names are historic on our stage.

Dunlap says that his object in writing his "History of the American Theatre" was to rescue from oblivion such facts relative to the drama in this country as could then be collected, and to combine them with his own knowledge of the players of the past. The only real monument to these early actors and actresses and their predecessors was the record of their work, and that could never "be swept from the memory of man," because the newspapers of the period preserved it for posterity.

# CHAPTER X.

----

## DOUGLASS IN NEW YORK.

A NEW THEATRE ON CRUGER'S WHARF—PERMISSION TO PERFORM DENIED—OPENING OF A HISTRIONIC ACADEMY ANNOUNCED— A BRIEF THEATRICAL SEASON FINALLY ALLOWED.

M R. DOUGLASS arrived in New York with his company in the autumn of 1758. As the old theatre in Nassau Street had been removed and a church built upon the site, Douglass built a new theatre on what was then known as Cruger's Wharf. It was near what is now called Old Slip, not far from the present Wall Street Ferry. Cruger's Wharf had water on both sides of it in what were called docks. The site does not seem to have been well chosen, but Mr. Douglass soon found other obstacles in the way of his enterprise, in comparison with which the situation was a matter of no great importance. He had built his theatre without obtaining the permission of the Magistracy to enact plays, and when he applied for it, it was refused. Thereupon he printed a card in Gaine's *Mercury*,[1] in which,

MR. DOUGLASS' CARD.—Mr. Douglass, who came here with a Company of Comedians having applied to the Gentlemen in Power for permission to play has (to his great mortification) met with a positive and absolute denial: He has in vain represented that such are his circumstances and those of the other members of his company that it is impossible for them to move to another place; and tho' in the humblest manner he begged the Magistrates would indulge him in acting as many Plays as would barely defray the expenses he and the Company have been at in coming to this city, and enable them to proceed to another, he has been unfortunate enough to be peremptorily refused it. As he has given over all thoughts of acting he begs leave to inform the Public that in a few days he will open an Histrionic Academy of which proper notice will be given in this Paper.

after pointing out that when he "applied to the gentlemen in power for permission to play," and had "met with a positive and absolute denial," he announced that he had given over all thoughts of acting, and in a few days would open a histrionic academy. This card was dated the 6th of November, but on the 8th of December[1] Douglass found it necessary to explain that his histrionic academy was not intended as an attempt to evade or resist the prohibition of the magistrates, but for dissertations on subjects moral, instructive and entertaining, and to endeavor to qualify such as would favor him with attendance to speak in public with propriety. It must be confessed that Mr. Douglass' first card does not read like the announcement of a manager with a company of comedians on his hands who had "given over all thoughts of acting," especially in an age when

---

[1] MR. DOUGLASS' EXPLANATION.—Whereas, I am informed that an advertisement of mine which appeared some time ago in this paper, giving notice that I would open an Histrionic Academy, has been understood by many as a declaration that I had proposed under that color to act plays without the consent of the Magistracy.

This is therefore, to inform the public that such a construction was quite foreign to my intent and meaning—that so vain, so insolent a project never once entered my head; it is an imputation on my understanding to imagine that I would dare in a public manner to aim an affront on gentlemen on whom I am dependent for the only means that can save us from utter ruin.

All that I proposed to do was to deliver dissertations on subjects MORAL, INSTRUCTIVE and ENTERTAINING and to endeavor to qualify such as would favor us with their attendance—TO SPEAK IN PUBLIC WITH PROPRIETY. But as such an undertaking might

have occasioned an Enquiry into my capacity I thought the public would treat me with greater favor when they were informed that I was deprived of any other means of getting my bread, nor would that have done more than barely supplied our present necessities.

The expenses of our coming here—our living since our arrival, with the charge of building, etc. (which, let me observe, we had engaged for before we had any reason to apprehend a denial) amounted to a sum that would swallow up the profits of a great many nights acting had we permission.

I shall conclude with humbly hoping that those gentlemen who have entertained an ill opinion of me from my supposed presumption will do me the favor to believe that I have truly explained the advertisement and that I am to them and the Public,

A very humble and devoted servant,

DAVID DOUGLASS.

Dec. 8, 1758.

"moral lectures" and "concerts of music" were the usual subterfuges in England for the presentation of unauthorized plays. It was by such a device that Garrick was enabled to make his *debut* as *Richard III*, at Goodman's Fields' Theatre, in 1741, and Mr. Douglass himself did not disdain to resort to a similar subterfuge some time afterward at Newport, R. I. The probability is that the explanation was made in return for a promise from the magistrates of permission to act, for after Douglass had been made to eat what was considered a sufficient quantity of humble pie, leave was graciously accorded him to perform thirteen nights, to enable him to pay his debts and get away.

The season, the first of many that were to follow under Mr. Douglass' management in New York, began December 28th, 1758, and closed on the 7th of February following. The list of performances shows a constant change of bill from night to night, the plays and farces comprising the most popular pieces of the time. Unfortunately no casts were printed in the advertisements, but it has been assumed, no doubt correctly, that Mrs. Douglass played the title role in "Jane Shore" on the opening night. Mrs. Harman was of course the *Alicia*, and Mr. Harman probably played *Hastings*. During the season Mrs. Douglass probably played *Lady Randolph* in "Douglas," *Arpasia* in "Tamer-

LIST OF PERFORMANCES.

1758.
Dec. 28—Jane Shore . . . . . . . Rowe
1759.
Jan.   1—Inconstant . . . . . . Farquhar
            Mock Doctor . . . . . Fielding
          3—Orphan . . . . . . . . Otway
          5—Spanish Fryar . . . . . Dryden
          8—Recruiting Officer . . . Farquhar
            Lovers' Quarrels.
        10—Othello . . . . . . . Shakspere
        12—Beaux' Stratagem . . . Farquhar
        15—Venice Preserved . . . . Otway
            Stage Coach . . . . . Farquhar
        24—Douglas . . . . . . . . Home
            Lethe . . . . . . . . Garrick
        26—Tamerlane . . . . . . . Rowe
        29—Drummer . . . . . . . Addison
            Damon and Phillida . . . Cibber
Feb.   7—Richard III . . . . . Shakspere
            Damon and Phillida.

lane," *Lady Truman* in the "Drummer," and *Queen Elizabeth* in "Richard III;" Mrs. Harman, *Anna, Selima, Abagail* and *Lady Anne;* Mr. Harman, *Old Norval, Tamerlane, Vellum* and *Richard;* Mr. Douglass, *Lord Randolph, Monesses,* and *Coachman;* and Mr. Hallam, *Young Norval, Bejazet, Tinsel* and *Richmond.* These assumptions are based upon the Philadelphia casts of the following season. As a specimen of Mr. Douglass' earlier advertisements in the New York papers, the one that is here reproduced is the most interesting, because it is the most comprehensive. It will be noticed that there is no mention of the company. There was no box-office; reserved seats were unknown, and people went to the play in the afternoon. Prices were then as high as now, while the hour of performance was the dinner-hour of the present time.

A DOUGLASS ADVERTISEMENT.

At the Theatre
on Mr. Cruger's Wharff

This present Monday will be presented a Comedy written by Captain Farquhar, call'd
THE INCONSTANT,
or
The Way to Win Him.
Farce,
THE MOCK DOCTOR.

\* \* \* \* \* \* \* \*

On Wednesday, the 3d Instant
a Tragedy called
THE ORPHAN,
or the
Unhappy Marriage.

\* \* \* \* \* \* \* \*

On Friday, the 5th Instant,
the comic scenes of
THE SPANISH FRYAR
with entertainments as will be expressed in the bills.

Tickets to be had at the Printing Office in Hanover Square, at the Coffee House, at the Fountain Tavern and nowhere else.

The doors of the Gallery will be opened at Four O'Clock, but the Pit and Boxes, that Ladies may be well accommodated with seats—not till Five—and the Play begins precisely at Six.

Box, 8 Shillings. Pit, 5 Shillings.
Gallery, 2 Shillings.

N.B.—No more tickets will be given out than the house will hold. And positively no money taken at the door.

On the opening night young Lewis Hallam was accorded the honor of speaking Singleton's prologue, and Mrs. Douglass recited Adam Thomson's epilogue, originally delivered in Philadelphia, in 1754. Both of these productions were transmitted by Mr. Douglass

to Gaine's *Mercury*, and the letter[1] and enclosures were printed in
that journal January 8th, 1759. In this letter Mr. Douglass conveys
the impression that both poems were the work of the same hand, and
that they had been specially written by the ingenious author for this
occasion. This led Dunlap, who was unacquainted with the previous
publication of Thomson's epilogue, to infer that it was Singleton who
was meant, and his error has been perpetuated ever since, even in the
collection of prologues and epilogues recently printed by the Dunlap
Society of New York. As this epilogue was frequently repeated
and underwent many changes, it is worth reprinting in its second
stage. It will be observed that the introductory lines are entirely new

THOMSON'S EPILOGUE.—SECOND VERSION.

Much has been said at this unlucky time,
To prove the treading of the stage a crime.
Mistaken zeal, in terms oft not so civil,
Consigns both play and players to the devil.
Yet wise men own, a play well chose may teach
Such useful moral truths as the parsons preach,

and that the first half of it is
remodeled and rewritten. The
second version, it must be
confessed, is a great improvement over the first, and it

[1] MR. DOUGLASS' LETTER. — Sir: Be pleased to give the enclosed Prologue and Epilogue, spoken at the opening of the New Theatre in this city a place in your columns. They were both written in North America and generously sent us by the ingenious author, to whom we acknowledge ourselves greatly obliged, and as we can not imagine the difficulty we met with in obtaining liberty to act here proceeded from any ill opinion those in authority had of a well regulated stage but rather from a tender regard for the mistaken opinions of others we humbly beg to embrace this opportunity of recommending this performance to the candid perusal of such unprejudiced though we doubt not well meaning minds.

They will be found, we imagine, on ex-

amination to contain a sensible, elegant and impartial statement of the true nature and use of theatrical entertainments, which, as the famous Mr. Addison expresses it, "were invented for the accomplishment and refining of human nature."

It would be ungrateful, likewise, on this occasion, to omit making our thankful acknowledgments to the Town for the generous encouragement given much beyond our merit by the crowded houses since we began to perform; but if the assiduous endeavors to the utmost of our ability to please, can make amends for our deficiencies, we flatter ourselves with the kind continuance of their favors which shall ever be gratefully acknowledged by Sir, (in the name of the Company)
The Town's most obedient Servant,
D. DOUGLASS.

would be interesting to know if the ingenious author of the original epilogue was allowed to revise his own work.

Mr. Douglass must have been a man of unusual energy and persistence, or he would not have continued his American theatrical campaign in the face of the obstacles that he found in his way at the outset. Not only was there a determined opposition to the theatre in the two leading cities, New York and Philadelphia, but there was not a building really adapted to theatrical purposes anywhere in the country. Wherever Douglass went it was first necessary for him to erect a temporary structure before it was possible for his company to perform at all. In New York, as we have seen, he built a so-called theatre on Cruger's Wharf. It must have been an exceedingly

May teach the heart another's grief to know,
And melt the soul in tears of generous woe.
So when the unhappy virtuous fair complains
In Shakspere's, Lee's or Otway's moving strains,
The narrowest hearts expanded wide appear,
And soft compassion drops the pitying tear.
Or would you warn the thoughtless youth to shun
Such dangerous arts which numbers have undone,
A Barnwell's fate can never fail to move,
And strike with shame and terror lawless love.
See, plunged in ruin, with a virtuous wife,
The Gamester weeps, despairs and ends his life.
When Cato bleeds he spends his latest breath,
To teach the love of country strong in death.
With such examples and a thousand more,
Of godlike men who lived in times before,
The tragic Muse renewing every age,
Makes the dead heroes tread the living stage.
But when to social gayety inclined
Our comic Muse shall feast the cheerful mind,
Fools of all sorts and fops a brainless crew,
To raise your mirth we'll summon to your view;
Make each pert coxcomb merry with his brother,
Whilst knaves conceal'd shall grin at one another.
'Tis magic ground we tread, and at our call
Those knights appear that represent you all.
Yet, hold! methinks I hear some snarler cry,
"Pray, madam, why so partial—rat me—why
Don't you do justice to your own sweet sex?
Are there no prudes, coquettes or jilts to vex?"
'Tis granted; vice and folly's not confined
To man alone, but spreads to womankind.
We frankly own—we may indeed, as well—
For every fluttering beau we've an affected belle,
Nor has dramatic Satire's candid page
Failed to chastise them justly on the stage.
Thus human life's our theme—a spacious field
Which the soul's noblest entertainments yield.
By men of worth admired from time,
Who nature's picture never judged a crime;
And if the soul in nature's cause we move,
The friends of nature cannot disapprove.
We trust they do not by the splendid sight
Of sparkling eyes that grace our scenes to-night;
Then bravely dare to assert the taste you've shown,
Nor be ashamed so just a cause to own;

And tell our foes what Shakspere said of old—
Our former motto spoke it, I am told—
That here the world in miniature you see,
And all mankind are players as well as we.

primitive affair, as it was demolished soon after he vacated
it. Before he could venture
into Philadelphia with his company, it was necessary for him to build
a new theatre there also. This required time, and nearly five months
elapsed after the close of the New York season before the Philadelphia
structure was ready for his accommodation. In the meantime, it is
not improbable that the company played a brief engagement at Perth
Amboy. Dunlap records his recollection of hearing old ladies of that
place speak in raptures of the beauty and grace of Mrs. Douglass, and
the pathos of her personation of *Jane Shore*. Perth Amboy was the
capital of the province of New Jersey, and a garrison town. There
were at that time not fewer than twenty-four New Jersey baronies—
lords-proprietors under the Berkeley and Cartaret grants—and Perth
Amboy was the social as well as political centre for this peculiar
aristocracy. Even now it is said, whimsically enough, it must be
confessed, that these Jersey barons or baronets meet once a year in
their ancient capital to consider the best interests of their order, on
which occasions they wear white wigs and address each other as "My
Lord." This annual assemblage seems to be a continuation of the
Council of Proprietors established in 1682. Previous to the Revolution the meetings of the Council were held twice a year, and as one
of these occurred on the second Tuesday in April, there was ample
time for a brief theatrical season at Perth Amboy, in 1759, between
the closing of the theatre on Mr. Cruger's Wharf and the opening
of the new theatre on Society Hill.

# CHAPTER XI.

## DOUGLASS IN PHILADELPHIA.

THE THEATRE ON SOCIETY HILL—OPPOSITION TO THE DRAMA—A LAW
AGAINST PLAYS—A BRILLIANT SEASON OF SIX MONTHS—THE
PLAYS AND THE CASTS.

M R. DOUGLASS, when he arrived in Philadelphia, in the
spring of 1759, showed that he had profited by his New York
experience, for his first act was to obtain the authority of Governor
Denny to perform, the Governor stipulating as a condition to his
assent that the company should give one night for the benefit of the
Pennsylvania Hospital. This was agreed to, but before the campaign
could begin it was necessary to have a theatre, and so Mr. Douglass
proceeded to build one at the south-west corner of Vernon and South
Streets, at what was known as " Society Hill," in the Southern Liberties. The building, which was of wood, was not well suited for theatrical purposes, and was used as a theatre for only one season. Subsequently it was turned into three dwelling-houses, which were finally
replaced by the brick structure that now stands on the site of the old
play-house. Mr. Douglass probably chose to begin his performances
in Philadelphia in a building so ill-suited to his purposes, instead of in
Plumstead's warehouse, because it was outside of the city limits, and
consequently beyond the control of the municipal authorities. There
was a determined opposition, however, and Judge Allen was applied

to for an injunction to restrain the players, but there is a story that the Judge replied that he had got more moral virtue from plays than sermons, and declined to grant the application.    To this it was added that as Judge Allen was prevented from attending the first performance through the death of his wife, his domestic misfortune was looked upon as in the nature of a judgment upon him for affording protection to profane stage-plays.    This assertion is made not only by Dunlap, but in some of the local histories of Philadelphia.    It is a pity to spoil such a nice story of the Chief Justice of Pennsylvania, whose wife was a sister of Governor Hamilton, but as Mrs. Allen died May 12th, 1760, when there were not only no players in the province, but when plays were prohibited by law, her death can not be looked upon as so clearly a judgment as if it had not been delayed for nearly a year.    Besides, if the judge made any such declaration he must have undergone a complete change of opinion in a few years, for the Chief Justice Allen of 1759 was the Recorder Allen of 1750, whose action led to the suppression of Murray and Kean's Company.

Mr. Douglass seems to have stolen a march upon the opponents of the theatre on this occasion, obtaining Governor Denny's authority to build a play-house and give performances before his purpose was known to the community.    It was no sooner announced, however, than all the religious bodies in the city were up in arms against him. The Quakers led off.    The journal of the General Assembly shows that on the 22d of May, 1759, an address from the Society called Quakers was presented to the House, setting forth that "they have, with real concern, heard that a company of stage-players are preparing to erect a theatre and exhibit plays to the inhabitants of this city, which they conceive, if permitted, will be subversive of the good order and

morals which they desire may be preserved in this Government."
They therefore prayed the House to frame and present to the Governor
for his assent "a bill to prohibit such ensnaring and irreligious entertainments." On the following day (May 23d) a Petition from the
Minister, Churchwardens and Elders of the Lutheran German Con-
gregation of Philadelphia was presented, praying "that a law may be
enacted to prevent the building of a play-house or theatre in or near
the said city, which the petitioners hear is intended and already
begun." This was referred for further consideration. The same day
an address was received from the Synod of New York and Philadelphia
(Presbyterian) to the same effect, and on the 26th, the Baptist Con-
gregation of Philadelphia was heard from, making a similar appeal.
It is evident that these addresses and petitions were not directed toward
deaf ears, for on the date last mentioned a Committee, comprising nine
members, was appointed to prepare and bring in a bill to prevent the
exhibition of theatrical entertainments and for suppressing lotteries.
Both the Committee and the House acted without a moment's unnecessary delay, the bill being presented
on the 28th, ordered to a third
reading on the 30th, and passed
on the 31st of May. A Committee
was immediately appointed to
wait on the Governor and ask his
assent to the measure, which reported that his Honor was pleased
to say that he would take the bill
under his immediate consideration. The object of this haste,

### The Law against Plays.

And Whereas, several companies of idle
persons and strollers have come into this
Province from foreign parts in the characters
of players, erected stages and theatres and
thereon acted divers plays by which the weak,
poor and necessitous have been prevailed on
to neglect their labor and industry and to give
extravagant prices for their tickets and great
numbers of disorderly persons have been
drawn together in the night to the great distress of many poor families, manifest injury of
this young colony and grievous scandal of
religion and the laws of this Government.

Be it Therefore Enacted, That every person and persons whatsoever that from and
after the First day of January which will be

A.D. 1760 shall erect, build or cause to be erected or built any play-house, theatre, stage or scaffold for acting, shewing or exhibiting any tragedy, comedy, tragi-comedy, farce, interlude, or other play, or part of a play whatsoever, or shall act, shew or exhibit them, or any of them, or be in any ways concerned therein or in selling any of the tickets aforesaid in any city, town or place within this Province and be thereof legally convicted in manner aforesaid shall forfeit and pay the sum of five hundred pounds lawful money aforesaid.

apparently, was to prevent the appearance of the players under the authority which the Governor had previously accorded them, but Governor* Denny kept the bill until the 15th of June, when he returned it with some amendments, which were accepted by

the House. The principal amendment, no doubt, was in regard to the time when the law should go into effect, so as to enable the Governor to keep faith with Mr. Douglass. The measure was finally passed, and received the Governor's sanction on the 20th of June, but it was set aside by the King in Council, September 2d, 1760.

As it was early summer before Mr. Douglass' season began, it is fair to assume that his plans were delayed by the uncertainties attendant upon the pending legislation, but the terms of the law once defined, there was no delay in opening the new theatre at Society Hill, and the utmost use was made of the intervening six months before the act went into effect, the house being kept open continuously from the 25th of June to the 28th of December. Originally the site of

LIST OF PERFORMANCES.

1759.

| June 25 | Tamerlane | Rowe |
|---|---|---|
| | Virgin Unmasked | Fielding |
| June 29 | Richard III | Shakspere |
| | Lethe | Garrick |
| July 6 | Provoked Husband | Vanbrugh |
| | Honest Yorkshireman | Carey |
| 13 | Douglas | Home |
| | Mock Doctor | Fielding |
| 20 | Recruiting Officer | Farquhar |
| | Advent's of Half an Hour | Bullock |
| 27 | Hamlet | Shakspere |
| | Stage Coach | Farquhar |
| Aug. 3 | The Drummer | Addison |
| | Anatomist | Ravenscroft |
| 10 | Theodosius | Lee |
| | Lethe. | |
| 17 | George Barnwell | Lillo |
| | Harlequin Collector. | |
| 24 | Beggars' Opera | Gay |
| | Lethe. | |
| 31 | Fair Penitent | Rowe |
| | School Boy | Cibber |

the theatre was a declivity on the bank of Dock creek, opposite the famous old Blue Anchor Inn, where Penn landed from his boat when he came from Chester, in 1682. Of this hill Spruce Street was the base, and Pine Street the summit. In 1730 and after, a flag was hoisted on the hill whenever the Assembly was in session, and on Sundays and holidays. There was also a redoubt there and a battery, the shot for the cannon being cast by John Pass, by whom was re-cast that national inheritance, the State House bell. At the time when Mr. Douglass built his theatre there, Society Hill was deserving of its name. There was a number of delightful dwellings in the neighborhood, and among others Alderman Plumstead had a beautiful descending garden in Union Street, which

Sept. 7—Douglas.
    14—Hamlet.
        Adventures of Half an Hour.
    26—Recruiting Officer.
        Stage Coach.
    28—Lear . . . . . . . . Shakspere
Oct. 5—Provoked Husband.
        Toy Shop . . . . . . . Dodsley
    12—Provoked Husband.
    26—Macbeth . . . . . . Shakspere
Nov. 2—Romeo and Juliet . . . Shakspere
        Miss in her Teens . . . Garrick
        (Benefit of Mr. Douglass.)
    9—Beggars' Opera.
        Harlequin Collector.
        (Benefit of Mrs. Love.)
    16—Theodosius.
        Lying Valet.
        (Benefit of Mr. Scott.)
    23—Provoked Husband.
        Harlequin Collector.
        (Benefit of Mr. Hallam.)
Dec. 1—Macbeth.
        Stage Coach.
        (Benefit of Mr. Allyn.)
    7—Suspicious Husband . . . Hoadly
        Virgin Unmasked.
        (Benefit of Adam Hallam.)
    14—Gamester . . . . . . . . Moore
        School Boy.
        (Benefit of Mr. Reed.)
    21—Romeo and Juliet.
        Harlequin Collector.
        (Benefit of Mr. Palmer.)
    27—George Barnwell.
        Lethe.
        (A charity performance.)
    28—Hamlet.
(Benefit of the Pennsylvania Hospital.)

was the admiration of the town. It was in part, perhaps, because of these surroundings that there was such violent opposition to the theatre at that time.

The cast of "Tamerlane," the piece with which Mr. Douglass

began his first season in Philadelphia, shows the new company in definite roles.    Harman had the part originally played here by Singleton, and Mrs. Harman suc-

### TAMERLANE.

Tamerlane . . . . . . . . . Mr. Harman
Bejazet . . . . . . . . . . Mr. Hallam
Monesses . . . . . . . . . Mr. Douglass
Axalla . . . . . . . . . . . Mr. Reed
Omar . . . . . . . . . . Mr. Tomlinson
Prince of Tanais . . . . . . . Mr. Horne
Dervise . . . . . . . . . . Mr. Morris
Haly . . . . . . . . . . Mr. A. Hallam
Arpasia . . . . . . . . . Mrs. Douglass
Selima . . . . . . . . . . Mrs. Harman

ceeded Mrs. Beccely. Douglass himself filled Rigby's part, and, oddly enough, young Lewis Hallam was the successor of Malone. Five years before Mr. Hallam had been content with *Haly*, now played by his brother, Adam Hallam, who had none of his genius.    The only name in the farce, "Virgin Unmasked," that is recorded is Mrs. Harman as *Lucy*.

The second play on record as produced this season was "Richard III." It was the first of five of Shakspere's tragedies presented in Philadelphia in the summer and autumn of 1759. The cast shows Mr. Harman still

### RICHARD III.

Richard . . . . . . . Mr. Harman
Richmond . . . . . . Mr. Hallam
King Henry . . . . . Mr. Douglass
Prince Edward . . . Mr. A. Hallam
Duke of York . Miss Nancy Hallam
Buckingham . . . . . . Mr. Reed
Catesby . . . . . . Mr. Tomlinson
Stanley . . . . . . . Mr. Morris
Oxford . . . . . . . Mr. Horne
Queen Elizabeth . . Mrs. Douglass
Lady Anne . . . . . Mrs. Harman
Duchess of York . . . . Mrs. Love

### LEAR.

Lear . . . Mr. Harman
Gloster . . . . Mr. Scott
Kent . . Mr. Tomlinson
Edgar . . . Mr. Hallam
Edmund . . . Mr. Reed
Cornwall . . Mr. Horne
Albany . . . Mr. Morris
Burgundy . Mr. Douglass
Usher . . . . Mr. Allyn
Goneril . . . Mrs. Love
Regan . . Mrs. Harman
Cordelia . Mrs. Douglass

in the lead, with Mrs. Harman as the successor of Mrs. Adcock. Mr. Hallam was second in rank, a part better adapted to his youth than the heavier role of *Richard*.    On this occasion the name of Miss Nancy Hallam first occurs as the *Duke of York*.    She subsequently played *Fleance* in "Macbeth," and other children's parts.    She has never been mentioned by any of the annalists.    The production of

" Hamlet." this season was probably the first presentation of Shakspere's masterpiece in America. Fortunately the cast has been preserved. It is especially remarkable in showing the great stride Mr. Hallam had made in his profession. But to Mr. Harman, perhaps as a recompense for the Hallam stride, was accorded the next great Shaksperean role, *King Lear.* Then to the

HAMLET.

Hamlet . . . . Mr. Hallam
Polonius . . . . Mr. Harman
Ghost . . . . Mr. Douglass
Laertes . . . . . Mr. Reed
Horatio . . . . . Mr. Morris
King . . . . Mr. Tomlinson
Gravediggers . { Mr. Allyn / Mr. Harman
Player King . . . Mr. Scott
Osric . . . . Mr. A. Hallam
Guildenstern . . . Mr. Horne
Ophelia . . . Mrs. Harman
Queen . . . . Mrs. Douglass
Player Queen . . Mrs. Love

MACBETH.

Macbeth . . . . . Mr. Hallam
Duncan . . . . . Mr. Harman
Donaldbane . . Mr. A. Hallam
Lenox . . . . . . Mr. Morris
Banquo . . . . . . Mr. Scott
Macduff . . . . Mr. Douglass
Seyton . . . . Mr. Tomlinson
Fleance . . Miss Nancy Hallam
Lady Macbeth . Mrs. Douglass
Lady Macduff . . . Mrs. Love
Hecate . . . . . Mrs. Harman
Witches . . . { Mr. Allyn / Mr. Harman / Mr. Tomlinson

dignity of *Hamlet* Hallam added *Macbeth*, being, as in the master role, the first tragedian seen in the part in America.

Later on, for Mr. Douglass' benefit, Hallam played *Romeo* to his mother's *Juliet,* perhaps the only instance in the history of the drama where a son was the lover and his mother the girlish heroine in Shakspere's love tragedy. This season, when " Lethe " was given as the afterpiece to " Richard III," *Lord Chalkstone,* played by Mr. Allyn, was introduced into the farce for the first time in this

ROMEO AND JULIET.

Romeo . . . . . . . . . . . Mr. Hallam
Mercutio . . . . . . . . . Mr. Harman
Montague . . . . . . . . . Mr. Douglass
Capulet . . . . . . . . . Mr. Tomlinson
Paris . . . . . . . . . . . . Mr. Horne
Friar Laurence . . . . . . . . Mr. Scott
Tybalt . . . . . . . . . . . Mr. Reed
Apothecary . . . . . . . . Mr. Allyn
Juliet . . . . . . . . . Mrs. Douglass
Lady Capulet . . . . . . Mrs. Love
Nurse . . . . . . . . . Mrs. Harman

country. The farce was exceedingly popular at that time, as will be observed from the number of times it served as the afterpiece at the theatre on Society Hill.

When Vanbrugh's "Provoked Husband" was produced in Philadelphia, on the 6th of July, it was its first representation, so far as the record shows, since its production in New York by Upton and his "sett of pretenders." This comedy, being left imperfect by Vanbrugh, Mr. Cibber completed it. When it was first produced, the "journey to London," which was Vanbrugh's, was condemned, because it was believed to be

PROVOKED HUSBAND.

| | |
|---|---|
| Lord Townly | Mr. Douglass |
| Manly | Mr. Hallam |
| Sir Francis Wronghead | Mr. Harman |
| Squire Richard | Mr. Morris |
| Count Bassett | Mr. Reed |
| John Moody | Mr. Tomlinson |
| Constable | Mr. Horne |
| Lady Townly | Mrs. Douglass |
| Lady Grace | Mrs. Harman |
| Lady Wronghead | Mrs. Love |
| Myrtilla | Mrs. Tomlinson |

Cibber's. For his benefit Mr. Hallam played *Lord Townly*, and Mr. Harman, as *Sir Francis*, was replaced by Mr. Scott.

Among the pieces presented by Murray and Kean's Company Farquhar's "Recruiting Officer" held a favorite place, but it is not known to have been produced by Hallam's Company at all. A characteristic anecdote is told of Quin in this comedy. On one occasion, having taken a little more wine than usual after dinner, he thus addressed Mrs. Woffington, who, as *Justice Balance*, was his daughter: "Sylvia, how old were you when your mother was married?"

RECRUITING OFFICER.

| | |
|---|---|
| Justice Balance | Mr. Reed |
| Captain Plume | Mr. Hallam |
| Captain Brazen | Mr. Harman |
| Mr. Worthy | Mr. Morris |
| Sergeant Kite | Mr. Douglass |
| Mr. Scale | Mr. Scott |
| Constable | Mr. Allyn |
| Recruits | { Mr. Tomlinson / Mr. Allyn |
| Bullock | Mr. Tomlinson |
| Melinda | Mrs. Harman |
| Sylvia | Mrs. Douglass |
| Rose | Mrs. Love |
| Lucy | Mrs. Tomlinson |

"What, Sir!" exclaimed the actress. "Pshaw!" he said, "I mean how old were you when your mother was born?" The only change in Philadelphia was Horne for Allyn as the *Constable* on one occasion.

Home's tragedy of "Douglas" was produced the first time in New York the previous season, but this is the first cast of it that has come down to us. The plot of this tragedy was suggested by the pathetic old Scotch ballad of "Gil Morrice." It was originally produced at Edinburgh, in 1756, and played at Covent Garden for the first time the next year. On this occasion Mr. Harman spoke the original prologue, from which the following extract was printed in the *Pennsylvania Gazette:*

DOUGLAS.

| | |
|---|---|
| Lord Randolph | Mr. Douglass |
| Glenalvon | Mr. Reed |
| Norval | Mr. Hallam |
| Old Norval | Mr. Harman |
| Lady Randolph | Mrs. Douglass |
| Anna | Mrs. Harman |

> This night a Douglass your protection claims;
> A wife! A mother! Pity's softest names—
> The story of her woes indulgent hear,
> And grant your suppliant all she begs—a tear.

The quotation was remarkably apposite.

Addison's "Drummer" still held the boards this season, but the cast was entirely different from that of four years before. Mr. Hallam now played the fop, Mr. Harman was the faithful steward, Mrs. Douglass took the role that she had before yielded to Mrs. Beccely, and Mrs. Harman, who was proving herself a very useful actress, replaced Mrs. Adcock as the sprightly maid.

DRUMMER.

| | |
|---|---|
| Sir George Truman | Mr. Reed |
| Fantome | Mr. Morris |
| Tinsel | Mr. Hallam |
| Vellum | Mr. Harman |
| Butler | Mr. Tomlinson |
| Coachman | Mr. Douglass |
| Gardener | Mr. Allyn |
| Lady Truman | Mrs. Douglass |
| Abagail | Mrs. Harman |

This comedy when it was originally produced without the name of the author, failed utterly although exquisitely acted; afterward it succeeded because it was believed that Addison had written it.

Dunlap asserts, on the authority of the younger Lewis Hallam, that Lee's tragedy, "Theodosius," named in the original Hallam repertoire, was always a great favorite everywhere. Be this as it may, this apparently was its first production. On its second representation Mr. Douglass played the title-role, and Mr. Horne took his original part. This tragedy was Lee's masterpiece. One great reason for its marked success on

#### THEODOSIUS.

Theodosius . . . . . . . . . . Mr. Reed
Varanes . . . . . . . . . . . Mr. Allyn
Marcian . . . . . . . . . . Mr. Hallam
Atticus . . . . . . . . . Mr. Harman
Leontine . . . . . . . Mr. Tomlinson
Lucius . . . . . . . . . . Mr. Douglass
Aranthes . . . . . . . . . Mr. Morris
Pulcheria . . . . . . . . Mrs. Harman
Athenais . . . . . . . . Mrs. Douglass
Marina . . . . . . . . Mrs. Tomlinson
Flavilla . . . . . . . . . . Mrs. Love

the American stage was, no doubt, the solemn church music composed for it by Henry Purcell, the first he ever furnished to the stage.

Upon the production of the "Beggars' Opera" in mid-summer a quaint distribution of parts will be noticed, not only in the cast of Gay's work, but of the pantomime that followed. The assumption of *Macheath* by Mr. Harman does not seem exactly in his line, but even that is not so surprising as the transition of Mrs. Douglass from *Mrs. Coaxer* to *Columbine*. Mrs. Love's assumption of *Polly*, the favorite singing role of the time, shows that she must have possessed merit as a singer what-

#### BEGGARS' OPERA.

Macheath . . . . . . . . . Mr. Harman
Peachum . . . . . . . Mr. Tomlinson
Moll Brazen . . . . . . . Mr. Douglass
Lockit . . . . . . . . . . . Mr. Scott
Mat o' the Mint . . . . . . . Mr. Reed
Beggar . . . . . . . . . . Mr. Morris
Player . . . . . . . . . Mr. Douglass
Jemmy Twitcher . . . . . . Mr. Allyn
Filch . . . . . . . . . Mr. A. Hallam
Harry Paddington . . . . . Mr. Horne
Polly . . . . . . . . . . . Mrs. Love
Mrs. Peachum } . . . . . Mrs. Harman
Diana Trapes }
Mrs. Coaxer . . . . . . Mrs. Douglass
Mrs. Slammekin . . . . Mrs. Tomlinson

#### HARLEQUIN COLLECTOR.

Harlequin . . . . . . . . Mr. Hallam
Miller . . . . . . . . . . . Mr. Allyn
Clown . . . . . . . . . Mr. Douglass
Conjuror . . . . . . . . Mr. Harman
Doctor . . . . . . . . Mr. Tomlinson
Columbine . . . . . . . Mrs. Douglass

ever her qualifications as an actress. Mr. Douglass evidently had a taste for *outre* parts as indicated by his appearance as *Moll Brazen* in the opera and the *Clown* in the pantomime.

Rowe's " Fair Penitent " and Dr. Hoadly's " Suspicious Husband " were both played, Mrs. Harman taking Mrs. Hallam's former role, and Mrs. Douglass contenting herself with Mrs. Adcock's part in the former and Mrs. Harman playing Mrs. Beccely's in the latter. Mr. Hallam's role in the one had been played by Rigby and in the other by Miller. In Hoadly's comedy Rigby was the original *Strictland*, now played by Palmer. Powell was the first *Lothario* in the "Fair Penitent" and the first Mrs. Barry the original *Calista*. Garrick's performance of *Ranger* in the comedy was inimitable and Bridgewater's *Mr. Strictland* was scarcely inferior in merit.

FAIR PENITENT.

| | |
|---|---|
| Sciolto . | Mr. Tomlinson |
| Altamont . | . Mr. Reed |
| Lothario . | . Mr. Harman |
| Horatio . | . Mr. Hallam |
| Rossano . | . Mr. Morris |
| Calista . | . Mrs. Harman |
| Lavinia . | Mrs. Douglass |
| Lucella . | . . Mrs. Love |

SUSPICIOUS HUSBAND.

| | |
|---|---|
| Mr. Strictland . | . . Mr. Palmer |
| Frankly . | . . . Mr. Douglass |
| Bellamy . | . . . . Mr. Morris |
| Ranger . | . . . . Mr. Hallam |
| Tester . | . . . Mr. Tomlinson |
| Jack Meggot . | . . . Mr. Reed |
| Buckle . | . . . . . Mr. Horne |
| Chairman . | . . . . . Mr. Scott |
| Mrs. Strictland . | Mrs. Harman |
| Jacintha . | . . . . . Mrs. Love |
| Lucetta . | . . . Mrs. Tomlinson |
| Clarinda . | . . . Mrs. Douglass |

Moore's " Gamester " was presented only once, and then, like the "Suspicious Husband," at a benefit. The noteworthy thing in the cast was the fact that Mr. Hallam, young as he was, found in the play another of those strong parts which he retained for many years. The most interesting fact connected with this production was the appearance of Palmer as

GAMESTER.

| | |
|---|---|
| Beverly . | . . . . . . . . . Mr. Hallam |
| Jarvis . | . . . . . . . . . Mr. Tomlinson |
| Lewson . | . . . . . . . . . Mr. Harman |
| Bates . | . . . . . . . . . . Mr. Morris |
| Stukely . | . . . . . . . . . Mr. Palmer |
| Dawson . | . . . . . . . . . . Mr. Allyn |
| Mrs. Beverly . | . . . . . . Mrs. Douglass |
| Charlotte . | . . . . . . . . Mrs. Harman |

*Stukely*, a part of which it was said when John Palmer died that *Stukely* died with him.

These casts, which comprise the names and show the rank of the members of Douglass' company in 1759, are also a proof of the carelessness with which American theatrical history has been written. In "Watson's Annals of Philadelphia" Misses Cheer and Morris are named as among the performers, and it is said that Francis Mentges (William Francis) was the dancing performer. Neither of these ladies appeared at that time, and the dancer was a Mr. Abbington, not impossibly the man who afterward gave his name to the celebrated Mrs. Abington. When Mr. Palmer, of whom no mention is made by any of the historians, had his benefit he played *Romeo*, "the first time in that character in this city," and Mr. Hallam appeared as *Mercutio*. Mr. Palmer's name occurs in the bills only for benefits, when, besides playing *Romeo* in his own behalf, he appeared as *Mr. Strictland* in the "Suspicious Husband" for Adam Hallam, *Macbeth* for Mr. Allyn and *Stukely* in the "Gamester" for Mr. Reed. It is not unlikely that this Mr. Palmer was the distinguished London actor John Palmer, the original *Joseph Surface* in the "School for Scandal," who made his first London appearances the next year.

When Mrs. Douglass had her benefit, Mr. Douglass spoke a prologue in the character of a Master Mason, and Mrs. Douglass an epilogue in the character of a Mason's wife. The manager announced on that occasion that it was his intention to wait upon as many ladies and gentlemen as possible, "but intreats those whom it may be his misfortune to neglect, rather to attribute it to his care in preparing for their entertainment in the most compleat manner in his power than to disrespect." Because the feast of St. Andrew occurred on Friday, the

30th of November, Mr. Allyn's benefit took place on Saturday, instead of the regular play-day. On that occasion the beneficiary appeared as *Macahone*, the brave Irishman, in which he introduced " The History of Mr. Allyn and the Three Lawyers." Adam Hallam, for his own benefit, performed a grotesque dance in the character of *Punch*.

What was called in the bills the closing performance " at the theatre on Society Hill " took place on the 27th of December, 1759, when " George Barnwell " and " Lethe " were given, " for a fund for purchasing an organ to the College Hall and instructing the children in Psalmody." On this occasion a prologue in praise of music was spoken by Mr. Hallam, and the occasional epilogue above printed was again recited by Mrs. Douglass. But in reality it was not the last, as on the following evening a performance was given for the benefit of the Pennsylvania Hospital, in pursuance of the agreement with Governor Denny. The advertisements for these benefits give a curious insight into the tastes and feelings of the time. That for the College was elaborate in the extreme, while the other, which appeared only in

CHARITY ADVERTISEMENT.

———

Philadelphia, December 27, 1759.
By PERMISSION and by Particular Desire Towards the raising a Fund for purchasing an ORGAN to the College-Hall in this city and instructing the Charity Children in Psalmody.
At the Theatre on *Society Hill*, this evening will be presented the tragical and interesting History of
GEORGE BARNWELL
Thorowgood by Mr. Douglass; Uncle, Mr. Morris; George Barnwell, Mr. Hallam; Blunt, Mr. Harman; Trueman, Mr. Tomlinson; Millwood, Mrs. Douglass; Maria, Mrs. Love; Lucy, Mrs. Harman.
Before the Play and between the Acts several celebrated Pieces of Concert Music will be performed by some Gentlemen of this city, who have kindly consented to promote the Design of this Entertainment ; for which Purpose a neat Harpsichord will be provided.
Also a Prologue in praise of MUSIC will be spoken by *Mr. Hallam* and an occasional Epilogue by *Mrs. Douglass*.
To which will be added a FARCE called
LETHE, or ÆSOP in the Shades.
In which the character of Lord *Chalkstone* will be introduced by Mr. *Allyn*.
N.B.—As this Benefit is wholly intended for improving our Youth in the divine Art of PSALMODY and CHURCH MUSIC in order to render the entertainment of the Town more

compleat at Commencements, and other public occasions in our College, it is not doubted but it will meet with all due encouragement from the inhabitants of this Place.

To begin exactly at Six O'Clock.

Tickets to be had of Mr. *Dunlap*, Mr. *Hurry* and of several Gentlemen.

Bradford's *Journal*, was as meagre as it was possible to make it. This was because of the difference of sentiment in the two institutions toward the "stage-players." Indeed, the Hospital authorities were even urged to refuse the money, as appears by an advertisement of the 10th of January, 1760, in which it is explained that it was not in the power of the Treasurer to commit this act of folly, notwithstanding it was "raised by exhibiting a stage-play near this city, which was done without the consent of the said managers, in con-

HOSPITAL ADVERTISEMENT.

For the Benefit of
THE PENNSYLVANIA HOSPITAL
To-morrow night at the Theatre on Society Hill will be presented the celebrated Tragedy of
HAMLET, PRINCE OF DENMARK.
Tickets will be sold by William Dunlap, W. Bradford, at the London Coffee House, Thomas Gordon and Evan Morgan.

sequence of the injunction of the late Governor Denny, at the time he granted liberty to the stage-players to erect the theatre near this city." When this card was printed, Pennsylvania had a law against such sinful indulgences as the "stage-play" of "Hamlet," under which the Hospital was to receive the forfeitures and penalties. The Act, however, failed to take cognizance of Mr. Douglass' losses, as at the time of its passage he had already incurred a debt of £300 and upward to Alexander Alexander, a builder, and £100 and upward to Willian Williams, a painter, for scenery.

# CHAPTER XII.

## DOUGLASS AT ANNAPOLIS.

THE PLAYERS IN MARYLAND—A COMPLETE LIST OF PERFORMANCES— MORE THEATRICAL VERSE—CHANGES IN MR. DOUGLASS' COM- PANY—GUESSES CONCERNING THE PLAYERS.

FROM Philadelphia Mr. Douglass made his way into Maryland, where there were no laws prohibiting " stage-plays," and at once began to give performances in the smaller towns of that Province. This is apparent from an announcement in the *Maryland Gazette* of the 7th of February, 1760, in which it was said, " by permission of his excellency the governor a theatre is erecting in this city which will be opened soon by a company of comedians who are now at Chester-Town." In spite of what Dunlap wrote about Annapolis having the luxury of a brick theatre as early as 1752, it is plain from this that there, as at New York, at Philadelphia, indeed everywhere, Mr. Douglass was compelled to build a play-house before he could give plays. By the 3d of March, however, he was ready to begin his season, and he continued the campaign until the middle of May. The season was a long one for a little city such as Annapolis was at that time—it would be far too long for Annapolis as it is to-day. The list of performances is the most interesting in our early theatrical history, because it is the only one before the Revolution, with the exception of that at Charleston, in 1773–4, that is complete. This completeness is due to the publisher of the Maryland *Gazette*, who printed, when the season closed, a full list of the pieces produced.    In this way a record was preserved that is interesting, not only because it is the first one of its kind, and consequently an almost unique contribution to history, but as the first instance in which an American journalist showed that he possessed an appreciation of the fact that matters relating to the theatre are news.    Even the *Pennsylvania Gazette* seldom mentioned the theatre at all, and never once did it condescend in these early days of the American drama to comment on the merits of the performers.    The same thing was true of Gaine's *Mercury*.    As sources of information for the historian it is only their advertising columns that contain the facts that comprise the history of the American theatre.    There is no reason to doubt that the prologues and epilogues that occasionally appeared in them were paid for, as were also the communications

LIST OF PERFORMANCES.

1760.

March 3—Orphan . . . . . . . . Otway
Lethe . . . . . . . . . Garrick
6—Recruiting Officer . . . Farquhar
Miss in her Teens . . . Garrick
8—Venice Preserved . . . . Otway
Mock Doctor . . . . . Fielding
10—Richard III . . . . . Shakspere
Miller of Mansfield . . Dodsley
13—Provoked Husband . . Vanbrugh
Stage Coach . . . . . Farquhar
15—Fair Penitent . . . . . . Rowe
Anatomist . . . . . Ravenscroft
20—Beaux' Stratagem . . . Farquhar
Lethe.
22—George Barnwell . . . . . Lillo
Lying Valet . . . . . . Garrick
24—Busybody . . . . . . Centlivre
Mock Doctor.
27—Revenge . . . . . . . Young
Lying Valet.
29—A Bold Stroke for a Wife, Centlivre
Damon and Phillida . . . Cibber
April 7—Romeo and Juliet . . Shakspere
Stage Coach.
8—Provoked Husband.
Honest Yorkshireman . . Carey
9—Othello . . . . . . . Shakspere
Devil to Pay . . . . . . Coffey
10—Constant Couple . . . Farquhar
Devil to Pay.
11—Romeo and Juliet.
Miss in her Teens.
12—Suspicious Husband . . Hoadly
Mock Doctor.
14—Richard III.
Hob in the Well . . . . Cibber
(Mr. Douglass' Benefit.)
15—Fair Penitent.
Lying Valet.
(Mr. Palmer's Benefit.)

in defence of the drama, whatever may have been the case with the dull essays that were often printed against it. A more liberal spirit prevailed in the office of the Maryland *Gazette*. When Douglass' company appeared in the " Orphan " at Annapolis there was for the first time in any American newspaper an article[1] upon the performance in the nature of dramatic criticism. It is, to be sure, only hearty commendation, but it is something to know that Douglass' company was able to please its Maryland patrons. This criticism, together with the prologue and epilogue,

16—Venice Preserved.
 Devil to Pay.
 (Mr. Murray's Benefit.)
17—Provoked Husband.
 Honest Yorkshireman.
 (Mrs. Douglass' Benefit.)
19—Revenge.
 Lethe.
 (Mr. Hallam's Benefit.)
22—Beaux' Stratagem.
 Lying Valet.
(Mrs. and Miss Dowthwaite's Benefit.)
23—Orphan.
 Lethe.
 (Miss Crane's Benefit.)
24—Constant Couple.
 Honest Yorkshireman.
 (Mr. Morris' Benefit.)
May 5—Douglas.
 Virgin Unmasked . . . Fielding
 (Mr. A. Hallam's Benefit.)
 8—Merchant of Venice . . Shakspere
 Lethe.
 (Mrs. Morris' Benefit.)
12—Gamester . . . . . . Moore
 Toy Shop . . . . . . Dodsley
 (Mr. Scott's Benefit.)

was printed on the 6th of March. The prologue was spoken by Mr. Douglass and the epilogue by Mrs. Douglass. The name of the local poet, who was so highly praised in the *Gazette,* has not been preserved. While no great literary merit can be claimed for these productions they were creditable to their author and to the occasion for

---

[1] CRITIQUE.—Monday last the Theatre in this city was opened when the tragedy of Orphan and Lethe (a dramatic satire) was performed in the presence of his Excellency the Governor to a polite and numerous audience who all expressed their satisfaction. The principal characters both in the play and entertainment were performed with great justice, and the applause which attended the whole representation did less honor to the abilities of the actors than to the taste of their auditors. For the amusement and emolument of such of our readers as were not present we here insert the Prologue and Epilogue, both written by a gentleman of this Province whose poetical works have rendered him justly admired by all encouragers of the liberal arts.

which they were written.   They are both racy of the soil.   To the players they must have proved an unexpected pleasure after the severity of their experiences in New York and Philadelphia.   They at last found themselves in a community where the drama was not only not despised but which took a hearty and generous interest in them as the exponents of dramatic art.   Even the lines themselves show that in "Maria's land" at that time badinage was not looked upon as necessarily bad, and, perhaps, upon the whole, the verses are more characteristic than any that were spoken from the American stage before the Revolution.   The allusion in the prologue to "Garrick thundering

THE MARYLAND POEMS.

*Prologue spoken by Mr. Douglass.*

Lo ! to new worlds th'' adventurous muse conveys
The moral wisdom of dramatic lays !
She bears thro' ocean Phœbus' high command,
And tunes his lyre in fair Maria's land ;
O'ertakes his sun, communicates his fires,
And rising bards in Western climes inspires.
   See ! Genius wakes, dispels the former gloom,
And sheds light's blaze, derived from Greece and Rome.
With polished arts wild passions to control ;
To warm the breast and humanize the soul ;
By magic sounds to vary hopes and fears ;
Or make each eye dissolve in virtuous tears ;
'Til sympathizing youths in anguish melt,
And virgins sigh for woes before unfelt !
Here as we speak each heart-struck patriot glows
With real rage to crush Britannia's foes !
To quell bold tyrants, and support the laws,
Or, like brave Wolfe, bleed in his country's cause !
   Europe no more sole arbitress shall sit,
Or boast the proud monopoly of wit ;
Her youngest daughter here with filial claim,
Asserts her portion of maternal fame !
   Let no nice sparks despise our humble scenes,
Half buskin'd monarchs and itin'rant queens !
Triflers ! who boast they once in tragic fury
Heard Garrick thund'ring on the stage of Drury !
Or view'd, exulting, o'er each gay machine,
The feats of Govent Garden's Harlequin !
   Athens, from such beginnings mean and low,
Saw Thespis' cart a wondrous structure grow ;
Saw theatres aspire, and with surprise,
Ghosts, gods or demons, or descend or rise.
   To taste, from censure draw no rash pretence,
But think good nature the sure test of sense.
As England's sons attend to reason's strains,
And prove her blood flows richly in your veins ;
Be what we act, the heroes of our parts,
And feel that Britons here have Roman hearts.

*Epilogue spoken by Mrs. Douglass.*

Well !—since the dreadful business is all over,
How strange a creature is your furious lover ?

on the stage of Drury" was evidently aimed at the American or Anglo-American boasters, who arrogated to themselves superior dramatic taste, because they had seen the greatest actor of that age in England. These, of course, would admit no excellence on the Colonial boards. The epilogue, on the contrary, compliments the "provincial fair ones" because of their freedom from metropolitan vices and the false spirit of British belles. Local allusions in a newly settled country are always gratefully accepted, and so these productions of the Maryland muse, coming as they did from the lips of Mr. and Mrs.

Your hot-brained spark! who for a little jilting,
Blasphemes the sex, swaggers and runs a tilting!
Without the least regard to virgin-fear,
As tho' he had been married—a whole year.
  " Why sure—we now must lead most happy lives,—
If slaves rebel against their sovereign wives!—
Had poor Monimia been like one of us
The wretch had never dared to use her thus!
By marriage-articles we stand prepared,
And fellows by our settlements are scared!
Th' exclusion of a night shall they take ill,—
Or, for a husband—must we quit quadrille?
When pin-money's secur'd if they turn Hectors,
We'll plague them worse than by stale curtain-lectures,
With play, rout, op'ra, masquerade and ball,
And the nocturnal joys of dear Vauxhall."
  But you, provincial fair ones, with meek merit
Detest such practices of female spirit!
*Here* none but planters of a field are found,
While there the planters of the head abound!
From whence arise such plenteous crops of horn
As well may vie in growth with Indian corn.
  You saw how fortune favors younger brothers,
The finer gentlemen and brisker lovers!
Sly Polydore!—he stole into her arms,
While the delicious theft improv'd her charms.
From such a feat, pray, how could she defend her,
Or know by instinct spouse from a pretender?
  Reasons like these, Ladies, I own are strong,
And all confess Castalio in the wrong!
Yet, think, he came with beauty's charm inspir'd,
By love and glowing expectation fired—
Then—then—to meet a balk—in such a season!—
Ah!—it might well deprive him of his reason!
Yet still,—impatience causes man's undoing!—
Next night had been as well and saved his ruin!
The bride might sure have kept th' affair unknown,
And told all other secrets—but her own!
Then the good man, ere honey-moon was past,
Might find his fit too violent to last,
And grown at once most careless and well-bred,
In the fifth week sneak to a sep'rate bed.

Douglass, must have seemed to the good people of Annapolis more complimentary and significant than they really were. Besides, they have interest in the fact that they were the first original productions recited on the stage under the Douglass management.

The casts of the Annapolis season that were preserved are only five in number, but they give an interesting insight into the resources that were open to an energetic manager even at that early period. The first of these is the cast of Otway's "Venice Preserved," produced on the third acting night. Apart from the names it contains it has interest as the first American cast extant of this tragedy.

### VENICE PRESERVED.

| | |
|---|---|
| Duke | Mr. Morris |
| Pruili | Mr. Douglass |
| Jaffier | Mr. Palmer |
| Pierre | Mr. Hallam |
| Renault | Mr. Scott |
| Conspirators | Mr. A Hallam<br>Mr. Douglass<br>Mrs. Morris |
| Belvidera | Mrs. Douglass |

It had been previously produced at New York at the theatre on Cruger's Wharf, with Mrs. Douglass as *Belvidera*, as a matter of course. Mr. Harman was probably the *Jaffier*. The next cast is that of the "Fair Penitent," which was presented a week later. On this occasion Mrs. Douglass resumed the part of *Calista*, which had been played in Philadelphia by Mrs. Harman. This is the first occasion, also, when Mrs. Morris is set down for an important role, and it is the first mention of Miss Dowthwaite. "George Barnwell" was the third of the pieces advertised. In this occurs the suggestive name of Mr. Murray, and for the first time the name of Miss

### FAIR PENITENT.

| | |
|---|---|
| Sciolto | Mr. Scott |
| Altamont | Mr. Hallam |
| Horatio | Mr. Palmer |
| Lothario | Mr. Douglass |
| Rossano | Mr. Morris |
| Calista | Mrs. Douglass |
| Lavinia | Mrs. Morris |
| Lucilla | Miss Dowthwaite |

### GEORGE BARNWELL.

| | |
|---|---|
| Thorowgood | Mr. Douglass |
| George Barnwell | Mr. Hallam |
| Trueman | Mr. Morris |
| Uncle | Mr. Murray |
| Blunt | Mr. Scott |
| Millwood | Mrs. Douglass |
| Maria | Mrs. Morris |
| Lucy | Miss Crane |

Crane, who played *Lucy*. The cast of "A Bold Stroke for a Wife," which followed, reveals apparently the full strength of the company at this time, with the exception of Miss Crane. Mrs. Dowthwaite's first recorded appearance was made in this piece. The cast of "Othello" is especially noteworthy, this being the first time Mr. Douglass is positively known to have played the *Moor*. Besides the parts indicated by these casts we know only that Mr. Palmer played *Townly* in the "Provoked Husband," and Mr. Hallam *Shylock* in the "Jew of Venice." Had these casts, few as they are, been lost we should have missed a peculiar phase in our early theatrical history. They show that with the exception of Mr. Morris and the immediate members of Mr. Douglass' family the company was entirely different from the original organization. Instead of Mr. Harman was Mr. Palmer, who had previously appeared only for benefits; Mrs. Harman was succeeded by Mrs. Morris, and for Messrs. Allyn and Tomlinson and their wives were substituted Mr. Murray and Mrs. and Miss Dowthwaite and Miss Crane. Mrs. Morris was the wife of the comedian, Owen Morris. It would be interesting to know more of this actress than the destroying hand of time has left to us. Whether she came to the Colonies with her

### A BOLD STROKE FOR A WIFE.

| | |
|---|---|
| Sir Philip Morelove | . . . . . Mr. Murray |
| Periwinkle | . . . . . . . . . Mr. Palmer |
| Tradelove | . . . . . . . . . . Mr. Morris |
| Obadiah Prim | . . . . . . . . . Mr. Scott |
| Colonel Fainwell | . . . . . . Mr. Douglass |
| Freeman | . . . . . . . . . . Mr. Hallam |
| Sackbut | . . . . . . . . . . . Mr. Scott |
| Quaking Boy | . . . . . . . Mr. A Hallam |
| Mrs. Lovely | . . . . . . . Mrs. Douglass |
| Mrs. Prim | . . . . . . . . . Mrs. Morris |
| Betty | . . . . . . . . . Mrs. Dowthwaite |
| Masked Lady | . . . . . Miss Dowthwaite |

### OTHELLO.

| | |
|---|---|
| Duke | . . . . . . . . . . . Mr. Murray |
| Othello | . . . . . . . . . . Mr. Douglass |
| Iago | . . . . . . . . . . . . Mr. Palmer |
| Cassio | . . . . . . . . . . . Mr. Hallam |
| Roderigo | . . . . . . . . Mr. A. Hallam |
| Desdemona | . . . . . . . . Mrs. Douglass |
| Emilia | . . . . . . . . . . . Miss Crane |

husband or whether her Annapolis appearances were her first season on the stage is not told anywhere, but from this time until her death she was a regular member of the company.   Mr. Murray may have been the Murray who was 'Ihomas Kean's partner, in 1750–52. Some reason for this supposition may be found in the fact that he seems to have made Annapolis his home.   The Dowthwaites and Miss Crane continued with the company for some time.   From her parts Miss Crane seems to have been an actress of experience, whatever may have been her merit.   How came Mr. Douglass to secure these recruits, and why were the members of his company, who were with him before and afterward, absent from Annapolis?   These questions are not easily answered, but the Annapolis season shows that even at that early period, it was possible to reorganize a theatrical company in America upon short notice.

When the season at Annapolis closed on the 8th of May, an epilogue addressed to the ladies was spoken by Mrs. Douglass.   This,

ADDRESS TO THE LADIES.

Ye gen'rous fair, ere finally we part,
Accept the tribute of a grateful heart;
O'erlooking faults, and lib'ral of your favors
You've smiled indulgent on our weak endeavors.
Our wand'ring theatre, o'erpaid and graced
Now hails your bounty and proclaims your taste,
While all those charms of person, so refined,
Shine brighter from the splendor of your mind.
    Blush not to own you caught the noble fire,
Which high-wrought scenes and tragic strains inspire.
Blush not, that for imaginary woes,
Your tender bosoms heav'd with real throes.
Think, while those tears in humid lustre roll,
They testify benevolence of soul.
These, flowing for heroic worth distrest,
Speak the rich virtues of a female breast!
—Should lovers sneer at these,—oh, scorn their suit,
The worst of coxcombs is the unfeeling brute.

like the prologue and epilogue spoken on the opening night, was also printed in the *Maryland Gazette*. As no mention is made of its having been specially written for the occasion, it may be assumed it was the same Mrs. Douglass was accustomed to speak at similar farewells.   If this was so, however, the address must have been adapted to the occasion, in order to pay a compliment to "fair Maryland." It may be said here, as a logical deduction of this thought, that Mr. Douglass in no way showed his skill as a manager more clearly than in the flattery he was careful to prepare for his patrons. His desire to please made him subservient, but in this no doubt was the secret of his success.

—Nay—should the formal prude in peevish age
Rail at the comic humors of the stage;
—Then say—you're proud those patterns to enjoy,
Who teach the world and rationally toy.
Say that true mirth, to vicious minds unknown
Is the just claim of innocence alone;
That characters of jilt, rake, knave and fool
Are best expressed by moral ridicule!
And maids are arm'd by each instructive plan
'Gainst all the wily arts of dang'rous man.
　Oh, may your influence still propitious prove,
To cheer our distant labors as we rove!
Till sister colonies assert our cause
And their's resound fair Maryland's applause.
　To aid the muse, if still such circles shine,
Brave youths shall glow with sentiments divine,
Love's vot'ries thence shall merit Britain's praise,
And kindle into patriots as they gaze!
　While gen'rous excellence their heart inflames
France shall droop conscious of her painted dames,
And still deplore the triumphs of our arms
Till Gallic beauty rivals English charms.

In spite of Mrs. Douglass' allusion to the "distant labors" of their "wandering theatre," the thespians went no further than Upper Marlborough as their first stage. The company remained at that place more than six weeks, advertising one performance weekly in the *Maryland Gazette* during their stay. After the close of the Upper Marlborough season a hiatus occurs in the recorded wanderings of Mr. Douglass and his forces, but subsequently they made their way to Williamsburg, playing there in the winter of 1760–61.

UPPER MARLBOROUGH PERFORMANCES.

1760.

| | | |
|---|---|---|
| May 22—Douglas | . . . . . . . . | Home |
| | Lethe | . . . . . . . Garrick |
| 26—Provoked Husband | . . | Vanbrugh |
| | Virgin Unmasked | . . . Fielding |
| June 2—Beaux' Stratagem | . . . | Farquhar |
| | Miss in her Teens | . . . Garrick |
| 9—Richard III | . . . . . | Shakspere |
| | Miller of Mansfield | . . . Dodsley |
| 16—Revenge | . . . . . . . | Young |
| | Devil to Pay | . . . . . Coffey |
| 24—Gamester | . . . . . . | Moore |
| | Lethe. | |
| July 1—Romeo and Juliet | . . . | Shakspere |
| | Miller of Mansfield. | |

# CHAPTER XIII.

———

## DOUGLASS IN, RHODE ISLAND.

A SUCCESSFUL SEASON AT NEWPORT IN 1761—TWO BENEFITS FOR THE POOR—PLAYING IN DISGUISE—WERE THERE TWO NEWPORT SEASONS?—THE COMPANY AT PROVIDENCE—ACT AGAINST STAGE-PLAYS.

WHEN the Williamsburg season closed Mr. Douglass and his company made their way to Newport, Rhode Island, where they played during the summer of 1761. Imitating the example of his predecessor, Hallam, Douglass seems to have provided his company with a certificate vouching for their conduct and capacity, for it was said in a letter from Newport, dated November 3d and printed in Gaine's *Mercury* on the 9th, that " the character they brought from the Governor and gentlemen of Virginia" had been fully verified.. This certificate was that " they were capable of entertaining a sensible and polite audience," and the Newport writer adds that the behavior of the company at that place was irreproachable; " and with regard to their skill as players the universal pleasure and satisfaction they have given is their best and most honorable testimony."

Notwithstanding this satisfactory testimony to the presence of the players at Newport in the summer and autumn of 1761, it has been found impossible to obtain anything like a complete account of w at was unquestionably the first theatrical incursion into New England. No file of the Newport *Mercury* for that year exists, and owing to a visit which Douglass made to Providence, and perhaps to Newport, in 1762, there is a confusion of dates in the local histories that it is difficult to unravel.

There are only three publications extant in relation to the drama at Newport at this early period. The first of these is a play-bill, which John Bernard copied many years afterward from one that had been preserved by Mr. Morris. As the year is not given there is a doubt whether it applies to 1761 or 1762. The names in the cast afford no assistance in determining the question. The only one in the list that is new is that of Mr. Quelch, who succeeded Adam Hallam as *Roderigo*. Quelch was with the company in New York during the season of 1761–2, and so he may have been at Newport either year or both. Indeed it is certain that he was at Providence in the latter year. Was this an announcement of a play in disguise? It is evident that "Moral Dialogues in Five Parts" meant a play, but it does not follow that this disguise was due to

A NEWPORT PLAY-BILL.

———

King's Arms Tavern, Newport, Rhode Island.

On Monday, June 10, at the Public Room of the Above Inn, will be delivered a Series of

MORAL DIALOGUES,
IN FIVE PARTS,

Depicting the Evil Effects of Jealousy and other Bad Passions, and Proving that Happiness can only Spring from the Pursuit of Virtue.

MR. DOUGLASS will represent a noble and magnanimous Moor named Othello, who loves a young lady named Desdemona, and after he has married her, harbors (as in too many cases) the dreadful passion of jealousy.

Of jealousy, our being's bane,
Mark the small cause, and the most dreadful pain.

MR. ALLYN will depict the character of a specious villain, in the regiment of Othello, who is so base as to hate his commander on mere suspicion, and to impose on his best friend. Of such characters, it is to be feared, there are thousands in the world, and the one in question may present to us a salutary warning.

The man that wrongs his master and his friend,
What can he come to but a shameful end?

MR. HALLAM will delineate a young and thoughtless officer, who is traduced by Mr. Allyn, and, getting drunk loses his situation, and his general's esteem. All young men, whatsoever, take example from Cassio.

The ill effects of drinking would you see?
Be warned and keep from evil company.

MR. MORRIS will represent an old gentleman, the father of Desdemona, who is not cruel or covetous, but is foolish enough to dislike the noble Moor, his son-in-law, because his face is not white, forgetting that we all spring from one root. Such prejudices are very numerous and very wrong.

Fathers beware what sense and love ye lack,
'Tis crime, not color, makes the being black.

MR. QUELCH will depict a fool, who wishes to become a knave, and trusting one gets killed by him. Such is the friendship of rogues—take heed.

When fools would knaves become, how often you'll
Perceive the knave not wiser than the fool.

MRS. MORRIS will represent a young and virtuous wife, who being wrongfully suspected gets smothered (in an adjoining room) by her husband.

Reader, attend; and ere thou goest hence
Let fall a tear to hapless innocence.

MRS. DOUGLASS will be her faithful attendant, who will hold out a good example to all servants, male and female and to all people in subjection.

Obedience and gratitude
Are things as rare as they are good.

Various other dialogues, too numerous to mention here, will be delivered at night, all adapted to the improvement of the mind and manners. The whole will be repeated on Wednesday and Saturday. Tickets, six shillings each, to be had within. Commencement at 7, conclusion at half-past 10, in order that every spectator may go home at a sober hour and reflect upon what he has seen before he retires to rest.

God save the king
And long may he sway
East, North, and South,
And fair America.

legal prohibition. A comparison with the Providence bill after the passage of the Rhode Island Act to prohibit plays shows no similarity between the two announcements. The play and farce were given "gratis" at the new schoolhouse in Providence, but the "Concert of Music," as a matter of course, was not free. It was only possible to witness the dramatic performances by paying for the concert. As there is nothing of this in the Newport bill, it seems probable that "Othello" and the other pieces given at the King's Arms were called "Moral Dialogues" only because they were not produced in a theatre. As there probably was neither stage nor scenery, no better description of the performances was possible than that of "moral dialogues." The second publication shows conclusively that the company was at Newport in 1761, but it sheds no light upon the date of the play-bill. As will be seen, it is an account of a charity performance which took place at Newport, September 7th, 1761. The letter was dated at Boston, and was printed in Parker's *Gazette*[1] (New York) on the 1st of October. The part in brackets is apparently Parker's comment. This shows that there was a building called the theatre in Newport, in September, 1761, whatever may have been the case in June. The play-house stood at Easton's Point, near Dyer's Gate, in the north part of the town. It is said this theatre was blown down in a gale, the company narrowly escaping with their lives. The gale must have occurred in May, or early in June, 1762, as the season for 1761 closed without mention of any such catastrophe.[2] It is evident from all this, especially from the ac-

---

[1] FIRST NEWPORT BENEFIT. — Boston, Sept. 21. We hear from Newport, Rhode Island, that on Monday the 7th inst. the comedy of the Provoked Husband, or Journey to London was acted at the theatre by the company of comedians in that town for the benefit of the poor; when the sum of One thousand and thirty pounds, Old Tenor (about fifty pounds Massachusetts lawful money) was raised for that charitable purpose and the money paid by Mr. Douglass in behalf of the company into the hands of Mr. George Gibbs who has undertaken to lay it out in corn which he is to store till the winter and then deal it out to such of the poor as shall be judged worthy to receive. [This money is surely well applied as the drought of the summer it is feared will render the article of corn scarce and dear the ensuing winter: And what will be the distress of the poor on that account is matter worthy of attention —— Railing against vice, luxury and debauchery is a cheap and empty sacrifice; but to relieve the distresses of our fellow creatures and to visit the widow and fatherless are the happy effects of the only true and undefiled religion; for without benevolence and charity every pretension to reformation will be as sounding brass or a tinkling cymbal.]

[2] SECOND NEWPORT BENEFIT. Newport, Nov. 3. On Friday evening last the company of comedians finished their performances in this town by enacting the tragedy of "Douglas" for the benefit of the poor. This second charity is undoubtedly meant as an expression of gratitude for the countenance and favor the town has shown them; and it cannot without an uncommon degree of malevolence be ascribed to an interested or selfish view, because it is given at a time when the company are just leaving the place, and consequently can have neither fear nor hope from the public. In return for this generosity it ought in justice to be told, that the behaviour of the company here has been irreproachable: and with regard to their skill as players the universal satisfaction they have given is their best and most honorable testimony. The character they brought from the Governor and gentlemen of Virginia has been fully verified, and therefore we shall run no risk in pronouncing "that they are capable of entertaining a sensible and polite audience."

count of his second benefit for the poor in Gaine's *Mercury*, that Mr. Douglass had a prosperous season in Newport in 1761, and it is not unlikely that his success tempted him to make a return visit to Rhode Island's capital the next year.

It is assumed by some of the local historians that when Mr. Douglass first applied for permission to act at Newport a license was refused, but afterward granted. This may have been in 1761. When "Othello" was presented at the King's Arms Inn in disguise, there is some reason for believing the year was 1762, as the statement is made that the company went from Newport to Providence. In Providence the opposition to stage-plays was very pronounced, but Douglass built "the new school-house" in Meeting Street, east of Benefit Street, as appears from an advertisement in the Newport *Mercury* on the 10th of August, and gave performances for several weeks in defiance of the popular sentiment and a vote of the town. What information we have in regard to this Providence season is derived from William Goddard, afterward publisher of the Pennsylvania *Chronicle*, who opened a printing office in Providence in 1762. One of the first

PROVIDENCE ADVERTISEMENT.

At the New School House in Providence on Thursday next, being the 12th of August will be performed,
A CONCERT OF MUSICK,
Vocal and Instrumental
to begin exactly at Seven O'Clock.
*Vivat Rex.*
Between the several Parts of the Concert will be presented (gratis) A Tragedy, call'd the
FAIR PENITENT.

Sciolto . . . . . . . . . . . Mr. Allyn
Altamont . . . . . . . . . . Mr. Quelch
Lothario . . . . . . . . . . Mr. Hallam
Horatio . . . . . . . . . . Mr. Douglass
Rossano . . . . . . . . . Mr. A. Hallam
Calista . . . . . . . . . . Mrs. Douglass
Lavinia . . . . . . . . . . Mrs. Morris
Lucilla . . . . . . . . . . Mrs. Hallam
To which will be added (gratis) A
Pastoral FARCE call'd
DAMON AND PHILLIDA.
Damon . . . . . . . . . . Mr. Sturt
Mopsus . . . . . . . . . . Mr. Quelch
Cymon . . . . . . . . . Mr. A. Hallam
Phillida . . . . . . . . . . Mrs. Morris
Arcas . . . . . . . . . . . Mr. Allyn
Corydon . . . . . . . . . Mr. Morris
N.B. There will be a Concert on Friday and on every Day next week except Saturday.

things that Goddard printed was a play-bill.  This was in June, the
month of the disguised performance at Newport.  In a letter to
Isaiah Thomas, the author of the " History of Printing," Mr. Goddard
says, "much company from Boston, etc., attended the theatre and
were highly gratified.  The theatrical campaign was short.  Party
politics occasioned the suppression of plays."  It is asserted in Peterson's " History of Rhode Island " that when the Act[1] demanded by the
people of Providence was passed Paul Tew brought it in his pocket
from Newport and the same evening, at the close of the performance,
proclaimed it from the stage.  If Mr. Peterson had taken the trouble
to examine the original authorities he would have found that the

[1] An Act to Prevent Stage Plays and other
Theatrical Entertainments within this Colony.

For preventing and avoiding the many mis-
chiefs which arise from public stage-plays, interludes and other theatrical entertainments which
not only occasion great and unnecessary expenses and discourage industry and frugality
but likewise tend generally to increase immorality, impiety and contempt of religion.

Be it therefore enacted by this General
Assembly and by the authority thereof it is
enacted that immediately from and after the
publication of this Act, no person or persons
whatsoever shall or may for his or her gain
or any price or valuable consideration, by or
under any pretence whatsoever, let or suffer
to be used or improved, any house room or
place whatsoever in this colony, acting or
carrying on any stage-plays, interludes or
other theatrical entertainments, on pain of
forfeiting and paying for each and every day
or time such house room or place shall be let,
used or improved, contrary to the true intent
and meaning of this Act £50 lawful money.
\* 　 \* 　 \* 　 \* 　 \* 　 \* 　 \* 　 \*
And whereas by a petition preferred to this

Assembly by a number of inhabitants of the
County of Providence setting forth that a
number of stage-players have lately appeared
and a play-house hath lately been built in
said town of Providence;  that the inhabitants
of said town, being legally called by warrant,
did at their late town meeting by a great
majority pass a vote that no stage-plays be
acted in said town;  yet the actors thereof, in
defiance of said vote and in defiance of the
public authority of said town have been and
are now daily continuing to exhibit stage-
plays and other theatrical performances;—

Be it therefore further enacted by the
authority aforesaid that in order more speed-
ily to cause this Act to be proclaimed where
those present may have the earliest notice
thereof, that his Honor the Governor be and
is hereby requested to issue a warrant directed
to a proper officer or officers in said county
of Providence directing him or them on sight
or receipt thereof to immediately proclaim the
aforesaid Act by beat of drum through the
streets of the compact part of said town of
Providence;  any law, custom or usage to the
contrary hereof in any wise notwithstanding.

Act was passed at East Greenwich on the 30th of August, 1762, not at Newport. According to the Act of the Rhode Island Assembly "a play-house hath lately been built in said town of Providence"; while according to Mr. Douglass' advertisement, the concerts for which he charged and the plays and farces that were performed "gratis" were given in "the new school-house." There is no reason to doubt that the school-house was in fact a theatre, being so called as part of the scheme to evade the town prohibition. This is probably the only time in the history of the drama when a theatre was called a school-house, but what seems humorous now must have been exceedingly serious in 1762.

These two seasons at Newport and Providence were the first and last times that a company of comedians was able to obtain a hearing in any part of New England before the Revolution.

# CHAPTER XIV.

---

## CHAPEL STREET THEATRE, NEW YORK.

MR. DOUGLASS BUILDS ANOTHER NEW THEATRE—THE SEASON OF
1761–2 IN NEW YORK—BALANCE-SHEET OF A BENEFIT FOR THE
POOR—CURIOUS GLIMPSES OF THE THEATRICAL MANNERS AND
CUSTOMS OF THE TIME.

BETWEEN his first and last campaign in Rhode Island Mr.
Douglass played a brief season in New York.  As early as the
20th of August, 1761, the New York *Gazette* announced that the
previous week Mr. Douglass had obtained permission from the
Lieutenant-Governor, Cadwallader Colden, " to build a theatre to perform in this city the ensuing winter."  Thus we see that while the
company was still playing a summer engagement at Newport Mr.
Douglass was in New York, making preparations for the work of the
winter.  Theatre-building was an essential part of these preparations,
even in New York.  The building on Cruger's Wharf had been
abandoned, and the new theatre was erected in Beekman Street, a
short distance below Nassau, on the south side of what was then
called Chapel Street.  The Chapel or Beekman Street Theatre was the
third theatre erected in New York.  When Mr. Douglass made his
application for authority to build this theatre, one of the New York
papers opposed to the enterprise declared that if the request was
acceded to the company would cost the city £6,000.  To this Mr.

Douglass replied with an array of figures that is as interesting as it is curious. He estimated the cost of the theatre at $1,625. The house held only £180, or $450. For a season limited to two months or sixteen nights—the limit was rigidly insisted upon—the average receipts were estimated at $300 per night, a total of only $4,800. The outlay of the season was set down at $1,000 for scenery and $39.07 per night for current expenses, amounting for the sixteen nights to £250, or $625. These figures may be tabulated as follows:

| | | |
|---|---:|---:|
| Probable receipts, 16 nights, | | $4,800 |
| Cost of the theatre, | $1,625 | |
| Cost of scenery, | 1,000 | |
| Current expenses, | 625 | 3,250 |
| Balance, | | $1,550 |

As salaries and living expenses are not included in this estimate, it will be seen that the expectations of both the manager and the actors were very moderate.

The season, which began on the 19th of November and lasted five months, was the last Mr. Douglass was to give in New York for a number of years. Originally it was the intention to limit the season to sixteen nights, only two performances a week being given. Even the partial list of plays produced, which it is possible to recover from the newspapers of the time, exceeds the limit. This list, it will be observed, includes only plays and farces of the highest character, but notwithstanding

LIST OF PERFORMANCES.

1761.

Nov. 19—Fair Penitent . . . . . . Rowe
　　　　Lethe . . . . . . . . Garrick
　　23—Provoked Husband . . Vanbrugh
　　26—Hamlet . . . . . . . Shakspere
　　　　Honest Yorkshireman . . Carey
Dec. 4—Tamerlane . . . . . . Rowe
　　　　Toy Shop . . . . . . Dodsley
　　18—King Henry IV . . . Shakspere
　　　　Hob in the Well . . . . Cibber
　　26—George Barnwell . . . . . Lillo
　　　　Lethe.

1762.

Jan. 1—Beggars' Opera . . . . . . Gay
　　4—Venice Preserved . . . . Otway
　　7—Cato . . . . . . . . Addison

this the opposition to the theatre was as determined and bitter as at any time before or since.

The controversy was carried on in the columns of Parker's *Gazette*. "Philodemus" opened the ball with an essay on "Theatrical Entertainments," in which he charged all ladies who attended the theatre as lacking in modesty, and declared that play-going had often proved fatal to the reputations of women by criminal assignations and lascivious intrigues. This was answered by "Amanda" on the 14th of December. "Amanda" declared that she could only recall one play, the " Fair Penitent," in which a loose *amour* was carried on, and pointed out how often in plays vice is painted in its most glaring colors. She called " Philodemus"

| | |
|---|---|
| Jan. | 7—Honest Yorkshireman. |
| | 11—Romeo and Juliet . . . Shakspere |
| | 20—Recruiting Officer . . . Farquhar |
| | Harlequin Collector. |
| | 25—Othello . . . . . . . Shakspere |
| | Lying Valet . . . . . . Garrick |
| | (Benefit of the Poor.) |
| Feb. | 1—Richard III . . . . . Shakspere |
| | Lethe. |
| | (Benefit of Mrs. Douglass.) |
| | 4—Theodosius . . . . . . . ; Lee |
| | Virgin Unmasked . . . Fielding |
| | (Benefit of Mrs. Morris.) |
| | 15—Committee . . . . . . Howard |
| | (Benefit of Adam Hallam.) |
| | 18—Douglas . . . . . . . Home |
| | Harlequin Collector. |
| | (Benefit of Mr. Douglass.) |
| March | 1—Romeo and Juliet. |
| | (Benefit of Mr. Quelch.) |
| | 15—Love for Love . . . . Congreve |
| | Harlequin Collector. |
| | (Benefit of Mr. Hallam.) |
| | 22—Beaux' Stratagem . . . Farquhar |
| | Hob in the Well. |
| | (Benefit of Mr. Morris.) |
| | 29—Inconstant . . . . . . Farquhar |
| | Miss in her Teens . . . Garrick |
| | (Benefit of Mrs. Hallam.) |
| April | 12—Hamlet. |
| | Devil to Pay . . . . . Coffey |
| | (Benefit of Mr. Tomlinson.) |
| | 19—Distressed Mother . . . . Philips |
| | Mock Doctor . . . . . Fielding |
| | (Benefit of Mr. Reed.) |
| | 26—Committee. |
| | Honest Yorkshireman. |
| | (Benefit of the Charity School.) |

an "impudent fellow," and said, "he is some superannuated animal that has past his grand climacteric, and whose earlier time of life has been employed in luxury and debauchery, and now being satiated, concludes that all is vanity and every pleasure criminal."

The following week " Philodemus " in a long letter, which the publisher of the *Gazette* said was well paid for, asked "Amanda" which was the best teacher, the play-house or the Bible? He resented "Amanda's" stigma upon himself, but was very bitter toward "play-house ladies." Indeed, he even intimated that "Amanda" was herself "a strolling player," an aspersion that she was not slow to resent, saying she had written in favor of the theatre some months before the players came. This communication seems to have been printed in Weyman's *Gazette*, for "Dolly Blithe" next undertook to ridicule "Amanda," telling her that by referring to her former piece in Weyman's paper, she had discovered herself, since most people knew who it was that laughed so prettily in church and wrote so handsome a vindication of the decency and propriety of it.

The opposition to the theatre in New York at this time had two curious phases. One was the readiness with which the opponents of the drama paid for the insertion of their "pieces" in Parker's paper; the other was a surprising fatality among play-goers to lose articles of value at the play-house, and to advertise for them with the intimation that they were stolen. When Dolly Blithe sent her letter to Parker, she remarked that some weighty arguments were enclosed with it. Parker said these arguments were the weight of a dollar. In the dearth of news he hoped his readers would think his being paid for such pieces a sufficient apology for inserting them. At the same time he announced that he had on hand another piece in vindication of the stage, but as it wanted the "proper arguments for its admission," he was in doubt whether he would use it. As it was not used, it may be assumed that no arguments of the weight of a dollar were forthcoming. While this controversy was going on, Thomas Harrison, organist of Trinity Church, advertised for a ring that had been lost coming from the play.[1] His advertisement, without doubt, was genuine, but it was almost immediately followed by another,[2] which suggests an effort to bring the theatre into disrepute. It is impossible to imagine anything more injurious to Mr. Douglass' prospects, especially at a time of bitter hostility to the theatre, than mention of the play-house, so soon after Mr. Harrison's advertisement, as if it was the resort of thieves and pickpockets.

One of the few play-bills of these early performances which were preserved, was one for the 26th of November, when "Hamlet," and the "Honest Yorkshireman" were given. This bill was exhibited for many years at Windust's Restaurant, at one time a noted theatrical resort, in Park Row, New York. It is especially valuable

ADVERTISEMENT IN THE NEWSPAPERS.

———

Theatre in Chapel Street.
By Permission of his Honor the LIEUTENANT-GOVERNOR
*By a* Company *of* Comedians *at the* New Theatre *in* Chapel Street
This day will be presented a Tragedy written by Shakspere, call'd
H A M L E T
Prince of Denmark
And a Baled Farce, call'd A
WONDER ! AN HONEST YORKSHIREMAN
No Person to be admitted without tickets, which are sold by Mr.
Hugh Gaine, Printer in Hanover Square.
Boxes 8*s*. Pit 5*s*. Gallery 3*s*.
No MONEY to be received at the DOORS, which will be open'd
at Four and the Play begin exactly at Six o'Clock. No
Person to be admitted behind the scenes.

[1] (From PARKER'S GAZETTE, Dec. 10, 1761.)—Lost coming from the play or concert a lady's hoop-ring with one stone out; whoever will bring the same to Thomas Harrison, organist of Trinity Church, near Mr. Reed's in King Street will have 3 dollars reward and no questions ask'd.

[2] A LOST LETTER CASE.—New York, December 31, 1761. Lost at the Play-House, on Monday the 28th instant a double black leather Letter Case containing New York and Jersey bills and some Letters and Papers of no use to any Person but the Owner. Whoever has found the said letter case and bills and will bring them to the Printer of this Paper shall receive Five Pounds reward and no questions asked.
N.B. Particulars of the Bills will be left with the Printer.

CASTS FROM THE WINDUST PLAY-BILL.

### HAMLET.

| | | | |
|---|---|---|---|
| Hamlet | . . . . . . . . . . . . . . Mr. Hallam | | |
| King | . . . . . . . . . . . . . . . . Mr. Douglass | | |
| Horatio . . . . . Mr. Reed | Marcellus . . Mr. A. Hallam | | |
| Ghost . . . . . Mr. Quelch | Guildenstern . . . . Mr. Sturt | | |
| Polonius . . . . Mr. Morris | Lucianus . . . Mr. Tomlinson | | |
| Laertes . . . . . Mr. Allyn | Francisco . . . Mr. Tremaine | | |
| Gravediggers { Mr. Quelch / Mr. Tomlinson | Queen . . . . Mrs. Douglass / Player Queen . . Mrs. Hallam | | |
| Ophelia | . . . . . . . . . . . . Mrs. Morris | | |

### HONEST YORKSHIREMAN.

| | |
|---|---|
| Gaylove . . . . Mr. Quelch | Muckworm . . . Mr. Morris |
| Blunder . . . . . Mr. Allyn | Sapscull . . . . . Mr. Sturt |
| Slango . . . Mr. A. Hallam | Arabella . . . . . Mrs. Morris |
| Combrush | . . . . . . . . . . Mrs. Douglass |

because it was the means of preserving the cast of "Hamlet" when Shakspere's masterpiece was produced for the second time on the American stage. The play-bill also contained a curious announcement,[1] not printed in the newspapers, which is interesting because it shows the theatrical customs of the period. Later on, Mr. Douglass' advertisements contained a notice[2] even more curious. It was aimed at the vice of crowding the stage during the performance, which was copied in this country from a pernicious custom that then prevailed in England. It would be difficult to determine which is the more remarkable, the abuse to which attention is called, or the obsequiousness of the manager. It was impossible in those days to give the stage to the actors without offense

---

[1] MR. DOUGLASS TO HIS PATRONS.—Mr. Douglass will be obliged to those Ladies and Gentlemen who had not an opportunity to deliver their tickets at the "Provoked Husband" to send them to his lodgings at Mr. Keen's, Confectioner on Hunter's Quay. Those Ladies who would have places kept in the boxes will please send a sensible servant to the theatre at 3 o'clock every play-day.

New York, November 24, 1761.

[2] A NOTICE. — Complaints having been several times made that a number of gentlemen crowd the stage and very much interrupt the performance, and as it is impossible the actors, when thus obstructed, should do that justice to their parts they otherwise would, it will be taken as a particular favor if no gentleman will be offended that he is absolutely refused admittance at the stage door, unless he has previously secured himself a place in either the stage or upper boxes.

and loss of patronage, and it is only reasonable to suppose that the egg-throwing episode, a few weeks afterward, grew out of this pernicious practice. Mr. Douglass made that episode historical by a card which he printed in Gaine's *Mercury*, a few days after the close of the season of 1761–2. This card proves that the egg, as a vehicle of dramatic criticism, came into use early on this Continent. It does not follow, however, that on this occasion the eggs were thrown as an expression of disapprobation with the performance or the performers.

MR. DOUGLASS' CARD.

Theatre in New York, May 3, 1762.

A Pistole Reward will be given to whoever can discover the person who was so very rude as to throw Eggs from the Gallery upon the stage last Monday, by which the Cloaths of some Ladies and Gentlemen were spoiled and the performance in some measure interrupted, D. DOUGLASS.

The probability is that they were aimed at some of the beaus of the period, who, with their powdered wigs, long, stiff-skirted coats, and waistcoats with flaps reaching nearly to the knees, silk stockings, short-quartered shoes, and silver or paste buckles, were in the habit of crowding the stage or ogling the actresses during the play. That this custom should lead to the resentments of the "gallery gods" was only natural; but it was also the subject of complaints from theatre-goers who went to see the play and the players, and not the fops of the town, as is apparent from Mr. Douglass' half-hearted appeal to the bucks of the town not to take it amiss if he compelled them to pay more than pit prices for the privilege of crowding his stage.

In the early part of the season the newspaper advertising was limited and only partial casts were printed. As these included the principal performers in the plays and sometimes in the farces, they will, however, be found interesting. These casts, meagre as they are, show that Mrs. Douglass was still the principal attraction of the company; Mrs. Morris had attained

*Beaux' Stratagem.*
  Archer . . . . . . . . Mr. Hallam
  Aimwell . . . . . . . Mr. Douglass
  Scrub . . . . . . . . Mr. A. Hallam
  Mrs. Sullen . . . . . Mrs. Douglass
*Beggars' Opera.*
  Captain Macheath . . . . Mr. Quelch
  Peachum . . . . . . . A Gentleman
  Polly . . . . . . . . . Mrs. Hallam
  Lucy . . . . . . . . . Mrs. Morris
*Cato.*
  Cato . . . . . . . . . Mr. Douglass
  Sempronius . . . . . . Mr. Hallam
  Marcia . . . . . . . Mrs. Douglass
  Lucia . . . . . . . . Mrs. Morris
*Devil to Pay.*
  Jobson . . . . . . . Mr. Tomlinson
  Nell . . . . . . . . . Mrs. Morris
*Distressed Mother.*
  Orestes . . . . . . . Mr. Hallam
  Pyrrhus . . . . . . . Mr. Douglass
  Hermione . . . . . . Mrs. Morris
  Andromache . . . . Mrs. Douglass
*Hob in the Well.*
  Flora . . . . . . . . Mrs. Hallam
  Hob . . . . . . . . . Mr. Quelch
*Inconstant.*
  Mirabel . . . . . . . Mr. Hallam
  Old Mirabel . . . . . . Mr. Morris
  Bissarre . . . . . . Mrs. Douglass
*King Henry IV.*
  King Henry . . . . . . Mr. Quelch
  Hotspur . . . . . . . Mr. Hallam
  Sir John Falstaff . . . . Mr. Douglass
*Love for Love.*
  Valentine . . . . . . Mr. Douglass
  Ben, the Sailor . . . . . Mr. Hallam
  Angelica . . . . . . Mrs. Douglass
*Miss in her Teens.*
  Captain Flash . . . . Mr. Hallam
  Captain Loveit . . . . Mr. Tomlinson
  Miss Biddy . . . . . Mrs. Hallam

the second place as an actress; and Mr. Douglass held the front rank, sharing the best roles with Mr. Hallam. Douglass, it will be observed, was the original *Falstaff* on the American stage. From their parts in the "Beggars' Opera," Mr. Quelch and Mrs. Hallam must have had some claim to consideration as singers. In the farces Mrs. Hallam and Mrs. Morris shared the best roles between them. Notwithstanding the opportunities afforded to these actors and actresses at this period, Mr. Hallam was the only member of the company who earned constant appreciation and continued promotion by actual merit. The others, including Mr. and Mrs. Douglass, were possessed of respectable talents only, a judgment for which there is ample contemporary evidence. Even in her prime Mrs. Douglass was not an actress of the highest rank, and before her career closed she sank into a subordinate place.

When the benefits began some of the beneficiaries printed full casts, both of the play and farce that comprised their bills. The first of these was Mrs. Douglass', on the 1st of February, 1762, when "Richard III" and "Lethe" were played. A month later, when Mr. Quelch had his benefit, he printed the cast of "Romeo and Juliet" as the parts were distributed this season.

MRS. DOUGLASS' BILL.

RICHARD III.

| | |
|---|---|
| Richard . . . . . . | Mr. Douglass |
| Richmond . . . . . . | Mr. Hallam |
| King Henry . . . . . . | Mr. Allyn |
| King Edward V . . | Mr. A. Hallam |
| Duke of York . . . | A young master |
| Buckingham . . . . | Mr. Tomlinson |
| Stanley . . . . . . . | Mr. Morris |
| Lieutenant of the Tower . . | Mr. Sturt |
| Catesby . . . . . . . | Mr. Reed |
| Tressel . . . . . . . | Mr. Hallam |
| Duchess of York . . . . | Mrs. Crane |
| Lady Anne . . . . . | Mrs. Morris |
| Queen Elizabeth . . | Mrs. Douglass |

LETHE.

| | |
|---|---|
| Lord Chalkstone . . . . | Mr. Allyn |
| Æsop . . . . . . . | Mr. Douglass |
| Mercury . . . . . . . | Mr. Sturt |
| Charon . . . . . . | Mr. Tomlinson |
| Tattoo . . . . . . . . | Mr. Reed |
| Fine Gentleman . . . . | Mr. Hallam |
| Frenchman . . . . . . | Mr. Allyn |
| Old Man . . . . . . | Mr. Morris |
| Bowman , . . . . | Mr. Tomlinson |
| Drunken Man . . . . | Mr. Hallam |
| Mrs. Riot . . . . . | Mrs. Douglass |

ROMEO AND JULIET.

| | |
|---|---|
| Romeo . . | Mr. Hallam |
| Prince . . | Mr. Douglass |
| Paris . . | Mr. Tomlinson |
| Montague . . | Mr. Sturt |
| Mercutio . | Mr. Douglass |
| Benvolio . | Mr. A. Hallam |
| Tybalt . . . | Mr. Reed |
| Friar Laurence . | Mr. Allyn |
| Friar John . | Mr. Tremaine |
| Juliet . . | Mrs. Douglass |
| Lady Capulet . | Mrs. Allyn |
| Nurse . . . | Mrs. Morris |

A curious fact that is revealed by these bills is the manner in which the parts were doubled. Neither Hallam nor Douglass disdained to appear as two characters in the same play, and Hallam even played the *Fine Gentleman* and *Drunken Man* in "Lethe." Taken in connection with the cast of "Hamlet" these bills show the changes that had occurred in the company since the Philadelphia season of 1759. Mr. and Mrs. Harman, Mrs. Love and Messrs. Horne and Scott have disappeared from the casts. Mr. Morris took Harman's place as *Polonius* in "Hamlet," and Mrs. Morris was the *Ophelia* instead of Mrs. Harman. Mr. Reed played *Laertes* instead of *Horatio*, and Mr. Douglass played the *King* instead of the *Ghost*, the latter part going to Mr. Quelch, a new member of the company. Mr. Sturt, who was also new, took Mr. Horne's place as

*Guildenstern.*   Mrs. Hallam was the *Player Queen* instead of Mrs. Love.   The *Francisco*, Mr. Tremaine, was probably the ambitious cabinet-maker of Murray and Kean's Company.   In "Romeo and Juliet" Mrs. Morris was the *Nurse*, instead of Mrs. Harman, and Mrs. Love gave place to Mrs. Allyn as *Lady Capulet*.   Mrs. Douglass was still the *Juliet* to her son's *Romeo*.   From this it will be seen that the only important changes were the loss of the Harmans.   Quelch, Sturt and Tremaine were probably residents of New York, and Scott and Horne of Philadelphia, who were called upon to play small parts in their respective cities.   Whoever they were, they were performers of little merit, as is evident from their parts and the fact that after a brief service their names disappear from American dramatic history.

Mrs. Morris, for her benefit on the 4th of February, published the full casts of "Theodosius" and the "Virgin Unmasked," which comprised her bill, as did also Mr. Douglass, on the 18th, of the tragedy of "Douglass" and the pantomime, "Harlequin Collector." It will be seen that Mr. Morris took advantage of his wife's benefit to appear in a tragedy role. As he was fitted only for comedy parts, his performance of *Theodosius* could

MR. DOUGLASS' BILL.

———

DOUGLAS.

Douglas . . . . Mr. Hallam
Lord Randolph . Mr. Douglass
Glenalvon . . . . Mr. Reed
Norval . . . . . Mr. Morris
Officer . . . Mr. Tomlinson
Attendant . . Mr. Tremaine
Anna . . . . . Mrs. Morris
Lady Randolph . Mrs. Douglass

HARLEQUIN COLLECTOR.

Harlequin . . . Mr. Hallam
Miller . . . . . . Mr. Allyn
Magician . . . . . Mr. Sturt
Anatomist . . . . Mr. Morris
Porter . . . . Mr. Tomlinson
Clown . . . . Mr. Douglass
Columbine . . Mrs. Douglass

MRS. MORRIS' BILL.

———

THEODOSIUS.

Varanes . . . . Mr. Hallam
Theodosius . . . Mr. Morris
Marcian . . . Mr. Douglass
Lucius . . . . . . Mr. Sturt
Leontine . . Mr. Tomlinson
Aranthes . . Mr. A. Hallam
Pulcheria . . . Mrs. Morris
Marina . . . . Mrs. Hallam
Flavilla . . . . . Mrs. Allyn
Julia . . . . . . Mrs. Crane
Athenais . . . Mrs. Douglass

VIRGIN UNMASKED.

Miss Lucy . . . Mrs. Morris
Goodwill . . . . Mr. Morris
Coupee . . . Mr. A. Hallam
Quaver . . . Mr. Tomlinson
Thomas . . . . . Mr. Read

scarcely fail to be funny. The incident proves that Morris, like most comedians, was ambitious to play tragedy. Besides these casts the only one for the season of 1761–2 that has come down to us was that of the " Mock Doctor," printed in the advertisement of Mr. Reed's benefit. In this cast occurs the name of Mrs. Crane, who played small parts on several occasions during the season. She was probably identical with Miss Crane, who was with the company at Annapolis, in 1760.

MOCK DOCTOR.

Gregory . . . . . . . . . Mr. Douglass
Sir Jasper . . . . . . . . . Mr. Morris
Leander . . . . . . . . . . Mr. Sturt
Robert . . . . . . . . Mr. A. Hallam
Davy . . . . . . . . . . . Mr. Allyn
Hellebore . . . . . . . Mr. Tremaine
Harry . . . . . . . . . . Mr. Tomlinson
James . . . . . . . . . . . Mr. Reed
Charlotte . . . . . . . . . Mrs. Crane
Dorcas . . . . . . . . . Mrs. Morris

One of the most interesting incidents of these early days of the American stage was the account rendered by Mr. Douglass of the receipts and disbursements of the " Othello" night for the benefit of " such poor families as are not otherwise provided for." In dollars the expenses were $46.31 and the receipts $332.56, leaving as the fund for the poor $286.25. All that the actors obtained from the performance was wine to the amount of two

A BENEFIT ACCOUNT.

|  | £. | s. | d. |
|---|---|---|---|
| Box tickets sold at the door, 116 at 8s. | 46 | 8 | |
| Pit tickets sold at the door, 146 at 5s. | 36 | 10 | |
| Gallery tickets sold at the door, 90 at 3s. | 13 | 10 | |
| Cash received at the doors | 36 | 12 | 6 |
| | £133 | | 6 |

CHARGES.

| | £ | s. | d. |
|---|---|---|---|
| To candles, 26 lb. spermaceti, at 3s. 6d. } To candles, 14 lb. tallow, at 1s. } | | 5 | 5 |
| To music, Messrs. Harrison & Van Dienval | | 3 | 12 |
| To the front doorkeeper, 16s., stage doorkeeper, 8s. | 1 | 4 | |
| To the assistants, 13s., bill-sticker, 4s. | | 17 | |
| To the men's dressers, 4s. } To the stage-keeper, 32s. } To the drummer, 4s. } | | 2 | |
| To wine in the second act | | 2 | 6 |
| To Hugh Gaine for two sets of bills, advertisements and commissions | | 5 | 10 |
| | | £18 10 | 6 |

Balance, £114, 10s.

and six. It is not likely their own benefits brought to any one of them anything like this sum. To their benefit announcements, however, we owe all that we know of the personal history of these forgotten actors and actresses. From Mrs. Douglass' advertisement it is learned that Mr. and Mrs. Douglass no longer lodged at Mr. Keen's, confectioner, on Hunter's Quay, but were living in Chapel Street, near the theatre. Mr. and Mrs. Hallam, on the contrary, had lodgings in Nassau Street. These facts, apparently so unimportant, settle the question of the identity of the Mrs. Hallam in the casts, showing that she was Mrs. Hallam, the wife, not Miss Hallam, the sister, of Lewis Hallam. We learn also that Adam Hallam's benefit was postponed in consequence of the illness of Mrs. Morris, his announcement[1] to this effect being made in Parker's *Gazette*, February 11th, 1762. The advertisement was printed in two lines across the bottom of the page of Parker's paper. Mr. Quelch lodged " at Captain Crew's next door but one to the theatre," and Mr. and Mrs. Morris " at Mr. Earle's, Hatter, at Beekman's Slip." On the 18th of March, Mr. Morris announced a change of mind in the choice of a play for his benefit, worded in the quaint phraseology of the time. That a comedian

By Particular Desire Mr. Morris has changed his Play from RICHARD to the BEAUX' STRATAGEM. The Entertainment as before mentioned; and hopes it will be agreeable to the Ladies and Gentlemen of the City.

should have selected a tragedy in the first instance for such an occasion is one of those incongruities of which theatrical history is full. It is not likely that any of the benefits this season yielded a rich harvest, for it must be confessed that players were not popular at that

[1] A. HALLAM'S ANNOUNCEMENT.—Mr. A. Hallam is sorry to acquaint the town that he is under the disagreeable necessity of again postponing his Play till Monday next, when it will certainly be acted, as another Performer will be ready in the character of MRS. DAY should Mrs. Morris's indisposition continue.

time, except among a small class of play-goers. Opposition to the drama was not the only cause of hostility to the stage. Even before the passage of the Stamp Act a strong republican sentiment had grown up in America and especially in New York. Actors were not only unpopular as actors, but, being English, they were looked upon as sympathizing with British aggression. As early as 1764 this feeling took offensive shape in wrecking the theatre in Chapel Street, which Douglass had built in 1761, and in which his company played during the season of 1761–62. Dunlap had the story of the destruction of the theatre from a gentleman residing on Long Island, who, as a boy, had helped to pull down the structure. According to this gentleman a number of persons assembled in a yard or open space opposite the theatre and set on some boys to begin the work, which, once begun, found hands enough to aid in it. This was the first American mob that directed its fury against the theatre, but as the company was absent at the time and had been for two years, it is not very clear what the impelling motive of the rioters was.

Dunlap assumes, with his usual confidence, that the theatre was utterly wrecked, but such could not have been the case, for on the 10th of April, 1765, "George Barnwell" and the "Brave Irishman" were played in "the theatre in Chapel Street" for the benefit of the prisoners in the gaol. This was probably the effort of a company of amateurs. Only one name was mentioned in the advertisement— Mr. Walsh as *Captain O'Blunder*, in the farce. A year later, on the 9th of April, 1766, the "Twin Rivals" and the "Miller of Mansfield" were announced, but it seems the performance was not allowed, because of the excited condition of political feeling. This inference follows from the fact that the same bill was advertised for the 6th of

May, the advertisement stating: "As the packet is now arrived and has been the messenger of good news relative to repeal, it is hoped that the public has no objection to the above performance." Whether this was Douglass' company, then about to change its name and become "the American Company," instead of the Company of Comedians from London, there is no means of knowing, but it seems likely, as during the summer of 1766, Mr. Douglass built a new theatre in Philadelphia preparatory to another campaign in the city of "Brotherly Love." As Dunlap is the only authority for the year of the destruction of the Chapel Street Theatre, it will be doing no violence to his accuracy by changing the date from 1764 to 1766. In that case the company may have been in New York and the mob would then have had a motive, in the excited feelings of the time, for pulling it down, in order to prevent the players from occupying it.

# CHAPTER XV.

## A REVIEW.

DRAMATIC PROGRESS IN AMERICA FROM 1752 TO 1766—WHAT IS
KNOWN OF THE EARLY PLAYERS—CHARLOTTE CHARKE'S SON-IN-
LAW—GOOD-BYE TO DOUGLASS' FIRST COMPANY.

IN the fourteen years that intervened between the performance of
the "Merchant of Venice," at Williamsburg, on the 5th of
September, 1752, and the opening of the old Southwark Theatre on
the 21st of November, 1766, many changes had occurred, not only in
the company, but in the Hallam family. Lewis Hallam, the elder,
had died and his widow had married again. For nearly ten years she
had been known to the American public as Mrs. Douglass, and was
now about to yield many of her best roles to a younger actress.
From a stammering boy young Lewis Hallam had become the leading actor on the American stage, with a long theatrical history behind
him at the age of twenty-six, and a still longer career, both as actor
and manager, before him. In his later years Mr. Hallam was accustomed to say that he owed whatever success he was able to achieve
to the early instructions of Rigby. Mr. Douglass, too, now also
about to yield his supremacy, had succeeded to the great Shaksperean
roles of Malone and Harman, and had proved himself a man of much

capacity, both as actor and manager. The other members of the family had not been so fortunate. Miss Helen Hallam had advanced slowly, and despite her opportunities had not been able to achieve distinction as an actress. She left the stage in 1754. Miss Nancy Hallam was never heard of again after being seen in children's parts in Philadelphia in 1761. If she lived to womanhood it may be accepted as established that she was the Miss Hallam of later years. Mrs. Hallam's name was never in the bills after 1762. It is probable that her separation from her husband occurred before 1766. The Mrs. Hallam of 1761–62 and the Miss Hallam of 1766–74 were musical, which the Miss Hallam of 1752–54 was not in any marked degree. It seems proper, in view of these considerations, that their parts should be summarized in this

PARTS OF MISS, MRS. AND NANCY HALLAM.

MISS HALLAM.
*Plays.*

Beaux' Stratagem . . . . . . . . . Cherry
Beggars' Opera . . . . . . . Mrs. Coaxer
Careless Husband . . . . . . . . Edging
Constant Couple . . . . . . . . . Parly
Distressed Mother . . . . . . . . Cleone
Love for Love . . . . . . . . Miss Prue
Merchant of Venice . . . . . . . Jessica
Suspicious Husband . . . . . . Lucetta
Tunbridge Walks . . . . . . . . Lucy
Woman is a Riddle . . . . . Necessary

*Farces.*

Anatomist . . . . . . . . Waiting Maid
Hob in the Well . . . . . . . . . Betty
Lying Valet . . . . . . . . . . Kitty Fry
Miss in her Teens . . . . . Miss Biddy
Stage Coach . . . . . . . . . . Dolly
Tom Thumb . . . . . . . . . . Cleora
Virgin Unmasked . . . . . . Miss Lucy

MRS. HALLAM.
*Plays.*

Beggars' Opera . . . . . . . . . Polly
Hamlet . . . . . . . . . Player Queen
Theodosius . . . . . . . . . . Marina

*Farces.*

Hob in the Well . . . . . . . . Flora
Miss in her Teens . . . . . Miss Biddy

MISS NANCY HALLAM.

Macbeth . . . . . . . . . . . Fleance
Richard III . . . . . . . Duke of York

place, and that we should take a final leave of them. The Mrs. Hallam of later years, who was said to be a niece of Mrs. Douglass, became an actress of decided merit, and was celebrated down to the Revolution for youth and beauty as well as strong dramatic powers.

Another Hallam of whom there is no further account is Adam, the younger brother of Lewis Hallam. Mr. Ireland, in his "Record of the New York Stage," says he found the name of Adam Hallam, shoemaker, in a New York Directory for 1798. It is improbable, though not impossible, that a poor actor left the stage to become a good shoemaker.

The best actor seen in America during these fourteen years was Mr. Rigby of the original company. While young Lewis Hallam had succeeded to his parts, all the evidence goes to show that the pupil had not yet become the equal of his master.

ADAM HALLAM'S PARTS.

*Plays.*

| | |
|---|---|
| Beaux' Stratagem | Scrub |
| Beggars' Opera | Filch |
| Bold Stroke for a Wife | Quaking Boy |
| Hamlet | Osric / Marcellus |
| Lear | Attendant |
| Macbeth | Donaldbain |
| Othello | Roderigo |
| Richard III | Duke of York / Prince Edward |
| Romeo and Juliet | Benvolio |
| Tamerlane | Hali |
| Theodosius | Aranthes |
| Venice Preserved | Conspirator |

*Farces*

| | |
|---|---|
| Honest Yorkshiremen | Slango |
| Mock Doctor | Robert |
| Tom Thumb | Tom Thumb |
| Virgin Unmasked | Coupee |

Mr. Harman, who succeeded Malone in the heavy fathers, but who was a more versatile actor than his predecessor, must have died or retired soon after the Philadelphia season of 1759, for he was never seen in New York and never appeared with the company afterward, while Mrs. Harman resumed her connection with it with reduced consequence in 1766. The only knowledge we have of Harman is that derived from Charlotte Charke's Memoirs. "Though I had no fortune to give her," Charlotte Charke writes, "without any partiality I look on her as a more advantageous match for a discreet man than a woman who might bring one and confound it in unnecessary expenses, which, I am certain, Kitty never will do; and had she met with as sober and respectable a creature as herself in the few years they have had a company might have been worth a considerable sum of money, to have set them up in some creditable business that might have redounded more to their quiet and reputation." Harman married Kitty Charke at Symington, and they played together as strolling actors for several years in and about Bath and the Isle of Wight. While Mrs. Charke never mentions the man whom her daughter "imprudently married" by name, she does not fail to do

MR. HARMAN'S PARTS.

| | |
|---|---|
| Beggars' Opera | Macheath |
| Douglas | Old Norval |
| Drummer | Vellum |
| Fair Penitent | Lothario |
| Gamester | Lewson |
| Hamlet | Polonius |
| Harlequin Collector | Conjurer |
| Lear | Lear |
| Macbeth | Duncan |
| Provoked Husband | Sir Francis Wronghead |
| Recruiting Officer | Captain Brazen |
| Richard III | Richard |
| Romeo and Juliet | Mercutio |
| Tamerlane | Tamerlane |
| Theodosius | Atticus |

justice to Mrs. Harman's talents. Among other parts she praises her daughter's acting as *Horatia* in the "Roman Father," and as *Boadicea*, wishing "she was so settled as to constantly play in that walk." The little we know of Harman and his wife is so interesting that it is to be regretted that so little was recorded of the personal history and professional merits of these forgotten actors.

Another interesting figure of this period, who has been utterly ignored, is Mr. Palmer. In Philadelphia, in 1759, he played only at benefits, but singularly enough he was himself accorded a benefit. At Annapolis, in 1760, he was a regular member of the company. Then he disappeared, but the next year, 1761–62, John Palmer, the younger, appeared in

MR. PALMER'S PARTS.

| | |
|---|---|
| Bold Stroke for a Wife | Periwinkle |
| Fair Penitent | Horatio |
| Gamester | Stukely |
| Macbeth | Macbeth |
| Othello | Iago |
| Romeo and Juliet | Romeo |
| Suspicious Husband | Mr. Strictland |
| Venice Preserved | Jaffier |

similar roles at Drury Lane on benefit occasions. Did Palmer find his
way to the Colonies in his strolling days? Dates and circumstances
coincide with this theory. There is no account of John Palmer before
1761, except the general assertion of Dr. Doran and others, that, previous to this time, he had been a stroller. In those days Englishmen
of his class were apt to find their way to America only to return to
England with unpleasant recollections of the New World. That
Palmer should have tried his fortunes here is not more remarkable
than the advent of Lewis Hallam, the elder, or the presence of Mr.
and Mrs. Harman. They were, in fact, all strollers, to whom the
provincial boards in England gave little reward and the London stage
no encouragement. There is, perhaps, in all English dramatic history
no more forcible example of this than Palmer. He was nearly ten
years in London before he began to make his mark. Garrick decried
him. Anything like a fair opportunity was denied him. In spite of
every obstacle he obtained the favor of the town and attained the high
distinction of being the best general actor of his time. Comedy was
his forte, but he was able to perform the tyrannical parts of tragedy
with great effect. His *Villeroy* in "Isabella" and *Stukely* in the
"Gamester" were excellent. "When shall we see such a *Villeroy* and
*Stukely* again?" Mrs. Siddons once asked. His *Sneer* in the "Critic"
and *Joseph Surface* in the "School for Scandal" were the complete
embodiments of the characters, for Palmer's strength lay in the
delivery of sarcasm and irony, insincere humility and hypocritical self-
reproach. It is scarcely assuming too much to conclude that the
*Stukely* of Mr. Reed's benefit in Philadelphia was the *Stukely* whose
demise Mrs. Siddons lamented.

Among these early actresses was Mrs. Love, whose career

furnishes some interesting features. She was the wife of Charles Love, a teacher of music, located in New York as early as 1753. When the original Hallam Company first gave performances in Nassau Street, Mrs. Love was engaged to sing between the acts, and she had the little part of *Jenny Diver* in the "Beggars' Opera." Before the close of Mr. Douglass' first campaign she had developed into an actress of considerable prominence, as will be seen from her parts, and from *Jenny* had become the *Polly* of Gay's work. As an actress, her training must have been entirely American. Another actress of the period known also to the American stage was Miss or Mrs. Crane. She was with Douglass at Annapolis, in 1760, as Miss Crane, and in New York, in 1761–62, as Mrs. Crane. She was probably an old-time amateur, "desirous of making the stage a profession," who found herself inadequate to the undertaking and soon retired.

MRS. LOVE'S PARTS.

*Plays.*

| | |
|---|---|
| Beggars' Opera | { Polly<br>{ Jenny Diver |
| Fair Penitent | Lucilla |
| Hamlet | Player Queen |
| Lear | Goneril |
| Macbeth | Lady Macduff |
| Provoked Husband | Lady Wronghead |
| Recruiting Officer | Rose |
| Richard III | Duchess of York |
| Romeo and Juliet | Lady Capulet |
| Suspicious Husband | { Maid<br>{ Jacintha |
| Theodosius | Flavilla |

*Farce.*

| | |
|---|---|
| Devil to Pay | Lucy |

MRS. CRANE'S PARTS.

*Plays.*

| | |
|---|---|
| George Barnwell | Lucy |
| Othello | Emilia |
| Richard III | Duchess of York |
| Theodosius | Julia |

*Farce.*

| | |
|---|---|
| Mock Doctor | Charlotte |

The actors who bade a final farewell to the American stage with the close of Mr. Douglass' first campaign were Reed, Horne, Scott, Quelch, Sturt, Tremaine and Murray. Mr. Reed was a useful member of Mr. Douglass' company, as his parts show, and so, also, in a lesser degree, was Mr. Horne. To the same category belong both Mr. Scott and Mr. Quelch. Beyond their parts nothing whatever is known of any of them. This remark applies also to Sturt, Tremaine and Murray. Reed was the successor of Bell, of the original company, although he occasionally filled parts that fell to the lot of Clarkson. Horne played only walking gentlemen, generally in the tragedies. Horne was Miller's successor, but he had few parts. Quelch, on the contrary, had now and then a good role in the singing pieces, but, singularly enough, while he was the *Macheath* in the "Beggars' Opera" he was only the *Mopsus* in the ballad-farce of "Damon and Phillida." Quelch was apparently the only one of these minor actors who accompanied Mr. Douglass' company in the visits to Rhode Island. He is not mentioned in the Annapolis casts of 1760. Scott not only formed part of the Annapolis contingent, but he was with Murray and Kean in 1750. In the advertisement for his benefit Scott is described as a "Naadecker," whatever that may

MR. REED'S PARTS.

*Plays.*

| | |
|---|---|
| Beggars' Opera | Mat o' the Mint |
| Douglas | Glenalvon |
| Drummer | Sir George Truman |
| Fair Penitent | Altamont |
| Hamlet | Laertes |
| Lear | Edmund |
| Provoked Husband | Count Basset |
| Recruiting Officer | Justice Balance |
| Richard III | { Buckingham / Catesby |
| Romeo and Juliet | Tybalt |
| Suspicious Husband | Jack Meggot |
| Tamerlane | Axalla |
| Theodosius | Theodosius |

*Farces.*

| | |
|---|---|
| Lethe | Tattoo |
| Mock Doctor | James |
| Virgin Unmasked | Thomas |

MR. QUELCH'S PARTS.

*Plays.*

| | |
|---|---|
| Beggars' Opera | Macheath |
| Fair Penitent | Altamont |
| Hamlet | { Ghost / Gravedigger |
| Henry IV | King Henry |
| Othello | Cassio |

*Farces.*

| | |
|---|---|
| Damon and Phillida | Mopsus |
| Hob in the Well | Hob |
| Honest Yorkshireman | Gaylove |

MR. HORNE'S PARTS.

*Plays.*

| | |
|---|---|
| Beggars' Opera | Paddington |
| Hamlet | Guildenstern |
| Lear | Cornwall |
| Richard III | Oxford |
| Romeo and Juliet | Paris |
| Suspicious Husband | Buckle |
| Tamerlane | Prince |

mean. Sturt appeared only a few times, in small parts, Tremaine had still fewer and smaller parts, and Murray was in the bills only thrice.

If these players, playing only the smaller roles of the drama, belonged to a later epoch, they would scarcely be worthy of mention; but as parts of the theatrical machinery of their own time they are exceedingly interesting, because they show us that Manager Douglass was never at a loss for actors. There is a little reason to doubt that, with the exception of the Hallams and English strollers, like Palmer and the Harmans, his company was made up from time to time of thespians of West India and colonial manufacture. Who or what they were, or how Mr. Douglass found them, we may never know, but they are entitled to remembrance for their share in laying the foundations of the American theatre. They strutted their brief hour and disappeared, but their names and their parts belong to the theatrical record of their time.

MR. SCOTT'S PARTS.

| | |
|---|---|
| Beggars' Opera | Lockit |
| Bold Stroke for a Wife | { Obadiah Prim / Sackbut } |
| George Barnwell | Blunt |
| Hamlet | Player King |
| Lear | Gloster |
| Macbeth | Banquo |
| Recruiting Officer | Mr. Scale |
| Romeo and Juliet | Friar Lawrence |
| Suspicious Husband | Chairman |
| Venice Preserved | Renault |

MR. STURT'S PARTS.

*Plays.*

| | |
|---|---|
| Hamlet | Guildenstern |
| Richard III | Lieutenant |
| Romeo and Juliet | Montague |
| Theodosius | Lucius |

*Farces.*

| | |
|---|---|
| Harlequin Collector | Magician |
| Honest Yorkshirem'n | Sapscull |
| Lethe | Mercury |
| Mock Doctor | Leander |

MR. TREMAINE'S PARTS.

*Plays.*

| | |
|---|---|
| Douglas | Attendant |
| Hamlet | Francisco |
| Romeo and Juliet | Friar John |

*Farce.*

| | |
|---|---|
| Mock Doctor | Hellebore |

MR. MURRAY'S PARTS.

| | |
|---|---|
| Bold Stroke | Sir Philip |
| George Barnwell | Uncle |
| Othello | Duke |

# CHAPTER XVI.

## THE SOUTHWARK THEATRE.

BUILDING OF THE FIRST PERMANENT PLAY-HOUSE IN AMERICA—A NEW
AND STRONG COMPANY AND BRILLIANT REPERTOIRE—SEASON OF
1766–7 IN PHILADELPHIA—THE PLAYS AND THE CASTS.

ALL the theatres built in America previous to the year 1766 were temporary structures and soon ceased to be used for theatrical purposes. In that year, however, a theatre was built in Philadelphia that continued to be used for dramatic representations until the beginning of the present century. This was what is known in history as the old Southwark Theatre, in South Street, above Fourth, the original walls of which are still standing. The upper part of the building was of wood, only the walls of the first story being of brick. It was partly destroyed by fire in 1821. Soon afterward the walls were raised to their present height and it is now and has been known for many years as Young's Distillery. Even Dunlap, whose book was published in 1832, notes the uses to which it had been put. "Once pouring out a mingled strain of good and evil," he says, and it may be said still, "it now dispenses purely evil." These old walls, now of 120 years' duration, for 55 years the foundation of a theatre, have been for nearly 65 years a temple on which was inscribed Y. P. M.—Young's Pure Malt.

This theatre, which may claim the honor of being the first real temple of the drama in America, was an ugly, ill-contrived affair, both outside and inside. The brick-work was rude but strong, and the wooden part of the building rough and primitive. The whole was painted a glaring red. The stage was lighted by plain oil-lamps, without glasses, and the view from the boxes was intercepted by large wooden pillars supporting the upper tier and the roof. " It was contended by many at the time," wrote a chronicler who had been there, " that the front bench in the gallery was the best seat in the house for a fair view of the whole stage." Unsatisfactory as this theatre must have been, it was in every way superior to the temporary structures that had preceded it, and it was the forerunner of the theatres that Mr. Douglass was soon to build in New York, Annapolis and Charleston.

It was scarcely to be expected that the new theatre should be built and opened without opposition. There was in Philadelphia at that time a spirit of hostility to the stage that could be deterred by no discouragement, and the Assembly was in sympathy with the narrow views of the Quakers and other sects opposed to the drama. In view of all this it is not surprising that a Remonstrance[1] was presented to

[1] A REMONSTRANCE.—A Remonstrance from a great number of the inhabitants of the City and County of Philadelphia of several religious denominations was presented to the House and read, setting forth that they have with much concern observed the design to establish stage-playing by erecting a theatre in the suburbs of this city, and being apprehensive of the pernicious consequences thereof, conceive it necessary to express their earnest desire that every lawful measure may be taken to discourage the continuance of those attempts that are now made to promote such a design.—That the direct tendency of stage-plays to divert the minds of the people and more especially of the unwary youths from the necessary application of the several employments by which they may be qualified to become useful members of society, renders it expedient for every well wisher to our trade and commerce to exert his endeavors to suppress them.—And when these Remonstrants consider the greater and more dangerous consequences of their enervating those sentiments and principles of the Holy Religion they profess and their direct repugnance to the spirit, temper and precepts of the Gospel— they hope this request from a number of the citizens and others of the several different denominations of Christians united in a desire to promote the cause and interest of religion and virtue, will engage the endeavors of the House to suppress these ensnaring entertainments by such an application to the Governor as on mature consideration they may judge will be most effectual.

the Assembly as soon as possible when the House convened after the building of the theatre. The Remonstrance was received on the 16th of February, 1767. On the 18th a committee was appointed to draft an Address to the Governor. This Address was reported on the 19th, and presented to Governor John Penn the same day. The Address, like the Remonstrance, was as illogical in its arguments as it was bigoted in its views, but the Governor received it unfavorably, and refused to give it his sanction or to seek to enforce its recommendations. Governor Penn returned for answer that he should consider the said Remonstrance and act agreeably to his judgment, "without regard to persons or parties." As a matter of fact he never interfered with the players, and so the Remonstrance came to naught.

The Southwark Theatre was first opened to the public on the 21st of November, 1766. It was on this occasion that the company was first called "The American Company." The plays that were advertised in the *Pennsylvania Gazette* and the *Pennsylvania Chronicle* make up a long and interesting list. The season was a long one, lasting until the 6th of July, 1767, and the productions were remarkable for their variety and importance. After an experience of four years as a manager in the colonies, followed by an absence of four years, Mr. Douglass had returned with a new company, in which,

LIST OF PERFORMANCES.

1766.
Nov. 21—Douglas . . . . . . . . Home
Catherine and Petruchio. Shakspere
24—School for Lovers . . Whitehead
26—Jane Shore . . . . . . . Rowe
28—Beggars' Opera . . . . . . Gay
Old Maid . . . . . . Murphy
Dec. 5—Richard III . . . . . Shakspere
Oracle . . . . . . Mrs. Cibber
12—Merchant of Venice . . Shakspere
Miller of Mansfield . . Dodsley
19—Constant Couple . . . Farquhar
Devil to Pay . . . . . . Coffey
26—Theodosius . . . . . . . . Lee
Lethe . . . . . . . . Garrick
1767.
Jan. 2—Tamerlane . . . . . . Rowe
Oracle.
9—Hamlet . . . . . . . Shakspere
Mock Doctor . . . . . Fielding

Jan.  16—Orphan of China . . . . Murphy
        Devil to Pay.
     23—Beaux' Stratagem . . . Farquhar
        Upholsterer . . . . . . Murphy
     26—Mourning Bride  . . . Congreve
        High Life Below Stairs . Townley
     30—Lear . . . . . . . . Shakspere
        Citizen . . . . . . . . Murphy
Feb.  2—Cato . . . . . . . . Addison
        Reprisal  . . . . . . Smollet
     6—Orphan of China.
        High Life Below Stairs.
     9—Miser . . . . . . . Fielding
        Reprisal.
    13—Romeo and Juliet . . Shakspere
        Catherine and Petruchio.
    16—Conscious Lovers . . . . Steele
        Damon and Phillida . . . Cibber
    20—Inconstant . . . . . Farquhar
        Thomas and Sally . . Bickerstaff
    23—George Barnwell . . . . . Lillo
        Mayor of Garratt . . . . . Foote
    27—Love for Love . . . . Congreve
        Damon and Phillida.
March 3—Provoked Husband . . Vanbrugh
        Harlequin Collector.
     5—Miser.
        Harlequin Collector.
     9—All for Love . . . . . Dryden
        Harlequin Collector.
    14—Love Makes a Man . . . Cibber
        Deuce is in Him . . . . Colman
    17—Richard III.
        Brave Irishman.
    19—Love in a Village . . Bickerstaff
        Mayor of Garratt.
    23—Earl of Essex . . . . . Jones
        Harlequin Collector.
    28—Macbeth . . . . . Shakspere
        Oracle.
    30—Macbeth.
        Lying Valet.
April  2—Gamester . . . . . Moore
        The Witches (a pantomime) Love
     7—Romeo and Juliet.
        Lethe.

however, were several members of his old corps, including Morris, Allyn and Tomlinson, and their wives. It is evident that he had returned determined to stay, a purpose that was only thwarted by the Revolution. The company became the American Company not only in name, but in fact. Most of its members made this country their home, and at least one of those who made his first appearance during this period became a distinguished officer in the patriot army. Having come to stay, Mr. Douglass naturally brought with him as strong a company as possible; but not only was the company a vast improvement on its predecessor, but the list of plays shows that the repertoire had been greatly increased since 1762. Among the pieces played for the first time, so far as is known, were the " Orphan of China," the " Miser," " Love Makes a Man," " Love in a Village," the " Jealous Wife," " Country Lasses," " School for Lovers," the "Wonder," and the "Roman Father." Many of the farces were new, notably the "Old Maid," the "Oracle," the "Upholsterer," "High Life Below Stairs," the "Deuce is in Him," "Mayor of Garratt," the "Spirit of Contradiction," the "Contrivances," the "Chaplet," the "Double Disappointment" and "Neck or Nothing." There was also a new pantomime, the "Witches," to supplement the well-worn "Harlequin Collector." But the season was especially noteworthy for the production of the first American play ever seen on the stage, the "Prince of Parthia," which apparently was not a success, as it certainly did not deserve to be. All this goes to show that since Mr. Douglass' company was last seen in Philadelphia and New York it had met with good fortune elsewhere, for the enterprising spirit it exhibited could only come with prosperity. The most important addition to the company, as it was

April 9—Hamlet.
Witches.
20—Mourning Bride.
Contrivances . . . . . . Carey
24—Prince of Parthia . . . . Godfrey
Contrivances.
27—A Bold Stroke for a Wife. Centlivre
Devil to Pay.
May 1—All for Love.
Hob in the Well.
4—A Bold Stroke for a Wife.
Apprentice.
7—Jealous Wife . . . . .*Colman
Lying Valet . . . . . . Garrick
(Miss Cheer's Benefit.)
11—Committee.
Picture of a Playhouse.
Spirit of Contradiction.
(Mr. Douglass' Benefit.)
14—Romeo and Juliet.
Reprisal.
(Mrs. Morris' Benefit.)
18—Drummer . . . . . Addison
Catherine and Petruchio.
(Mrs. Harman's Benefit.)
21—Beaux' Stratagem.
Don Quixote in England.
(Mr. Morris' Benefit.)
25—Cymbeline . . . . . Shakspere
Mayor of Garratt.
(Mr. Hallam's Benefit.)
28—Love in a Village.
High Life Below Stairs.
(Mr. Woolls' Benefit.)
June 1—Revenge.
Tom Thumb . . . . . Fielding
(Mr. Wall's Benefit.)
4—Country Lasses . . . . Johnson
Chaplet . . . . . . . Mendez
(Miss Wainwright's Benefit.)
8—Coriolanus . . . . . . Thomson
Contrivances.
(Mr. Tomlinson's Benefit.)
12—School for Lovers.
Neck or Nothing . . . . Garrick
(Miss Hallam's Benefit.)

June 15—Miser.
      Double Disappointment . Mendez
      (Mr. Allyn's Benefit.)
   18—Roman Father  . . . Whitehead
      Hob in the Well.
      (Mrs. Douglass' Benefit.)
   22—Merchant of Venice.
      Lying Valet.
      (Mrs. Tomlinson's Benefit).
   25—Wonder . . . . . . . Centlivre
      Citizen.
      (Mr. Greville's Benefit.)
   29—Cymbeline.
      Neck or Nothing.
      (Miss Hallam's Benefit.)
July   2—Gamester.
      Reprisal.
      (Mr. Broadbelt's Benefit.)
    6—Constant Couple.
      Apprentice.
      (Mrs. Wall's Benefit.)

then organized, was the acquisition of Miss Cheer. As she succeeded to most of Mrs. Douglass' former roles, and had the choice of parts in the new plays, it follows that her engagement was due to the advancing age of the manager's wife. Miss Wainwright was next in importance. These ladies were probably engaged in the West Indies. Another important acquisition was Mr. Woolls, a good actor, an excellent singer and an honest man. Except the few people who can only be described as useful the rest of the company comprised the previous members, all well known to American theatre-goers.

The season began with the tragedy of "Douglas," and Garrick's version of "Catherine and Petruchio" as an afterpiece. In previous years it had been performed with Mr. Harman as *Norval,* Mr. Reed as *Glenalvon* and Mrs. Morris as *Anna.* In the other parts the cast was the same as

### DOUGLAS.

| | |
|---|---|
| Douglas . . .  . . . . . . | Mr. Hallam |
| Lord Randolph . . . . . . | Mr. Douglass |
| Glenalvon . . . . . . . . . | Mr. Wall |
| Norval . . . . . . . . . . | Mr. Morris |
| Anna. . . . . . . . . . | Mrs. Harman |
| Lady Randolph . . . . . | Mrs. Douglass |

when the tragedy was played for Mr. Douglass' benefit in New York, in 1762. It is a singular fact that the Shakspere comedy, or rather farce, was not only originally played in America as arranged by Garrick for Drury Lane, in 1754, but that it continued to be so played until 1887, when the "Taming of the Shrew" was produced for the first time in its entirety by Augustin Daly, in New York. Since the appearance of Mr. Hallam and Miss Cheer in the two title roles, the parts have been filled by such noted players as Cooper and Mrs. Mason (1814); Macready and Mrs. Darley (1827); W. B. Wood and Mrs. Sharpe (1839); Vandenhoff and his daughter, Miss Vandenhoff (1839); Couldock and Mrs. Hoey (1850); Edwin Booth and Ada Clifton (1862); and finally (1887) John Drew and Ada Rehan in the "Taming of the Shrew." But only the original *Catherine* in this country, Miss Cheer, chose the part for her *debut*.

### CATHERINE AND PETRUCHIO.

| | |
|---|---|
| Catherine | Miss Cheer |
| Petruchio | Mr. Hallam |
| Hortentio | Mr. Douglass |
| Grumio | Mr. Morris |
| Baptista | Mr. Tomlinson |
| Biondello | Mr. Wall |
| Music Master | Mr. Allyn |
| Peter | Mr. Woolls |
| Bianca | Mrs. Wall |
| Curtis | Mrs. Harman |

Whitehead's "School for Lovers" at this time was still a new play in London. It was played only once in Philadelphia during the season of 1766–7, so far as the records show, for although announced for Miss Hallam's benefit, the benefit was postponed. Garrick was the original *Sir John*, Mrs. Clive the *Araminta* and Mrs. Cibber the *Celia.*

### SCHOOL FOR LOVERS.

| | |
|---|---|
| Sir John Dorilant | Mr. Douglass |
| Modely | Mr. Hallam |
| Belmour | Mr. Wall |
| Araminta | Miss Cheer |
| Lady Beverly | Mrs. Harman |
| Celia | Miss Hallam |

It is probable that "Jane Shore," the play announced for the third night of the season, was not performed, a notice appended to the advertisement of the "Beggars' Opera" indicating that want of patronage had caused it to be postponed. In those days theatre-goers re-

### NOTICE.

\*\*\* The Director of the Theatre begs leave to assure the Town that for the future no audience be it ever so small will be disappointed upon any account whatsoever, and that the play advertised will be certainly performed.

fused to be trifled with, as is shown by Mr. Douglass' apology. The cast of Gay's work on this occasion was noteworthy for the introduction of Mr. Woolls as *Macheath*, and Miss Wainwright as *Polly*. These singers were both pupils of the celebrated Dr. Arne. Mr. Murphy's two-act comedy, the "Old Maid," originally produced at Drury Lane, in 1761, had its first presentation in America as the afterpiece to the "Beggars' Opera," on this occasion. It is worthy of particular mention as the first of Murphy's many pieces produced on the American stage before the Revolution.

### BEGGARS' OPERA.

| | |
|---|---|
| Macheath | Mr. Woolls |
| Peachum | Mr. Allyn |
| Lockit | Mr. Tomlinson |
| Filch | Mr. Wall |
| Beggar | Mr. Morris |
| Jemmy Twitcher | Mr. Matthews |
| Moll Brazen | Mr. Douglass |
| Lucy | Mrs. Morris |
| Mrs. Peachum | Mrs. Harman |
| Mrs. Coaxer | Mrs. Tomlinson |
| Mrs. Slammekin | Miss Dowthwaite |
| Polly | Miss Wainwright |

### OLD MAID.

| | |
|---|---|
| Old Maid | Mrs. Harman |
| Captain Cape | Mr. Douglass |
| Clerimont | Mr. Hallam |
| Mr. Harlow | Mr. Allyn |
| Mr. Heartly | Mr. Morris |
| Trifle | Mrs. Morris |
| Mrs. Harlow | Miss Cheer |

The first of Shakspere's tragedies presented this season was "Richard III," with Mrs. Cibber's little farce, the "Oracle," as the afterpiece. The cast of the tragedy is only important in showing the re-arrangement of the parts since its last production. Mr. Douglass had succeeded Mr. Harman as *Richard*, but Hallam now succeeded Douglass, the two latter exchanging parts. Instead of Mrs. Morris, Miss Cheer was the *Lady Anne*. The afterpiece was a translation from the French, executed by Mrs. Cibber for her

### RICHARD III.

| | |
|---|---|
| Richard | Mr. Hallam |
| Richmond | Mr. Douglass |
| King Henry | Mr. Morris |
| Prince Edward | Mr. Godwin |
| Duke of York | Miss Dowthwaite |
| Buckingham | Mr. Wall |
| Stanley | Mr. Allyn |
| Tressel | Mr. Douglass |
| Catesby | Mr. Tomlinson |
| Ratcliff | Mr. Woolls |
| Lady Anne | Miss Cheer |
| Duchess of York | Mrs. Harman |
| Queen Elizabeth | Mrs. Douglass |

benefit at Covent Garden, in 1752. The character of *Cynthia* was little more than a transcript from Shakspere's *Miranda*. Mr. Hallam was evidently determined to shine in Shaksperean parts this season; for a week after his first appearance as *Richard* he played *Shylock*, and followed this part two weeks later with *Hamlet*. In the meantime,

ORACLE.

| | |
|---|---|
| Cynthia | Miss Hallam |
| Oberon | Mr. Wall |
| Fairy Queen | Mrs. Douglass |

however, he appeared both in comedy and tragedy, and in farce — as *Sir Harry Wildair* in the "Constant Couple," played originally in this country by Mr.

MERCHANT OF VENICE.

| | |
|---|---|
| Shylock | Mr. Hallam |
| Bassanio | Mr. Douglass |
| Antonio | Mr. Tomlinson |
| Gratiano | Mr. Allyn |
| Launcelot | Mr. Morris |
| Lorenzo | Mr. Woolls |
| Salanio | Mr. Wall |
| Salarino | Mr. Matthews |
| Jessica | Miss Wainwright |
| Nerissa | Mrs. Harman |
| Portia | Miss Cheer |

CONSTANT COUPLE.

| | |
|---|---|
| Sir Harry Wildair | Mr. Hallam |
| Colonel Standard | Mr. Douglass |
| Beau Clincher | Mr. Allyn |
| Young Clincher | Mr. Wall |
| Alderman Smuggler | Mr. Morris |
| Vizard | Mr. Tomlinson |
| Dickey | Mr. Woolls |
| Angelica | Miss Cheer |
| Lady Darling | Mrs. Tomlinson |
| Parly | Miss Wainwright |
| Mob's Wife | Mrs. Harman |
| Lady Lurewell | Mrs. Douglass |

Singleton, when, as Master Lewis Hallam, he was only the *Dickey;* as *Varanes* in Lee's tragedy of "Theodosius," advertised for the 26th of December, a part he had played in New York four years before for Mrs. Morris' benefit, Mr. Morris then, as now, having the title-role; and as *Bajazet* in Rowe's "Tamerlane," another

THEODOSIUS.

| | |
|---|---|
| Varanes | Mr. Hallam |
| Theodosius | Mr. Morris |
| Marcian | Mr. Douglass |
| Atticus | Mr. Tomlinson |
| Leontine | Mr. Allyn |
| Aranthes | Mr. Wall |
| Lucius | Mr. Woolls |
| Pulcheria | Mrs. Harman |
| Marina | Miss Hallam |
| Flavilla | Miss Wainwright |
| Julia | Miss Dowthwaite |
| Delia | Mrs. Tomlinson |
| Athenais | Miss Cheer |

TAMERLANE.

| | |
|---|---|
| Monesses | A Gentleman |
| Bajazet | Mr. Hallam |
| Tamerlane | Mr. Douglass |
| Axalla | Mr. Wall |
| Dervise | Mr. Morris |
| Omar | Mr. Tomlinson |
| Prince | Mr. Allyn |
| Zama | Mr. Platt |
| Mirvan | Mr. Woolls |
| Haly | Mr. Godwin |
| Selima | Miss Cheer |
| Arpasia | Mrs. Douglass |

part which he had previously made his own. As a rule Mr. Hallam kept aloof from the afterpieces as not comporting with his position in the company. The afterpiece to Farquhar's comedy on this night, December 19th, was the popular farce of the "Devil to Pay," in which

DEVIL TO PAY.

Sir John Loverule . Mr. Woolls
Jobson . . . . Mr. Tomlinson
Butler . . . . . . Mr. Morris
Coachman . . . . Mr. Allyn
Footman . . . . . Mr. Wall
Doctor . . . . . Mr. Douglass
Lady Loverule . Mrs. Harman
Lucy . . . . Mrs. Tomlinson
Lettice . . . Miss Dowthwaite
Nell . . . . . . Mrs. Morris

Mrs. Morris was compensated with the part of *Nell,* for having been left out of the comedy, but Mr. Hallam contented him-

LETHE.

Drunken Man . Mr. Hallam
Æsop . . . . Mr. Douglass
Frenchman . . . Mr. Allyn
Old Man . . . Mr. Morris
Mercury . . . Mr. Woolls
Fine Gentleman . Mr. Wall
Charon . . Mr. Tomlinson
Mrs. Tattoo . Mrs. Harman

self with his role in the comedy. Oddly enough, however, he played the *Drunken Man* in "Lethe," after appearing as *Varanes* in "Theodosius." It was probably his desire to show his versatility that

HAMLET.

Hamlet . . . Mr. Hallam
King . . . . Mr. Douglass
Horatio . . . A Gentleman
Laertes . . . . . Mr. Wall
Polonius . . . Mr. Morris
Ghost . . . Mr. Tomlinson
Osric . . . . Mr. Godwin
Player King . . Mr. Allyn
Bernardo . . . . Mr. Platt
Rosencranz . . Mr. Woolls
Player Queen . Mrs. Harman
Queen . . . Mrs. Douglass
Ophelia . . . . Miss Cheer

induced him to play such diverse parts on the same evening. But in "Hamlet" he was only *Hamlet.* He was twenty-six, but he had played the

MOCK DOCTOR.

Mock Doctor . . Mr. Allyn
Sir Jasper . . . Mr. Morris
Leander . . . Mr. Woolls
Squire Robert . . Mr. Wall
James . . . . . Mr. Platt
Harry . . . . Mr. Godwin
Helebore . . Mr. Tomlinson
Charlotte . . . Mrs. Wall
Dorcas . . . . Mrs. Morris

part five years before at the Chapel Street Theatre in New York, when he was only twenty-one, with Mrs. Morris as *Ophelia,* instead of Miss Cheer, and Mrs. Hallam, his wife, as the *Player Queen,* instead of Mrs. Harman. The tragedy was followed by the farce of the "Mock Doctor," but while the *Dorcas* was the same as before, the *King* in the play now refrained from appearing as *Gregory* in the farce.

After "Hamlet" the next full piece in the list was Murphy's "Orphan of China," which was then produced for the first time in America. It was characteristic of the theatrical taste of the time that Arthur Murphy's only tragedy, which was far inferior in merit to his comedies, should precede them on the American stage. Its production was due, perhaps, to Mrs. Douglass' desire to appear in a role in which Mrs. Yates had found her first opportunity to display her tragic powers. A week later Farquhar's masterpiece, the "Beaux' Stratagem," was again reproduced, and with it Murphy's farce, the "Upholsterer." This farce, first acted at Mr. Mossop's benefit at Drury Lane, was founded on Nos. 155, 160 and 178 of *The Tattler*. No cast of its first production in this country has been found. Farquhar's comedy had now been familiar to play-goers for the long period of sixty years.

### ORPHAN OF CHINA.

| | |
|---|---|
| Zamti | Mr. Douglass |
| Zapheniri | Mr. Hallam |
| Timurkan | Mr. Allyn |
| Hamet | Mr. Wall |
| Mirvan | Mr. Morris |
| Octar | Mr. Tomlinson |
| Orasming | Mr. Greville |
| Zimventi | Mr. Woolls |
| Messenger | Mr. Godwin |
| Mandare | Mrs. Douglass |

### BEAUX' STRATAGEM.

| | |
|---|---|
| Archer | Mr. Hallam |
| Aimwell | Mr. Douglass |
| Sullen | Mr. Wall |
| Foigard | Mr. Allyn |
| Freeman | Mr. Greville |
| Scrub | Mr. Morris |
| Gibbet | Mr. Woolls |
| Boniface | Mr. Tomlinson |
| Honslow | Mr. Godwin |
| Bagshot | Mr. Platt |
| Dorinda | Miss Hallam |
| Lady Bountiful | Mrs. Harman |
| Cherry | Miss Wainwright |
| Gipsy | Mrs. Wall |
| Mrs. Sullen | Miss Cheer |

When it was originally produced at the Haymarket in 1707 the dramatist attributed its success to the acting of Mr. Wilks. The fact that it held the stage for more than a century after Farquhar's death and continued to be frequently acted both in England and America is a proof how little it owed to any actor.

When Mr. Congreve's "Mourning Bride" was announced for the 26th of January, the advertisement was accompanied by a curious note of explanation. It is to be regretted that there was no capable dramatic critic in Philadelphia at that time to put on record his opinion of the manner in which Mr. Congreve's tragedy was cropped on that occasion. This was the great dramatist's only tragedy, but while it was inferior to his comedies it was even more popular.

### AN EXPLANATION.

*** Mr. Congreve's comedies are allowed to abound with genuine wit and true humor; but in compliance with the licentious taste of the time in which they were written the author has in some places given the rein to his wanton muse and deviated from those rules a more refined age and chaste stage require: The reviser of this play has taken the freedom to crop such luxuriances and expunge every passage that might be offensive either to decency or good manners.

*Zara* was one of Mrs. Siddons' great parts. As the afterpiece to Congreve's tragedy Townley's farce, "High Life Below Stairs," was presented. The author of this farce was a clergyman. It was at this time comparatively new, having been originally produced in 1759. It was a very diverting picture of life in the servants' hall at the

### MOURNING BRIDE.

| | |
|---|---|
| Osmyn | Mr. Hallam |
| King | Mr. Douglass |
| Gonzales | Mr. Morris |
| Garcia | Mr. Wall |
| Hali | Mr. Tomlinson |
| Selim | Mr. Godwin |
| Alonzo | Mr. Greville |
| Perez | Mr. Allyn |
| Mutes | { Mr. Woolls / Mr. Platt |
| Zara | Mrs. Douglass |
| Almeria | Miss Cheer |
| Attendants to Zara | { Mrs. Tomlinson / Mrs. Wall |
| Attendants to Almeria | { Miss Wainwright / Miss Hallam |

### HIGH LIFE BELOW STAIRS.

| | |
|---|---|
| Lovel | Mr. Hallam |
| Freeman | Mr. Douglass |
| Lord Duke | Mr. Wall |
| Sir Harry | Mr. Allyn |
| Philip | Mr. Morris |
| Coachman | Mr. Woolls |
| Tom | Mr. Tomlinson |
| Kingston | Mr. Matthews |
| Cloe | Mr. Platt |
| Lady Charlotte | Miss Wainwright |
| Lady Bab | Miss Hallam |
| Cook | Mrs. Harman |
| Kitty | Miss Cheer |

period when it was written. Mr. Lovel, a wealthy commoner, pretending to go to his country-seat in Devonshire, assumes the character of a country bumpkin from Essex, and puts himself under the charge of his own butler. In this character he participates in a large supper-party given by Philip, the butler, at which his servants assume the titles of his friends. In the midst of the feast he reveals himself and dismisses all his domestics, except Tom, who has received scant courtesy from the rest. This was one of the few farces in which both Mr. Hallam and Miss Cheer condescended to appear.

The next bill on the list comprised "King Lear" and another of Murphy's farces presented for the first time, the "Citizen." As with the "Upholsterer," no cast of this farce has been preserved. In the tragedy Mrs. Douglass now yielded *Cordelia* to Miss Cheer, and Mr. Hallam appeared for the first time in the mighty title-role, in succession to Mr. Harman. Hallam retained the part for many years, but finally

### KING LEAR.

| | |
|---|---|
| Lear | . . . . . . . . . . Mr. Hallam |
| Edgar | . . . . . . . . . . Mr. Douglass |
| Edmund | . . . . . . . . . . . Mr. Wall |
| Gloster | . . . . . . . . . . . Mr. Morris |
| Albany | . . . . . . . . . . . Mr. Allyn |
| Cornwall | . . . . . . . . . Mr. Greville |
| Kent | . . . . . . . . . . Mr. Tomlinson |
| Usher | . . . . . . . . . . . Mr. Godwin |
| Burgundy | . . . . . . . . . . Mrs. Wall |
| Goneril | . . . . . . . . Miss Wainwright |
| Regan | . . . . . . . . . . . Mrs. Harman |
| Arante | . . . . . . . . . . Mrs. Tomlinson |
| Cordelia | . . . . . . . . . . Miss Cheer |

was compelled to concede it to younger and more powerful actors.

A week later (February 2d) came Addison's "Cato" and Dr. Smollett's farce, the "Reprisal." In the tragedy Miss Cheer succeeded Mrs. Douglass as *Marcia*, but Messrs. Douglass and Hallam retained the roles they had previously

### CATO.

| | |
|---|---|
| Cato | . . . . Mr. Douglass |
| Sempronius | . . Mr. Hallam |
| Portius | . . . A Gentleman |
| (Being his first appearance.) | |
| Juba | . . . . . . Mr. Wall |
| Syphax | . . . . Mr. Allyn |
| Marcus | . . . . Mr. Godwin |
| Lucius | . . . Mr. Tomlinson |
| Decius | . . . . Mr. Woolls |
| Lucia | . . . . Mrs. Harman |
| Marcia | . . . . Miss Cheer |

### REPRISAL.

| | |
|---|---|
| M. Champignon | . . Mr. Allyn |
| Lieut. O'Claber | . . Mr. Morris |
| Ens'n McClaymore. | Mr. Douglass |
| Block | . . . . . . Mr. Hallam |
| Lieut. Lyon | . . Mr. Broadbelt |
| Heartly | . . . . . Mr. Greville |
| Brush | . . . . . . Mr. Wall |
| Hallyard | . . . . Mr. Woolls |
| Miss Harriet | . . Miss Hallam |

played. In the farce Allyn played the Frenchman, Morris the Irishman, Douglass the Scotchman and Hallam the Englishman.

Upon the production of "Romeo and Juliet" Mrs. Douglass for the first time relinquished Shakspere's youthful heroine, which was in keeping with her general surrender of her parts to Miss Cheer this season. In the "Miser," the production of which preceded that of "Romeo and Juliet," she was announced for *Mrs. Wisely*, but gave up the part, and in the "Conscious Lovers," which followed, she played *Isabella*, instead of her previous role of *Indiana*. As Miss Wainwright was excluded from acceptable roles in the tragedies and comedies, Cibber's ballad farce was given as the afterpiece to the "Conscious Lovers," to afford her an opportunity in a singing part. The only new piece among these productions was the "Miser." There are a number of comedies called by this name, beginning with one by Shadwell, 1672. They were all based on the *"Avare"* of Moliere. This was Fielding's version, of which Mr. Murphy said it had the value of a copy from a great painter by an eminent hand.

ROMEO AND JULIET.

| | |
|---|---|
| Romeo | Mr. Hallam |
| Mercutio | Mr. Douglass |
| Capulet | Mr. Morris |
| Friar Lawrence | Mr. Allyn |
| Montagu | Mr. Tomlinson |
| Escalus | Mr. Broadbelt |
| Tybalt | Mr. Wall |
| Paris | Mr. Woolls |
| Benvolio | Mr. Godwin |
| Balthazar | Mr. Greville |
| Friar John | Mr. Platt |
| Lady Capulet | Mrs. Douglass |
| Nurse | Mrs. Harman |
| Juliet | Miss Cheer |

MISER.

| | |
|---|---|
| Lovegold | Mr. Allyn |
| Frederick | Mr. Douglass |
| Clerimont | Mr. Wall |
| James | Mr. Tomlinson |
| Decoy | Mr. Morris |
| Sattin | Mr. Greville |
| Sparkle | Mr. Woolls |
| Furnish | Mr. Platt |
| Bubbleby | Mr. Godwin |
| Ramillie | Mr. Hallam |
| Harriet | Miss Hallam |
| Mrs. Wisely | Mrs. Tomlinson |
| Lappet | Mrs. Harman |
| Wheedle | Mrs. Wall |
| Mariana | Miss Cheer |

CONSCIOUS LOVERS.

| | |
|---|---|
| Young Bevil | Mr. Hallam |
| Sealand | Mr. Douglass |
| Myrtle | Mr. Wall |
| Sir John Bevil | Mr. Broadbelt |
| Cymberton | Mr. Allyn |
| Tom | Mr. Morris |
| Humphrey | Mr. Tomlinson |
| Daniel | Mr. Godwin |
| Isabella | Mrs. Douglass |
| Phillis | Mrs. Harman |
| Mrs. Seal'nd | Miss Wainwright |
| Lucinda | Miss Hallam |
| Indiana | Miss Cheer |

DAMON AND PHILLIDA.

| | |
|---|---|
| Damon | Mr. Woolls |
| Mopsus | Mr. Hallam |
| Cimon | Mr. Wall |
| Arcas | Mr. Allyn |
| Corydon | Mr. Morris |
| Phillida | Miss Wainwright |

The next bill (February 20th) comprised Farquhar's " Inconstant," a comedy requiring a strong cast, and Bickerstaff's "Thomas and Sally," then given for the first time. In the comedy Mr. Hallam played one of those handsome, dashing young rakes that could not fail to satisfy any actor, but his *Oriana*, being no longer young, was some excuse for his inconstancy. Although the plot turns upon *Oriana's* love for *Young Mirabel*, and she saves him from the *Bravos* in the house of *Lamorce*,

### INCONSTANT.

| | |
|---|---|
| Young Mirabel | Mr. Hallam |
| Old Mirabel | Mr. Morris |
| Capt. Duretete | Mr. Douglass |
| Dugard | Mr. Wall |
| Petit | Mr. Tomlinson |
| First Bravo | Mr. Allyn |
| Second Bravo | Mr. Broadbelt |
| Third Bravo | Mr. Woolls |
| Fourth Bravo | Mr. Greville |
| Oriana | Mrs. Harman |
| Lamorce | Miss Wainwright |
| Bizarre | Miss Cheer |

Miss Cheer's role of *Bizarre* has always been the favorite one with leading actresses, and it was in this part that Mrs. Yates took her farewell of the stage in 1799. The farce was a musical entertainment, for which the celebrated Dr. Arne, the instructor of Mr. Woolls and Miss Wainwright, composed the music.

### THOMAS AND SALLY.

| | |
|---|---|
| Dorcas | Miss Cheer |
| Sally | Miss Wainwright |
| Squire | Mr. Woolls |
| Sailor | Mr. Wall |

This season was remarkable for the number of new comedies produced as afterpieces, Foote's "Mayor of Garratt," presented with the tragedy of "George Barnwell," being among them. The tragedy, as produced this season, is only interesting to the student of dramatic history because of the changes in the cast, but the comedy was a novelty, and it was the first of Foote's works seen on

### GEORGE BARNWELL.

| | |
|---|---|
| George Barnwell | Mr. Hallam |
| Thorowgood | Mr. Douglass |
| Truman | Mr. Morris |
| Uncle | Mr. Allyn |
| Blunt | Mr. Tomlinson |
| Maria | Miss Hallam |
| Lucy | Mrs. Harman |
| Millwood | Miss Cheer |

the American boards.    Foote played *Major Sturgeon* when the piece was originally produced at the Haymarket in 1763, but *Jerry Sneak,* frequently played in this country by the elder Booth, became in the hands of Russell — Jerry Sneak Russell—the part of the piece as a type of the henpecked husband. The part of *Matthew Mug* was intended as a caricature of the Duke of Newcastle.  The origin of the *Sneaks* and *Bruins,* it has been claimed, is found in *Bisket* and *Fribble,* and their respective wives in the "Epsom Wells" of Shadwell, which, by the way, Shadwell's contemporaries said was not his.

MAYOR OF GARRATT.

| | |
|---|---|
| Major Sturgeon . . . . . . | { Mr. Hallam |
| Matthew Mug . . . . . . | |
| Jerry Sneak . . . . . . . . | { Mr. Wall |
| Lint . . . . . . . . . . . . | |
| Sir Jacob Jollop . . . . . . | Mr. Tomlinson |
| Bruin . . . . . . . . . . | Mr. Douglass |
| Crispin Heel-tap . . . . . . . | Mr. Morris |
| Roger . . . . . . . . . . . | Mr. Godwin |
| Snuffle . . . . . . . . . . . . | Mr. Platt |
| First Mob . . . . . . . . . | Mr. Woolls |
| Second Mob . . . . . . . | Mr. Matthews |
| Third Mob . . . . . . . . | Mr. Broadbelt |
| Fourth Mob . . . . . . . . . | Mr. Allyn |
| Mrs. Bruin . . . . . . . . | Mrs. Harman |
| Mrs. Sneak . . . . . . . . | Miss Cheer |

The second of Congreve's pieces produced at the Southwark Theatre was "Love for Love." This comedy long continued to hold the stage, *Ben,* the sailor, being a favorite part with Jack Bannister and *Miss Prue* with Mrs. Jordan.   It was acted in this country almost as often as in England, being originally produced by Murray and Kean's Company. Afterward the elder Hallam played *Ben* and Rigby *Valentine.* The cast on this occasion showed

LOVE FOR LOVE.

| | |
|---|---|
| Valentine . . . . . . . . . | Mr. Douglass |
| Ben . . . . . . . . . . . | Mr. Hallam |
| Sir Sampson Legend . . . . | Mr. Tomlinson |
| Foresight . . . . . . . . . | Mr. Morris |
| Scandal . . . . . . . . . . | Mr. Allyn |
| Tattle . . . . . . . . . . . | Mr. Wall |
| Jeremy . . . . . . . . . | Mr. Godwin |
| Buckram . . . . . . . . . | Mr. Greville |
| Angelica . . . . . . . . . | Miss Hallam |
| Mrs. Frail . . . . . . . | Mrs. Douglass |
| Mrs. Foresight . . . . . . . | Mrs. Wall |
| Nurse . . . . . . . . . | Mrs. Harman |
| Miss Prue . . . . . . . . . | Miss Cheer |

Mr. Hallam in his father's part, but is especially noteworthy because of Mrs. Douglass' acceptance of *Mrs. Frail,* the part in which Mrs. Adcock made her American *debut.* The next piece on the list was Vanbrugh and Cibber's " Provoked Husband," with the pantomime of the " Harlequin Collector." In the tragedy Miss Cheer was the *Lady Townly* for the first time. It will be observed that she appeared also in the pantomime. Dry-

PROVOKED HUSBAND.

Lord Townly . . . Mr. Hallam
Manly . . . . . Mr. Douglass
SirFrancisWronghead Mr.Morris
Squire Richard . . . Mr. Allyn
Count Basset . . . . Mr. Wall
John Moody . . Mr. Tomlinson
Lady Grace . . Mrs. Douglass
Lady Wronghead . Mrs. Harman
Miss Jenny . . . Miss Hallam
Mrs. Motherly . Miss Wainwright
Myrtilla . . . . . . Mrs. Wall
Trusty . . . . . Mrs. Morris
Lady Townly . . . Miss Cheer

HARLEQUIN COLLECTOR.

Harlequin . . Mr. Hallam
Clown . . . . Mr. Morris
Miller . . . . . Mr. Allyn
Magician . . . Mr. Woolls
Doctor . . . Mr. Douglass
Porter . . . Mr. Tomlinson
Baboon . . . . . Mr. Wall
Skeleton . . Mr. Matthews
Miller's Men } Mr. Broadbelt
Mr. Appleby
Columbine . . . Miss Cheer

den's version of the love episode of Antony and Cleopatra, " All for Love," had its first representation in America this season, with Mr. Hallam as the Roman conqueror, who lost all for love of the beautiful Egyptian, and Miss Cheer in the part in which Mrs. Oldfield and Peg Woffington were unrivaled. There were two *debuts* in this piece—those of Master Hallam and Miss Tomlinson as Antony's children. It will be readily supposed that Miss Tom-

ALL FOR LOVE.

Marc Antony . . . . . . . Mr. Hallam
Ventidius . . . . . . . . Mr. Douglass
Dolabella . . . . . . . . . . Mr. Wall
Alexas . . . . . . . . . . . Mr. Morris
Serapion . . . . . . . . Mr. Tomlinson
Myris . . . . . . . . . . Mr. Woolls
Octavia . . . . . . . . Mrs. Douglass
Charmion . . . . . . . Miss Wainwright
Iras . . . . . . . . . . . Mrs. Wall
Cleopatra . . . . . . . . . . Miss Cheer
Antonius . . . . . . . . Master Hallam
(His first appearance on any stage.)
Agrippina . . . . . . . . Miss Tomlinson
(Her first appearance on any stage.)

linson was the daughter of Mr. and Mrs. Tomlinson, of the company, but this Master Hallam has never been mentioned by any of the American historians. The inference is that he was the son of Lewis Hallam and of the Mrs. Hallam who was with the company in 1761-2.

One of the most interesting bills of the season was the production, for the first time in this country, of Cibber's "Love Makes a Man" and Colman's farce, the "Deuce is in Him." The comedy was one of Cibber's earlier productions, its first performance at Drury Lane being as early as 1701. The sprightliness of *Clodio* and the manly tenderness and openness of *Carlos* were, no doubt, temptations to Hallam and Douglass, and it may be that its first production in this country was

LOVE MAKES A MAN.

Clodio . . . . . . . . . . . Mr. Hallam
Carlos . . . . . . . . . . Mr. Douglass
Don Lewis . . . . . . . . Mr. Morris
Antonio . . . . . . . . . . Mr. Allyn
Charius . . . . . . . . . Mr. Tomlinson
Don Duart . . . . . . . . . Mr. Wall
Governor . . . . . . . . Mr. Greville
Monsieur . . . . . . . . Mr. Godwin
Priest . . . . . . . . . . Mr. Woolls
Page . . . . . . . . Miss Dowthwaite
Lawyer . . . . . . . . . . Mr. Platt
Louisa . . . . . . . . Mrs. Douglass
Elvira . . . . . . . . Miss Wainwright
Honoria . . . . . . . . . . Mrs. Wall
Angelina . . . . . . . . . Miss Cheer

so long delayed because of the elder Lewis Hallam's misfortune in the part of *Don Lewis* at Covent Garden. The farce was new, having been first acted at Covent Garden, in 1762, where it met with a success almost as great as that of the "Beggars' Opera" in its first season. But even more interesting was the first production, in America, this season of "Love in a Village." According to the *Pennsylvania Gazette* Bickerstaff's comic opera was "done here beyond expectation," and the critic says "Miss Wainwright is a very good singer and her action exceeds the famous Miss Brent;

DEUCE IS IN HIM.

Colonel Tamper . . . . . . . Mr. Hallam
Major Belfort . . . . . . . Mr. Douglass
Prattle . . . . . . . . . . . . Mr. Wall
Mad. Florival . . . . . . . Mrs. Harman
Bell . . . . . . . . . . Miss Wainwright
Emily . . . . . . . . . . Miss Hallam

LOVE IN A VILLAGE.

Justice Woodcock . . . . . Mr. Douglass
Hodge . . . . . . . . . . . Mr. Hallam
Hawthorn . . . . . . . . Mr. Woolls
Sir William Meadows . . . . . Mr. Morris
Young Meadows . . . . . . . Mr. Wall
Eustace . . . . . . . . . . . Mr. Allyn
Rosetta . . . . . . . Miss Wainwright
Lucinda . . . . . . . . . . Miss Hallam
Margery . . . . . . . . . Mrs. Harman
Mrs. Deborah . . . . . . Mrs. Douglass

Mr. Hallam exceeds everything in the character of *Hodge*, and Mr. Woolls almost equals Beard in *Hawthorn*." The piece was still new, even in London, having been originally presented at Drury Lane in 1763. It is based upon the episode of "Lindor," in Marmontel's "Tales," but the character of *Madame Florival* was taken from a story originally published in the *British Magazine*.

A number of pieces which the American Company had made familiar to the play-going public were reproduced in quick succession, among them the "Earl of Essex," "Macbeth," the "Gamester," and "A Bold Stroke for a Wife." In all these the casts were almost completely remodeled, Miss Cheer obtaining the leading female roles. With the "Gamester" a new pantomime, "The Witches," was given for the first time. A new pantomime was certainly needed, the well-worn "Harlequin Collector" having become threadbare. This was the piece invented by Mr. Love, and acted at Drury Lane in 1762. It seems identical with "Harlequin Restored."

MACBETH.

| | |
|---|---|
| Macbeth | Mr. Hallam |
| Macduff | Mr. Douglass |
| Duncan | Mr. Allyn |
| Banquo | Mr. Morris |
| Lenox | Mr. Wall |
| Seyton | Mr. Tomlinson |
| Witches | Mrs. Harman, Miss Wainwright, Mrs. Tomlinson |
| Malcolm | Mr. Godwin |
| Donaldbain | Mr. Platt |
| Fleance | Miss Dowthwaite |
| Officer | Mr. Greville |
| Hecate | Mrs. Harman |
| Lady Macduff | Mrs. Douglass |
| Lady Macbeth | Miss Cheer |

WITCHES.

| | |
|---|---|
| Harlequin | Mr. Hallam |
| Pantaloon | Mr. Morris |
| Petit Maitre | Mr. Allyn |
| Statuary | Mr. Douglass |
| Constable | Mr. Broadbelt |
| Cook | Mrs. Harman |
| Mercury | Mr. Woolls |
| Pierot | Mr. Tomlinson |
| Valet | Mr. Wall |
| Necromancer | Mr. Woolls |
| Columbine | Miss Cheer |

EARL OF ESSEX.

| | |
|---|---|
| Essex | Mr. Hallam |
| Southampton | Mr. Douglass |
| Burleigh | Mr. Morris |
| Sir Walter Raleigh | Mr. Tomlinson |
| Lieutenant of the Tower | Mr. Woolls |
| Queen Elizabeth | Mrs. Douglass |
| Countess of Nottingham | Miss Hallam |
| Countess of Rutland | Miss Cheer |

GAMESTER.

| | |
|---|---|
| Beverly | Mr. Hallam |
| Stukely | Mr. Douglass |
| Lewson | Mr. Wall |
| Jarvis | Mr. Morris |
| Dawson | Mr. Allyn |
| Bates | Mr. Tomlinson |
| Charlotte | Mrs. Harman |
| Lucy | Miss Wainwright |
| Mrs. Beverly | Miss Cheer |

When the benefits began a number of new pieces were produced. Miss Cheer chose for her night Colman's "Jealous Wife," making her first appearance as *Mrs. Oakley*. The comedy had been originally produced at Drury Lane, in 1761, with prodigious success, Mr. Garrick playing *Oakley*. The groundwork of the play was taken from Fielding's "Tom Jones," the episode of Sophia taking refuge at Lady Bellaston's house serving as an underplot for the exhibition of the henpecked husband and his domineering and termagant rather than jealous wife.

#### JEALOUS WIFE.

| | |
|---|---|
| Jealous Wife | Miss Cheer |
| Oakley | Mr. Hallam |
| Major Oakley | Mr. Douglass |
| Charles | Mr. Wall |
| Russet | Mr. Morris |
| Sir Harry Beagle | Mr. Allyn |
| Lord Trinket | Mr. Hallam |
| Captain O'Cutter | Mr. Allyn |
| Tom | Mr. Woolls |
| John | Mr. Tomlinson |
| William | Mr. Matthews |
| Harriet | Miss Hallam |
| Toilet | Mrs. Harman |
| Betty | Miss Wainwright |
| Lady Freelove | Mrs. Douglass |

Mr. Douglass for his benefit, besides Howard's familiar play, the "Committee," and a recitation by Mr. Hallam of "Bucks, have at ye all," generally called in the bills of the time a "Picture of a Playhouse," presented for the first time in America an English farce in

#### COMMITTEE.

| | |
|---|---|
| Colonel Careless | Mr. Douglass |
| Colonel Blunt | Mr. Hallam |
| Teague | Mr. Allyn |
| Abel | Mr. Woolls |
| Bailiff | Mr. Platt |
| Soldier | Mr. Matthews |
| Mrs. Day | Mrs. Douglass |
| Arabella | Miss Hallam |
| Mrs. Chat | Mrs. Tomlinson |
| Ruth | Miss Cheer |

#### DRUMMER.

| | |
|---|---|
| Tinsel | Mr. Hallam |
| Sir George Truman | Mr. Douglass |
| Vellum | Mr. Allyn |
| Gardener | Mr. Morris |
| Butler | Mr. Wall |
| Coachman | Mr. Greville |
| Abagail | Mrs. Harman |
| Lady Truman | Miss Cheer |

two acts, called the "Spirit of Contradiction." This was a piece of inferior merit which met with little success at Covent Garden, where it was originally produced, and with no favor here, *Mrs. Partlett*, for which Mrs. Harman was well adapted, being the only good part in the farce. That excellent actress for her own benefit contented herself with Addison's " Drummer," its first production this season, and a repetition of " Catherine and Petruchio," and Mr. Morris followed with the "Beaux' Stratagem"

### SPIRIT OF CONTRADICTION.

| | |
|---|---|
| Randal | Mr. Hallam |
| Steer | Mr. Douglass |
| Lovewell | Mr. Wall |
| Mr. Partlett | Mr. Morris |
| Ruin | Mr. Allyn |
| Miss Harriet | Miss Wainwright |
| Betty | Mrs. Morris |
| Mrs. Partlett | Mrs. Harman |

and " Don Quixote in England " as the afterpiece. Although Fielding's comedy had long been a favorite in London, where it was

### DON QUIXOTE IN ENGLAND.

| | |
|---|---|
| Don Quixote | Mr. Hallam |
| Sancho Panca | Mr. Morris |
| Grizzel | Mr. Douglass |
| Squire Badger | Mr. Wall |
| Sir Thomas | Mr. Tomlinson |
| Fairlove | Mr. Greville |
| John | Mr. Allyn |
| Cook | Mr. Woolls |
| Jezebel | Mrs. Morris |
| Dorothea | Miss Wainwright |

acted at the little theatre in the Haymarket as early as 1733, this was its first production in America. Macklin, it will be remembered, was the *Squire Badger* the night he killed Thomas Hallam at Drury Lane.

Mr. Hallam in his own behalf, eager, no doubt, to appear as *Posthumus*, presented Shakspere's " Cymbeline " for the first time in this country. As with " Catherine and Petruchio," it was the Garrick version produced at Drury Lane in 1761 that was first seen on the American stage. Although Miss Cheer was the original *Imogen* in this country, the part was that in which Miss Hallam was destined to win her chief renown.

### CYMBELINE.

| | |
|---|---|
| Posthumus | Mr. Hallam |
| Iachimo | Mr. Douglass |
| Cymbeline | Mr. Allyn |
| Cloten | Mr. Wall |
| Belarius | Mr. Morris |
| Caius Lucius | Mr. Tomlinson |
| Guiderius | Mr. Greville |
| Arviragus | Mr. Woolls |
| Doctor | Mr. Platt |
| Philario | Mr. Morris |
| Pissanio | Mrs. Harman |
| Queen | Mrs. Douglass |
| Helen | Mrs. Tomlinson |
| Imogen | Miss Cheer |

Miss Wainwright, not content with a comedy, the "Country Lasses," new to American theatre-goers, gave also a new farce, the "Chaplet." The comedy, which had been originally acted as early as 1715, comprised two distinct plots, one borrowed from Fletcher's "Custom of the Country," and the other from Mrs. Behn's "City Heiress," who, in her turn, had appropriated Middleton's "Mad World, my Masters." In this piece the character of *Farmer Freehold,* played by Mr. Morris, was the most admirable. The after-piece was a musical entertainment with some excellent music by Boyce. It was first given at Drury Lane, in 1749. The "Chaplet" belonged to a class of performance now unfortunately banished from the stage altogether, but presenting the combination of

COUNTRY LASSES.

| | |
|---|---|
| Modely | Mr. Hallam |
| Heartwell | Mr. Douglass |
| Sir John English | Mr. Allyn |
| Freehold | Mr. Morris |
| Lurcher | Mr. Wall |
| Vulture | Mr. Tomlinson |
| Sneak | Mr. Woolls |
| Longbottom | Mr. Greville |
| Carbuncle | Mr. Broadbelt |
| Shacklefigure | Mr. Platt |
| Countryman | Mr. Matthews |
| Flora | Miss Wainwright |
| Aura | Miss Cheer |

CHAPLET.

| | |
|---|---|
| Damon | Mr. Woolls |
| Palemon | Mr. Wall |
| Pastora | Mrs. Harman |
| Laura | Miss Wainwright |

pleasing poetry and exquisite music, in itself an argument for the restoration of the afterpiece. This production was of course due to the *Laura.* In the advertisement of her benefit Miss Wainwright announced that, having lost a number of tickets, "none but the stamped ones will be received." A like misfortune befell Mr. Wall, who advertised the loss of his chest, which contained almost all of his apparel and nearly a thousand tickets. In consequence he had a new set printed, on which were engraved the emblems of masonry, to distinguish them from the stolen ones.

Mr. Tomlinson's choice of Thomson's "Coriolanus" was, it must be confessed, an odd selection. and Mr. Allyn's presentation of Moses Mendez' "Double Disappointment" could only have been intended to afford him an opportunity to play the *Frenchman*, a class of parts that he affected. Mrs. Douglass made a happier choice in adding Whitehead's "Roman Father" to the repertoire

ROMAN FATHER.

| | |
|---|---|
| Roman Father | . . . . . . . Mr. Hallam |
| Publius Horatius | . . . . . . Mr. Douglass |
| Tullus Hostilius | . . . . . . . Mr. Allyn |
| Valerius | . . . . . . . . . . . Mr. Wall |
| First Citizen | . . . . . . . . . Mr. Morris |
| Second Citizen | . . . . . . . Mr. Greville |
| Third Citizen | . . . . . . . . Mr. Woolls |
| Fourth Citizen | . . . . . . . . Mr. Platt |
| Valeria | . . . . . . . . . Mrs. Douglass |
| Horatia | . . . . . . . . . Miss Cheer |

of the American Company. In no tragedy, except Shakspere's, have so many actors been seen to advantage as in the title-role of this great play. On this occasion Mr. and Mrs. Parker, from the theatre in Jamaica, appeared as *Hob* and *Flora* in the afterpiece. Finally, as the last new piece of the season, Miss Hallam selected the farce "Neck or Nothing," as the afterpiece for her night, and notwithstanding the performance for her benefit was postponed from the 12th to the 29th of June, because of the weather, she retained it, while substituting "Cymbeline" for the

NECK OR NOTHING.

———

| | |
|---|---|
| Slip | . . . . . . . . . . . Mr. Hallam |
| Martin | . . . . . . . . . . Mr. Morris |
| Belford | . . . . . . . . . . Mr. Wall |
| Sir William | . . . . . . . . Mr. Allyn |
| Mr. Stockwell | . . . . . Mr. Tomlinson |
| Miss Nancy | . . . . . . . Miss Hallam |
| Jenny | . . . . . . . . Miss Wainwright |
| Mrs. Stockwell | . . . . . Mrs. Douglass |

"School for Lovers." This farce, if it was Garrick's, had not met with the usual success of his pieces at Drury Lane, where it was laid aside after being acted only six or eight times.

The heat in Philadelphia in the second week of June, 1767, must have been intense. Notwithstanding it was said in the announcement of Miss Hallam's benefit, "there are some alterations made in

the house in order to render it cool," the weather caused its postponement, and some of the company determined not to take benefits
at all.  Miss Hallam's was consequently advertised as the last of the
season, but later on the heat moderated, and Mr. Broadbelt and Mrs.
Wall reconsidered their .determination.  It thus happened that the
Fourth of July had passed before the theatre closed for the summer.

The incidents of the first season at the Southwark Theatre, of
which the prints of the time give a hint, were not of a startling character.  As to the patronage, it was not great, as we learn from the
critic of the *Pennsylvania Gazette*, already quoted, who regretted that
he could not see the house better filled.  One reason for this was that
the old spirit of opposition to the drama was still active.  On the 9th of
February, 1767, Goddard's *Pennsylvania Chronicle* contained the first
of a series of articles trying to prove the absolute unlawfulness of stage
entertainments.  These papers were signed "Philadelphus," and they
were not concluded till the 4th of May.  As a matter of fact these
articles were only reprints of the writings against the theatre of William Jay, an English clergyman.  According to Mr. Jay, as quoted
by "Philadelphus," theatrical representations are akin to image worship, and contrary to the spirit of religion.   "You go to hear a play,"
he exclaimed, "I tell you, you go to hear ribaldry and profaneness;
that you entertain your mind with extravagant thoughts, wild rants,
blasphemous speeches, wanton amours, profane jests and impure
passions."   The editor, however, was careful to explain that the on-
slaught on the worship of images was "no reflection on the Roman
Catholics of this city and Province," but it was boldly asserted that
no actor could be a Christian.  The same journal on the 16th of
February contained an article by "Eugenio," who believed he would

not stand single when he asserted that plays have an evil tendency to corrupt and debauch the mind, and he declared that even in Shakspere the sublime flights of poesy scarcely atone for the low, droll buffoonery with which his best pieces abound. These attacks drew an answer from Mr. Douglass, who wrote to the *Chronicle* in regard to " the torrent of incomprehensible abuse of late so plentifully bestowed upon the theatre." " I should look forward with terror," he said, " if I thought myself engaged in a business that could be productive of the horrid consequences imputed to it." He enclosed an essay, dated New York, March 17th, 1762, which he considered an answer to those who had attacked him " in so indecent and illiberal a manner." This essay, which was printed for the first time, was intended for New York, but had not been published because the opposition subsided. On the same day that the letter of " Eugenio " was published, the remonstrance against the new theatre, in the usual terms of denunciation, was presented to the General Assembly. As every other means of suppressing the play-actors failed Goddard's *Chronicle* on the 6th of April was enriched with a satirical description of a strolling company of players, which, like nearly everything else printed in this country against the theatre at that time, was conveyed from a London journal.

# CHAPTER XVII.

## "THE DISAPPOINTMENT."

THE FIRST AMERICAN COMEDY ACCEPTED FOR PRODUCTION—A SATIRE
ON THE SEARCHERS AFTER HIDDEN TREASURE—AN ACCOUNT
OF THIS FORGOTTEN PLAY—WHY IT WAS DETERMINED NOT TO
PRODUCE IT.

THE first American comedy, or comic opera, as it was called, that was accepted by a manager and put into rehearsal for a speedy production, was a local satire intended to ridicule an idea then prevalent that Blackbeard, the pirate, had concealed much of his ill-gotten treasure on the banks of the Delaware, in the neighborhood of Cooper's Point. The popular conceit was that the pirates sometimes killed a prisoner and buried his body with the treasure, so that his " spook," or ghost, keeping its vigils over the grave might frighten away intruders. Naturally, the reported presence of a ghost at a particular spot was a sufficient incentive to dig there for hidden wealth. As one superstition always begets others the professors of the black art of the period were in great demand, both to discover the places where the treasure was concealed and to put a " magic ring " round the spot to keep the searchers harmless while digging. These superstitions sometimes led to practical joking by the young wags of the time, and it is understood that it was one of these practical jokes that supplied the story for the " comic opera " put in rehearsal by Mr.

Douglass' company in the winter and spring of 1767 and announced for production at the Southwark Theatre. The announcement was printed in Goddard's *Pennsylvania Chronicle* for the 18th of April, 1767.

It was, it must be confessed, an exceedingly modest advertisement of the intended production of the first American comedy ever prepared for the stage. It was not even said that it was American in authorship or local in theme. These important facts

ADVERTISEMENT.

BY AUTHORITY.
By the American Company,
At the New Theatre in *Southwark* on Monday next, being the 20th of April, will be presented a new COMIC OPERA, called
THE DISAPPOINTMENT;
or, the
*Force of Credulity.*
To which will be added a farce called
THE MAYOR OF GARRATT.

only appeared by implication in the notice of its withdrawal printed in the *Pennsylvania Gazette* on the following Wednesday by way of explanation. As it was not produced, although it came so near production that it was only

"The Disappointment" (that was advertised for Monday), as it contains personal reflections, is unfit for the stage.

withdrawn between Saturday and Monday, one might be tempted to believe it was published in consequence, but that such was not the case appears from the following advertisement printed in the *Pennsylvania Chronicle* simultaneously with the announcement of its intended production. This so-called comic opera is now so scarce that a copy was recently sold in New York at auction for $13. The

ADVERTISEMENT.

Just published and to be sold at
Samuel Taylor's,
Book-Binder, at the Corner of *Market* and *Water Streets*, price One Shilling and Sixpence, a new *American* COMIC OPERA of two Acts, called
THE DISAPPOINTMENT;
or, the
Force of Credulity.
By ANDREW BARTON, Esq.

piece was originally printed in New York, as appears from the title-page of the first edition, but it was reprinted in Philadelphia after the

Revolution, where its local interest caused it to be sought after for many years. The "personal reflections" that induced Mr. Douglass to withdraw it were evidently well-founded, for it is described in the preface as a "local piece," and the publication was explained as due to the following reasons:

1. The infrequency of dramatic compositions in America.

2. The torrent of solicitations from all quarters.

3. The necessity of contributing to the entertainment of the city.

4. To put a stop, if possible, to the foolish and pernicious practice of searching after supposed hidden treasure.

Evidently the name of Andrew Barton, Esq., on the title-page is an assumed one, and in the Ridgway Library copy the name of Colonel Thomas Forrest, of Germantown, is written in ink as the author. Colonel Forrest, at one time captain of a company of Revolutionary scouts dressed as Indians, and later on a colonel in the War for Independence, died in 1828, at the age of eighty-three. In his youth he was a noted wag, and it is said of him in Watson's "Annals of Philadelphia" that when he was about twenty-one

TITLE-PAGE.

The
DISAPPOINTMENT;
or, the
*Force of Credulity.*
A New
AMERICAN COMIC OPERA
of Two Acts.
By ANDREW BARTON, ESQ.
Enchanting gold! thou dost conspire to blind
Man's erring judgment, and misguide the mind;
In search of thee the wretched worldling goes,
Nor dangers fears, tho' fiends of night oppose.
NEW YORK.
Printed in the Year M, DCC, LXVII.

years of age a tailor who was measuring him for a coat happened to remark, "Ah, Thomas, if you and I could only find some of the money of the sea-robbers we might drive our coach for life." Forrest pretended to take the suggestion seriously, and through the tailor they were joined by one Ambruster, a printer, who believed he could conjure the pirate and compel him to give up the treasure. Forrest made an engagement to meet Ambruster and the tailor at a public-house in the city, where the printer was to show Forrest and several other persons, who were to share in the hidden wealth, a proof of his powers. By an arrangement with the innkeeper preparation was made to lower from the room above, by means of a pulley, the ghost of the pirate at Ambruster's invocation. The company assembled and the conjuror began to "hex," as the process of incantation was called. When Ambruster finally invoked the pirate, "*du Verfluchter, komm heraus,*" the pulley began to reel and the ghost, with staring eyes and a ghastly countenance, was among them. The whole company fled dismayed, except Forrest. The apparition only served to whet the appetite of those who had taken part in the incantation for possession of the treasure, and Forrest's joke was carried out very much in the way described in the play.

In turning a joke of this kind into a play the situations could not fail to be irresistibly comic, but the prologue seems to have been designed to relieve the piece from the imputation that finally caused its withdrawal. A much graver objection to the comedy, and one that should have prevented its acceptance in the first instance, was its coarseness and immorality, making it unfit for the stage. In the plot of the comedy the scheme was planned

### PROLOGUE.

Tho' distant far from fam'd Britannia's isle,
Where comic scenes call cynics forth to smile;
Our artless muse hath made her first essay
T' instruct and please you with a modern play.
Theatric business was and still shou'd be
To point out vice in its deformity;
Make virtue fair! shine eminently bright,
Rapture the breast and captivate the sight.
No matter which, the pulpit or the stage,
Condemn the vice and folly of the age;
These are our boast and on sure ground we stand,
Plead virtue's cause throughout this infant land;
We mount the stage and lend an helping hand.
Wits, fools, a knave and conjuror to-night,
The objects make both of your ears and sight,
A band of dupes are humm'd with idle schemes,

Quit solid sense for airy golden dreams.
Our flatt'ring muse think's she's some merit gain'd,
Pursuing truth and things, like truth, well feign'd.
The subjects suited to our present times,
No person's touch'd, altho' she lash their crimes;
Nor gall or copp'ras tincture her design,
But gay, good humor breathe in every line.
If you condemn her—she for censure stands;
But if applaud—then thund'ring clap your hands.

by four humorous gentlemen, *Hum, Parchment, Quadrant* and *Rattleirap*, the last-named being a supposed conjuror. The dupes were *Raccoon*, an old debauchee; *Washball*, an avaricious barber; *Trusthoop*, a cooper, and *McSnip*, a tailor. The other characters were *Meanwell*, a gentleman in love with *Washball's* niece; *Topinloft*, a sailor; *Spitfire, Rattletrap's* assistant; *Moll Placket*, a dissolute woman; *Mrs. Trusthoop*, and *Lucy, Washball's* niece. When the curtain rises on the first act, *Hum, Parchment* and *Quadrant* are discovered seated around a table in a tavern, where they are drinking and discussing their scheme. *Raccoon*, who, "though great coward as they say he is," will "venture to the gates of hell" for money, is expected. *Hum* announces that he has contrived matters so that *Raccoon* "shall make the discovery himself." *Quadrant* informs the others that he has drawn in both *Trusthoop* and *McSnip*. With his share of the treasures, *Quadrant* says *Trusthoop* "talks of building a chapel at his own expense and employing a score of priests to keep up a continual rotation of prayers for the repose of the souls of those poor fellows who buried it." As for *McSnip*, he "intends to knock off business, go home to England and purchase a title." *Mr. Parchment* prepared the papers which were duly enclosed in a letter to *Mr. Hum*, purporting to come from his sister in England. One of these papers, that looked old enough to have been "preserved in the Temple of Apollo or the Tower of Babel," contained a list of the treasure buried by Edward Teach, *alias* Blackbeard: "*Imprimis*, 17 golden candlesticks, chalices and crucifixes; 30,000 Portugal pieces; 20,000

Spanish pistoles, 470,000 pistareens, 73 bars of gold, a small box of diamonds, 60,000 pieces of eight and 150 pounds weight of gold dust." There was, of course, a draft of the place where the treasure lies, almost as ingenious as that introduced by Poe into his story of " The Gold Bug." This leads *Quadrant* to sing to his fellow-conspirators to the air of " I am a brisk and lively lass:"

> In all the town there's none like you,
> When you're on mischief bent, sirs;
> With pen and ink one well can write
> What you do both invent, sirs.

When *Raccoon* enters *Hum* steps out for a moment, dropping the papers. *Raccoon* picks them up, looks over them and crams them into his bosom. *Hum* returns lamenting the loss of his papers, and declaring that the drawer must have picked his pocket. The poor servant is roughly handled and searched. At the beginning of this scene *Washball, Trusthoop* and *McSnip* enter. Finally *Raccoon* gives up the papers, on condition that *Hum* lets him in for a share. *Parchment* pretends to know nothing of the papers, and declares that if they contain any scheme, plot, combination, rout, riot or unlawful assembly—in fine, anything against his most sacred Majesty, George II, etc., etc.—he'll at once to the Attorney-General and lodge an information against every man in the company and hang every mother's son of them. *Parchment* is finally convinced and then wishes he had been "in such a plot twenty years ago."

"By my saul," cries *McSnip*, "I'll away we all me dranken joorneymen and keck the shap-boord oot a' the wandow."

"I'll shave no more," exclaims *Washball*—"No, not I—I'll keep my hands out of the suds."

"Dis will make me cut de figure in life," says *Raccoon*, "and appear in de world de proper impotance; and den I'll do someting for my poor ting."

The conspirators obtain two pistoles each from the dupes, and the scene closes with a solo from *Parchment:*

AIR—"*How Blest Has My Time Been.*"

Now let us join hands and unite in this cause,
'Tis glorious gold that shall gain us applause;
How blest now are we with such treasure in store,
We'll clothe all the naked and feed all the poor.

How happy for me to this country I came,
You all, my dear friends, now can witness the same;
In wealth to abound—oh, the thought is most sweet,
No more will I write for one farthing a sheet.

In the second scene of the first act *Trusthoop* finds himself locked out by his wife. The old reprobate, *Raccoon*, in the third scene carries a spit, pick-axe and spade into *Moll Placket's* house and puts them under the bed. *Moll* calls him her "dear Cooney," and he not only tells his "pet" and "dear ting" all about the treasure, but promises her £500 a year for pin money when it is obtained. The fourth is a street scene where *Hum, Rattletrap* and *Quadrant* agree to assemble their dupes at the Ton Tavern. In the fifth scene *McSnip* turns his journeymen out of the shop. Then comes a love-scene between *Lucy* and *Meanwell*. *Lucy* tells her lover that her uncle, *Washball*, has ordered her to discard him, and promised her a marriage portion of £10,000 if she marries agreeably to his wishes. The seventh scene— think of seven scenes in the first act of a comic opera—shows the conspirators and dupes at the tavern, and the act closes with a song sung by *Rattletrap* to the air of "The Jolly Toper."

The second act opens with a broad, coarse scene that would be inadmissible nowadays between *Topinloft*, the sailor, and *Moll Placket*, during which *Raccoon* comes for his spit, pick-axe and spade.  *Topinloft* conceals himself under the bed where the implements were placed, but to prevent *Raccoon* from going there for them *Moll* pretends that she is about to raise a familiar spirit, and the sailor makes his escape as a ghost, knocking *Raccoon* over as he rushes out.  The next scene is " the place of action near the Stone Bridge."  *Rattletrap* draws "the magic circle" and pronounces the words of incantation—"*Diapaculum interravo, testiculum stravaganza.*"  While the digging proceeds the convulsions of nature are rather queer, and finally the ghost of the pirate appears and spits fire.  *Trusthoop* says the spook "looks like no slouch of a fellow."  *Washball*, thoroughly frightened, prays " *Mea culpa,*" and *Raccoon*, who now wishes he had lived a better life, asks him to pray in English, saying " dese spirits don't understand de Latin."  The ghost resists the search for the treasure, but in vain, and when the chest is secured *Rattletrap* sings:

> Tho' my art some despise, I appeal to your eyes
>     For a proof of my magical knowledge ;
> Tho' the wisdom of schools damn our art and our tools,
>     We can laugh at the fools of the college.
>
> Now, my friends, we're possessed of the glorious chest,
>     Join hands and rejoice without measure ;
> Let it be our first care that great blessing to share
>     Whose contents are an infinite treasure.

The piece ought to end with the opening of the chest, which is found to contain only stones, but it does not, for *Lucy* and *Meanwell* have eloped and are to to be forgiven, and there is besides an epilogue in which all the characters, including *Moll* and the sailor, appear.  The

" local reflections " in this piece are only such as would belong to an actual event.

Although without merit as a dramatic composition, "The Disappointment" is worthy of preservation as a picture of a credulous and superstitious epoch in the history of Pennsylvania. In casting the piece it is probable that Hallam was to have played *Rattletrap*, Woolls *Parchment*, Douglass *Raccoon*, Morris *McSnip*, Mrs. Harman *Moll* and Miss Wainwright *Lucy*. Beyond these it is not easy to guess at the distribution of the parts. By some the authorship of the comedy was attributed to Joseph Leacock, who was a jeweler and silversmith in Philadelphia at the time, and by others to John Leacock, who became Coroner after the Revolution. There is no reason to doubt, however, that the author was Colonel Forrest.

# CHAPTER XVIII.

---

## "THE PRINCE OF PARTHIA."

THE FIRST AMERICAN PLAY EVER PRODUCED—THOMAS GODFREY'S
TRAGEDY—WHO THE ACTORS WERE—ALL THAT IS KNOWN IN
REGARD TO THE PIECE.

WHILE the comic opera, "The Disappointment," was the first American play announced for production, the first American play written for the stage and actually produced was "The Prince of Parthia," a tragedy by Thomas Godfrey, the younger. The elder Godfrey was a poor glazier, but he was remarkable as a mathematician, and was the original inventor of the quadrant that came to be known as Hadley's. He died in Philadelphia in the month of December, 1749. The announcement of his death, in which it was said that he had a genius for all kinds of mathematical knowledge, was printed in the *Pennsylvania Gazette* for the 19th. Thomas Godfrey, the younger, was born in Philadelphia in 1736. As a lad he was apprenticed to a watchmaker. In 1758 he served as a lieutenant in the Pennsylvania forces that formed a part of the expedition against Fort Duquesne. Subsequently, in 1759, young Godfrey went to North Carolina, where he gave his leisure during the summer and autumn to completing his tragedy, intending it for production in Philadelphia by Douglass' company. "By the last vessel from this place," he wrote to a Philadelphia friend in a letter dated November 17th, 1759, "I sent you the copy of a tragedy I finished here, and desired your interest in bringing it on the stage; I have not yet heard of the vessel's arrival, and believe if she is safe it will be too late for the company now in Philadelphia." This letter proves conclusively that Godfrey wrote the " Prince of Parthia " with a view to its production, and as it was printed in the introduction to Godfrey's poems, of which the tragedy formed a part, published in 1765, there is no excuse for Mr. Dunlap's ignorance in regard to the author's intentions respecting it.

Young Godfrey had many influential friends in Philadelphia. Among them were Dr. Smith, the first principal of the Philadelphia Academy; Francis Hopkinson, the author of " The Battle of the Kegs;" Benjamin West, the distinguished artist, and Nathaniel Evans, a young clergyman, who also aspired to be a poet. It was through Dr. Smith's influence that Godfrey obtained his lieutenant's commission in the Pennsylvania forces in the Duquesne expedition. In August, 1758, the young soldier wrote a poetical epistle from Fort Henry, which is a favorable specimen of Godfrey's versification, and a striking picture of the deep distress that overwhelmed the frontier settlements in that epoch of unsparing savage warfare. But Dr. Smith not only promoted Godfrey's military ambition— he was the young poet's literary sponsor as well. As the editor of the *American Magazine* he printed the earlier productions of Godfrey's muse

A SPECIMEN OF GODFREY'S VERSE.

Here no enchanting prospect yields delight,
But darksome forests intercept the sight;
Here, filled with dread, the trembling peasants go,
And start with terror at each nodding bough,
Nor as they trace the gloomy way along,
Dare ask the influence of a cheering song.

If in this wild a pleasing spot we meet,
In happier times some humble swain's retreat;
Where once with joy he saw the grateful soil
Yield a luxuriant harvest to his toil.
[Blest with content, enjoyed his solitude,
And knew his pleasures, though of manners rude;]
The lonely prospect strikes a secret dread,
While round the ravag'd cot we silent tread,
Whose owner fell beneath the savage hand,
Or roves a captive on some hostile land,
While the rich fields with Ceres' blessings stor'd,
Grieve for their slaughter'd, or their absent lord.

and extolled the verses of his aspiring contributor. It was not Dr. Smith who collected Godfrey's productions and secured their publication after the author's death, as his biographer asserts, but the Rev. Mr. Evans. The collection, to which Mr. Evans contributed a life of the poet, and Dr. Smith a critical estimate of Mr. Godfrey's writings, fails to sustain the opinions of the critic as to their merits. The best of Godfrey's poems unquestionably was his "Court of Fancy," first published in 1762. As a specimen of his versification the description of Fancy, printed herewith, will serve. Godfrey was almost without education, but his poems are chiefly remarkable for an affectation of learning that he did not have. In the estimation of his friends he was an untutored child of genius. His friend Evans, in a doggerel ode beginning:

### FANCY.

"High in the midst, rais'd on her rolling throne,
Sublimely eminent bright Fancy shone:
A glitt'ring tiara her temples bound,
Rich set with sparkling rubies all around,
Her azure eyes rolled with majestic grace,
And youth eternal bloom'd upon her face.
A radiant bough, ensign of her command,
Of polish'd gold, waved in her lily hand;
The same the sybil to Eneas gave,
When the bold Trojan cross'd the Stygian wave.
In silver traces fix'd unto her car,
Four snowy swans, proud of th' imperial fair,
Wing'd lightly on, each in gay beauty drest,
Smooth'd the soft plumage that adorn'd her breast,
Sacred to her the lucent chariot drew,
Or whether wildly through the air she flew,
Or whether to the dreary shades of night,
Oppress'd with gloom, she downwards bent her flight,
Or, proud, aspiring, sought the blest abodes,
And boldly shot among the assembled gods."

While you, dear Tom, are forc'd to roam
In search of fortune far from home,

invoked him to renounce the muse and

With me henceforward join the crowd,
And, like the rest, proclaim aloud
That money is all virtue.

Prefixed to Godfrey's poems is an elegy to his memory by Evans, in which the most appropriate lines were as follows:

> Stranger, whoe'er thou art, by fortune's hand
> Lost on the baleful Carolinian strand,
> Oh ! if thou see'st perchance the Poet's grave
> The sacred spot with tears of sorrow lave.
> Oh ! shade it, shade it with ne'erfading bays—
> Hallow'd the place where gentle Godfrey lays.

John Green, a portrait-painter, who was also one of the poet's early friends, contributed an additional elegy to the memorial volume of Godfrey's verse. Green's lines, although they show little poetic merit, are superior in tender sympathy and appreciation to the halting numbers of Godfrey's literary executor. Young Godfrey, on his part, in his poem, en-

EXTRACT FROM GREEN'S ELEGY.

> Ye gentle swains on Carolina's shore,
> Who knew my Damon, (now alas, no more),
> By moonlight round his hallow'd grave repair,
> Strew sweetest flow'rs and drop a sorrowing tear,
> With never fading laurel shade his tomb,
> And bid the rising bay forever bloom,
> Teach springing flow'rs their purpl'd heads to rise,
> And sweetly twining write, " Here virtue lies."
> Sing in sad strains each venerable name,
> In Fortune's spite that struggled up to fame;
> By Virtue led life's rugged road along,
> Their lives instructive as their sweetest song.
> Say while their praises tremble on the tongue,
> Thus lived this youthful Bard—thus gentle Damon sung.

titled " A Night Piece," paid this compliment to Green :

> What hand can picture forth the solemn scene,
>     The deep'ning shade and glimm'ring light !
> How much above the expressive art of Green,
>     Are the dim beauties of the dewy night !

Still another evidence of the esteem in which Godfrey was held by his friends is found in the fact that his portrait was painted by Benjamin West. The picture was among the earliest efforts of that great painter. It has been described as " indicative of talent neither in the artist nor the person delineated." Godfrey died in North Carolina, August 3d, 1763. His poems, including "The Prince of Parthia," were then collected and published in a small folio volume, in 1765. The book has long been regarded as a scarce one, but may be found occasionally on the shelves of the second-hand dealers. Among the original subscribers were Chief Justice William Allen and William Plumstead, the latter taking two copies. Benjamin Franklin's private copy with his autograph—he subscribed for twelve copies— was on sale at Scribner's, in New York, a few years ago.

As an acting play "The Prince of Parthia" has no merit whatever. The speeches are long and are in blank verse, remarkable only for its measured dulness. All the characters are on stilts. There is little plot to the piece and no action. As a first attempt at play-writing in America by a young man who had had few opportunities of seeing plays acted, the tragedy is not without interest. It has none of the interest, however, that makes it readable as a poem or presentable as a play. That it ever should have met with favor on the stage is impossible, and it is probable that its production was in the nature of a peace-offering to the Philadelphia public for the failure to produce "The Disappointment." The tragedy followed immediately upon the withdrawal of the comedy, as the announcement printed in the *Pennsylvania Gazette* on the 23d of April shows. It is in the face of this advertisement that Dunlap asserts with his usual inaccuracy, "Whether intended for the stage or only for the closet is unknown; that it was not performed by the players is certain."

ADVERTISEMENT.

By authority.
By the American Company.
At the new Theatre in *Southwark*, to-morrow, being the 24th of April, will be presented a Tragedy, written in America by the late ingenious Mr. GODFREY, of this city, called
THE PRINCE OF PARTHIA;
To which will be added
THE CONTRIVANCES.
To begin precisely at seven o'clock.
Vivant Rex et Regina.

The plot of the tragedy, such as it is, is not well-knit nor well wrought out. Arsaces, son of Artabanes, King of Parthia, has just returned from a successful campaign

against Arabia.   The play opens in the Temple of the Sun at Ctesi-
phon.   The opening scene is between Gotarzes, the youngest brother
of Arsaces, and Phraates, a courtier.   It requires a number of long
speeches in blank verse to enable Gotarzes to inform his friend that
his gallant brother

> Triumphant enters now our joyful gates;
> Bright Victory waits on his glittering car
> And shows her fav'rite to the wond'ring crowd.

Thereupon Phraates takes occasion in fifteen lines to answer that

> Glad Ctes'phon
> Pours forth her numbers like a rolling deluge
> To meet the blooming Hero.

With more than doubtful grammar and in lame measure Gotarzes exclaims:

> Happy Parthia!
> Now proud Arabia dreads her destined chains,
> While shame and rout disperses all her sons.
> Barzaphernes pursues the fugitives,
> The few whom fav'ring night redeem'd from slaughter.

There is, of course, just there no lack of praises of the victorious
Prince of Parthia.   According to Phraates:

> In blest Arsaces every virtue meets;
> He's generous, brave and wise and good,
> Has skill to act and noble fortitude
> To face bold danger in the battle firm,
> And dauntless as a lion fronts his foe.

This panegyric reminds Gotarzes of "one luckless day" when
"in the eager chase"

> A monstrous leopard from a bosky den
> Rushed forth, and foaming lash'd the ground.

As was to be expected, Gotarzes' "treach'rous blade" snapped
short, and of course

> Arsaces then,
> Hearing the din, flew like some pitying power,
> And quickly freed me from the monster's jaws,
> Drenching his bright lance in his spotted breast.

Arsaces has a wicked brother, Vardanes, who hates the elder prince,

> For standing 'twixt him and the hope of empire.

This Vardanes was seized with a cramp while bathing in the Euphrates, but his cries

> Arsaces heard,
> And thro' the swelling waves he rushed to save
> His drowning brother, and gave him life;
> And for the boon the ingrate pays him hate.

The poetic license allowed only to young men of genius enabled the author of "The Prince of Parthia" to represent the Queen as the widow of Tissaphesenes and the mother of the fierce Vonones when she became the wife of Artabanes. Vonones conspired against the King's life, and the Queen resolved to ruin Arsaces—

> Because, that fill'd with filial piety,
> To save his royal Sire, he struck the bold
> Presumptuous traitor dead.

The second scene is between Vardanes and his friend, Lycias. Vardanes takes occasion to say—

> I hate Arsaces
> Tho' he's my mother's son, and churchmen say
> There's something sacred in the name of brother,
> My soul endures him not, and he's the bane
> Of all my hopes of greatness. Like the sun
> He rules the day and like the night's pale queen
> My fainter beams are lost when he appears.

Vardanes had still another reason to hate his brother, and he declares:

> In love as well as glory he's above me;
> I dote on fair Evanthe, but the charmer
> Disdains my ardent suit; like a miser
> He treasures up her beauties to himself.

The Queen and Edessa have the third scene, in which the former gives expression to her discontent with Arsaces, and utters a curse that comprises the most satisfactory lines in the play:

> O may he never know a father's fondness,
> Or know it to his sorrow; may his hopes
> Of joy be cut like mine, and his short life
> Be one continued tempest; if he lives
> Let him be cursed with jealousy and fear,
> And vext with anguish of neglecting scorn;
> May torturing hope present the flowing cup,
> Then hasty snatch it from his eager thirst,
> And when he dies base treach'ry be the means.

She announces that

> "Vardanes is the minister of vengeance."

The fourth scene is between Evanthe and Cleone. Evanthe, in speeches not fewer than sixteen lines in length, says:

> Twice fifteen times
> Has Cynthia dipt her horns in beams of light,
> Twice fifteen times has wafted all her brightness,
> Since first I knew to love; 'twas on that day
> When curs'd Vonones fell upon the plain—
> The lovely victor doubly conquer'd me.

She was a captive of Vonones, and, of course, the daughter of Bethas. The King and Arsaces are seen in the last scenes of the act, where Bethas is shown in chains. Arsaces asks for the life of the captive and the King grants it. In the second act the lovers meet in the cell of the captive father, while Vardanes and Lycias begin to scheme to overthrow Arsaces and

> To gain a crown or else a glorious tomb.

The third act opens with a scene between the King and Queen, in which she accuses him of a guilty design upon Evanthe, which he does not deny, but as he retires, exclaims:

> No more I'll wage a woman's war with words.

Then Vardanes enters, asking the Queen—

> Dread Thermusa,
> Say, what has roused this tumult in thy soul?

She informs him that his father is his rival. Not suspecting his father's passion, Arsaces asks the hand of Evanthe as a reward for his services, but Evanthe lets him know how she is persecuted by the King. The King plots with Vardanes against Evanthe, saying:

> Indulge thy father with this one request,
> Seize with some horse Evanthe, and bear her
> To your command. Oh, I'll own my weakness,
> I love her with a fondness mortal never knew.

Lycias murders the King at the instigation of the Queen, and in the fourth act Vardanes imprisons his brother Arsaces, and the Queen plots the assassination of the Prince. While she is in his cell, intending to stab him, the Ghost of Artabanes rises, and at once proceeds to make a speech eighteen lines in length. This deters her, as well it might. To close the fourth act Barzaphernes returns with his army from Arabia and releases Arsaces. In the last act Vardanes makes love to Evanthe, much against her will, in the royal palace, but the palace is assaulted by Arsaces and captured. Evanthe, unfortunately hearing that Arsaces has fallen in the battle, takes poison, and is dying when her lover succeeds in rescuing her. It only remains for Arsaces also to commit suicide.

After one hundred and twenty years the first production of an

American play is a matter of great interest to students of American theatrical history; but beyond the fact of the production of the " Prince of Parthia," on the 24th of April, 1767, and the play itself, which has come down to us as a token of the first attempts at dramatic authorship in America, nothing is known of the event. There was, however, a second advertisement printed in the *Pennsylvania Chronicle*, which contained a list of the performers who had parts in Godfrey's tragedy. Mr. Hallam, apparently, never mentioned the fact of its production to Dunlap—indeed, he may have forgotten it altogether. The newspapers of the time are silent in regard to it.

THE CHRONICLE ADVERTISEMENT.

*By Authority.*
Never Performed Before.
By the American Company.
At the New Theatre in Southwark
On Friday the Twenty-fourth of April will be
presented a Tragedy written by the late
ingenious Mr. Thomas Godfrey of
this city called The
PRINCE OF PARTHIA.
The principal characters by Mr. Hallam, Mr. Douglass, Mr. Wall, Mr. Morris, Mr. Allyn, Mr. Tomlinson, Mr. Broadbelt, Mr. Greville, Mrs. Douglass, Mrs. Morris, Miss Wainwright and Miss Cheer.

As no second edition of the tragedy was ever printed, no information in regard to the play or the cast has been preserved in that way. The only thing that is possible under the circumstances is to make up a probable cast from the list of names in the advertisement. There is no reasonable doubt that the roles taken by Douglass and Hallam and Mrs. Douglass and Miss Cheer were as indicated in this " Probable Cast." By whom the minor characters were actually played is not a matter of great importance, especially as we have the names of all the performers in the piece.

PROBABLE CAST.

| | |
|---|---|
| Artabanes, King of Parthia | . Mr. Douglass |
| Arsaces, | . . . . Mr. Hallam |
| Vardanes, } his sons, } | . . . Mr. Tomlinson |
| Gotarzes, | . . . . . Mr. Wall |
| Barzaphernes, lieutenant-general under Arsaces | . . . . . . . Mr. Allyn |
| Lysias, } officers at court, } | Mr. Broadbelt |
| Phraates, | Mr. Greville |
| Bethas, a noble captive | . . . . Mr. Morris |
| Thermusa, the queen | . . . . Mrs. Douglass |
| Evanthe, beloved by Arsaces | . . Miss Cheer |
| Cleone, her confidant | . . Miss Wainwright |
| Edessa, attendant on the queen | . Mrs. Morris |

As the work of a young man of twenty-three, without education and without a knowledge of stage requirements, "The Prince
of Parthia" is not discreditable to its author.  Neither as a poem nor
as an acting play has it any merit that would cause it to be remembered, were it not for the fact that it was the first American play ever
written as well as the first actually produced.  The absence of comment in the newspapers is not surprising, since to the journalists of
that day the first production of an American play, or a play of any
kind, was not a matter of any public interest or importance.  In
society, however, there was a deep interest in plays.  In the "Journal
of William Black" it is said that in the society of some fair Philadelphia ladies the talk turned to "criticising on plays" and their
authors, Addison, Prior, Otway, Congreve, Dryden, Pope and Shakspere being among the poets criticised.  "The words genius," wrote
Mr. Black, in 1744, "and no genius—invention, poetry, fine things,
bad language, no style, charming writing, imagery, and diction (as the
author of 'Dr. Simple' says), with many more expressions which swim
on the surface of criticism, seemed to have been caught by those female
fishers for the reputation of wit."  In 1773, Miss Sarah Eve recorded
in her journal that she had just read the "Fashionable Lover," a
"prodigious, fine comedy, wrote by Cumberland;" and shortly afterwards she says she was reminded of "those lines of our poet Godfrey:"

> Curiosity's another name for man;
> The blazing meteor streaming thro' the air,
> Commands our wonder, and admiring eyes.
> With eager gaze we trace the lucent paths,
> Till spent at last it shrinks to native nothing,
> While the bright stars, which ever steady glow,
> Unheeded shine and bless the world below.

# CHAPTER XIX.

———

## THE AMERICAN COMPANY.

A SUPPLEMENTARY SEASON AT THE SOUTHWARK THEATRE—STRENGTH
OF THE COMPANY—JOHN HENRY AND THE STORER SISTERS—
MISS CHEER AND HER ROMANTIC MARRIAGE—MR. HALLAM—MISS
WAINWRIGHT, MR. WOOLLS AND THE OTHERS.

DURING the summer and autumn of 1767 Mr. Douglass was
busy building a theatre in New York that was almost identical
in plan and appearance with the old Philadelphia theatre. This was
the house that became known in American theatrical history as the
John Street Theatre. While it was in course of construction the
Southwark Theatre was re-opened for a brief period, during which
the American Company was seen at its best at any time before the
Revolution. The supplementary season lasted from the 24th of
September to the 23d of November, during which new members of
the company were introduced to the public and the company's large
repertoire presented in rapid succession. But strangely enough, this
year spent at the Southwark Theatre is utterly ignored by most of
those who write about the early American stage, the re-organized
American Company being treated as if its history began with the New
York season of 1767-8. This is due to the assumption in Ireland's
" Records of the New York Stage " that what was first in New York

was first in America, although in reality that city played a secondary part in the early development of the American stage.

The list of performances of the brief supplementary season of the autumn of 1767 shows only two pieces that had not already been given in the Southwark Theatre. One of these was "Venice Preserved" and the other the "Clandestine Marriage." The reproductions, however, were pieces that required strong casts, including as they did the "Roman Father," "Jealous Wife," "Gamester," "Theodosius," "Beaux' Stratagem," "Wonder" and "Love in a Village," together with three of Shakspere's tragedies, "Hamlet," "Romeo and Juliet" and "Lear." Besides, the list of performances shows a change of farce every acting night, some of the farces, as the "Mayor of Garratt," being in reality comedies. These performances, so remarkable for their extent and variety, are in themselves evidence of the merit of the performers.

LIST OF PERFORMANCES.

1767.
Sept. 24—Lecture on Heads.
Oct.   6—Roman Father . . . . Whitehead
         Miss in her Teens  . . . Garrick
       9—Jealous Wife . . . . . . Colman
         Harlequin Restored.
      12—Hamlet . . . . . . . Shakspere
         Citizen . . . . . . . . Murphy
      16—Romeo and Juliet . . . Shakspere
         Mayor of Garratt . . . . . Foote
      19—Beaux' Stratagem . . . Farquhar
         High Life Below Stairs . Townley
      23—Gamester . . . . . . . . Moore
         Harlequin Collector.
      26—Love in a Village . . . Bickerstaff
         Oracle . . . . . . . Mrs. Cibber
      30—Wonder . . . . . . . Centlivre
         Devil to Pay . . . . . . Coffey
Nov.  2—Venice Preserved . . . . Otway
         Neck or Nothing . . . . Garrick
       9—Lear . . . . . . . . Shakspere
         Miller of Mansfield . . . Dodsley
      13—Theodosius . . . . . . . . Lee
         Chaplet . . . . . . . Mendez
      19—Clandestine Marriage.
                      Garrick and Colman
         Brave Irishman. . . . . Sheridan
      23—Clandestine Marriage.
         Lying Valet . . . . . . Garrick

All that is known of the "Lecture on Heads" is contained in the advertisement for the opening night, as it was printed in Goddard's *Pennsylvania Chronicle.* Mr. Hallam also recited "Bucks Have at

Ye All." On the first play-night, October 6th, when the "Roman Father" was repeated, Mr. Henry played *Publius Horatius*, instead of Mr. Douglass, and Mr. Douglass was *Tullius Hostilius*, instead of Mr. Allyn. This was John Henry, who was set down in the housebills and in the newspaper advertisements as "from the theatre in Jamaica." Mr. Henry was born in Dublin, and it is said that he made his *debut* at Drury Lane, in 1762, meeting with little success. Dunlap says that his introduction to the stage was under the auspices of Thomas, the father of Richard Brinsley Sheridan, but Dunlap was

LECTURE ON HEADS.

———

For that Night only,
At the THEATRE in SOUTHWARK,
(By particular desire)
On Thursday next being the 24th instant,
Messrs. DOUGLASS and HALLAM
will deliver
A LECTURE ON HEADS, etc.,
and
THE DISSECTION of THE HEARTS of a British
Sailor and his Agents for PRIZE MONEY
With several pieces of Music between the
Parts of the LECTURE by
Mr. Woolls,
Miss Hallam and
Miss Wainwright, &c., &c.
To begin at half an hour after six o'clock.
Tickets are sold at the London Coffee
House and at Mr. Douglass' in Lombard
street, where Places in the Boxes may be had.
Boxes 5s., Pit 3s., Gallery 2s.

so uniformly inaccurate that it is impossible to accept anything he asserts as a fact. It certainly was not a fact, as stated in Dunlap's " History of the American Theatre," that Henry made his first appearance in America at the John Street Theatre, in New York, on the 7th of December, 1767, as *Aimwell* in the "Beaux' Stratagem," for, as has been shown, he appeared in Philadelphia for the first time two months previously. Besides *Publius Horatius* and other parts, Mr. Henry appeared during the brief Philadelphia season as *Charles*, in the "Jealous Wife;" *Lovewell*, in the "Clandestine Marriage;" *Jaffier*, in "Venice Preserved," and *Edmund*, in "King Lear." He also played *Captain O'Blunder*, in the farce of the "Brave Irishman." At this time Hallam always had the best parts in everything, and it was not often that Henry was accorded a good role, but notwithstanding this it was not long until he proved himself one of the best performers ever seen in the Colonies. He was tall and commanding in person, and it is possible to agree with Dunlap for once when he says that Henry must have been as handsome an *Aimwell* as ever trod the stage.

On the same night that Mr. Henry made his first appearance at the Southwark Theatre in the "Roman Father" Miss Storer, also from the theatre in Jamaica, made her American *debut* as *Biddy Belair* in "Miss in her Teens." This was Ann Storer, who, as Mrs. Hogg, was a great favorite at the old Park Theatre in New York in the beginning of the present century. Though often played by the American Company there is no record of Garrick's farce having been given during the

MISS IN HER TEENS.

Miss Biddy Belair . . . . . . Miss Storer
(From the theatre in Jamaica.)
Captain Flash . . . . . . . . Mr. Hallam
Fribble . . . . . . . . . . . Mr. Allyn
Captain Loveit . . . . . . Mr. Tomlinson
Jasper . . . . . . . . . . . Mr. Woolls
Puff . . . . . . . . . . . . Mr. Morris
Tag . . . . . . . . . Miss Wainwright

previous season at the Southwark Theatre. It was probably presented on this occasion to allow Miss Storer to make her *debut* as *Biddy*. It is a tradition that Miss Storer's mother was the Mrs. Storer (Miss Clark) of Covent Garden, of whom some poetaster sang :—

> Then Storer, with her sweet enchanting strains,
> Steals to our hearts, and o'er our senses reigns;
> With ravished ears we hear the pleasing sounds,
> And heavenly joys the vaulted roof resounds

The Storer family in Jamaica comprised Mrs. Storer and her four daughters. Henry married the eldest, but the vessel on which she made the voyage from Jamaica was burnt and she was lost at sea. Henry subsequently lived with Ann Storer as his wife, by whom he had a son, who afterward became the captain of a ship. Ann after-

ward married John Hogg, who was the comic old man when she was
the comic old woman of the New York Theatre. As Mrs. Hogg she was
the mother of a number of sons and a daughter, who was known on the
stage as Mrs. Claude. After the death of Mr. and Mrs. Hogg the family
name was changed to Biddle by an act of the New York Legislature.
George Edgar Biddle, professionally known as George Edgar, is her
grandson, and consequently he can lay claim to the earliest theatrical
descent of any living American actor. The third sister, Fanny Storer,
became Mrs. Mechler, and Maria Storer, the youngest, was the last
Mrs. Henry. At this time she was still a child. The late William B.
Wood, speaking of Mrs. Henry in his " Personal Recollections of the
Stage," says of her in the last decade of the last century: "She usually
came full-dressed to the theatre in the old family coach; and the
fashion of monstrous hoops worn at that day made it necessary for
Mr. Henry to slide her out sideways, take her in his arms and carry
her like an infant to the stage entrance. The carriage was a curious
and rather crazy-looking affair, and lest the gout, which rendered it
indispensable to him, might not be generally known as an excuse for
such a luxury, he decorated the panels with two crutches crossed—
the motto, 'This, or These.'" Mrs. Henry was described by Wood
as a perfect fairy in person. Even before the Revolution as Miss M.
Storer and Miss Storer she acquired a place second only to the front
rank. In the succeeding pages the sisters must not be confounded
with each other.

The only piece presented for the first time in this country this
season was the "Clandestine Marriage." It was advertised as produced
"by particular desire." It was still a new comedy, having been
originally produced at Drury Lane in 1765. According to Mr. Galt,

in his "Lives of the Players," the "Clandestine Marriage" was a
plagiarism from a piece called the "False Concord," written by the
Rev. James Townley, author of
"High Life Below Stairs." The
characters of Lord Lavendre, Mr.
Suds—a soap-boiler, of course—
and a pert valet in Mr. Townley's
comedy, were, it is said, "transplanted with the dialogue of some
scenes in the 'Clandestine Marriage' under the names of *Lord
Ogelby, Mr. Sterling* and *Mr.
Brush.*" It has always been

CLANDESTINE MARRIAGE.

| | |
|---|---|
| Lord Ogelby | Mr. Hallam |
| Sir John Melvil | Mr. Douglass |
| Lovewell | Mr. Henry |
| Sterling | Mr. Morris |
| Brush | Mr. Wall |
| Canton | Mr. Allyn |
| Sergeant Flower | Mr. Tomlinson |
| Traverse | Mr. Malone |
| Truman | Mr. Greville |
| Mrs. Heidelberg | Mrs. Douglass |
| Fanny | Miss Hallam |
| Betty | Miss Storer |
| Chambermaid | Miss Wainwright |
| Trusty | Mrs. Morris |
| Miss Sterling | Miss Cheer |

claimed, however, and Colman admits in a letter to Garrick, dated
December 4th, 1765, that "it is true, indeed, that by your suggestion
Hogarth's proud lord"—from the first plate of the 'Marriage *a la
Mode*'—"was converted into Lord Ogelby." The part is an expansion
of the idea of *Lord Chalkstone* in "Lethe," and was for the most part
written by Garrick for himself. Owing to his advanced age and fre-
quent attacks of the gout Garrick relinquished the part to King, whose
*Ogelby* proved to be one of his most meritorious characters. In *Mrs.
Heidelberg* Mrs. Clive almost closed her long list of comic characters—
indeed it was her last except one, *Lady Fuss* in the "Peep Behind the
Curtain."

A third pantomime, "Harlequin Restored," was added to the
company's repertoire this season, and Otway's "Venice Preserved"
was presented for the first time by the American Company, as it was
then organized. On this occasion Miss Cheer made her first appear-

ance as *Belvidera*. These two casts—that of the " Clandestine Marriage " and this of "Venice Preserved"—are important in showing the strength of the company as a whole and the relative rank of its members.

It is not surprising that the newspapers from

VENICE PRESERVED.

| | |
|---|---|
| Pierre | Mr. Hallam |
| Jaffier | Mr. Henry |
| Priuli | Mr. Douglass |
| Bedamar | Mr. Wall |
| Renault | Mr. Morris |
| Duke | Mr. Tomlinson |
| Spinosa | Mr. Malone |
| Eliot | Mr. Greville |
| Theodore | Mr. Woolls |
| Durand | Mr. Roberts |
| Officer | Mr. Allyn |
| Belvidera | Miss Cheer |

HARLEQUIN RESTORED.

| | |
|---|---|
| Harlequin | Mr. Hallam |
| Pantaloon | Mr. Morris |
| Petit Mache | Mr. Allyn |
| Statuary | Mr. Douglass |
| Cook | Mrs. Harman |
| Mercury | Mr. Woolls |
| Pierot | Mr. Tomlinson |
| Valet de Chambre | Mr. Wall |
| Necromancer | Mr. Woolls |
| Columbine | Miss Cheer |

1749 to 1767, except in their advertising columns and through paid-for contributions, were silent in regard to the theatre. In that age players were considered as little better than vagabonds—strollers—were looked upon as tramps. To condemn profane stage-plays was part of the cant of the epoch. Even Captain Graydon, in his "Memoirs of a Life Chiefly Passed in Pennsylvania," [1]

[1] EXTRACT FROM GRAYDON'S MEMOIRS.— A short time before the epoch of my becoming a student of law, the city was visited by the company of players since styling themselves the old American Company. They had for several years been exhibiting in the islands, and now returned to the continent in the view of dividing their time and labors between Philadelphia and New York. At Boston,

They did not appear,
So peevish was the edict of the may'r,

or at least of those authorities which were charged with the custody of public morals. The manager was Douglass, rather a decent than shining actor, a man of sense and discretion, married to the widow Hallam, whose son, Lewis, then in full culmination, was the Roscius of the theatre. As the dramatic heroes were all his without a competitor, so the heroines were the exclusive property of Miss Cheer, who was deemed an admirable performer. The singing department was supplied and supported by the voices of Woolls and Miss Wainwright, said to have been pupils of Dr. Arne; while in the tremulous drawl of the old man, in low jest and buffoonry, Morris, thence the minion of the gallery, stood first and unrivaled. As for the Tomlinsons, the Walls, the Allyns, etc., they were your *Bonifaces*, your *Jessamys*, your *Mock Doctors*, and what not. On the female side Mrs. Douglass was a respectable, matron-like dame, stately or querulous as occasion required, a very good *Gertrude*, a truly appropriate *Lady Randolph*, with her white handkerchief and her weeds; but then, to applaud, it was absolutely necessary to forget

speaks of the American Company with an apology for introducing the players into his narrative. Fortunately he did not consider the merits of the performers comprising the American Company, when it was first called by that name, unworthy of his pen, and to him posterity owes the only creditable characterization of the players at the Southwark Theatre in 1766–67 that has been preserved—perhaps the only one ever written. The minor actors and actresses who were with the company at this time Captain Graydon does not mention at all. Among these were Godwin, a dancer, who played insignificant roles, such as *Haly* in "Tamerlane," *Honslow* in the "Beaux' Stratagem,"

that to touch the heart of the spectator had any relation to her function. Mrs. Harman bore away the palm as a duenna, and Miss Wainwright as a chambermaid. Although these were among the principal performers at first, the Company was from time to time essentially improved by additions. Among these the Miss Storers, Miss Hallam and Mr. Henry were valuable acquisitions, as was also a Mr. Goodman, who had read law in Philadelphia with Mr. Ross. This topic may be disgusting to persons of gravity, but human manners are my theme, as well in youth as in age. Each period has its playthings; and if the strollers of Thespis have not been thought beneath the dignity of Grecian history, this notice of the old American stagers may be granted to the levity of memoirs.

Whether there be any room for comparison between these, the old American Company and the performers of the present day, I venture not to say. Nothing is more subject to fashion than the style of public exhibitions; and as the excellence of the Lacedemonian black broth essentially depended, we are told, on the appetite of the feeder, so, no doubt, does the merit of theatrical entertainments. I can not but say, however, that in my opinion

the old company acquitted themselves with most animation and glee—they were a passable set of comedians. Hallam had merit in a number of characters, and was always a pleasing performer. No one could tread the stage with more ease. Upon it, indeed, he might be said to have been cradled and wheeled in his go-cart. In tragedy it can not be denied that his declamation was either mouthing or ranting; yet a thorough master of all the tricks and *finesse* of his trade, his manner was both graceful and impressive, "tears in his eyes, distraction in his aspect, a broken voice, and his whole function suiting with forms to his conceit." He once ventured to appear in *Hamlet*, either at Drury Lane or Covent Garden, and was endured. In the account given of his performance he is said not to have been to the taste of a London audience, though he is admitted to be a man of pleasing and interesting address. He was, however, at Philadelphia as much the soul of the Southwark Theatre as ever Garrick was of Drury Lane, and if, as Dr. Johnson allows, popularity in matters of taste is unquestionable evidence of merit, we cannot withhold a considerable portion of it from Mr. Hallam, notwithstanding his faults.

*Selim* in the "Mourning Bride," the *Messenger* in the "Orphan in China," and *Osric* in "Hamlet;" Matthews, Greville and Platt, of whom there is no information, apart from the unimportant roles that they filled; Broadbelt, who seldom played, but was apparently employed in the business office of the theatre; Malone, who was a dancer and juggler, and whose name is only interesting from the fact that it was the same as the original *Shylock* and *Lear* in this country; and the Dowthwaites, mother and daughter, of whom we know nothing. Two of these, Messrs. Matthews and Platt, withdrew after the close of the Southwark Theatre, in 1767, when their theatrical careers ended. Their lists of parts are short ones, and the parts were in themselves unimportant, but the summaries are worth making, in order to show the roles that were filled at this time under Mr. Douglass' management by prentice hands.

It is a curious fact in connection with these early actors and actresses that nearly everything that has passed for history in regard to them is inaccurate. All the historians unite in saying that Miss Cheer made her *debut* December 7th, 1767, at the John Street Theatre, New York, as *Mrs. Sullen* in the "Beaux' Stratagem." This error is due to Dunlap, from whom it has been copied by all his successors. "The name of Miss Cheer," he says, "appears for the first time on

MR. PLATT'S PARTS.

*Plays.*

| | |
|---|---|
| Beaux' Stratagem | Bagshot |
| Committee | Bailiff |
| Country Lasses | Shacklefigure |
| Cymbeline | Doctor |
| Hamlet | Bernardo |
| Macbeth | Donaldbain |
| Miser | Furnish |
| Mourning Bride | Mute |
| Roman Father | Fourth Citizen |
| Romeo and Juliet | Friar John |
| Tamerlane | Zama |

*Farces.*

| | |
|---|---|
| High Life Below Stairs | Cloe |
| Mayor of Garratt | Snuffle |
| Mock Doctor | James |

MR. MATTHEWS' PARTS.

*Plays.*

| | |
|---|---|
| Beggars' Opera | Jemmy Twitcher |
| Committee | Soldier |
| Country Lasses | Countryman |
| Jealous Wife | William |
| Merchant of Venice | Salarino |

*Farces.*

| | |
|---|---|
| Harlequin Collector | Skeleton |
| High Life Below Stairs | Kingston |
| Mayor of Garratt | Second Mob |

occasion of opening the house in John Street. She played the part of *Mrs. Sullen,* and from this time shared the first rank of characters with Mrs. Douglass." The surprise is not that Dunlap blundered. He was a failure in every undertaking of his long and laborious career— as a dramatist, as a theatrical manager, as an artist, as a novelist and as a historian. On the contrary, the wonder is that what he wrote should have been accepted as authentic for so many years. It must be conceded that it was worth the historian's while to ascertain the fact that Miss Cheer, the second leading lady of prominence on the American stage, made her first appearance in this country, at the Southwark Theatre, November 21st, 1766, as *Catherine,* in "Catherine and Petruchio," and had been in possession of nearly all of Mrs. Douglass' parts for more than a year before the John Street house was opened. Nearly all the parts in which she was ever seen she created at the Southwark Theatre. Of the role in which Miss Cheer made her first appearance at the John Street Theatre it is only necessary to say that she played *Mrs. Sullen* in Philadelphia as early as January 23d, 1767, and repeated the part nearly two months before she was seen in it in New York.

When Miss Cheer made her American *debut* as *Catherine* to Mr. Hallam's *Petruchio,* she was already an actress of established reputation, as is evident from the indorsement of the *Pennsylvania Gazette,* which described her as one of the best players in the empire. This was, no doubt, an over-statement of her claims to professional standing, but in this country her rank was undisputed. Among the parts in which she was seen in her first season in Philadelphia were *Lady Anne,* in "Richard III;" *Portia,* in the "Merchant of Venice;" *Ophelia,* in "Hamlet;" *Juliet,* in "Romeo and Juliet;" *Imogen,* in "Cymbeline;" *Cordelia,* in "Lear," and *Lady Macbeth* in the Shaksperean repertoire;

as *Almeria*, in the "Mourning Bride;" *Marcia*, in "Cato;" *Angelica*, in the "Constant Couple;" *Mrs. Sullen*, in the "Beaux' Stratagem;" *Millwood*, in "George Barnwell," *Bisarre*, in the "Inconstant;" *Miss Prue*, in "Love for Love;" *Angelina*, in "Love Makes a Man;" *Indiana*, in the "Conscious Lovers;" *Mariana*, in the "Miser;" *Mrs. Beverly*, in the "Gamester;" *Mrs. Oakley*, in the "Jealous Wife;" *Aura*, in "Country Lasses;" *Cleopatra*, in "All for Love;" *Countess of Rutland*, in "Earl of Essex;" *Ruth*, in the "Committee;" *Ann Lovely*, in "A Bold Stroke for a Wife;" *Lady Townly*, in the "Provoked Husband;" *Araminta*, in the "School for Lovers," and *Horatia*, in the "Roman Father," in the plays, and as *Mrs. Harlow*, in the "Old Maid;" *Mrs. Sneak*, in the "Mayor of Garratt," and *Dorcas*, in "Thomas and Sally," among the farces. In the supplementary season, in November and December, she added to the parts in which she had been previously seen *Violante*, in the "Wonder;" *Belvidera*, in "Venice Preserved;" *Pulcheria*, in "Theodosius," and *Miss Sterling*, in the "Clandestine Marriage." During the New York season of 1767–8 she added to these parts *Miranda*, in the "Busybody;" *Clarinda*, in the "Suspicious Husband;" *Sylvia*, in the "Recruiting Officer;" *Calista*, in the "Fair Penitent;" *Desdemona*, in "Othello;" *Monimia*, in the "Orphan;" *Hermione*, in the "Distressed Mother," and *Lady Percy*, in "Henry IV." To these parts she finally contributed *Lady Constance* in "King John," the title-role in "Zara," *Roxana* in "Alexander the Great," and *Lady Betty Lambton* in "False Delicacy." This, it must be confessed, is a wonderful showing for two years' work for an actress.

Whether Miss Cheer's withdrawal from the American Company was due to her marriage it is impossible to say, especially as she remained on the stage for nearly a year after it was announced. That event was one of the most romantic in dramatic history. In the *Penn-sylvania Chronicle* for the 28th of August, 1768, it is reported in the concise terms characteristic of the journalism of that period. Lord Rosehill was the son and heir of the sixth Earl of North-esk in the Scotch peerage. In

MISS CHEER'S MARRIAGE.

———

Last week was married in Maryland the Right Honorable Lord Rosehill to Miss Margaret Cheer, a young lady much admired for her theatrical performances.

Burke's " Peerage " it is said that Lord Rosehill married Catherine Cameron in 1768. This indicates either that Margaret Cheer was only the stage name of the actress, or that the young Lord was twice married within a year. At the time of his marriage Lord Rosehill had just entered upon his twentieth year, and it may be assumed that Miss Cheer was several years his senior, and that the union was the result of a boyish passion for the leading lady of the American Company. The young nobleman was in Philadelphia in 1768, where he was much petted by society. Lord Rosehill's father was a naval officer of distinction, who attained the rank of Admiral of the White. Of the motives that brought the young lord to America, thus making possible his marriage with Miss Cheer-Cameron, there is no account, nor have we any account of the length of his stay. If Lady Rosehill lived with her husband during his lifetime, it is certain they did not return to Scotland immediately after her retirement, for she played *Queen Elizabeth*, in "Richard III," for Mrs. Douglass' benefit in New York as late as 1773. David Carnegie, Lord Rosehill, died in France without issue in 1788. As the Earl, who was succeeded by his second son, William, also a distinguished naval officer, lived until 1792, Lady Rosehill never became a countess. Dunlap is authority for the statement that she was afterward known as Mrs. Long. Miss Cheer was

the only actress on the American stage who ever succeeded in captur-
ing a lord for a husband, and after Lavinia Fenton, who became
Duchess of Bolton, she was the first actress to marry a title.   At a
later period it was not unusual for favorite actresses to become the
wives of noble lords, Miss Eliza Farren becoming Countess of Derby
in 1797, Miss Louisa Brunton, sister of our own Mrs. Warren, Countess
of Craven in 1807, and Mrs. Coutts, known to the stage as Miss Mellon,
Duchess of St. Albans in 1827.   It is surprising that Miss Cheer's
marriage to Lord Rosehill should have passed at the time with no
other public mention than the brief announcement in the *Pennsylvania
Chronicle* and should afterward have been completely lost sight of by
the historians of the American theatre.

According to another historian of the American theatre, Colonel
Brown, Miss Wainwright also made her American *debut* in New York,
December 7th, 1767, as *Cherry* in the "Stratagem."   She, too, had
played her first New York role in Philadelphia nearly a year before
she appeared in it in New York, and when the John Street Theatre was
opened she was already an established Philadelphia favorite in the
more important parts of *Polly* in the "Beggar's Opera," and *Rosetta*
in "Love in a Village."   Colonel Brown also makes the astounding
declaration that Ann Storer (Mrs. Hogg) made her *debut* as a child in
1767 at the John Street Theatre.   It is not likely that a child who had
already played *Miss Biddy Belair* in "Miss in her Teens," *Regan* in
"King Lear" and *Betty* in the "Clandestine Marriage" in Philadelphia
should become an infantile *Betty* in New York a few weeks later.

It is unnecessary to follow the mistakes of the historians further
in this chapter, and so it only remains to be added that during the
supplementary season of 1767 tickets were advertised to be had "at

the London Coffee House and at Mr. Allyn's, next door but one to the theatre." The prices were: Boxes 7s. 6d., pit 5s., gallery 2s. With a brief interval during the summer of 1767 Philadelphia had had a long series of theatrical performances at the new theatre in Southwark, beginning with " Douglas," November 21st, 1766, and finally closing with the " Clandestine Marriage," November 23d, 1767. It was now to be New York's turn, and a long period elapsed before the players returned to the Quaker City.

# CHAPTER XX.

———

## JOHN STREET THEATRE, NEW YORK.

AMUSEMENTS WHILE THE PLAYERS WERE ABSENT—DESCRIPTION OF
THE NEW THEATRE—THE FIRST SEASON IN THE NEW PLAY-
HOUSE—DEATH OF MRS. MORRIS—FATAL ACCIDENT TO A CAR-
PENTER—RENEWED OPPOSITION TO PLAYS AND PLAYERS.

WHILE the Philadelphians were enjoying the acting of the
American Company, whatever its quality, in the winter and
spring and again in the autumn of 1767, the New Yorkers were
determined not to be entirely bereft of amusements. On the 14th
of April there was a concert of music at the New Assembly Room,
for the benefit of Mr. Leonard, whoever he may have been, and the
same evening Mr. Bayly, a sleight-of hand performer, took what was
called a benefit, the bill comprising " a new farce called the 'Enchanted
Lady of the Grove,'" the "Drunken Peasant" and the "Miller." Mr.
Tea was the *Peasant* and Mr. Bayly the *Clown* in the former of the
last two pieces, and Mr. Bayly the *Miller* and Mr. Tea the *Harlequin*
in the latter. The entertainment closed with " a negro dance," in
character, by Mr. Tea. Strangely enough, although the entertainment
was frequently repeated, the place where it was given was not named
in the announcements until the 18th of May, when it was said that the
performance would take place " at the Orange Tree on Golden Hill."

On the 5th of May "Harlequin's Escape" was in the bills with this cast: *Pantaloon*, by a Gentleman; *Spaniard*, Mr. Bayly; *Harlequin*, by a Gentleman; *Clown*, Mr. Tea.

On the 18th Otway's "Orphan" was played "by Gentlemen and Ladies for their amusement," and "Harlequin Statue" was given, thus cast: *Pantaloon*, Mr. Shaw; *Harlequin*, Mr. Martin; *Clown*, Mr. Tea; *Columbine*, Mrs. Bayly.

The Royal American Band of Music had a benefit at Burns' New Assembly Room on the 20th of April, and on the 13th of August the first of a series of concerts was given at Ranelagh Garden. During the summer Mr. Douglass visited New York, probably to superintend the building of his new theatre. During his visit he gave the celebrated "Lecture on Heads" in three parts at Burns' Assembly Room, beginning July 17th, with singing between the parts and at the end of the lecture by Mr. Woolls. Tickets were one dollar, but the price being objected to "as rather too high" Mr. Douglass lowered it after the first night to half a dollar. The lecture was delivered every Tuesday and Friday evening, the last performance taking place on the 6th of August. William C. Hulett, who was the dancer of the original Hallam Company, had a benefit at Burns' on the 2d of December, at which he was assisted by Mr. Woolls and Miss Hallam.

In the first American play produced in New York, and the first comedy by an American that was American in theme—"The Contrast," by Judge Tyler, of Vermont—the original *Jonathan* is made to describe the theatre in New York at the time it was re-opened after the Revolution. "As I was looking here and there for it," *Jonathan* says, "I saw a great crowd of folks going into a long entry that had lanterns over the door, so I asked the man if that was the place they played hocus pocus? He was a very civil kind of a man, though he did speak like the Hessians; he lifted up his eyes and said: 'They play hocus pocus tricks enough there, Got knows, mine friend.' So I went right in and they showed me away clean up to the garret, just like a meeting house gallery. And so I saw a power of topping folks, all sitting around in little cabins just like father's corn-crib."

This was the theatre in John Street, which for a quarter of a century was to New York what the Southwark Theatre was to Philadelphia. Both houses were alike in appearance, but the New York theatre stood back about sixty feet from the street, with a covered way of rough wooden materials from the sidewalk to the doors. It was principally of wood and was painted red. It had two rows of boxes and a pit and gallery, the capacity of the house when full being about eight hundred dollars. The stage was sufficiently large for all the requirements of that theatrical era, and the dressing-rooms and green-room were in a shed adjacent to the theatre.

The theatre in John Street was opened to the public on the 7th of December, 1767, the season lasting until the 2d of June, 1768. Some idea of the work performed by the American Company in New York during the season may be gathered from the list of pieces known to have been produced. Even now the list is not complete, but as it stands it shows thirty-eight full pieces—tragedies and comedies, including eight of Shakspere's masterpieces — and twenty-six farces. This, it must

LIST OF PERFORMANCES.

1767.
Dec. 7—Beaux' Stratagem . . . Farquhar
Lethe . . . . . . . . Garrick
11—School for Lovers . . Whitehead
Mayor of Garratt . . . . . Foote
14—Richard III . . . . . Shakspere
Oracle . . . . . Mrs. Cibber
18—Clandestine Marriage .
Garrick and Colman
Old Maid . . . . . . Murphy
21—Hamlet . . . . . . . Shakspere
Thomas and Sally . . Bickerstaff
28—Cymbeline . . . . . Shakspere
30—Mourning Bride . . . Congreve
Upholsterer . . . . . . Murphy
(Benefit of debtors in the City Gaol.)

be confessed, is a remarkable showing, to which no modern company would be equal. Although most of the pieces had been previously presented at the Southwark Theatre, none of them had been played more than two or three times, and so every play must have required a fresh study from all concerned. How exacting these studies were may be gathered from the delays in producing Murphy's All in the Wrong," which was originally announced for production, and is set down by Mr. Ireland as presented in New York on the 6th of April, 1768. This was intended to be the first production of the comedy, but owing to the pressure of the regular repertoire it was found necessary to postpone its presentation until a later date. There is no existing record of its actual production this season. Murphy's comedy was produced by command of Lady Moore, the wife of Sir Henry Moore, at that

1768.
Jan.  1—Busybody . . . . . . Centlivre
       Deuce is in Him . . . . . Colman
      4—Romeo and Juliet . . Shakspere
       Miss in her Teens . . . Garrick
      7—Gamester . . . . . . . Moore
       Catherine and Petruchio. Shakspere
     11—Love in a Village . . Bickerstaff
       Contrivances . . . . . . Carey
     15—Earl of Essex . . . . . . Jones
       Witches.
     18—Wonder . . . . . . . Centlivre
       Witches.
     22—A Bold Stroke for a Wife. Centlivre
       Reprisal . . . . . . . Smollett
     25—King Lear . . . . . Shakspere
       Hob in the Well . . . . Cibber
     28—Merchant of Venice . . Shakspere
Feb.  1—Suspicious Husband . . Hoadly
       Devil to Pay . . . . . . Coffey
      4—George Barnwell . . . . . Lillo
       Catherine and Petruchio.
      8—Love in a Village.
       High Life Below Stairs . Townley
     11—Orphan . . . . . . . . Otway
       Harlequin Collector.
     15—Recruiting Officer . . . Farquhar
       Citizen . . . . . . . Murphy
     18—Recruiting Officer.
       Citizen.
     22—Venice Preserved . . . . Otway
     25—King Henry IV . . . Shakspere
       Old Maid.
     29—Committee . . . . . . Howard
March 3—Macbeth . . . . . . Shakspere
       Oracle.
      7—School for Lovers.
       Apprentice . . . . . . Murphy
     10—Roman Father . . . Whitehead
       Catherine and Petruchio.
     14—Miser . . . . . . . . Fielding
       Chaplet . . . . . . . Mendez
     19—Cato . . . . . . . . Addison
       Witches.
     24—Fair Penitent . . . . . Rowe
       Neck or Nothing . . . . Garrick

April  4—Constant Couple  . . . Farquhar
High Life Below Stairs.
6—All in the Wrong  . . . Murphy
8—Wonder.
Harlequin Collector.
11—Othello . . . . . . . Shakspere
14—Romeo and Juliet.
Catherine and Petruchio.
(Miss Cheer's Benefit.)
18—Country Lasses  . . . . Johnson
Citizen.
(Miss Wainwright's Benefit.)
21—Conscious Lovers  . . . . Steele
Polly Honeycomb  . . . Colman
(Mr. Morris' Benefit.)
25—Cymbeline.
High Life Below Stairs.
(Mr. Hallam's, Benefit.)
28—All for Love . . . . . . Dryden
Upholsterer.
(Mr. Douglass' Benefit.)

May  2—Richard III.
Taste (Interlude)  . . . . Foote
(Benefit of the Misses Storer.)
5—Hamlet.
Miller of Mansfield  . . Dodsley
(Mr. Tomlinson's Benefit.)
9—Orphan of China . . . . Murphy
Brave Irishman.
(Mr. Hallam's Benefit.)
13—Venice Preserved.
Love a la Mode . . . . Macklin
(Mr. Henry's Benefit.)
16—Distressed Mother  . . . Philips
Thomas and Sally.
(Mrs. Harman's Benefit.)
19—Love in a Village.
Lying Valet . . . . . . Garrick
(Miss Hallam's Benefit.)
23—Jane Shore . . . . . . Rowe
Miss in her Teens.
(Mrs. Douglass' Benefit.)
26—Provoked Husband . . Vanbrugh
Honest Yorkshireman.
(Mr. and Mrs. Wall's Benefit.)

time Governor of New York. Besides this the only new comedy presented this season was Macklin's "Love a la Mode."

Although Mr. Hallam was first in everything from *Hamlet, Macbeth* and *Lear*, and *Marc Antony*, in "All for Love," and *Don Felix*, in the "Wonder," to *Slip*, in "Neck or Nothing," and *Harlequin*, in the "Witches," and Mr. Henry's parts, as a rule, were little above "responsible utility"— *Tybalt*, in "Romeo and Juliet," *Tubal*, in the "Merchant of Venice," *Malcolm*, in "Macbeth," the *Tailor*, in "Catherine and Petruchio," and *Crispin Heel-Tap*, in the "Mayor of Garratt"—the latter showed not only a worthy ambition but sound judgment in taking advantage of his benefit to be seen as *Sir Callaghan O'Brallaghan*, in Macklin's comedy. After Henry's death Hallam was accustomed to describe him as "a splendid amateur actor," but in many parts he was beyond doubt

Hallam's superior. In Irish characters especially he was unexcelled by any actor who appeared on the American stage previous to the Revolution or after it as

May 30—Gamester.
Devil to Pay.
(Mr. Tomlinson's Benefit).
June 2—Earl of Essex.
Cock-lane Ghost.
Catherine and Petruchio.
(Mrs. Douglass'Benefit.)

*Patrick* in the " Poor Soldier," in which he was a great favorite with General Washington, who first saw him in the role in Philadelphia, during the sittings of the Federal Convention, in 1787.

In Macklin's comedy an Irish officer, a Jew broker, a Scotch baronet and an English squire are addressing a young lady of very great fortune, but only one of them, the Irishman, is a disinterested lover — Macklin was an Irishman. The character of the Irishman bears a strong resemblance to the elder Sheridan's *Captain O'Blunder*—a part in which Henry delighted—and the thought of the catastrophe is borrowed from Theophilus Cibber's comedy, " The Lover." The piece was originally brought out at Drury Lane in 1760. Besides this two other farces that were new to the American stage were presented this season. One of these was the elder Colman's " dramatic novel," as it was called, " Polly Honeycomb." It was aimed at the evil effects of the fashionable taste for mischievous

LOVE A LA MODE.

| | |
|---|---|
| Sir Callaghan O'Brallaghan | . . Mr. Henry |
| Sir Archy MacSarcasm | . . . Mr. Douglass |
| Squire Groom | . . . . . . . Mr. Hallam |
| Beau Mordecai | . . . . . . . Mr. Morris |
| Sir Theodore Goodchild | . . Mr. Tomlinson |
| Charlotte | . . . . . . . . . Miss Hallam |

POLLY HONEYCOMB.

| | |
|---|---|
| Mr. Honeycomb | . . . . . . . Mr. Morris |
| Scribble | . . . . . . . . . . . Mr. Wall |
| Ledger | . . . . . . . . . Mr. Tomlinson |
| Mrs. Honeycomb | . . . . . . Mrs. Harman |
| Nurse | . . . . . . . . . Mrs. Tomlinson |
| Polly | . . . . . . . . . Miss Wainwright |

novels, and met with amazing success when it was first produced at Drury Lane. It owed much of its success, however, to the exquisite absurdity of the fulsome tenderness of Mr. and Mrs. Honeycomb.

The other, "Fanny, the Phantom; or, the Cock-lane Ghost," was presented for Mrs. Douglass' benefit on the closing night of the season.

### COCK-LANE GHOST.

The Orator }
Peter Paragraph } . . . . . . . Mr. Wall
Irish Sergeant . . . . . . . Mr. Douglass
Counsellor Prosequi . . . . Mr. Tomlinson
Shadrach Bodkin . . . . . . . Mr. Morris
The Justice . . . . . . . . . Mr. Woolls

It was, no doubt, an interlude based on the episode of 1762 in Cocklane, Stockwell, which, for awhile engrossed the attention of all London.

The repertoire of the New York season of 1767–8 included nine pieces, more or less familiar, that had not been seen in Philadelphia in 1766–7. Among these was Mrs. Centlivre's "Busybody," first played in this country by Murray and Kean's company in 1751. It was originally acted at Drury Lane in 1709. Wilks had such a mean opinion of his own part, *Sir George,* that one morning at rehearsal he threw it into the pit and swore nobody should sit out such silly stuff. The actors reported that it was a silly thing written by a woman, and so when it was produced there was only a small audience. In spite of the poor opinion the players had of it it was successful. Pack was the original *Marplot,* but the following year Dogget played the part at the Haymarket. Another play acted this season that was in the Murray and Kean repertoire was Philips'

### BUSYBODY.

Marplot . . . . . . . . . . Mr. Hallam
Sir George Airy . . . . . . Mr. Henry
Sir Francis Gripe . . . . . . Mr. Morris
Charles . . . . . . . . . . Mr. Wall
Sir Jealous Traffic . . . . . Mr. Douglass
Whisper . . . . . . . . . . Mr. Allyn
Butler . . . . . . . . . . . Mr. Greville
Isabinda . . . . . . . . . Miss Hallam
Patch . . . . . . . . . . Mrs. Harman
Scentwell . . . . . . . . Mrs. Tomlinson
Mirinda . . . . . . . . . . Miss Cheer

### DISTRESSED MOTHER.

Pyrrhus . . . . . . . . . Mr. Douglass
Orestes . . . . . . . . . . Mr. Hallam
Pylades . . . . . . . . . . Mr. Morris
Phœnix . . . . . . . . . Mr. Tomlinson
Hermione . . . . . . . . . Miss Cheer
Cephisa . . . . . . . . . . Miss Storer
Cleone . . . . . . . . . Miss Hallam
Andromache . . . . . . . Mrs. Harman

"Distressed Mother." This tragedy had been long laid aside by the American Company, and it was only revived on this occasion to allow Mrs. Harman to play *Andromache* for her benefit. The third of the Murray and Kean repertoire by alphabetical arrangement in the list of pieces this season was Rowe's "Fair Penitent." It was probably produced to give the amateur who played *Altamont* an opportunity to appear in New York. Still another piece from the same repertoire was Otway's

FAIR PENITENT.

| | |
|---|---|
| Altamont | A Gentleman |
| (Being his first appearance on this stage.) | |
| Lothario | Mr. Hallam |
| Horatio | Mr. Douglass |
| Sciolto | Mr. Henry |
| Rossano | Mr. Woolls |
| Lavinia | Mrs. Douglass |
| Lucilla | Miss F. Storer |
| Calista | Miss Cheer |

"Orphan." Miss Cheer probably desired its production in order to try her powers as *Monimia.* Then came Farquhar's "Recruiting Officer." Although this comedy is named in the Dunlap repertoire of the original Hallam Company there is no evidence that it was played, except by "the com-

ORPHAN.

| | |
|---|---|
| Chamont | Mr. Hallam |
| Castalio | Mr. Henry |
| Polydore | Mr. Wall |
| Acasto | Mr. Morris |
| Chaplain | Mr. Tomlinson |
| Ernesto | Mr. Allyn |
| Page | Miss M. Storer |
| Serina | Miss Storer |
| Florella | Mrs. Harman |
| Monimia | Miss Cheer |

RECRUITING OFFICER.

| | |
|---|---|
| Captain Plume | Mr. Hallam |
| Captain Brazen | Mr. Henry |
| Justice Balance | Mr. Morris |
| Sergeant Kite | Mr. Douglass |
| Worthy | Mr. Woolls |
| Bullock | Mr. Wall |
| Melinda | Miss Storer |
| Rose | Miss Wainwright |
| Lucy | Mrs. Harman |
| Sylvia | Miss Cheer |

pany of comedians from Philadelphia," until the arrival of Douglass in New York, in 1758. The first American cast on record is that of the theatre on Society Hill, Philadelphia, in 1759. The characters are drawn from life, *Captain Plume* being a portrait of the author; *Worthy* of a Mr. Owen, of Russason; *Justice Balance* of Mr. Berkely, Recorder of Shrewsbury; *Sylvia* of Mr. Berkely's daughter, and *Melinda* of a Miss Harnage, of Balsadine, near the Wrekin.

Two of Shakspere's tragedies seldom played by the American Company, "Othello" and the first part of "King Henry IV," were produced this season. The former was played by Upton in New York and the elder Hallam at Williamsburg as early as 1752. The earliest cast of it extant was that at Annapolis in 1760, when Palmer played *Iago* to Douglass' *Moor*. The latter was first played at the Chapel Street Theatre, New York, in 1761, with Mr. Douglass, as now, as the fat knight This is the first full cast of the tragedy that has been preserved.

KING HENRY IV.

| | |
|---|---|
| Sir John Falstaff | Mr. Douglass |
| Hotspur | Mr. Hallam |
| King Henry | Mr. Morris |
| Prince of Wales | Mr. Wall |
| Sir Walter Blunt | Mr. Henry |
| Worcester | Mr. Tomlinson |
| Sir Richard Vernon | Mr. Greville |
| Northumberland | Mr. Woolls |
| Westmoreland | Mr. Raworth |
| Poins | Mr. Malone |
| Peto | Mr. Roberts |
| Prince John | Mrs. Wall |
| Hostess | Mrs. Harman |
| Lady Percy | Miss Cheer |

OTHELLO.

| | |
|---|---|
| Othello | Mr. Douglass |
| Iago | Mr. Hallam |
| Cassio | Mr. Henry |
| Brabantio | Mr. Morris |
| Roderigo | Mr. Wall |
| Duke | Mr. Greville |
| Ludovico | Mr. Tomlinson |
| Montano | Mr. Malone |
| Emilia | Mrs. Harman |
| Desdemona | Miss Cheer |

Only one more full play, Hoadly's "Suspicious Husband," and one farce, Carey's "Honest Yorkshireman," remain to be noticed as not in the list of pieces played by the American Company in Philadelphia, but given in New York this season. No interest attaches to these casts except as part of the record. Hallam had a fondness for the roles that Garrick had made famous, which was probably the reason for the revival of the comedy, but on this occasion he played *Gaylove* in the farce as well as *Ranger* in the comedy.

SUSPICIOUS HUSBAND.

| | |
|---|---|
| Ranger | Mr. Hallam |
| Strictland | Mr. Douglass |
| Frankly | Mr. Wall |
| Jack Meggot | Mr. Allyn |
| Mrs. Strictland | Miss Storer |
| Clarinda | Miss Cheer |
| Jacintha | Miss F. Storer |
| Lucetta | Miss Wainwright |

HONEST YORKSHIREMAN.

| | |
|---|---|
| Gaylove | Mr. Hallam |
| Sapscull | Mr. Wall |
| Muckworm | Mr. Morris |
| Slango | Mr. Tomlinson |
| Blunder | Mr. Raworth |
| Arabella | Miss Hallam |
| Combrush | Miss Cheer |

Only three plays were presented in New York in 1767–8 that had been played in Philadelphia in 1766–7, without advertisement

BOLD STROKE FOR A WIFE.

Col. Feignwell . Mr. Hallam
Obadiah Prim . . Mr. Allyn
Sir Philip . . . Mr. Douglass
Tradelove . . . . Mr. Henry
Periwinkle . . . Mr. Morris
Freeman . . . . Mr. Wall
Simon Pure . . Mr. Woolls
Sacbut . . . Mr. Tomlinson
Mrs. Prim . Mrs. Douglass
Betty . . Miss Wainwright
Masked Lady . . Mrs. Wall
Ann Lovely . . Miss Cheer

of the casts in the newspapers. These were Mrs. Centlivre's two comedies, "A Bold Stroke for a Wife" and the "Wonder: A Woman Keeps a Secret," and Rowe's tragedy, "Jane Shore." Both of Mrs. Cent-

WONDER.

Don Felix . . Mr. Hallar
Colonel Blinker . Mr. W.
Gibby . . . Mr. Douglass
Don Lopez . . Mr. Morris
Don Pedro . Mr. Tomlinson
Lissardo . . . Mr. Greville
Frederick . . . Mr. Woolls
Isabella . . . Miss Hallam
Flora . . Miss Wainwright
Iris . . . . . Mrs. Harman
Violante . . . Miss Cheer

livre's comedies had held the stage over fifty years, the former being especially popular with American audiences, while in the latter many of the great lights of the English stage made reputation, from Wilks to Garrick as *Don Felix*, and from Mrs. Oldfield to Mrs. Abington as *Violante*. On the occasion of the production of the "Wonder" in New York, in 1768, the audience, however, was more noteworthy than the play. Toward the close of the year 1767 an Indian delegation visited New York.[1] It comprised the famous Attakullakulla, or the Little Carpenter; Onconostota, or the Great Warrior, and the Raven King of Toogoloo, with six other chiefs. They were Cherokees from South Carolina, who had come to see General Gage to ask his interposition

---

[1] PENNSYLVANIA GAZETTE'S REPORT. — New York, December 17. The expectation of seeing the Indian chiefs at the play on Monday night occasioned a great concourse of people. The house was crowded, and it is said great numbers were obliged to go away for want of room.

The Indians regarded the play, which was "King Richard III," with seriousness and attention, but, as it cannot be supposed that they were sufficiently acquainted with the language to understand the plot and design and enter into the spirit of the author, their countenances and behavior were rather expressive of surprise and curiosity than any other passions. Some of them were much surprised and diverted at the tricks of *Harlequin*.

in mediating a peace with the Six Nations. Hearing that there was a theatre in New York, they expressed a desire to see a play acted, whereupon the General caused places to be taken for them. This was the second time an Indian delegation was entertained with a theatrical representation, the first, as already mentioned, being at Williamsburg, Va., during the first season of the original Hallam Company. To meet the tastes of these untutored theatre-goers, a pantomime was substituted for the "Oracle," which had been announced as the afterpiece for the evening. The substitution was no doubt in consequence of Mr. Hallam's recollection of what pleased the savages at Williamsburg, in 1752. This performance took place on the 14th of December, 1767, and on the 8th of April following the Indians paid a second visit to the theatre. This was the night when Mrs. Centlivre's comedy, the "Wonder," was produced. The quaint language of the part of the bill relating to the entertainment of the Cherokees will be found the best possible description of the event. So strong was the reverence for royalty in those

EXTRACT FROM ADVERTISEMENT.

For the Entertainment of the Cherokee Chiefs and Warriors.

HARLEQUIN COLLECTOR;
Or,
The Miller Deceived.

Harlequin . . . . . . . . . Mr. Hallam
Clown . . . . . . . . . . Mr. Morris
Miller . . . . . . . . . . Mr. Tomlinson
Magician . . . . . . . . . Mr. Woolls
Baboon . . . . . . . . . . Mr. Wall
Anatomist . . . . . . . . Mr. Douglass
Porter . . . . . . . . . . Mr. Roberts
Haymakers by Mr. Henry, Mr. Malone, Mr. Greville, Mr. Raworth, Mr. Roberts, Miss Hallam, Miss Storer, Miss F. Storer, Miss Wainwright, Mrs. Harman, Mrs. Tomlinson, Mrs. Wall, etc.
Columbine . . . . . . . . Miss Cheer
*⁎* The Cherokee Chiefs and Warriors, being desirous of making some return for the friendly Reception and Civilities they have received in this city, have offered to entertain the Public with the
War Dance,
Which they will exhibit on the stage after the Pantomime.

☞ It is humbly presumed that no part of the audience will forget the proper Decorum so essential to all public Assemblies, particularly on this Occasion, as the Persons who have condescended to contribute to their entertainment are of Rank and Consequence in their own country.

days that even respect for rank and consequence in savages was insisted upon. The most interesting feature of the second entertainment, however, was that provided by the savages themselves, this being the first time an Indian war-dance was danced on any stage by native performers.

The tragedy of "Jane Shore" was evidently selected by Mrs. Douglass for her benefit to afford her an opportunity to repeat the title-role. It was only natural that the actress who had been the acknowledged star of the American stage from 1752 to 1766 should wish to put aside such subordinate roles as *Mrs. Heidelberg* and *Mrs. Wisely* to appear on her benefit night in one of the parts in which she had been a favorite, and this in itself will account for her re-appearance as the merriest and most unfortunate of the mistresses of Edward IV.

JANE SHORE.

| | |
|---|---|
| Hastings | Mr. Hallam |
| Gloster | Mr. Morris |
| Dumont | Mr. Wall |
| Belmour | Mr. Woolls |
| Jane Shore | Mrs. Douglass |
| Alicia | Miss Cheer |

Nothing relating to the early history of the American stage is more interesting than the farces presented from time to time by the American Company. In that age these delicious *morceaux* were as carefully cast as the full pieces, and so there was occasion to regret that Mr. Douglass refrained from advertising the performers in so many of them in his first season at the Southwark Theatre. In New York, however, he repaired this omis-

CITIZEN.

| | |
|---|---|
| Citizen | Mr. Wall |
| Young Wilding | Mr. Henry |
| Old Philpot | Mr. Douglass |
| Sir Jasper | Mr. Tomlinson |
| Beaufort | Mr. Woolls |
| Quilldrive | Mr. Malone |
| Dapper | Mr. Greville |
| Corunna | Mrs. Tomlinson |
| Maria | Miss Wainwright |

APPRENTICE.

| | |
|---|---|
| Dick | Mr. Wall |
| Wingate | Mr. Morris |
| Gargle | Mr. Henry |
| President | Mr. Woolls |
| Simon | Mr. Tomlinson |
| Charlotte | Miss Wainwright |

sion in a great degree. Arthur Murphy's farces were just coming into vogue, and we thus have the casts, slightly modified, of three of them, the "Apprentice," the "Citizen" and the "Upholsterer." The "Apprentice" was written in derision of the "spouting clubs" then so common in London and thence transplanted to the Colonies. The "Citizen" was originally produced as a comedy, making the reputation of a new London actress, Miss Elliot, as *Maria*, but it was printed as a farce, and it was as a farce that it was always played in this country. The young girl who escaped an unwelcome lover by passing herself on him for a fool must have afforded Miss Wainwright excellent scope for her talents. The "Upholsterer" was taken from *The Tattler*, Nos. 155, 160 and 178, and was first acted for Mr. Mossop's benefit at Drury Lane, in 1758. All the characters are *outre*, the old upholsterer, when he is declared bankrupt, showing no concern for himself or his family, but busying himself with schemes for the payment of the national debt. This farce, which was very funny, had great success both in England and America.

#### UPHOLSTERER.

| | |
|---|---|
| Upholsterer | Mr. Douglass |
| Barber | Mr. Wall |
| Pamphlet | Mr. Hallam |
| Bellman | Mr. Henry |
| Rovewell | Mr. Woolls |
| Feeble | Mr. Morris |
| Maria | Mrs. Wall |
| Termagant | Mrs. Harman |

The "Brave Irishman" was written by Thomas Sheridan, the father of Richard Brinsley Sheridan, when a mere boy at college. It was originally produced in Dublin. As Henry was an Irishman, and always took kindly to Irish parts, the coura-

#### BRAVE IRISHMAN.

| | |
|---|---|
| Capt. O'Blunder | Mr. Henry |
| Dr. Clyster | Mr. Hallam |
| Dr. Gallipot | Mr. Douglass |
| Cheatwell | Mr. Wall |
| Tradewell | Mr. Morris |
| Marquis | Mr. Roberts |
| Lucy | Miss Hallam |
| Betty | Miss Wainwright |

#### CONTRIVANCES.

| | |
|---|---|
| Rovewell | Mr. Woolls |
| Argus | Mr. Morris |
| Hearty | Mr. Allyn |
| Robin | Mr. Tomlinson |
| Betty | Mrs. Harman |
| Arethusa | Miss Wainwright |

geous but blundering Captain was just in his way.   Another interesting farce, of which we have this season the first American cast that was
preserved, was the " Contrivances," by Henry Carey, the author of " Sally
in our Alley."   A fact worth recalling in connection with this farce is
that *Arethusa* used to be the probationary part for female singers
before they were allowed to venture upon characters of more consequence.   But a still more interesting cast of this season was that of

the " King and the Miller of

Mansfield."   Dodsley's dramatic

tale, based on the well-known

story of Henry II and the miller,

had been played ever since the

dawn of the drama in this country,

MILLER OF MANSFIELD.

The King . . . . . . . . . . Mr. Henry
The Miller . . . . . . . . . . Mr. Hallam
Dick . . . . . . . . . . . . Mr. Morris
Lord Lovewell . . . . . . . . Mr. Wall
Joe . . . . . . . . . . . . . Mr. Woolls
Peggy . . . . . . . . . . . . Mrs. Wall
Kate . . . . . . . . . . . Mrs. Tomlinson
Margary . . . . . . . . . Mrs. Harman

but this is the first cast apparently ever printed in the newspapers.
It is noteworthy also that of the two men who played the *King* and
the *Miller*, the *King* was afterward to become the king of the American stage.

This season also gave us the first casts by the American Company, since its reorganization in 1766, of two familiar farces, Garrick's

LYING VALET.

Lying Valet . . Mr. Hallam
Beau Trippet . Mr. Greville
Gayless . . . . . Mr. Wall
Drunken Cook . Mr. Morris
Justice Guttle . Mr.Tomlinson
Melissa . . . Mrs. Harman
Kitty Pry . Miss Wainwright

" Lying Valet " and
Cibber's " Hob in the
Well."   These are
only introduced as
part of the record

HOB IN THE WELL.

Hob . . . . . . Mr. Allyn
Friendly . . . . Mr.Woolls
Hob's Mother . Mrs. Harman
Flora . . . . Miss Hallam

which it is the aim of this
work to preserve with as much completeness
as possible.   Hallam it will be noticed played *Sharp* in Garrick's farce.

An interesting study of the methods and conditions of theatrical management in America in the earlier years of the old Ameri

can Company is afforded by the indented table, showing the modifications the Philadelphia casts of 1766–7 underwent in New York in 1767–8. It will be observed, first of all, that Mr. Henry only succeeded to the roles of the actors of inferior position, as Broadbelt, Wall and Allyn. Mr. Hallam's name appears in this list only once, because he had already possessed himself of all the best roles, except *Lovegold* in the "Miser," which he now added to his own repertoire. Miss Cheer's name occurs only four times, once because it had not been printed, probably by mistake, in the Philadelphia ad-

CONTRASTED CASTS.

| PLAYS. | NEW YORK. | PHILADELPHIA. |
|---|---|---|
| *All for Love.* | | |
| Octavia | Miss Storer | Mrs. Douglass |
| *Beaux' Stratagem.* | | |
| Aimwell | Mr. Henry | Mr. Douglass |
| Sullen | Mr. Tomlinson | Mr. Wall |
| Sir Charles | Mr. Malone | Mr. Greville |
| Boniface | Mr. Douglass | Mr. Tomlinson |
| Scrub | Mr. Wall | Mr. Morris |
| *Cato.* | | |
| Portius | Mr. Henry | A Gentleman |
| Syphax | Mr. Morris | Mr. Allyn |
| Marcus | Mr. Greville | Mr. Godwin |
| Lucia | Miss Hallam | Mrs. Harman |
| *Clandestine Marriage.* | | |
| Trusty | Mrs. Tomlinson | Mrs. Morris |
| *Committee.* | | |
| Teague | Mr. Henry | Mr. Allyn |
| Mr. Day | Mr. Morris | |
| Obadiah | Mr. Tomlinson | |
| *Conscious Lovers.* | | |
| Sir John Bevil | Mr. Henry | Mr. Broadbelt |
| Cymberton | Mr. Greville | Mr. Allyn |
| Daniel | Mr. Roberts | Mr. Godwin |
| Isabella | Miss Storer | Mrs. Douglass |
| *Constant Couple.* | | |
| Beau Clincher | Mr. Henry | Mr. Allyn |
| Tom Errand | Mr. Greville | |
| Parly | Miss F. Storer | Miss Wainwright. |
| *Country Lasses.* | | |
| Sir John English | Mr. Tomlinson | Mr. Allyn |
| Carbuncle | Mr. Henry | Mr. Broadbelt |
| Shacklefigure | Mr. Roberts | Mr. Platt |
| *Cymbeline.* | | |
| Bellarius | Mr. Henry | Mrs. Morris |
| Pissanio | Mr. Morris | Mrs. Harman |
| *Earl of Essex.* | | |
| Countess of Nottingham | Miss Storer | Miss Hallam |

vertisement of the "Orphan of China," and once because she had turned over the part of *Kitty* in "High Life Below Stairs" to Miss Storer, *Mrs. Sneak* in the "Mayor of Garratt" to Miss Wainwright, and *Dorcas* in "Thomas and Sally" to Mrs. Harman. It will be seen also that, as Mrs. Douglass had previously yielded up her great roles to Miss Cheer, so now she gave up many of her smaller parts to Miss Storer. The minor changes in these casts are only important in showing the ease with which small

*Gamester.*

| | | |
|---|---|---|
| Charlotte | Miss Hallam | Mrs. Harman |

*Hamlet.*

| | | |
|---|---|---|
| Horatio | Mr. Henry | A Gentleman |
| Osric | Mr. Roberts | Mr. Godwin |
| Marcellus | Mr. Greville | |
| Player King | Mr. Malone | Mr. Allyn |
| Queen | Mrs. Harman | Mrs. Douglass |
| Player Queen | Miss Storer | Mrs. Harman |

*King Lear.*

| | | |
|---|---|---|
| Edmund | Mr. Henry | Mr. Wall |
| Kent | A Gentleman | Mr. Morris |
| Albany | Mr. Allyn | Mr. Wall |
| Usher | Mr. Wall | Mr. Godwin |
| Regan | Miss Storer | Mrs. Harman |

*Love in a Village.*

| | | |
|---|---|---|
| Eustace | Mr. Henry | Mr. Allyn |

*Macbeth.*

| | | |
|---|---|---|
| Duncan | Mr. Greville | Mr. Allyn |
| Malcolm | Mr. Henry | Mr. Godwin |
| Donaldbain | Mr. Malone | Mr. Platt |
| Fleance | Miss M. Storer | Miss Dowthwaite |
| Hecate | Mr. Woolls | Mrs. Harman |

*Merchant of Venice.*

| | | |
|---|---|---|
| Salarino | Mr. Malone | Mr. Matthews |
| Gobbo | Mr. Raworth | |
| Tubal | Mr. Henry | |

*Miser.*

| | | |
|---|---|---|
| Lovegold | Mr. Hallam | Mr. Allyn |
| Ramillie | Mr. Morris | Mr. Hallam |
| Decoy. | Mr. Raworth | Mr. Morris |
| List | Mr. Henry | |
| Furnish | Mr. Malone | Mr. Platt |
| Charles | Mr. Roberts | Mr. Godwin |
| Mrs. Wisely | Mrs. Douglass | Mrs. Douglass Mrs. Tomlinson |

*Orphan of China.*

| | | |
|---|---|---|
| Timurkan | Mr. Henry | Mr. Allyn |
| Octar | Mr. Greville | Mr. Tomlinson |
| Morat | Mr. Tomlinson | |
| Mandare | Miss Cheer | |

*Provoked Husband.*

| | | |
|---|---|---|
| Squire Richard | Mr. Woolls | Mr. Allyn |
| Lady Grace | Mrs. Harman | Mrs. Douglass |

| | | |
|---|---|---|
| Lady Wronghead . . | Miss Wainwright. | Mrs. Harman . . |
| Mrs. Motherly . . . | Mrs. Tomlinson . | Miss Wainwright. |

*Richard III.*

| | | |
|---|---|---|
| Richmond . . . . . | Mr. Henry . . . | Mr. Douglass . . |
| Buckingham . . . . | Mr. Douglass . . | Mr. Wall . . . . |
| Prince of Wales . | Mr. Wall . . . . | Mr. Godwin . . |

*Romeo and Juliet.*

| | | |
|---|---|---|
| Escalus . . . . . . | Mr. Malone . . | Mr. Broadbelt . |
| Friar Laurence . . . | Mr. Greville . . | Mr. Allyn . . . |
| Benvolio . . . . . . | Mr. Wall . . . | Mr. Godwin . . |
| Tybalt . . . . . . . | Mr. Henry . . . | Mr. Wall . . . |
| Friar John . . . . . | Mr. Roberts . . | Mr. Platt . . . . |
| Lady Capulet . . . . | Miss Storer . . . | Mrs. Douglass . |

*School for Lovers.*

| | |
|---|---|
| Steward . . . . . . | Mr. Tomlinson . |

### FARCES.

*Catherine and Petruchio.*

| | | |
|---|---|---|
| Music Master . . . . | Mr. Raworth . . | Mr. Allyn . . . |
| Tailor . . . . . . { | Mr. Henry . . . <br> Mr. Malone . . | Mr. Henry . . . |
| Bianca . . . . . . . | Miss Storer . . . | Mrs. Wall . . . |

*Devil to Pay.*

| | | |
|---|---|---|
| Nell . . . . . . . | Miss Wainwright. | Mrs. Morris . . |

*High Life Below Stairs.*

| | | |
|---|---|---|
| Sir Harry . . . . . | Mr. Henry . . . | Mr. Allyn . . . |
| Tom . . . . . . . . | Mr. Malone . . | Mr. Tomlinson . |
| Kingston . . . . . . | Mr. Tomlinson . | Mr. Matthews . |
| Robert . . . . . . | Mr. Greville . . | |
| Lady Charlotte . . . | Miss F. Storer . | Miss Wainwright. |
| Cloe . . . . . . . | Mr. Roberts . . | Mr. Platt . . . . |
| Kitty . . . . . . . | Miss Storer . . . | Miss Cheer . . . |

*Lethe.*

| | | |
|---|---|---|
| Tattoo . . . . . . . | Mr. Malone . . | |
| Mrs. Tattoo . . . . | Miss Hallam . . | Mrs. Harman . . |
| Mrs. Riot . . . . . | Miss Wainwright. | |

*Mayor of Garratt.*

| | | |
|---|---|---|
| Crispin Heel-tap . . | Mr. Henry . . . | Mr. Morris . . . |
| Roger . . . . . . . | Mr. Malone . . | Mr. Godwin . . |
| Snuffle . . . . . . | Mr Roberts . . | Mr. Platt . . . . |
| Mrs. Sneak . . . . . | Miss Wainwright. | Miss Cheer . . . |

*Miss in her Teens.*

| | | |
|---|---|---|
| Fribble . . . . . . | Miss M. Storer . | Mr. Allyn . . . |
| Flash . . . . . . . | Miss F. Storer . | Mr. Hallam . . |
| Miss Biddy . . . . | Miss Hallam . . | Miss Storer . . . |

parts were filled at a time when actors can not be supposed to have been numerous in the Colonies. The cast of "Miss in her Teens," for Mrs. Douglass' benefit, was an exceptional one for that time, the younger Storer sisters playing *Flash* and *Fribble.* Maria, the Mrs. Henry of a later period, made her first appearance in New York on the 7th of January, 1768, as a singer, between the play and the farce of the evening. Fanny, afterward Mrs. Mechler, remained on the stage for a comparatively brief period and was the least distinguished of the sisters. It may be well to add that all the parts omitted in this

*Neck or Nothing.*

| Sir William | . . . . | Mr. Henry . . . | Mr. Allyn . . . |
| Jenny | . . . . . . . | Miss Storer. . . | Miss Wainwright. |

*Old Maid.*

| Clerimont | . . . . . | Mr. Wall . . . | Mr. Hallam . . |

*Thomas and Sally.*

| Dorcas | . . . . . . . | Mrs. Harman . | Miss Cheer . . . |

*Witches.*

| Monsieur | . . . . . | Mr. Roberts . . | |

table were played in New York by the same actors and actresses by whom they had previously been performed in Philadelphia. A reference to the Southwark Theatre performances will in all cases give the New York casts.

The incidents of the season were not numerous, but some of the advertisements afford quaint glimpses of the company and the theatrical customs of the time. Early in the season the bills contained directions for carriages approaching and leaving the theatre, which in themselves suggest not only the interest that the wealth

REGULATIONS FOR CARRIAGES.

———

*⁎* To prevent accidents by carriages meeting it is requested that those coming to the House may enter John-street from the Broadway, and returning drive from thence down John-street into Nassau-street or forwards to that known as Cart and Horse street, as may be most convenient.

and fashion of New York felt in the play-house, but the manner in which the rich Knickerbockers went to the play. Another advertisement shows that printed plays, not even Shakspere's, were common at that period, for when "Macbeth" was produced, on the 3d of March, Hugh Gaine announced that copies of the tragedy might be had at the Bible and Crown, in Hanover Square. Generally the benefit bills were the most interesting. One or two of those of this season were particularly so. Mr. Hallam, for instance, boldly announced that as his benefit had not been up to his expectations, and as the rules of the theatre made it undesirable that he should take a second night, he had arranged with Mr. Woolls to have his night in return for the profits of "Cymbeline." Miss Hallam, too, met with a misfortune

MISS HALLAM'S CHANGE OF BILL.

*⁎* As the "Clandestine Marriage," which Miss Hallam designed for her benefit, can not be performed on account of Miss Cheer's indisposition, she flatters herself the Ladies and Gentlemen who intended to honor her with their countenance and interest will not let an unavoidable accident deprive her of their appearance in her favor, and that they will be kind enough to approve of her choice of "Love in a Village," as it is the only piece of any merit in which Miss Cheer does not appear.

that is apt to befall aspiring actresses with pretensions to the lead—the leading lady was ill. This announcement of the change of bill can only mean that Miss Cheer, notwithstanding her illness, would not allow Miss Hallam to assume any of her parts, thus imposing upon the beneficiary the necessity of substituting a piece in which the leading lady did not appear, for the comedy originally chosen for Miss Hallam's benefit. Mr. Wall, too, had his woes and consequent wail. One can not help wondering whether a report was really "propagated with intent to injure him," or whether this was a device on his part to fill the treasury with sympathetic coin of the realm — Boxes, 8 shillings;

MR. WALL'S WAIL.

☞ It having been reported about town that Mr. Wall intends to postpone his benefit of this evening, he takes this method to inform the public that such report is false and malicious and propagated with intent to injure him, being resolved not to defer it on any consideration whatever.

Pit, 5 shillings; Gallery, 3 shillings—tickets "to be had ot Mr. Wall at Mrs. Sproul's in De Peyster's Street near the Fly Market." After the regular season closed the famous "Lecture on Heads" was given, August 22d, by Messrs. Douglass and Hallam, supplemented by the singing of Miss Hallam.

The first secession among the members of Mr. Douglass' original company, who returned with him in 1766, was in the retirement of Mr. and Mrs. Allyn this season. Mr. Allyn was an actor who was ready to play anything at any time, as will be seen from the diverse characters in the list of his parts. Mrs. Allyn probably was not an actress at all, and it is likely she played the two roles credited to her because there was no one else at hand to play them. As to the causes of Allyn's retirement history is silent. All we know of him is his work as an actor, but of its quality we have no knowledge. Mr. Allyn must not be confounded with Mr. Allen, who came to America immediately before and was seen on the stage in this country immediately after the Revolution. The latter was the father of the self-styled Andrew Jackson Allen. An interesting fact in relation to Mr. Allyn was that he was the original in this country of *Lord Chalkstone* in " Lethe," after Garrick introduced the character into the farce. It is not improbable that Allyn was seen to best advantage in such roles, but as the *Miser* and *Iago* he must have been absurdly inadequate. It is evident, how-

MR. ALLYN'S PARTS.

*Plays.*

| | |
|---|---|
| A Bold Stroke for a Wife | . . Obadiah Prim |
| Beaux' Stratagem | . . . . . . . Foigard |
| Beggars' Opera . . . . | { Peachum / Jemmy Twitcher |
| Busybody | . . . . . . . . . . . Whisper |
| Cato | . . . . . . . . . . . . . Syphax |
| Clandestine Marriage | . . . . . . . Canton |
| Committee | . . . . . . . . . . . Teague |
| Conscious Lovers | . . . . . . . Cymberton |
| Constant Couple | . . . . . . Beau Clincher |
| Country Lasses | . . . . . Sir John English |
| Cymbeline | . . . . . . . . . . Cymbeline |
| Don Quixote in England | . . . . . . John |
| Drummer | { Vellum / Gardener |
| Fair Penitent | . . . . . . . . . Sciolto |
| Gamester | . . . . . . . . . . Dawson |
| George Barnwell | . . . . . . . . . Uncle |
| Hamlet | { Laertes / Player King / Gravedigger |
| Inconstant | . . . . . . . . First Bravo |
| Jealous Wife | { Sir Harry Beagle / Capt. O'Cutter |
| Lear | { Albany / Usher |
| Love for Love | . . . . . . . . Scandal |
| Love in a Village | . . . . . . . Eustace |
| Love Makes a Man | . . . . . . Antonio |
| Macbeth | { Duncan / Witch |
| Merchant of Venice | . . . . . . Gratiano |
| Miser | . . . . . . . . . . . Lovegold |
| Mourning Bride | . . . . . . . . . Perez |
| Orphan | . . . . . . . . . . . Ernesto |
| Orphan of China | . . . . . . Timurkan |
| Othello | . . . . . . . . . . . . Iago |
| Prince of Parthia | . . . . . Barzaphernes |
| Provoked Husband | . . . . Squire Richard |
| Recruiting Officer | . . . . . . Constable |
| Richard III | { Henry VI / Stanley |

Roman Father . . . . . . Tullus Hostilius
Romeo and Juliet . . . . { Apothecary / Friar Laurence
Suspicious Husband . . . . . Jack Meggot
Tamerlane . . . . . . . . . . Prince
Theodosius . . . . . . . . . { Varanes / Leontine
Venice Preserved . . . . . . . . Officer

*Farces.*

Catherine and Petruchio . . . Music Master
Contrivances . . . . . . . . . Hearty
Damon and Phillida . . . . . . . Arcas
Devil to Pay . . . . . . . . . Coachman
Harlequin Collector . . . . . . . Miller
Harlequin Restored . . . . . Petit Maitre
High Life Below Stairs . . . . . Sir Harry
Hob in the Well . . . . . . . . . Hob
Honest Yorkshireman . . . . . . Blunder
Lethe . . . . . . . . { Lord Chalkstone / Frenchman
Mayor of Garratt . . . . . Fourth Mob
Miss in her Teens . . . . . . . Fribble
Mock Doctor . . . . . . { Mock Doctor / Davy
Neck or Nothing . . . . . . Sir William
Old Maid . . . : . . . . . Mr. Harlow
Reprisal . . . . . . . M. Champignon
Spirit of Contradiction . . . . . . Ruin
Witches . . . . . . . . . Petit Maitre

MRS. ALLYN'S PARTS.

Romeo and Juliet . . . . . Lady Capulet
Theodosius . . . . . . . . . . Flavilla

ever, that he was useful because of his versatility, whatever his talents, and he is to be remembered by posterity as one of the most active of the pioneers of the drama in America. It is a noteworthy fact that Mr. Allyn's best roles were accorded him while Mr. Douglass' company was in Rhode Island, in 1761–2, his position in the stronger American Company of 1766–8 being a subordinate one. It is not impossible that he left the stage because of a want of managerial appreciation.

Early in this season the first recorded death occurred among the players of the American Company. It was that of Mrs. Morris,[1] who was drowned in crossing the ferry from Kill von Kull to New York, together with her maid servant. In a book entitled "Retrospections of America," published in 1887, but purporting to be compiled from the diary of John Bernard, an English comedian, who came to America

[1] DROWNING OF MRS. MORRIS.—(New York *Mercury*, December 14th, 1767.)—We hear that last week one of the stage-wagons, crossing the ferry at Kill von Kull in a scow, some of the passengers seated themselves in the wagon, but in approaching the shore the wagon was by some means overturned into the river, by which two women (Mrs. Morris, belonging to the play-house, and her maid) were drowned.

in 1797, and knew Mr. Morris in the closing years of his life, the statement is made that Morris told the story of his wife's death while crossing the Delaware with Bernard as occurring on that river. The statement is quoted here only to contrast an old man's recollections with the contemporary report of the accident. Mrs. Morris made her first appearance in this country at Annapolis, in 1760, as one of the *Conspirators* in "Venice Preserved," and her last part was *Trusty* in the "Provoked Husband," at the Southwark Theatre, November 19th, 1767. In the meantime, however, she had played some important roles, and in 1761 and 1762 she shared the lead with Mrs. Douglass in Rhode Island and New York. After Miss Cheer joined the company, in 1766, Mrs. Morris seldom appeared, and then apparently only to oblige the management.

Mrs. Morris' death was not the only fatal accident that marked the history of the John Street

MRS. MORRIS' PARTS.

*Plays.*

| | |
|---|---|
| A Bold Stroke for a Wife | Mrs. Prim |
| Beggars' Opera | Lucy |
| Cato | Lucia |
| Distressed Mother | Hermione |
| Don Quixote in England | Jezebel |
| Douglas | Anna |
| Fair Penitent | Lavinia |
| George Barnwell | Maria |
| Hamlet | Ophelia |
| Othello | Desdemona |
| Provoked Husband | Trusty |
| Richard III | Lady Anne |
| Romeo and Juliet | Nurse |
| Theodosius | Pulcheria |
| Venice Preserved | Conspirator |

*Farces.*

| | |
|---|---|
| Devil to Pay | Nell |
| Honest Yorkshireman | Arabella |
| Mock Doctor | Dorcas |
| Old Maid | Trifle |
| Spirit of Contradiction | Betty |
| Virgin Unmasked | Lucy |

Theatre in the month of December, 1767. On Monday, the 28th of December, John Abraham, a carpenter, went on the roof of the shed over the dressing-room to hang a window, when his foot slipped and he fell about twenty-eight feet into the yard. He was so terribly bruised that he died on the following Sunday. Because Hallam and

Henry, after the Revolution, built dressing-rooms and a green-room on the west side of the theatre, Dunlap assumes that previously they had been under the stage. The report of the accident by which the carpenter lost his life, in the newspapers of the beginning of January, 1768, shows that, as usual, his assumption was unfounded.

Mr. Greville left the company at this time. His history is in his parts.

A most determined attack was made upon the theatre this season, especially in the columns of Holt's *New York Journal.* On the 8th of January "Philander" wrote, saying: "The erecting of a play-house in this city has been and still is a matter of uneasiness to a very great part of the inhabitants," and hoping that those who were thus affected toward it would show their disapprobation by staying away. "Philander" kept up his assaults, and the following week he declared that he had confidence in the good wishes and endeavors of the opponents of the drama "for rendering the play-house in the city of New York a useless fabric, by letting it remain a monument of the rashness and folly of

MR. GREVILLE'S PARTS.

*Plays.*

| | |
|---|---|
| Beaux' Stratagem | Freeman |
| Busybody | Butler |
| Cato | Marcus |
| Clandestine Marriage | Truman |
| Conscious Lovers | Cymberton |
| Constant Couple | Tom Errand |
| Country Lasses | Longbottom |
| Cymbeline | Guiderius |
| Don Quixote in England | Fairlove |
| Drummer | Coachman |
| Hamlet | Marcellus |
| Henry IV | Sir Richard Vernon |
| Inconstant | Fourth Bravo |
| Lear | Cornwall |
| Love for Love | Buckram |
| Love Makes a Man | Governor |
| Macbeth | Duncan |
| Mourning Bride | Alonzo |
| Orphan of China | Orasming / Octar |
| Othello | Duke |
| Prince of Parthia | Phraates |
| Roman Father | Second Citizen |
| Romeo and Juliet | Balthazar / Friar Laurence |
| Venice Preserved | Eliot |
| Wonder | Lissardo |

*Farces.*

| | |
|---|---|
| Citizen | Dapper |
| High Life Below Stairs | Robert |
| Lying Valet | Beau Trippet |
| Reprisal | Heartly |

those who erected it against the general opinion and sentiments of the people."

A friend of the theatre, who signed himself "Dramaticus," undertook to defend the stage in Parker's *Gazette*, in reply to "Philander." Because this defender did not persist in the controversy he was assailed in the *Journal* in a communication that was only remarkable for its peculiar and flaming heading. Not only was a funeral eulogium pronounced upon young "Dramaticus," but the muse was invoked to sing his elegy. The eulogium was too dull to be preserved, and the elegy is only worthy of preservation because of its rancor and bitterness toward the stage and its defenders.

A
Funeral Eulogium
on
The Death of
DRAMATICUS,
Who departed this life in January, 1768,
Ætatis Suæ, 22.
By a friend of the Deceased.
Calcanda semel via lete—nec viteri mortem posse, nec retardari. HORACE.
We must all tread the valleys of the dead— we can neither escape *death* nor retard it.
TOWERS.

This was signed "T," to whom the editor apologized for omitting the lines indicated by asterisks, but he thought the charge beginning "Ye gentle nymphs" too general, as, in justice to the ladies, it must be acknowledged that a great number of them refrained from going to the playhouse on principle. Thereupon "Belinda" took up the pen to say that she was "one of those females" who were

ELEGY.
———

Ye daring witlings that infest this town,
Reflect upon the horrid deed you've done;
He's dead! he's dead! Dramaticus is dead!
From his pale cheek the rosy hue is fled;
His eyes are closed that sparkl'd once with fire;
His tongue is silent—that could mirth inspire,
Charm every ear—and in his comic vein
*    *    *    *    *    *    *
But now, behold, his death the gay deplore,
Absorbed in grief his corse stand weeping o'er;
Each gentle nymph gives vent to mournful sighs,
While pearly tears o'erflow the pitying eyes;
So great their sorrow at this fatal shock!
*    *    *    *    *    *    *    *

In sober sadness, beaus inclined the head,
And this their cry, Dramaticus is dead!
He's dead! alas! how awful is the sound!
Ye guilty wretches say, Who gave the wound?
To you, Philander, we his fall ascribe,
And your inhuman, wrong-head, scribbling tribe.
But if resentment can avenge his death,
Oh, tremble at each fop's and female's breath!
How much I pity and lament his fate,
In strains elegiac shall the muse relate;
While cypress wreaths around our brows shall twine
As wanton tendrils clasp the clust'ring vine.
And for his tomb these verses I'll compose,
To brand the name of his malignant foes:

Here lies a youth that once each grace adorn'd,
Belov'd by all but bigots, whom he scorn'd;
And who blind superstition did engage
With labor'd dullness and unmanly rage
To murder the great patron of the stage.

not ashamed to say they were enemies of the theatre.

A correspondent, signing his communication " R. S.," wrote on the 28th that he had not thought of troubling the public on the subject of the play-house, as he never imagined it could be so long supported against the wishes and inclinations of the most sober and respectable inhabitants. He computed the weekly receipts at £300, which he of course looked upon as a tax upon the community. The opposition was based upon both moral and economic grounds, and it was so bitter that, according to " Thrifty," whose letter was dated the 21st of January, some poor debtors, who were seen at the play, were sued by their creditors in consequence and sent to jail.

Notwithstanding the reputed tax of £300 a week upon the poor New Yorkers for tickets to the theatre, the management was so seriously embarrassed that it was proposed to keep the company together by selling thirty boxes in advance for the next season. This led " Democritus " to suggest the raising of a fund of £3,000 for the actors, in consideration of which they were to sink into non-existence as a company. He thought that as the money would be lost if they came back, it was better to pay them for not coming back.

# CHAPTER XXI.

---

## THE NEW VIRGINIA COMPANY.

A SEASON AT NORFOLK AND WILLIAMSBURG—THE COMPANY AND THE PLAYS—CASTS FROM THE VIRGINIA GAZETTE—AN ATTEMPT TO COMPETE WITH MR. DOUGLASS' AMERICAN COMPANY.

WHILE the American Company was performing in New York, in the season of 1767–8, the good people of Norfolk and Williamsburg were entertained by a number of players who styled themselves the "Virginia Company of Comedians." With one or two exceptions none of them had ever been heard of before, as they were destined never to be heard of afterward. The only knowledge we have of the Norfolk season is an allusion in the *Virginia Gazette* of February 4th, 1768, to a prologue spoken by Mrs. Osborne on the 19th of January, her benefit night. Mrs. Osborne was the leading lady, and she may have been identical with Miss Osborne who played in New York with Murray and Kean in 1750–51. This is not clear, but the fact that there was no Mr. Osborne in the company suggests the adoption of the maturer title, as was customary at that time.

The season at Williamsburg began on the 4th of April, 1768, and lasted until June. The record is far from being complete, but as it stands it will afford a fair idea of the material composing the Virginia Company of Comedians, and the scope and character of their work. The titles of only six plays and as many farces have come down to us as the list of performances of the season, but these comprise in the full pieces tragedy, comedy and musical comedy. The repertoire of the Virginia Company of Comedians, so far as it is known, is surprisingly similar to that of the American Company, even down to the pantomime, "Harlequin Skeleton." From all this it is evident that the manager in his selection of plays took a leaf from Mr. Douglass' book.

LIST OF PERFORMANCES.

1768.

April 4—Douglas . . . . . . . . Home
Honest Yorkshireman . . Carey
6—Drummer . . . . . . Addison
Miss in her Teens . . . Garrick
8—Venice Preserved . . . . Otway
Damon and Phillida . . . Cibber
5—Orphan . . . . . . . Otway
Harlequin Skeleton.
May 18—Constant Couple . . . Farquhar
Miller of Mansfield . . Dodsley
(Mrs. Osborne's Benefit.)
June 3—Beggars' Opera . . . . . . Gay
Anatomist . . . . . . Ravenscroft
(Mrs. Parker's Benefit.)

There was no announcement of the opening bill, but on the date of the initial performance the *Virginia Gazette* printed a full advertisement of the entertainment for the following Monday. We find from the casts contained in this announcement that Mr. Godwin, who was a member of the American Company at the Southwark Theatre in Philadelphia, in 1766–7, was now one of the Virginia Comedians, playing a better line of parts than had been accorded him by Mr. Douglass. Playing "old men" was Mr. Parker, who

A SPECIMEN BILL.

By permission of the Worshipful the Mayor of Williamsburg,
At the Old Theatre, near the Capitol
By the Virginia Company of Comedians,
On Monday the 4th of April will be presented a Tragedy called

DOUGLAS.

Lord Randolph . . . . . . Mr. Bromadge
Glenalvon . . . . . . . . . Mr. Godwin
Norval Douglas . . . . . . . Mr. Verling
Old Norval . . . . . . . . . Mr. Parker
Officer . . . . . . . . . . . Mr. Walker
Lady Randolph . . . . . . Mrs. Osborne
Anna . . . . . . . . . . . Mrs. Parker

An occasional Prologue by Mr. Verling, and after the Play a Dance by Mr. Godwin, To which will be added a Farce, called

was in Philadelphia with the American Company the next winter, where he was advertised as from the theatre in Jamaica. Mrs. Parker was the soubrette and leading singer. Of Mr. Verling, who played the juvenile, and Mr. Bromadge, who had the heavy lead, there are no previous accounts, but Mrs. Osborne's name has a familiar sound. Other names

### THE HONEST YORKSHIREMAN.

| | |
|---|---|
| Sir Penurious Muckworm | Mr. Bromadge |
| Gaylove | Mr. Verling |
| Sapscull | Mr. Parker |
| Slango | Mr. Godwin |
| Blunder | Mr. Walker |
| Arabella | Mrs. Osborne |
| Combrush | Mrs. Parker |

Tickets to be had of Mr. William Russell, at his store next door to the Post Office, and at the door of the Theatre.

Boxes 7s. 6d., Pit 5s., Gallery 3s. 9d.

*Vivant Rex & Regina.*

N.B.—No person whatever can be admitted behind the Scenes.

[On *Wednesday* the *Drummer*, with *Miss in her Teens.*]

occur in the later casts, so that the company seems to have been as fully organized, so far as numbers go, as that which it attempted to rival. William Russell was the publisher of the *Virginia Gazette*.

The second bill printed in the *Virginia Gazette* comprised "Venice Preserved," in which Mr. Godwin had the important part of *Jaffier*, and "Damon and Phillida," with the *Belvidera* of the evening as *Damon* and Mrs. Parker as *Phillida*.

### VENICE PRESERVED.

| | |
|---|---|
| Duke | Mr. Charlton |
| Priuli | Mr. Bromadge |
| Jaffier | Mr. Godwin |
| Pierre | Mr. Verling |
| Bedamer | Mr. Bromadge |
| Renault | Mr. Parker |
| Eliot | Mr. Walker |
| Belvidera | Mrs. Osborne |

### DAMON AND PHILLIDA.

| | |
|---|---|
| Arcas | Mr. Bromadge |
| Corydon | Mr. Godwin |
| Damon | Mrs. Osborne |
| Cymon | Mr. Parker |
| Mopsus | Mr. Verling |
| Phillida | Mrs. Parker |

It is only necessary to contrast the parts played by Messrs. Verling and Bromadge and Mrs. Osborne with those of Godwin and the Parkers to reach the conclusion that the company was composed of professional players. It would be interesting to compare the *Belvidera* of Mrs. Osborne, fond of coat and trousers as she was, with that of Miss Cheer, but not a line of criticism relating to either exists.

In the third bill that has come down to us, which comprised Otway's " Orphan," besides a dance called the " Bedlamites," and the pantomime, " Harlequin Skeleton," there are two names made familiar by the casts of the American Company in Philadelphia — those of Mrs. and Miss Dowthwaite. As in Philadelphia their parts at Williamsburg were unimportant, the chief interest of their presence with the Virginia Company being the tenacity with which they clung to the stage under the discouraging conditions of that time.

ORPHAN.

Acasto . . . . . . . . . . Mr. Bromadge
Castalio . . . . . . . . . . Mr. Verling
Polydore . . . . . . . . . . Mr. Parker
Chamont . . . . . . . . . . Mr. Godwin
Chaplain . . . . . . . . . Mr. Charlton
Ernesto . . . . . . . . . . Mr. Walker
Page . . . . . . . . . Miss Dowthwaite
Monimia . . . . . . . . . Mrs. Osborne
Serina . . . . . . . . . . . Mrs. Parker
Maid . . . . . . . . . Mrs. Dowthwaite

Mr. Godwin, in recompense perhaps for his increased importance as an actor, made himself exceedingly useful as a dancer, appearing between the play and the farce almost nightly, sometimes in a very elaborate terpsichorean production, as the "Bedlamites." In pantomime he was the *Harlequin*, showing a disposition on his part to rival Mr. Hallam in versatility, if not in talent.

HARLEQUIN SKELETON.

Harlequin . . Mr. Godwin
Pantaloon . . . Mr. Verling
Conjuror . . Mr. Bromadge
Merchant . . . Mr. Walker
Frenchman . . Mr. Charlton
Clown . . . . Mr. Parker
Scaramouch . . Mr. Walker
Columbine . . Mrs. Parker

BEDLAMITES.

Bedlamite . . Mr. Godwin
Mad Doctor . Mr. Charlton
Simon . . . . Mr. Walker

At the time of these performances Williamsburg society was very gay, as was shown by the fact that Peyton Randolph, who became the first President of Congress, a few months later gave a dinner that was the talk of the whole Province. If the players had the favor of this society their lives were cast in pleasant places.

Only two benefits were advertised this season, those of Mrs.

Osborne and Mrs. Parker. The former chose for her bill Farquhar's comedy, the "Constant Couple," and the familiar farce, "Miller of Mansfield." Mrs. Osborne's evident fondness for gay and dashing male roles, she manifested on this occasion by playing *Sir Harry* in the comedy and appearing as one of the *Courtiers* in the farce. In the fifth act of the play she danced a minuet in character with Miss Yapp. Between the first and second acts Mr. Parker recited a prologue in the character of a *Country Boy;* after the second act Godwin, Bromadge and others gave a dance called the "Coopers," and after the third act Mrs. Parker sang a cantata. Mrs. Parker for her benefit manifested an economical spirit, refraining from printing the casts either of the opera or the farce. It may be assumed, however, that she was the *Polly* of the evening, and it is not improbable that Mrs. Osborne played *Captain Macheath.*

It is clear that it was the Virginia Company of Comedians of 1768 and their advertisements in the *Virginia Gazette* that suggested to John Esten Cooke the theatrical atmosphere and local color of his novel, "The Virginia

CONSTANT COUPLE.

Sir Harry Wildair . Mrs. Osborne
Colonel Standard . Mr. Charlton
Wizard . . . . Mr. Bromadge
Alderman Smuggler . Mr. Parker
Beau Clincher . . Mr. Verling
Clincher, junior . . Mr. Godwin
Dicky . . . . . Mr. Farrell
Tom Errand . . . Mr. Walker
Lady Darling . Mrs. Dowthwaite
Angelina . . Miss Dowthwaite
Parley . . . . . Miss Yapp
Lady Lurewell . . Mrs. Parker

MILLER OF MANSFIELD.

King . . . . . Mr. Verling
Miller . . . . . Mr. Parker
Lord Lurewell . Mr. Godwin
First Courtier . Mrs. Osborne
Second Courtier . Mr. Charlton
Joe . . . . . . Mr. Farrell

MRS. PARKER'S BENEFIT.

For the Benefit of
MRS. PARKER.
By Permission
Of the Worshipful the Mayor of Williamsburg,
At the old Theatre near the Capitol,
By the VIRGINIA COMPANY OF COMEDIANS,
On Friday the 3d of June
will be presented
THE BEGGARS' OPERA,
and
THE ANATOMIST
or
*Sham Doctor.*

Comedians."   It was these advertisements, no doubt, that induced Mr. Cooke to give the name of the "Virginia Company of Comedians" to the original Hallam Company, and led him to describe the Hallam theatre as "the old Theatre near the Capitol."   It led, however, to his confounding the rival companies, but this is not surprising, because the files of the *Virginia Gazette* for 1768 are the earliest containing theatrical advertisements that have been preserved so far as the best informed librarians in the United States are aware.

# CHAPTER XXII.

## SOUTHWARK THEATRE, 1768-9.

A BRIEF SEASON IN PHILADELPHIA—HARD WORK FIGHTING AGAINST
ADVERSITY—MORE NEW PLAYS AND NEW ACTORS—AN EXHIBI-
TION OF FIREWORKS—ANOTHER SPECIMEN OF ANTI-THEATRICAL
CANT.

AFTER an absence of eleven months from Philadelphia, during
six of which the American Company gave performances at the
new John Street Theatre in New York, Mr. Douglass returned with
his forces to the Southwark Theatre, which was re-opened with the
"Spanish Fryar" and "Honest Yorkshireman" on the 21st of October,
1768. Originally this season was intended to last only three weeks,
and the announcement of the "Mourning Bride" and "Honest Yorkshireman" for the 28th of October was advertised as the "last week
but one." Subsequently, however, it was determined to extend it,
but so far as the newspapers are concerned there was no explanation
of this change of purpose. The reason was probably the sufficient
one of good business. The New York season had not been satisfactory, and when it closed the outlook for the future was a gloomy
one. Indeed it seemed as if the disbandment of the company was
impending. The cost of the New York theatre probably proved too
heavy a load for the management in the face of a most determined
effort to crush the enterprise. Never was the opposition to the drama
in New York so bitter as in the spring of this year. As far as possible,
the detested play-house was boycotted. Play-going was not only an

offense in the eyes of those who were opposed to the theatre, but it was punished as such, as is evident from the imprisonment of the poor debtors who were known to have been to the play. When the season closed Mr. Douglass was almost without money. In consequence, he was compelled to practice the most rigid economy in Philadelphia. Always before and always after this year his advertising was on an exceedingly liberal scale. This season, with a few exceptions, and in the following season in New York, it was confined to a mere mention of the pieces for the evening.

The list of productions of a brief season, lasting only little over two months, must necessarily be a short one; but, brief as this season was, four pieces never before acted in America were produced at the Southwark Theatre between the 12th and 30th of December, 1768. These were "King John,"·"False Delicacy," "Zara" and "Alexander the Great." Besides, the opening piece, the "Spanish Fryar," had not been played since its production at the theatre on Cruger's Wharf in New York, in 1759, when only the comic scenes were given. The first production of Shakspere's "King John" in this country, it will be observed, was followed four days later by the first production of Hugh Kelly's "False

LIST OF PERFORMANCES.

1768.

Oct. 21—Spanish Fryar . . . . . Dryden
            Honest Yorkshireman . . Carey
      28 · Mourning Bride . . . Congreve
            Miss in her Teens . . . . Garrick
Nov. 4—Cymbeline . . . . . . Shakspere
            Love a la Mode . . . . Macklin
      25—Clandestine Marriage . .
                        Garrick and Colman
            Lethe . . . . . . . . . Garrick
Dec. 2—Tamerlane . . . . . . . Rowe
            High Life Below Stairs . Townley
        9—Busybody . . . . . . Centlivre
            Contrivances . . . . . . Carey
      12—King John . . . . . . Shakspere
      14—Macbeth . . . . . . Shakspere
            Miss in her Teens.
      16—False Delicacy . . . . . Kelly
            Catherine and Petruchio Shakspere
      26—Zara . . . . . . . . . . Hill
      30—Alexander the Great . . . . Lee
            Dissertation upon Noses—(Wall).
            Neck or Nothing . . . Garrick

1769.

Jan. 6—Alexander the Great.
            Contrivances.

Delicacy" in America. But even apart from the novelties the season was a successful one. A company capable of playing Shakspere's "Cymbeline " and Macklin's " Love a la Mode" the same evening, with a change of bill every acting night, was something known only at that early period in the development of the American stage.

The first advertisement of the season that contained the names of the performers was that of Rowe's tragedy, " Tamerlane." Some changes had occurred in the company after the close of the New York season. Malone, Greville and Allyn gave up the modest line of parts they were accustomed to fill to Parker, Darby and Byerly. The newcomers are first noticed in the existing bills on this occasion. Mr. Parker, it will be remembered, was with the

### TAMERLANE.

| | |
|---|---|
| Bajazet | Mr. Hallam |
| Monesses | Mr. Henry |
| Axalla | Mr. Parker |
| Omar | Mr. Tomlinson |
| Dervise | Mr. Morris |
| Haly | Mr. Wall |
| Tamerlane | Mr. Douglass |
| Tanais | Mr. Darby |
| Mirvan | Mr. Woolls |
| Stratocles | Mr. Byerly |
| Zama | Mr. Raworth |
| Selima | Miss Cheer |
| Arpasia | Miss Hallam |

Virginia Company of Comedians at Williamsburg in the beginning of the year. Of Darby and Byerly we have no knowledge beyond the parts they played.

The production of a tragedy as elaborate as "King John" is at once a proof of the strength of the company and of the taste of the time. Many years afterward when it was revived by Charles Kean upon something like the splendid scale of his Shaksperian revivals in London, the undertaking was looked upon as an extraordinary theatrical event. It is not to be supposed that Mr. Douglass' production compared in *mise en scene* with Charles Kean's, but it is supposable that the acting of the earlier was fully equal to that of the later company.

No cast of "King John" was printed in the Philadelphia papers on the occasion of the first production of the tragedy in America.

KING JOHN.

| | |
|---|---|
| King John | . . . . . . . . . Mr. Douglass |
| Falconbridge | . . . . . . . . . Mr. Hallam |
| Hubert | . . . . . . . . . . . Mr. Henry |
| Pembroke | . . . . . . . . . Mr. Tomlinson |
| Salisbury | . . . . . . . . . . Mr. Parker |
| Robert Falconbridge | . . . . . Mr. Roberts |
| King Philip | . . . . . . . . . Mr. Byerly |
| Dauphin | . . . . . . . . . . . Mr. Wall |
| Austria | . . . . . . . . . . Mr. Darby |
| Pandulph | . . . . . . . . . Mr. Morris |
| Chatillon | . . . . . . . . Mr. Raworth |
| Melun | . . . . . . . . . . Mr. Woolls |
| Prince Arthur | . . . . . . . Miss M. Storer |
| Prince Henry | . . . . . . . Mrs. Harman |
| Queen Eleanor | . . . . . . Mrs. Douglass |
| Lady Constance | . . . . . . . Miss Cheer |
| Lady Falconbridge | . . . . . . Miss Storer |
| Blanche of Castile | . . . . . Miss Hallam |

Indeed, the only recognition of the importance of the production on the part of the management was in underlining the tragedy in the advertisements of the "Busy-body" in the *Pennsylvania Gazette* and the *Pennsylvania Journal*. As the cast was printed in the New York papers when "King John" was produced in that city just four weeks later, and as no changes had occurred in the company in the meanwhile, it may be assumed that the parts were played by the same players in the two cities.

The most interesting production of the season was, of course, Hugh Kelly's "False Delicacy." This comedy was published soon after its production at Drury Lane, and it had been in print only a few months when it was presented in Philadelphia by the American Company. Kelly was an Irishman, who had learned the business of a staymaker in Dublin, but being disinclined to an occupation so

FALSE DELICACY.

| | |
|---|---|
| Colonel Rivers | . . . . . . . . Mr. Douglass |
| Cecil | . . . . . . . . . . . Mr. Hallam |
| Lord Winworth | . . . . . . . Mr. Henry |
| Sir Harry Newburg | . . . . . . Mr. Wall |
| Sidney | . . . . . . . . . . . Mr. Byerly |
| Mrs. Harley | . . . . . . . Mrs. Douglass |
| Miss Marchmont | . . . . . . Miss Hallam |
| Miss Rivers | . . . . . . . . . Miss Storer |
| Sally | . . . . . . . . . . . Mrs. Harman |
| Lady Betty Lambton | . . . . . Miss Cheer |

humble he went to London in 1763, hoping to live by his pen. His first literary work to attract attention was a poem called "Thespis," in which he satirized Mr. Moody, Mrs. Clive and Mrs. Dancer among others, after the manner of Churchill's "Rosciad." This was an ill-judged beginning for a man who was soon to turn dramatic author, for when Garrick accepted his comedy neither Moody nor Mrs. Clive would consent to play in it, and Mrs. Dancer was with difficulty induced to accept the part of *Lady Betty*. The critics, too, were hostile and attacked the play as a dull, sentimental sermon,—

Vending in dialogue sermonic scenes,

sang one of them in dull verse,—but the piece was received with applause by the public. Its success was so great that it was almost immediately translated into most of the modern languages—Portuguese, French, Italian and German—and it had the unusual distinction of being played in America while it was still in the first flush of its European popularity.

In "Zara," a tragedy based on the "Zaire" of Voltaire, Miss Cheer had the title-role, with Hallam as *Ozman* and Douglass as *Lusignan*. "Alexander the Great" was Lee's tragedy known as the "Rival Queens." This piece, the scene of which is in Babylon, was revived at Drury Lane with great magnificence as late as 1795, when John Philip Kemble was *Alexander*. Although it shows evidences of Lee's madness, it has many merits, among them the admirable manner in which the steady *Clytus* is contrasted with

### ALEXANDER THE GREAT.

| | |
|---|---|
| Alexander | Mr. Hallam |
| Clytus | Mr. Douglass |
| Lysimachus | Mr. Henry |
| Hephestion | Mr. Wall |
| Cassander | Mr. Morris |
| Polyperchon | Mr. Parker |
| Philip | Mr. Tomlinson |
| Thessalus | Mr. Woolls |
| Perdiccus | Mr. Byerly |
| Eumenes | Mr. Roberts |
| Meleager | Mr. Raworth |
| Aristander | Mr. Darby |
| Statira | Miss Hallam |
| Lysigambis | Mrs. Douglass |
| Parisates | Miss Storer |
| Roxana | Miss Cheer |

the fiery *Alexander*, and the mild and secure *Statira* with the disappointed and raging *Roxana*. It may be added that this was the only period before the Revolution when the American Company could safely have ventured upon a production so elaborate and exacting.

Besides the pieces, old and new, presented this season, Mr. Douglass sought to please the Philadelphia public by an exhibition of fireworks on the stage after the farce, which was announced for the 9th of December. " It having been hinted to Mr. Douglass," the manager said in his advertisement, " that an exhibition of this kind (the first upon any stage in America) would be acceptable to the public ; he with pleasure embraced the opportunity of manifesting his zeal and attention by presenting them with this additional entertainment, for which, tho' the expense of the evening will be greatly increased, he demands no more than the usual prices." The fireworks were arranged by " the two Italian brothers," and comprised a large wheel illuminated with brilliant fire ; a triumphal arch with a globe in the middle; a tornant with variegated fire and several fountains of different composition. The experiment seems to have been eminently successful, for on the 14th the fireworks were repeated with new combinations, the management making an acknowledgment of past favors and indulging in cheerful promises for the future. It will be observed that down to "Nothing more than the usual prices will be demanded " Mr. Douglass' methods are identical with those of the modern manager.

An amusing specimen of the

AT GREAT EXPENSE.

---

*⁎⁎⁎* Mr. Douglass having with great pleasure observed the satisfaction which the Exhibition on Friday gave to the audience in general has, at much greater expense, engaged the conductors to prepare this act, which, he doubts not, will meet with that countenance and encouragement every attempt of his to entertain the town has been favored with.

Nothing more than the usual prices will be demanded.

cant of the period directed against the theatre found its way into print this season in the columns of the *Pennsylvania Gazette*. It was signed " J. R.," and described as a " genuine relation." [1] Anything more silly it is not easy to imagine. This man, who accepted a box-ticket to the play through " a principle of complaisance," had the bad taste to bestow it upon a negro, who, in turn, sold it for half price. As a consequence an intruder was introduced into the box, which evidently was intended only for the friends of the family where " J. R." found his way. It would not have been impolite for him to refuse the ticket, but the use to which he put it is surprising.

---

[1] A GENUINE RELATION.—Having been introduced a few evenings ago into the company of some ladies and gentlemen (to most of whom I was an entire stranger), after the tea equipage was removed, one of the gentlemen produced some box tickets for the play, which he generously bestowed on the company. I, as a stranger, being presented with one, which (having no taste for theatrical performances) a principle of complaisance prevailed on me to accept. What the unhappy consequence was of this piece of generosity in the gentleman follows : Some of the company who had before resolved to hear service at St. Paul's Church on that night found themselves now much straitened to put their pious resolution in practice, in short, a division in sentiment took place, some being strenuously bent to see the play and some to hear a sermon, and in order to reduce their versatile inclinations they agreed the matter should be determined by drawing cards, which was accordingly done, when giddy chance determined in favor of the theatre. Good God, gentlemen, what a degenerate age do we live in ! Into what a state of apostacy are we fallen, when our zeal for religion is actuated by the turn of a card and the mimicry of buffoons is put in competition with the sacred oracles of truth ! I had almost forgot to tell you that the ticket which was conferred on me I gave to a negro who attended me at tea, but the virtuous slave (as I have since understood) immediately sold it for half price, with which he purchased a prayer-book. An example of religion and virtue in a slave worthy the imitation of the greatest ruler upon earth.

PHILADELPHIA, December 19th, 1768.

# CHAPTER XXIII.

## JOHN STREET THEATRE, 1769.

A SEASON THAT WAS NOT PROSPEROUS—THE MANAGEMENT AND THE PLAYERS EMBARRASSED—EFFORTS TO RAISE MONEY—RETIREMENT OF MISS CHEER AND MISS WAINWRIGHT—THEIR PARTS.

JUST ten days after the close of the Southwark Theatre for the season of 1768–9 Mr. Douglass' company re-opened the John Street Theatre, in New York. The season was not a prosperous one, but the players remained in New York until the middle of June, when they went to Albany, where they opened with "Venice Preserved," on the 3d of July, according to Dunlap. This reputed visit of the players to the ancient city of Albany is based upon tradition only and can not be verified, as no newspaper was printed there at that time. According to this tradition the performances were given in the hospital. The tradition is probably well founded, as Mr. Douglass had learned that neither Philadelphia nor New York could support a prolonged theatrical season every year, in consequence of which the necessity of seeking fresh pastures would force itself upon him. The Albany experiment does not appear to have proved satisfactory, however, and Mr. Douglass afterward looked to the South for new theatrical cities. Business embarrassments this season also taught him, apparently, to look to public subscriptions, as at Annapolis and Charleston, for the means with which to build new theatres.

Among the pieces acted in New York this season were many old favorites, and the new plays presented in Philadelphia the preceding December. Besides, there were several productions then seen for the first time in America. Steele's " Tender Husband," Garrick's " Guardian " and Bickerstaff's " Padlock " comprised the list of new productions. In Steele's comedy there was genuine humor without indelicacy, which until his time was thought to be inseparable from wit. The "Guardian " was still a new piece, having been first acted at Drury Lane, in 1759, for the benefit of Christopher Smart, a poet, at that time in jail for debt. In the " Padlock," which was newer still, having had a run of fifty-three nights at Drury Lane, in 1768, when it was originally produced, Mr. Hallam made a great "hit" as *Mungo.* He continued to be unrivaled in the part until his death, surpassing even Dibdin, the original, who also composed the music for the piece. It has

LIST OF PERFORMANCES.

1769.

Jan. 16—King John . . . . . . . Shakspere
　　20—Jealous Wife . . . . . . . Colman
　　　　Picture of a Playhouse.
　　　　Miss in her Teens . . . . Garrick
　　27—Beaux' Stratagem . . . Farquhar
　　　　Citizen . . . . . . . . . Murphy
　　30—Zara . . . . . . . . . . . Hill
Feb. 2—Romeo and Juliet . . . Shakspere
　　　　Guardian . . . . . . . Garrick
　　9—Cymbeline . . . . . Shakspere
　　　　Miller of Mansfield . . . Dodsley
　　17—Orphan . . . . . . . . Otway
　　　　Lethe . . . . . . . . Garrick
　　24—Alexander the Great . . . . Lee
　　　　Contrivances . . . . . . . Carey
March 3—Beggars' Opera . . . . . . Gay
　　　　Witches.
　　10—King Henry IV . . . Shakspere
　　　　Guardian.
　　17—Busybody . . . . . . Centlivre
　　　　Brave Irishman . . . . Sheridan
　　20—Tender Husband . . . . . Steele
　　27—Tender Husband.
　　　　Upholsterer . . . . . . Murphy
April 10—Othello . . . . . . . Shakspere
　　　　Hob in the Well . . . . Cibber
　　14—False Delicacy . . . . . Kelly
　　　　Catherine and Petruchio Shakspere
　　27—King John.
　　　　Thomas and Sally . . Bickerstaff
(Mr. and Mrs. Tomlinson's benefit.)
May 1—Jane Shore . . . . . . Rowe
　　　　Devil to Pay . . . . . Coffev
(Benefit of Miss and Miss M. Storer.)
　　4—Maid of the Mill . . . Bickerstaff
　　8—Romeo and Juliet.
　　　　(Miss Hallam's benefit.)
　　11—Jane Shore.
　　　　Miss in her Teens

Harlequin Skeleton.
(Benefit of Mr. Henry and Miss and
        Miss M. Storer.)
May 25—Richard III . . . . . Shakspere
        Love a la Mode . . . . Macklin
        (Mrs. Douglass' benefit.)
    29—Constant Couple . . . Farquhar
        Padlock . . . . . . Bickerstaff
        (Mr. Hallam's benefit.)
June 1—Earl of Essex . . . . . . Jones
        Padlock.
        (Mr. Woolls' benefit.)
     9—Love Makes a Man . . . Cibber
        Lying Valet . . . . . . Garrick
    (Mr. and Mrs. Tomlinson's benefit.)
    15—Drummer . . . . . . . Addison
        Alexander's Feast (Byerly).
        Padlock.
        (Parker and Byerly's benefit.)
    17—Love for Love . . . . Congreve
        Padlock.
    29—An Entertainment by Mr. Henry.

been suggested that Mr. Hallam owed much of his excellence as *Mungo* to his study of the negro character and dialect in Jamaica and the Colonies.

All the indications seem to point to unusual embarrassment both on the part of the management and the members of the company individually. As early as the 10th of April, when "Othello" was in the bills, it was announced that the part of *Othello* would be "attempted by a gentleman, assisted by other gentlemen in the characters of the Duke and Senate of Venice, from a benevolent and generous design of encouraging the theatre and relieving the performers from some embarrassments in which they are involved." Mr. Ireland believes that the *Othello* on this occasion was Major Moncrief, a British officer, who was the most distinguished amateur actor in the Colonies before and during the Revolution. Even before this extraordinary efforts had been made to obtain good houses. On the 30th of March it was announced that the bill would be "performed by the particular desire of the Grand Knot of the Friendly Brothers of St. Patrick,"[1] on the follqwing

---

[1] NEW YORK JOURNAL, MARCH 30TH.— The *Friendly Brothers* of *St. Patrick*, and several Gentlemen of this City intend dining together at Bolton and Sigel's, next Monday, and from thence to go to the Play in the Evening; such Gentlemen as propose to join them will be pleased to send in their Names to the Bar of said Tavern two days before.
New York, March 28th, 1769.

Monday, the 3d of April. Dunlap gives the 17th of March as the date when the "Busybody" and the "Brave Irishman" were performed. The bill for the 3d of April was not advertised, but Sheridan's farce was probably the afterpiece. It may be that the Friendly Brothers encouraged the theatre both on St. Patrick's Day and afterward. A similar discrepancy exists in regard to a performance advertised for "the entertainment of the Right Worshipful the Grand Master, the Masters, Wardens and Brethren of the Ancient and Honorable Society of Free and Accepted Masons." According to the original advertisement the performance was set down for the 20th, but it was afterward announced for the 27th of March, without any explanation either of postponement or repetition. For the latter date, however, the "Upholsterer" was in the bill "by command," instead of the "pantomime entertainment" intended for the 20th. Previous to the performance of the 27th Mr. Douglass announced that it would be "taken as a favor if the ladies and gentlemen who desire to have places in the boxes reserved for them would send to bespeak 'em before Saturday evening at farthest, that proper lists may be made out for the boxkeepers and every possible care taken to prevent mistakes."

A MASONIC ENTERTAINMENT.

By Command of his Excellency the
GOVERNOR.
For the Entertainment of the Right Worshipful the Grand Master, the Masters, Wardens and Brethren of the Ancient and Honorable Society of Free and Accepted Masons;
*By the American Company*
At the Theatre in John-Street on Monday the 20th of March, Inst., will be presented a Comedy never acted there, call'd, The
TENDER HUSBAND
or the
ACCOMPLISHED FOOLS.
With a Prologue and Epilogue and several Songs proper for the Occasion.
*To which will be added a*
PANTOMIME ENTERTAINMENT.
The Company of *all the Brethren* in Town is earnestly requested to meet at Burns' at five o'clock on the day of Performance and walk from thence in *Procession* to the Theatre where the Pit will be reserved for their Accommodation.
BOXES and Pit, 8*s.* Gallery, 3*s.*

Although "a new set of scenes" was provided for the "Othello" night, when the part of *Othello* was "attempted by a gentleman, assisted by other gentlemen in the characters of the Duke and Senate of Venice, from a benevolent and generous design of encouraging the theatre and relieving the performers from some embarrassments in which they are involved," there were many signs of unusual poverty on the part of the company. Among these was the peculiar character of the benefits. Mr. and Mrs. Tomlinson had two, Woolls had two, the Misses Storer had one, and another in conjunction with Mr. Henry. Mrs. Harman made an extraordinary effort to raise the wind by giving a concert at Burns' Room on the 13th of June, at which she had the assistance of Miss Hallam, Miss M. Storer, Mr. Woolls and Miss Wainwright. Besides, Mr. Henry gave a monologue entertainment at the theatre on the 29th of June. His bill comprised a lecture on "Hearts," with an original prologue; Hippesley's *Drunken Man*, and some pantomimic bits which he called "Harlequin's Frolic." He announced, oddly enough, that as the late hours of the theatre had been complained of, he would begin at 8 o'clock, and assured the public that his entertainment would be over by half-past 10. On the day following, the 30th, Mr. Woolls and Miss Hallam assisted at a concert at Vauxhall Garden, Woolls singing "Black Sloven" and "Blest as the Immortal Gods is he," and Miss Hallam "Ye Men of Gaza" of Handel, and the two artists uniting in the duet "Fair Aurora" from "Artaxerxes." These later entertainments show that if Messrs. Henry and Woolls and Miss Hallam joined the company at Albany they gave themselves little time to make the journey.

A somewhat startling episode of the production of the "Beggars' Opera" this season in New York was Mr. Hallam's appearance as *Captain Macheath*, and another event of some importance was Miss Hallam's appearance for the first time as *Juliet*, on the 8th of May. After many years of steady work on the American stage she had at last become the leading lady of the company, as the successor of Miss Cheer. This position she continued to hold until the company finally disbanded in 1774.

The motives for Miss Cheer's retirement are not clear. If it was in consequence of her marriage to Lord Rosehill, it is singular that it did not take place sooner, that event having occurred nearly a year before. That Lady Rosehill did not go to England immediately after her retirement is evident from the fact that she played *Queen Elizabeth* in " Richard III," for Mrs. Douglass' benefit, in New York, in 1773. This may or may not be accounted for by a story that somehow found its way into print, that she had previously eloped with her father's coachman. In any case she must have been a woman of good birth and education, and to have possessed both experience and adaptability to enable her to play the long list of trying roles that must be put to her credit within the brief period of three

MISS CHEER'S PARTS.

*Plays.*

| | |
|---|---|
| A Bold Stroke for a Wife | Ann Lovely |
| Alexander the Great | Roxana |
| All for Love | Cleopatra |
| Beaux' Stratagem | Mrs. Sullen |
| Busybody | Miranda |
| Cato | Marcia |
| Clandestine Marriage | Miss Sterling |
| Committee | Ruth |
| Conscious Lovers | Indiana |
| Constant Couple | Angelica |
| Country Lasses | Aura |
| Cymbeline | Imogen |
| Distressed Mother | Hermione |
| Drummer | Lady Truman |
| Earl of Essex | Countess of Rutland |
| Fair Penitent | Calista |
| False Delicacy | Lady Betty Lambton |
| Gamester | Mrs. Beverly |
| George Barnwell | Millwood |
| Hamlet | Ophelia |
| Henry IV | Lady Percy |
| Inconstant | Bizarre |
| Jane Shore | Alicia |
| Jealous Wife | Mrs. Oakley |
| King John | Lady Constance |
| Lear | Cordelia |
| Love for Love | Miss Prue |
| Love Makes a Man | Angelina |
| Macbeth | Lady Macbeth |
| Merchant of Venice | Portia |

| | |
|---|---|
| Miser . . . . . . . . . . . . . | Mariana |
| Mourning Bride . . . . . . . . | Almeria |
| Orphan . . . . . . . . . . . . | Monimia |
| Orphan of China . . . . . . . . | Mandare |
| Othello . . . . . . . . . | Desdemona |
| Prince of Parthia . . . . . . . . | Evanthe |
| Provoked Husband . . . . . | Lady Townly |
| Recruiting Officer . . . . . . . | Sylvia |
| Richard III . . . . . . { | Queen Elizabeth / Lady Anne |
| Roman Father . . . . . . . . . | Horatia |
| Romeo and Juliet . . . . . . . . | Juliet |
| School for Lovers . . . . . . | Araminta |
| Suspicious Husband . . . . . . | Clarinda |
| Tamerlane . . . . . . . . . . | Selima |
| Theodosius . . . . . . . . . { | Athenais / Pulcheria |
| Venice Preserved . . . . . . | Belvidera |
| Wonder . . . . . . . . . . . | Violante |
| Zara . . . . . . . . . . . . . | Zara |

*Farces.*

| | |
|---|---|
| Catherine and Petruchio . . . . | Catherine |
| Harlequin Collector . . . . . . | Columbine |
| High Life Below Stairs . . . . . | Kitty |
| Honest Yorkshireman . . . . | Combrush |
| Mayor of Garratt . . . . . . | Mrs. Sneak |
| Old Maid . . . . . . . . . | Mrs. Harlow |
| Thomas and Sally . . . . . . . | Dorcas |
| Witches . . . . . . . . . . | Columbine |

years. During her short reign on the American stage, besides a few parts in pantomime and farce, she is known to have played exactly fifty of the leading characters of the drama. This, it must be confessed, is a wonderful showing and one which no modern actress has exceeded in a life-time. Whatever may have been Miss Cheer's artistic capabilities her industry is unquestionable, and she probably earned a greater reward than her exertions ever obtained for her. After the Revolution she reappeared upon one occasion but was coldly received.

A change almost equally important as the loss to the company of Miss Cheer was the retirement of Miss Wainwright. She did not appear in Philadelphia at all the previous season, and in New York in the beginning of 1769 she was seen only three times. Her services in two of the parts in which she appeared, *Polly* in the "Beggars' Opera" and *Patty* in the "Maid of the Mill," seem to have been gratuities, and she evidently appeared in "Thomas and Sally" for the Tomlinsons, on the 27th of April, as appears from a quaint notice annexed to the announcement of the production of the "Maid of the Mill," on the 4th of May.

Miss Wainwright's Farewell.

☞ Miss Wainwright's performance on Monday se'nnight was advertised for the last, and intended to be so; but at the particular desire of some persons of distinction she performs in this opera

Miss Wainwright was an accomplished actress and singer. She had been with the American Company two years, her most important roles being *Polly* in the "Beggars' Opera" and *Rosetta* in "Love in a Village," in both of which she appeared at the Southwark Theatre in 1766–7. Her American *debut* was made in the former, and she was the original *Rosetta* in America. After leaving the stage Miss Wainwright lived in retirement in Philadelphia for many years, appearing a few times afterward, out of compliment to her old manager, when the company played in the Southwark Theatre for the last time before the Revolution. Miss Wainwright's place was not filled, her parts being taken by the Storer sisters and Miss Hallam, as occasion required.

Whether the company went to Albany after the close of the New York season of 1769, as has been shown, is open to doubt. According to Dunlap the Albany season was announced as for one month only. This would have

MISS WAINWRIGHT'S PARTS.

*Plays.*

| | |
|---|---|
| All for Love | Charmian |
| Beaux' Stratagem | Cherry |
| Beggars' Opera | Polly |
| Clandestine Marriage | Betty |
| Conscious Lovers | Mrs. Sealand |
| Constant Couple | Parly |
| Country Lasses | Flora |
| Disappointment | Lucy |
| Don Quixote in England | Dorothea |
| Gamester | Lucy |
| Inconstant | Lamorce |
| Jealous Wife | Betty |
| Lear | Goneril |
| Love in a Village | Rosetta |
| Love Makes a Man | Elvira |
| Macbeth | Witch |
| Maid of the Mill | Patty |
| Merchant of Venice | Jessica |
| Mourning Bride | Attendant. |
| Prince of Parthia | Cleone |
| Provoked Husband | { Mrs. Motherley / Lady Wronghead |
| Recruiting Officer | Rose |
| Suspicious Husband | Lucetta |
| Wonder | Flora |

*Farces.*

| | |
|---|---|
| Apprentice | Charlotte |
| Brave Irishman | Betty |
| Chaplet | Laura |
| Citizen | Maria |
| Contrivances | Arethusa |
| Damon and Phillida | Phillida |
| Deuce is in Him | Bell |
| Devil to Pay | Nell |
| High Life Below Stairs | Lady Charlotte |
| Lethe | Mrs. Riot |
| Lying Valet | Kitty Pry |
| Mayor of Garratt | Mrs. Sneak |
| Miss in her Teens | Tag |
| Neck or Nothing | Jenny |

Polly Honeycomb . . . . . . . . . Polly
Spirit of Contradiction . . . . Miss Harriet
Thomas and Sally . . . . . . . . . Sally
Upholsterer . . . . . . . . . . . Harriet

given the players ample time to go to Philadelphia for the next season at the Southwark Theatre, which did not begin until November. It is unfortunate that Dunlap is so uniformly inaccurate that what was perhaps the first theatrical season at what is now the capital of the State of New York should not only be without a history, but in doubt. At that time Albany was only a village, as is shown in the pictures of the period, and it does not seem likely that it should have been able to support a theatrical company, even for a month. This fact in itself is not a proof, however, that it was not visited by the Thespians in 1769.

# CHAPTER XXIV.

## THE NEW AMERICAN COMPANY.

ANOTHER SEASON AT ANNAPOLIS—THE COMPANY A COMPOSITE ONE—
A STRIKING LIST OF PERFORMANCES—OLD PLAYS AND FARCES
AND NEW COMEDIES PRODUCED—SOME FULL AND MANY PARTIAL
CASTS—MALONE AND GODWIN'S PARTS.

WHILE the American Company was playing in New York, from January to June, 1769, another theatrical organization, styling itself the New American Company, was entertaining the good people of Annapolis, the season beginning on the 18th of February and lasting until the 13th of June. This company was apparently organized, or rather re-organized by Mr. Godwin, who was with the American Company in 1766-7, but had left it and joined the Virginia Company of Comedians in 1768. This assumption is based on the fact that Godwin now had better roles than he ever had before.

The new company was made up in part of the leading people of the Virginia Company, of some of the least important members of the American Company at the Southwark Theatre in 1768, and of fresh accessions. Among the actors from the American Company besides Godwin and Parker, both of whom had been with the Virginia Comedians, were Malone and Darby. Mr. Verling, of the Virginia Company, had the lead, and next in consequence to him was Godwin. Mrs. Parker was the leading actress early in the season, but subsequently Mrs. Osborne joined the company, assuming the heavy tragedy roles. With the exception of the Walkers the rest of the troupe was new to the American stage. Among the latter was a Mr. Jefferson, who, oddly enough, lodged with a Mr. Adams, at Annapolis. Who Mr. Jefferson was it is impossible to say. It is not likely, but he may have been John Jefferson, a son of the great Jefferson of Drury Lane, and the elder brother of Joseph Jefferson, afterward a favorite Philadelphia comedian. It was not uncommon for young English barnstormers to visit the Colonies at that time, and John Jefferson with Manager Godwin at Annapolis, in 1769, would not have been more out of place than he was with Manager Davis at Brixham, in 1786, as related by Ryley in the "Itinerant."

The Annapolis season of 1769 shows remarkable activity on the part of the company, such as it was, and a wide range of plays and farces for the entertainment of the patrons of the theatre. A noteworthy feature of the season was the number of amateurs who aspired to Thespian honors. On the 22d of February the part of *Othello* was "attempted by a gentleman for his amusement, being the first time of his ever appearing on the stage." The same gentleman played *Hamlet* on the 3d of April, and he repeated *Othello* on the 13th of May for Mrs. Walker's benefit. Another gentleman, on

LIST OF PERFORMANCES.

1769.
Feb. 18—Romeo and Juliet . . . Shakspere
        Virgin Unmasked . . . Fielding
     22—Othello . . . . . . . Shakspere
        Honest Yorkshireman . . . Carey
     24—Jealous Wife . . . . . . Colman
        Brave Irishman. . . . . Sheridan
     25—Beggars' Opera . . . . . . Gay
        Brave Irishman.
March 4—Douglas . . . . . . . . Home
        High Life Below Stairs . Townley
      6—Richard III . . . . . Shakspere
        Lethe . . . . . . . . Garrick
      9—Jealous Wife.
        Upholsterer . . . . . . Murphy
     11—Romeo and Juliet.
        Honest Yorkshireman.
     14—Inconstant . . . . . . Farquhar
        Merlin . . . . . . . . Hill
     15—Douglas.
        Mock Doctor . . . . . Fielding

one occasion, appeared as *Damon* in "Damon and Phillida," and still another was advertised for *Obadiah Prim* in "A Bold Stroke for a Wife." But perhaps the most daring of the amateurs was a gentleman who appeared "for his amusement" on the tight-rope for the benefit of Mr. Malone. The repertoire in its leading features was patterned after that of the American Company, but it comprised two pantomimes, two interludes, a farce and a comedy that were new in this country. The pantomime advertised as "Merlin" was probably Aaron Hill's "Merlin in Love," though it may have been Theobald's, or Giffard's alteration of Dryden's "King Arthur." It may be assumed that Henry Woodward's "Genii" was not the splendid spectacle at Annapolis, in 1769, that it was at Drury Lane when it was first acted, in 1752. The farce, "Wrangling Lovers," was taken by William Lyon from Vanbrugh's

Mar. 16—Beaux' Stratagem . . . Farquhar
Devil to Pay . . . . . . Coffey
17—Miser . . . . . . . . Fielding
High Life Below Stairs.
18—Revenge . . . . . . . . Young
Damon and Phillida . . . Cibber
April 1—Miser.
Devil to Pay.
3—Hamlet . . . . . . . Shakspere
Mayor of Garratt . . . . . Foote
8—Richard III.
Polly Honeycomb . . . . Colman
(Mr. Verling's benefit.)
18—Provoked Husband . . Vanbrugh
Miller of Mansfield . . . Dodsley
(Mr. Godwin's benefit.)
22—Busybody . . . . . . Centlivre
Genii (Pantomime) . . Woodward
(Mr. Spencer's benefit.)
25—Merchant of Venice . . Shakspere
Lying Valet . . . . . . Garrick
(Mr. Malone's benefit.)
29—Mourning Bride . . . . Congreve
Honest Yorkshireman.
(Mr. Jefferson's benefit.)
May 1—Suspicious Husband . . . Hoadly
Wrangling Lover . . . Vanbrugh
Lethe.
(Mr. Burdett's benefit.)
2—Richard III.
High Life Below Stairs.
3—Douglas.
Mayor of Garratt.
4—King Henry IV . . . Shakspere
Damon and Phillida.
9—Bold Stroke for a Wife . Centlivre
Farmer's Return from London
Garrick
(Mrs. Malone's benefit.)
13—Othello.
Trick upon Trick . . . . Yarrow
(Mrs. Walker's benefit.)
16—George Barnwell . . . . . Lillo
17—Conscious Lovers . . . . Steele
Citizen . . . . . . . Murphy
(Mrs. Osborne's benefit.)

May 18—Beggars' Opera.
　　Miss in her Teens . . . Garrick
　20—Distressed Mother . . . . Philips
　　Harlequin Skeleton.
　23—Way to Keep Him . . . Murphy
　　Mock Doctor.
　　(Mr. Darby's benefit.)
　27—Earl of Essex . . . . . . Jones
　　Chaplet . . . . . . . Mendez
　　(Mrs. Parker's benefit.)
　30—She Wou'd and She Wou'd Not
　　　　　　　　　Cibber
　　(Mrs. Jones' benefit.)
June　3—Conscious Lovers.
　　Catherine and Petruchio Shakspere
　　(Mrs. Walker's benefit.)
　6—A Bold Stroke for a Wife.
　　Upholsterer.
　　(Mr. Page's benefit.)
　10—Love in a Village . . . Bickerstaff
　　Anatomist . . . . . Ravenscroft
　　(Mr. Parker's benefit.)
　13—Theodosius . . . . . . . Lee
　　Devil to Pay.
　　(Mrs. Burdett's Benefit.)

"Mistake," printed in Edinburgh in 1745, and "Trick upon Trick" suggests R. Fabian's "Trick for Trick," during the first performance of which occurred the fatal quarrel between Macklin and Thomas Hallam, but the cast shows it was the piece published by Joseph Yarrow, at York, in 1742. The comedy new to the American stage was Cibber's "She Wou'd and She Wou'd Not," of which, unfortunately, no cast was printed in the newspapers. This is the only comedy of the many written by Colley Cibber that has been seen on the modern stage, Mr. Augustin Daly including it among the revivals which almost annually were a part of his policy as a manager. The piece was originally acted at Drury Lane. Cibber borrowed his plot from Leonerd's "Counterfeits." Mrs. Jones was probably the original *Hypolita* in this country.

In his advertisement of his benefit Mr. Malone supplied a quaint bit of autobiography. According to his announcement he must have been a more accomplished juggler than he was skillful as an actor. Malone was evidently an Irishman, and he utilized the opportunities afforded him by the An-

MALONE'S BIT OF AUTOBIOGRAPHY.

Between the Play and the Farce several performances on the slack rope in full swing by Mr. Malone—
　I. He vaults the rope.
　II. He lies on it at full length.
　III. He beats a drum.

napolis season to appear as *Captain O'Blunder* in Sheridan's farce, as well as to display his agility on the slack rope. In the full pieces Malone was generally content with very modest parts. He evidently belonged to the class of performers that in these latter

IV. He balances a pyramid of smoking pipes on the edge of a drinking glass.

V. He balances the pipes and a pyramid of thirty glasses of jelly in each hand.

VI. He stands on his head on a small pack-cord and holds a pistol in each hand, which he will fire, if agreeable to the Ladies.

N.B.—There will be several performances on the tight-rope by a Gentleman.

days are called variety actors, although in this age it is not often that the juggler is able to act even such small parts as were played by Malone during his brief career on the American stage.

Full casts of only five pieces produced at Annapolis by the New American Company were printed in the *Maryland Gazette*. The first of these was the "Beggars' Opera," in which Mr. Verling and Mrs. Parker had the favorite roles. They had had many predecessors, both on the English and American stage, as they were to have many successors. When Gay showed his musical comedy to Congreve before its production, that great dramatist said it would either take greatly or be damned confoundedly. It had now held the stage for half a century, and for almost half of that period there was no American company so

### BEGGARS' OPERA.

| | |
|---|---|
| Captain Macheath | Mr. Verling |
| Peachum | Mr. Darby |
| Lockit | Mr. Parker |
| Filch | Mr. Godwin |
| Robin of Bagshot / Drawer | Mr. Malone |
| Jemmy Twitcher | Mr. Page |
| Crook-Fingered Jack | Mr. Walker |
| Mat o' the Mint | Mr. Godwin |
| Ben Budge | Mr. Burdett |
| Nimming Ned | Mr. Jefferson |
| Beggar | Mr. Parker |
| Player | Mr. Burdett |
| Mrs. Peachum / Lucy Lockit | Mrs. Walker |
| (Her first appearance in these characters.) | |
| Diana Trapes / Mrs. Vixen | Mrs. Jones |
| Mrs. Slammekin | Mrs. Walker |
| Mrs. Coaxer | Mrs. Burdett |
| Jenny Diver | Mrs. Malone |
| Moll Brazen | Mr. Walker |
| Polly | Mrs. Parker |

"mean and contemptible" as not to sing or attempt to sing it.

If Mr. Godwin was the manager of the New American Company the advertisement of the full cast of the "Miser" is readily accounted for:

MISER.

| | |
|---|---|
| Lovegold . . . . . . . . . | Mr. Godwin |
| Frederick. . . . . . . . . . | Mr. Verling |
| Clerimont. . . . . . . . . . | Mr. Burdett |
| List . . . . . . . . . . . | Mr. Malone |
| Ramillie . . . . . . . . . | Mr. Darby |
| James ⎱ . . . . . . . . . | Mr. Parker |
| Decoy ⎰ | |
| Mercer . . . . . . . . . . | Mr. Page |
| Lawyer ⎱ . . . . . . . . | Mr. Walker |
| Sparkle ⎰ | |
| Furnish . . . . . . . . . . | Mr. Jefferson |
| Mrs. Wisely . . . . . . . . | Mrs. Burdett |
| Harriet . . . . . . . . . . | Mrs. Jones |
| Lappet . . . . . . . . . . | Mrs. Walker |
| Wheedle . . . . . . . . . | Mrs. Malone |
| Mariana . . . . . . . . . . | Mrs. Parker |

he was himself the *Lovegold*. In Philadelphia, in 1766, when the comedy was first played in this country, he was compelled to be satisfied with a very small part, while Mr. Allyn played the *Miser*. Hallam afterward played *Lovegold*, and now Godwin was, in one part at least, Hallam's rival. All this is guess-work, of course, but it is guess-work based on human nature—the human nature of the footlights, which is even more lasting than theatrical tradition. The performance must have been wretched.

Dr. Young's tragedy, the "Revenge," is a play that never proved attractive on the American stage. Why it should have been produced at Annapolis it is impossible to say, unless Mr. Ver-

REVENGE.

| | |
|---|---|
| Don Alonzo . | Mr. Godwin |
| Don Carlos . | Mr. Burdett |
| Alvarez . . . | Mr. Parker |
| Don Manuel | Mr. Malone |
| Zanga . . . | Mr. Verling |
| Isabella . . | Mrs. Walker |
| Leonora . . . | Mrs. Jones |

MARYLAND GAZETTE, March 9th, 1769.

The Public may be assured that the Company of Comedians in this city have gained great applause by their two last performances, Viz: the tragedies of "Douglas" and "Richard III."

ling was desirous of showing his great tragic powers as *Zanga*, as he had previously gained distinction as *Lord Randolph* and *Richard III*. Although the "Revenge" had been previously played by the American Company, this is the earliest cast of it that was preserved.

Mr. Darby for his benefit chose a comedy never before acted

in America, Arthur Murphy's "The Way to Keep Him," partly, perhaps, because it was a novelty, and partly to enable him and his wife to appear as *Sir Bashful* and *Lady Constant.* The piece, as it was now played at Annapolis, had been produced at Drury Lane as long before as 1761, but Mr. Darby was careful to announce that on that occasion it had run twenty-six nights without intermission. Subsequently the comedy became a favorite one in the repertoire of the American Company.

THE WAY TO KEEP HIM.

| | |
|---|---|
| Sir Bashful Constant | . . . . . . Mr. Darby |
| Sir Brilliant Fashion | . . . . . Mr. Spencer |
| William | . . . . . . . . . . Mr. Parker |
| Sideboard | . . . . . . . . . Mr. Burdett |
| Lovemore | . . . . . . . . . Mr. Verling |
| Mrs. Lovemore | . . . . . . . Mrs. Parker |
| Mignionet | . . . . . . . . . . Mrs. Jones |
| Muslin | . . . . . . . . . . Mrs. Walker |
| Lady Constant | . . . . . . . . Mrs. Darby |
| (Being her first appearance.) | |
| Widow Bellmore | . . . . . . Mrs. Osborne |

Mrs. Parker went further than any of her associates in the New American Company and printed the casts of both pieces in her benefit bill—Jones' tragedy, the "Earl of Essex," and Mendez' "musical entertainment," the "Chaplet." Both these pieces had been frequently acted by the American Company. These casts are only interesting for comparison and as part of the record.

EARL OF ESSEX.

| | |
|---|---|
| Earl of Essex | . . . . Mr. Verling |
| Southampton | . . . . . Mr. Darby |
| Lord Burleigh | . . . . Mr. Burdett |
| Sir Walter Raleigh | . . Mr. Spencer |
| Lieutenant | . . . . . . Mr. Parker |
| Queen Elizabeth | . . . Mrs. Jones |
| Countess of Nottingham | . Mrs. Parker |
| Countess of Rutland | . Mrs. Osborne |

CHAPLET.

| | |
|---|---|
| Damon | . . . . Mr. Spencer |
| Palæmon | . . . . Mr. Darby |
| Laura | . . . . Mrs. Osborne |
| Pastora | . . . . Mrs. Parker |

When Mrs. Malone took her benefit she announced Garrick's "Farmer's Return from London" as the afterpiece, but as "Thomas and Sally" was subsequently advertised without any mention of the interlude, it is not certain whether it

THOMAS AND SALLY.

| | |
|---|---|
| Squire | . . . . Mr. Spencer |
| Thomas | . . . . Mr. Verling |
| Sally | . . . . . Mrs. Parker |
| Dorcas | . . . Mrs. Osborne |

FARMER'S RETURN.

| | |
|---|---|
| Farmer | . . . . Mr. Parker |
| Farmer's Wife | . Mrs. Parker |
| Roger | . . . . . Mr. Malone |

was dropped from the bill or given between the play and the farce, as was the custom in London. Garrick originally wrote it to do Mrs. Pritchard a service at her benefit. It was a humorous description in rhyme of what the farmer saw in London—the coronation of George III and Queen Charlotte, the entertainments of the theatres and the famous imposition of the Cock-lane ghost.

The partial casts that were printed this season in the *Maryland Gazette* are interesting in showing who were the stars of the company.

PARTIAL CASTS.

*Plays.*

*A Bold Stroke for a Wife.*
Colonel Feignwell . . . . . Mr. Verling
Ann Lovely . . . . . . . Mrs. Osborne
*Busybody.*
Marplot . . . . . . . . . Mr. Spencer
Miranda . . . . . . . . . Mrs. Parker
*Conscious Lovers.*
Young Bevil . . . . . . . Mr. Verling
Indiana . . . . . . . . . Mrs. Osborne
*Distressed Mother.*
Pyrrhus . . . . . . . . . Mr. Verling
Orestes . . . . . . . . . Mr. Godwin
Hermione . . . . . . . . . Mrs. Jones
Andromache . . . . . . . Mrs. Osborne
*Douglas.*
Douglas . . . . . . . . Mr. Verling
Lady Randolph . . . . . Mrs. Osborne
*George Barnwell.*
Barnwell . . . . . . . . Mr. Godwin
Maria . . . . . . . . . . Mrs. Walker
Millwood . . . . . . . Mrs. Osborne
*King Henry IV.*
Prince of Wales . . . . . Mrs. Osborne
Poins . . . . . . . . . . Mrs. Parker
Falstaff . . . . . . . . . Mr. Verling
*Love in a Village.*
Young Meadows . . . . . Mr. Spencer
Hawthorn . . . . . . . Mr. Verling
Rosetta . . . . . . . . . Mrs. Parker
Lucinda . . . . . . . . Mrs. Osborne

These casts show that Mr. Verling was to this company what Mr. Hallam was to the one it attempted to rival—the first in everything. His parts ranged from *Shylock* and *Romeo* to *Falstaff* and *Petruchio;* from *Hawthorn* to *Captain O'Blunder*, for it is to be remarked that he did not allow Malone a monopoly of the brave Irishman.. He was, after Mr. Hallam, the first *Petruchio*, as Mrs. Walker was, after Miss Cheer, the first *Catherine*. This production of " Catherine and Petruchio" was the familiar farce, being advertised as "with alterations and additions by David Garrick." There were four ladies in the company who were accorded important roles. Of these, Mrs. Parker was apparently the most versatile, and Mrs. Osborne in possession of the greatest tragic force. It was, however, no mean distinction to Mrs. Walker to be given the part of *Catherine* in "Catherine and Petruchio," or to Mrs. Jones to be allowed to become the *Juliet* of the company.

The character of the theatre in which the New American Company played at Annapolis may be learned from a note appended to one of the advertisements. "Upper boxes," it was said, "are now preparing, the passage to which must be from the stage; 't is therefore hoped such ladies and gentlemen as choose to fix on *them* seats will come before the play begins, as it is not possible they can be admitted after the curtain is drawn up." The hour for beginning was six o'clock, and the prices were 7*s.* 6*d.* to the lower boxes, and 5*s.* to the pit and upper boxes. There was no

*Merchant of Venice.*
Shylock . . . . . . . . . Mr. Verling
Portia . . . . . . . . . . Mrs. Osborne
*Mourning Bride.*
Almeria . . . . . . . . . Mrs. Osborne
*Othello.*
Desdemona . . . . . . Mrs. Osborne
*Provoked Husband.*
Lady Townly . . . . . Mrs. Osborne
*Romeo and Juliet.*
Romeo . . . . . . . . Mr. Verling
Juliet . . . . . . . . . . Mrs. Jones
*Suspicious Husband.*
Ranger . . . . . . . . Mrs. Osborne

### Farces.

*Anatomist.*
M. le Medecin . . . . . Mr. Spencer
Crispin . . . . . . . . . Mr. Darby
Beatrice . . . . . . . . Mrs. Parker
*Brave Irishman.*
Capt. O'Blunder . . . . . Mr. Verling
*Catherine and Petruchio.*
Petruchio . . . . . . . Mr. Verling
Grumio . . . . . . . . . Mr. Parker
Catherine . . . . . . . Mrs. Walker
*Citizen.*
Maria . . . . . . . . . Mrs. Osborne
*Damon and Phillida.*
Damon . . . . . . . . Mr. Spencer
Phillida . . . . . . . . Mrs. Parker
*Genii.*
Genii . . . . . . . . . Master Knapp
Harlequin . . . . . . . Mr. Spencer
Columbine . . . . . . . Mrs. Parker
*Harlequin Skeleton.*
Harlequin . . . . . . . Mr. Godwin
Columbine . . . . . . . Mrs. Parker
*Lying Valet.*
Sharp . . . . . . . . . Mr. Verling
Melissa . . . . . . . . Mrs. Malone
Kitty Pry . . . . . . . . Mrs. Parker
*Merlin.*
Harlequin . . . . . . . Mr. Godwin
Clown . . . . . . . . . Mr. Malone
Columbine . . . . . . . Mrs. Parker

*Mock Doctor.*
Mock Doctor . . . . . . . . Mr. Darby
Dorcas . . . . . . . . . . Mrs. Parker
*Polly Honeycomb.*
Polly . . . . . . . . . . Mrs. Osborne
*Trick upon Trick.*
Vizard . . . . . . . . . . Mr. Verling
Mrs. Mixune . . . . . . . . Mrs. Jones

gallery. It can scarcely be claimed for a structure such as this must have been that it was, in the language of Charles Durang, "that old Temple of the Muses, known as the first theatre erected in America." "This theatre," Durang wrote, "was built of old-fashioned brick. It was not very lofty, and might be called a one-story edifice. It had a very good depth for its proportions. When I saw it years afterward it had the appearance of being at one period of time surrounded with a flower-garden, tastefully laid out. It was viewed with reverence, on account of its historical associations with the earliest efforts of the drama on this continent." As the theatre that Mr. Durang saw was not built until 1771, his reverence was wasted at a false shrine.

With the close of the season at Annapolis the New American Company apparently ceased to exist. With it Mr. Malone, whose versatile talents as actor and juggler must have been exceedingly useful in such an organization, disappeared also, and the name of Mr. Godwin does not afterward occur in American dramatic annals until after the Revolution. The parts filled by these two players, under the different conditions in which they appeared, afford an insight into the dramatic methods of the time that is deserv-

MR. MALONE'S PARTS.

*Plays.*
Beaux' Stratagem . . . . . . . Sir Charles
Beggars' Opera . . . . { Robin of Bagshot / Drawer
Clandestine Marriage . . . . . . Traverse
Hamlet . . . . . . . . . . Player King
Henry IV . . . . . . . . . . . Poins
Macbeth . . . . . . . . . Donaldbain
Merchant of Venice . . . . . . Salarino
Miser . . . . . . . . . . . { Furnish / List
Othello . . . . . . . . . . Montano
Romeo and Juliet . . . . . . . Escalus
Venice Preserved . . . . . . . Spinosa

*Farces.*
Catherine and Petruchio . . . . . Tailor
Citizen . . . . . . . . . . Quilldrive
Farmer's Return from London . . . Roger

ing of attention. In the American Company Malone and Godwin held the same rank. If there was any difference it was in Malone's favor. Under Mr. Douglass' management he played the *Player King* in "Hamlet," *Poins* in "Henry IV," and *Donaldbain* in "Macbeth," while Godwin's best parts were *Osric, Malcolm* and *Benvolio.* In the New American Company Malone obtained no advance, but while he made himself useful in such insignificant roles as *Tom,* in "High Life Below Stairs," and *Roger,* in the "Farmer's Return from London," Godwin leaped at a single bound from *Bubbleby* to *Lovegold,* in the "Miser," and accorded himself such parts as *Clincher, Jr.,* in the "Constant Couple," *Orestes,* in the "Distressed Mother," *Glenalvon,* in "Douglas," *Chamont,* in the "Orphan," and *Jaffier,* in "Venice Preserved." For an actor who had begun a few years before as *Daniel,* in the "Conscious Lovers," *Usher,* in "Lear," *Jeremy,* in "Love for Love," the *Messenger,* in the "Or-

MR. GODWIN'S PARTS.

*Plays.*

| | |
|---|---|
| Beaux' Stratagem | Honslow |
| Beggars' Opera | Filch |
| Cato | Marcus |
| Conscious Lovers | Daniel |
| Constant Couple | Clincher, Jr. |
| Distressed Mother | Orestes |
| Douglas | Glenalvon |
| George Barnwell | Barnwell |
| Hamlet | Osric |
| Lear | Usher |
| Love for Love | Jeremy |
| Love Makes a Man | Monsieur |
| Macbeth | Malcolm |
| Miser | { Bubbleby / Lovegold } |
| Mourning Bride | Selim |
| Orphan | Chamont |
| Orphan of China | Messenger |
| Revenge | Don Alonzo |
| Richard III | Prince Edward |
| Romeo and Juliet | Benvolio |
| Tamerlane | Haley |
| Venice Preserved | Jaffier |

*Farces.*

| | |
|---|---|
| Bedlamites | Bedlamite |
| Damon and Phillida | Corydon |
| Harlequin Skeleton | Harlequin |
| Honest Yorkshireman | Slango |
| Mayor of Garratt | Roger |
| Merlin | Harlequin |
| Miller of Mansfield | Lurewell |
| Mock Doctor | Harry |
| Harlequin Collector | Haymaker |
| High Life Below Stairs | Tom |
| Lethe | Tattoo |
| Mayor of Garratt | Roger |
| Merlin | Clown |

phan of China," and *Haly*, in " Tamerlane," Mr. Godwin's new line of parts ought to have been a sign of great advancement in his profession, but somehow it does not seem possible that an actor who played only the humblest roles with the American Company in 1766, and was retained only for a single season, should have been able to play acceptably the parts attempted by Godwin at Williamsburg and Annapolis. After the Revolution Godwin again tried his fortunes both as actor and manager, but none of the other members of the New American Company were ever heard of after this season.

# CHAPTER XXV.

SOUTHWARK THEATRE, 1769–70.

DUNLAP'S LOST PLAYERS—WHERE THEY WERE—ANOTHER BRILLIANT
SEASON IN PHILADELPHIA—MISS HALLAM THE LEADING LADY—
FIRST PRODUCTION OF A NUMBER OF NOTEWORTHY PLAYS.

AFTER the visit to Albany, in the summer of 1769, Dunlap finds no trace of the American Company until 1772, when it was playing at Annapolis. The fact was that Mr. Douglass once more transferred his forces to Philadelphia, where he reopened the Southwark Theatre, on the 8th of November, for a long and vigorous campaign. This season was one of the most brilliant in the history of the American stage. The repertoire was unusually attractive, and, although Miss Cheer and Miss Wainwright were no longer with the company, their absence does not seem to have proved a serious embarrassment. The older members had now had a sufficiently long experience to play almost any role acceptably, and fresh recruits were added from time to time. At last the American Company had reached that degree of perfection that its name was, in itself, a guarantee of a worthy entertainment in spite of the withdrawal of old favorites, and regardless of the addition of new candidates for public favor—that height of popularity that it was no longer necessary for

Mr. Douglass to resort to elaborate advertising.   As a consequence,

the announcements in the newspapers this season contained only the name of the company, the titles of the pieces to be performed and the dates of the performances.   This departure made it possible for the manager to advertise in the three papers published in Philadelphia at that time —the *Gazette*, the *Journal* and the *Chronicle*—and, consequently, the list of productions this season is nearly complete.   This list shows a number of important additions to the repertoire of the American Company—some full pieces never before acted in America, besides new farces and interludes.   These pieces, some of them produced with unusual elaboration, were Kane O'Hara's "Midas," one of the most delightful mythological burlesques ever written, and in which, at a later period, Madame Vestris was to become so great a favorite as *Apollo ;* Dryden's version of

Shakspere's "Tempest," an atrocity with its Caliban's sister, and the scarcely less acceptable sister of Miranda that, happily, has long been banished from the stage; the "Siege of Damascus," by John Hughes, first acted at Drury Lane, in 1720, on the night of the author's death; "Wit's Last Shift," which had been produced at Drury Lane only a few months before its production in Philadelphia; "Edward, the Black Prince," Shirley's, not the play of Mrs. Hofer, originally produced in a theatre in Goodman's Fields, in 1748, "by a patched-up, wretched set of performers"—if Dunlap is right—by William Hallam's company; Goldsmith's "Good-Natured Man," produced at Covent Garden, in 1768; Steele's "Funeral" and "Tender Husband," once popular, but now, happily, no longer on the boards, and Shakspere's "Merry Wives of Windsor." The new interludes and

Jan. 23—Tempest.
Neptune and Amphitrite.
Mayor of Garratt . . . . . Foote
29 Same bill as the 23d
Feb. 2—Tempest.
Neptune and Amphitrite.
Padlock.
6—Edward, the Black Prince . Shirley
Citizen . . . . . . . . . Murphy
9—Funeral . . . . . . . . . Steele
Damon and Phillida . . . Cibber
16—Orphan of China . . . . Murphy
Upholsterer . . . . . . . Murphy
19—Funeral
Upholsterer.
Mar. 2—Merry Wives of Windsor . Shakspere
High Life Below Stairs . Townley
6—Tempest.
Neptune and Amphitrite.
Padlock.
9—Comus . . . . . . . . . Milton
Edgar and Emmeline Hawkesworth
12—Edward, the Black Prince.
Edgar and Emmeline.
16—Revenge . . . . . . . . Young
· Harlequin Restored.
19—Tempest.
Neptune and Amphitrite.
Devil to Pay . . . . . . . Coffey
22—Beaux' Stratagem.
Edgar and Emmeline.
30—Tender Husband . . . . . Steele
Miss in her Teens . . . . Garrick
(Miss Storer's benefit.)
April 2—Fair Penitent . . . . . . Rowe
Harlequin Collector.
(Mrs. Henry's benefit.)
16—Alexander the Great . . . . Lee
Thomas and Sally. . . Bickerstaff
(Mrs. Harman's Benefit.)
20—Jane Shore . . . . . . . Rowe
Padlock.
(Miss Hallam's benefit.)
27—Good-Natured Man . . Goldsmith
Devil to Pay.
(Mr. Morris' benefit.)

May 3—Good-Natured Man.
  Catherine and Petruchio . Shakspere
  (Mr. Tomlinson's benefit.)
 10—Love for Love . . . . . Congreve
  Wit's Last Stake . . . . . . King
  (Mrs. Douglass' benefit.)
 17—Wild Irishman.
  High Life Below Stairs.
  (Benefit of Mr. and Mrs. Henry and
   Miss Storer.)
 24—Cymbeline . . . . . . Shakspere
  Guardian . . . . . . . . Garrick
  (Benefit of Parker and Broadbelt.)

afterpieces comprised Colman's "Musical Lady," Hawkesworth's "Edgar and Emmeline," and "Neptune and Amphitrite," a musical interlude popular in London, but never printed. It must be confessed that the presentation of so many new pieces by the American Company, at the time it was lost sight of by the historians, is some evidence that Mr. Dunlap, and those that came after him, might have found the players if they had looked for them.

The success of the season, judging from the number of times it was played and the commendations of an amateur critic[1] of the period, was the "Tempest." As no cast of the comedy was preserved, it is not possible to say how much of the Dryden version was retained. As, however, the whole of the Dryden title—"The Tempest, or the Enchanted Island"—was used, it is likely the excisions extended only to verbal "luxuriances." Apart from these, the Dryden version was more showy, more intricate, more ex-

---

[1] EXTRACTS FROM CANDIDUS' CRITIQUE.
—As the representation of this play is certainly the greatest attempt ever made by the performers in this part of the world, the curiosity of the town was very much excited, and I felt a secret satisfaction in seeing it honored with the appearance of a numerous American audience, who had taste enough to distinguish and relish the beauties of that immortal bard.

  *  *  *  *  *

It would be doing great injustice to the performers to pass unnoticed their manifest attention on this occasion to the entertain-ment of the audience, which, with the good taste shown in the disposition of the machinery and decorations, certainly rendered this play the most delightful entertainment ever exhibited on the American stage. The thanks of the public are due to the person who superintended the getting up of this piece for his good judgment and discretion in pruning it of many indecent luxuriances, which Dryden had introduced into it with the vitiated taste of the age in which he wrote. As there is nothing now to offend, but very much to delight, in this celebrated performance, I shall hope each evening it

tended in the musical parts, and better fitted to keep up the attention of an audience than Shakspere's delightful comedy. It may be assumed, therefore, that the "Tempest" produced on this occasion is to be credited to Dryden rather than to Shakspere, and it will be observed that there is nothing in the contemporary critique of "Candidus," printed in the *Pennsylvania Journal,* to contradict this assumption. Later the casts show the additional creations that Dryden added to Prospero's island thus settling the question definitely. The Dryden version was acted at Dorset Gardens as early as 1670. It is remarkable that such a production should have retained the stage for a century but such was the case not only in America but in England, even Kemble's revivals including some of Dryden's alterations.

As no casts were printed in the newspapers this season it is not easy to give a satisfactory account of the changes that had occurred in the company. It is not improbable that Mr. Goodman, who became an excellent actor, and the second Mrs. Morris, one of the most noted of the earlier actresses on the American stage, were brought forward at this time, and it is certain that Miss Richardson made her *debut* at the Southwark Theatre this season. The fact that Miss Richardson was

may hereafter be given to the town to see a numerous appearance of the friends to useful recreation, bearing testimony of their invaluable obligations to the great poet of nature, and endeavoring to make some return to the players for their assiduity and expense in procuring this great addition to our rational amusements. I am not insensible, gentlemen, in saying this much in favor of theatrical performances, how obnoxious I render myself to the censure of a few, who, being entirely ignorant of their nature or uses, are continually railing against them; but so careless am I of the evil report of such people, that I am not ashamed to own my admiration of dramatic performances hath induced me, now and then, to associate with some of the performers, from whose conversation I have often received both pleasure and advantage. It is this that gives me the satisfaction to advertise your readers, who are lovers of the drama, of another play which I think was never acted here, and will be highly interesting to every one zealous for the honor of his country. It is founded on the story of the immortal son of Edward III, surnamed the Black Prince, a man in whom innate courage shone with superior lustre. * * *

with the American Company in 1769–70 is established by a house-bill for Miss Storer's benefit, in the possession of the Pennsylvania Historical Society.    This bill contains the casts of the "Tender Hus-

TENDER HUSBAND.

Humphrey Gubbin . . . . . . . Mr. Hallam
Sir Harry Gubbin . . . . . . . Mr. Douglass
Mr. Clerimont . . . . . . . . . Mr. Henry
Captain Clerimont . . . . . . . Mr. Byerly
Mr. Tipkin . . . . . . . . . . Mr. Morris
Mr. Prince . . . . . . . . . . . Mr. Wall
The Niece . . . . . . . . . Miss Hallam
Aunt . . . . . . . . . Mrs. Tomlinson
Fainlove . . . . . . . . . Mrs. Harman
Jenny . . . . . . . . . Miss Richardson

band" and "Miss in her Teens," but is partially mutilated, so that it is uncertain whether Miss Richardson or Miss Hallam played *Miss Biddy.*    It is probable, how-ever, that the part was given to the former, as Miss Hallam was now fully installed as the leading lady

of the company.    Among the parts she is known to have played dur-ing the season were *Juliet* in "Romeo and Juliet" and *Mrs. Sullen* in the "Beaux' Stratagem."    Oddly enough she appeared as *Nell* and Mr. Hallam as *Jobson* in the "Devil to Pay" for the first time this season.    "A young gentle-

MISS IN HER TEENS.

Captain Flash . . . . . . . . Mr. Henry
Captain Loveit . . . . . . . . Mr. Parker
Fribble . . . . . . . . . . . Miss Storer
Puff . . . . . . . . . . . . Mr. Morris
Tag . . . . . . . . . . . . Mrs. Henry

woman" made her *debut* as *Dorinda* in the "Stratagem," December 12th, 1769.    It is of course impossible to say whether this was Miss Richardson.    The name of Mrs. Henry now occurs for the first time. Miss Storer was evidently Miss Maria Storer, the younger of the Storer sisters, while this Mrs. Henry was the Miss Storer of previous years. When she took her benefit Mr. Henry announced that as *Harlequin* in the pantomime he would "run up a perpendicular scene twenty feet high." History is silent as to the manner in which this remarkable feat was accomplished.    This, however, was not the only *outre* incident relating to the benefits, for in the announcement of Mrs. Douglass' it was promised that Mr. Wall would speak an epilogue, riding on an ass. Mr. Douglass sometimes indulged in advertisements that have a quaint sound to modern ears. One of these was as follows: "Mr. Douglass will be extremely obliged to any lady or gentleman who will lend him the burlesque of the 'Dragon of Wantley.'" At that time the newspapers gave little or no attention to the theatres, and consequently his advertisements are the only sources of information left to us in regard to the surroundings of the theatre in Southwark, or his foresight and energy in providing for the comfort of his patrons. "A foot-path is made," he announced in February, 1770, "across the common to the corner of Pine Street, in Fourth Street, on which those ladies who are not provided with carriages may come to the house without dirtying their feet." There is no attempt at fine writing in this announcement, but words could scarcely give a more vivid picture of the desolate and forbidding situation of the Southwark Theatre previous to the Revolution.

The peculiar relations of the theatre toward the public were frequently illustrated in the newspapers at that time. Everybody connected with the play-house was apparently outside of the pale of respectable society. According to his letter in the *Pennsylvania Journal* "Candidus" expected to be ostracised for writing it. Mr. Douglass evidently feared that some musical persons belonging to the city would be insulted for assisting his orchestra on opera nights. "As they have no view," he said in one of his advertisements, "but to contribute to the entertainment of the public, they certainly claim a protection from any manner of insult." After the close of the season Mr. Wall gave, on the 6th of June, a monologue entertainment made up from the writings of George Alexander Steevens, at the Lodge Room.

He called it "A Rhapsody," but even for this entertainment he thought it necessary to assure the public that no party, sect or denomination would be aimed at. But he must have horrified the good people who petitioned the General Assembly against the theatre, in 1759, by announcing that after the entertainment the music would be at the service of such ladies and gentlemen as might choose to dance. The Southwark Theatre was now closed, not to be re-opened again for many months, although at that time Philadelphia was certainly the best theatrical city in the Colonies.

# CHAPTER XXVI.

## IN MARYLAND AND VIRGINIA.

AFTER the close of the Philadelphia season in May, 1770, the
American Company went South, playing at Annapolis and
Williamsburg in the winter of 1770–1 and again the following year.
Unfortunately the material available for the history of these two years in
Maryland and Virginia is not so full as would be desirable. Announcements of the intended performances were not regularly made, either in
the *Maryland Gazette* at Annapolis or the *Virginia Gazette* at Williamsburg. This was owing, no doubt, to the small number of inhabitants in the two capitals and the necessity of depending upon the
planters in the vicinity of each for patronage, whom it was necessary
to reach by some other means than the tardy newspapers of the
period. It is likely that during these two years other places were
visited besides Annapolis and Williamsburg, but in that case all record
of the travels of the American Company has been hopelessly lost.
The first stop was at Annapolis, where the season began early and
was very short. It was announced at the outset that the company's

engagement at Virginia would prevent more than a month's stay at that time, and a careful examination of the files of the *Maryland Gazette* shows only the bills for three nights of that brief season. It is evident, however, from a communication printed in that journal on the 6th of September that Miss Hallam[1] succeeded in making a deep impression on the Marylanders as *Imogen* in "Cymbeline."  No modern actress, not even Miss Neilson, has been able to extort such unreserved praise from the critics as "Y. Z." bestowed on Miss Hallam.  So far as the actress is concerned the communication was not so much a criticism as a rhapsody.  Praise certainly could not go farther than a comparison of the unknown Miss Hallam with the celebrated Mrs. Cibber. Never before had an American actress called forth such eulogy, and, as will be seen hereafter, this was only the beginning of the high

PERFORMANCES—ANNAPOLIS.

1770.

Aug. 27—Suspicious Husband . . . Hoadly
        Thomas and Sally . . Bickerstaff
  30—Cymbeline . . . . . Shakspere
        Miller of Mansfield . . . Dodsley
Sept. 1—Love in a Village . . Bickerstaff

[1] MISS HALLAM AS IMOGEN.—*To the Printer :*—As I make it a matter of conscience to do justice to merit to the utmost of my abilities in whatever walk of life I chance to discover it, I shall take the liberty of publishing through the channel of your paper the observations which the representation at the Theatre on Thursday night drew from me.

I shall not at present expatiate on the merits of the whole performance, but confine myself principally to one object.  The actors are indubitably entitled to a very considerable portion of praise.  But by your leave, gentlemen (to speak in the language of *Hamlet*)—"Here's metal more attractive."  On finding that the part of *Imogen* was to be played by Miss Hallam I instantly formed to myself from my predilection for her the most

sanguine hope of entertainment.  But how was I ravished on experiment !  She exceeded my utmost idea !  Such delicacy of manner ! Such classical strictness of expression !  The music of her tongue—the *vox liquida*, how melting !  Notwithstanding the injuries it received from the horrid ruggedness of the roof and the untoward construction of the whole house, methought I heard once more the warbling of Cibber in my ear.  How true and thorough her knowledge of the part she personated !  Her whole form and dimensions how happily convertible and universally adapted to the variety of her part.

A friend of mine, who was present, was so deeply impressed by the bewitching grace and justness with which the actress filled the whole character, that immediately on going

regard in which Miss Hallam was to be held by the Maryland public. In *Imogen*, especially, their admiration for her was unbounded. Not only did the local poets sing her praises, comparing her face with Cytherea's and her form with the perfections of Diana, but they invoked their native artist, destined to become one of America's greatest painters, Charles Wilson Peale, to paint her in the part in which they best liked to see her, an invocation to which he gave heed. The poem of "Y. Z.'s" friend was, of course, printed in the *Maryland Gazette* at the same time with the critique. While it does not show a high order of poetic merit it is as gushing as anything in these latter days by unfledged singers to actresses of imagined charms and imaginary merits. But even fulsome praise is a sign that praise is not entirely undeserved, and it

To Miss Hallam.

———

Hail, wondrous maid!   I grateful hail
　　Thy strange dramatic power;
To thee I owe that Shakspere's tale
　　Has charmed my ears once more.
'Twas his to paint, with touch refined,
　　Beyond the rules of art,
Each varying passion of the mind,
　　And probe the human heart.

home he threw out, warm from the heart as well as brain, the verses I enclose.

The house, however, was thin for want of sufficient acquaintance with the general as well as particular merits of the performers. The characteristical propriety of Mrs. Douglass cannot but be too striking to pass unnoticed. The fine genius of that young creature, Miss Storer, unquestionably affords the most pleasing prospect of an accomplished actress. The discerning part of an audience must cheerfully pay the tribute of applause due to the solid sense which is conspicuous in Mrs. Harman, as well as to her perspicuity and strength of memory. The sums lavished on a late set whose merits were not of the transcendent kind, in whatever point of light they are viewed, are still fresh in our memories. And should these their successors, whose deportment, decency and unremitting study to please have ever been confessedly marked, meet with discountenance, methinks such a conduct would not reflect the highest honor either on our taste or spirit.

The merit of Mr. Douglass' company is notoriously in the opinion of every man of sense in America, whose opportunities give him a title to judge—take them all in all—superior to that of any company in England, except those of the metropolis. The dresses are remarkably elegant; the dispatch of the business of the theatre uncommonly quick; and the stillness and good order preserved behind the scenes are proofs of the greatest attention and respect paid to the audience.

Y. Z.

'Tis thine, with kindred reach of thought
    And magic powers to please,
What he, sweet child of Fancy, wrought
    To act with grace and ease.

Great Bard of Nature! Hard the part
    Thy forceful scenes to play;
And few like Hallam have the art
    To catch thy glowing ray.

Say! Does she plead as though she felt
    The tender tale of woe?
Our eyes, albeit unused to melt,
    With tears of pity flow.

Or does she charm the jocund hours
    With strokes of comic wit?
See, laughter holds his sides, and pours
    Full Ios round the pit.

She speaks!—What elocution flows!
    Ah! softer far her strains
Than fleeces of descending snows,
    Or gentlest vernal rains.

Do solemn measures slowly move?
    Her looks inform the strings:
Do Lydian airs invite to love?
    We feel it as she sings.

Around her, see the Graces play,
    See Venus' wanton doves;
And in her eye's pellucid ray,
    See little laughing loves.

Ye God's! 'Tis Cytherea's face;
    'Tis Dian's faultless form;
But hers alone the nameless grace
    That every heart can charm.

When laid along thy grassy tomb
    What pencil, say, can paint
Th' unlustrous but expressive gloom
    Of thee, fair sleeping saint.

Or thine, or none, self-tutored Peale!
    Oh! then, indulgent hear
Thy bard's request, and let him kneel
    A weeping hermit there!

may be assumed with safety that Miss Hallam had developed into an actress of more than usual ability. As an evidence that her Annapolis critic, who first sounded her praises, was a man of sound dramatic instinct his early appreciation of Miss Storer may be cited. This young girl, after the Revolution, completely fulfilled the predictions that were made by "Y. Z." concerning her future. Besides, his judgment of Miss Hallam is corroborated by the course pursued by the "self-tutored Peale." Charles Wilson Peale was born at Chestertown, near Annapolis. Early in life he was apprenticed to a saddler, and he subsequently carried on that business. Mr. Peale was "a jack-of-all-trades," being, besides, a silversmith, watchmaker and carver, sportsman, naturalist and preserver of animals. As an inventor he perfected some important improvements, and he was the first dentist in America who made sets of artificial teeth. As a portrait painter he showed remarkable proficiency, even before he received any instruction in the art. In the winter of 1770–71 Mr. Peale studied under Copley, at Boston, and it is likely that his picture of Miss Hallam as *Imogen* was painted in the summer and autumn of the latter year, after his return from New England. This assumption is based on the fact that the lines in which his skill and this painting were so highly praised were printed in the *Maryland Gazette*, November 7th, 1771. There is no evidence that the picture was ever exhibited at Peale's Museum, in Philadelphia, and all trace of it has been lost.

After the close of the short season at Annapolis the American Company went to Virginia, but there is no record of the tour nor even of the engagement at Williamsburg during the winter of 1770–71 beyond a reference in the *Virginia Gazette* to the production of the "Tender Husband" and the "Honest Yorkshireman," on the 22d

To MR. PEALE on his Painting Miss Hallam in the character of *Fedele* in "Cymbeline."

The grand design in Grecian schools was taught;
Venetian colors gave the pictures thought.
In thee, oh Peale, both excellences join ;
Venetian colors and the Greek design.
Thy style has matched what e'en the ancients knew,
Grand the design and as the coloring true.
Pursue the path thou hast so well begun,
And second be to nature's eldest son.
Shakspere's immortal scenes our wonder raise,
And next to him thou claim'st our highest praise.
When Hallam as *Fedele* comes distressed,
Tears fill each eye and passion heaves each breast;
View with uplifted eyes the charming maid,
Prepared to enter though she seems afraid.
And see, to calm her fears and soothe her care,
Bellarius and the royal boys appear.
Thy pencil has so well the scene conveyed,
Thought seems but an unnecessary aid.
How pleased we view the visionary scene,
The friendly cave and rock and mountain green;
Nature and art are here at once combined,
And all Elysium to one view confined.
Another scene still claims thy pencil's aid,—
Storer in *Ariel*—Enchanting maid !
Whose easy nature every grace affords,
And charms without the empty pomp of words;
The list'ning ear on every word intent,
Catches the sound and guesses what is meant.
" Her name, the boast of every tuneful choir,
Shall tremble on the strings of every lyre."
Accept, oh Peale, these friendly artless lays,
The tribute that a fond admirer pays;
Unrivaled, as unmatched, be still thy fame,
And Shakspere's scenes still raise thy envy'd name.

of April, 1771. It is not certain, however, that this production was by the American Company. On the contrary, the probability is that Mr. Douglass paid a brief visit to Jamaica early in 1771, while Mr. Henry went to England for recruits. This supposition is strengthened by an announcement in the *Maryland Gazette*, on the 19th of September, 1771, that Henry arrived at Norfolk on the 11th, a passenger on the brigantine "Jenny," Isaac Mitchenson, master, from Whitehaven. At this time the American Company was again at Annapolis, while a company of comedians without any distinctive name was playing at Williamsburg. The performance of the "West Indian" and the "Musical Lady," on the 23d of October, was the opening night, the season lasting two months. So far as is known these are the first performances of the "West Indian," and of one of Ben Jonson's plays in America, but it is probable they had previously been seen at Williamsburg, because no special mention of them was made in the advertisements, while "King Lear" was announced as "never performed in Virginia."

WILLIAMSBURG PERFORMANCES.

1771.
Oct. 23—West Indian . . . . Cumberland
　　　　Musical Lady . . . . . Colman
　　26—West Indian.
　　　　Musical Lady.
Nov. 12—King Lear . . . . . Shakspere
　　23—Every Man in his Humor . Jonson
　　　　Damon and Phillida . . . Cibber
Dec. 21—Jealous Wife . . . . . . Colman
　　　　Padlock . . . . . . Bickerstaff

When the American Company returned to Annapolis in the autumn of 1771 it was to dedicate a new temple to the drama. This was the theatre that Dunlap was led into accepting, on the authority of a writer in the *Maryland Gazette*, in 1828, as "the earliest temple reared in our country to the dramatic muse," and as being in existence in 1752. Contemporary authority in regard to the erection of the Annapolis theatre thus erroneously described is abundant. The clearest account of the building of the

Annapolis theatre of 1771 is contained in "Letters from America,"[1] 1769–77, by William Eddis (London, 1792), who was surveyor of the customs at Annapolis. There is internal evidence in this letter that Mr. Eddis was the critic who so favorably reviewed the performance of Miss Hallam as *Imogen*, already quoted, but his letter is chiefly valuable in showing how the funds were obtained for the erection of the new theatre. Although Mr. Eddis gives the credit of initiating the plan to the incumbent of the Province House there is no reason to doubt that it was suggested by Mr. Douglass. The manager had previously resorted to the same policy in New York to relieve himself from embarrassments incurred by the erection of the John Street Theatre. This is apparent from his appeal to the subscribers, dated nearly a fortnight before Mr. Eddis' letter was written. As has happened with subscriptions of every kind, in every age, some of Mr. Douglass' subscribers who were quick to sign were slow to pay, and he was consequently compelled to resort to a card in the *Maryland Gazette* to let them know that they were expected

---

[1] EDDIS' LETTER.—Annapolis, June 18th, 1771. — * * * When I bade farewell to England I little expected that my passion for the drama could have been gratified in any tolerable degree at a distance so remote from the great mart of genius; and I brought with me strong prepossessions in behalf of favorite performers whose merits were fully established by the universal sanction of intelligent judges. My pleasure and my surprise were therefore excited in proportion, on finding performers in this country equal at least to those who sustain the best of the first characters in your most celebrated provincial theatres. Our Governor, from a strong conviction that the stage, under proper regulations, may be rendered of general utility and made subservient to the great interests of religion and virtue patronizes the American Company; and as their present place of exhibition is on a small scale and inconveniently situated, a subscription by his example has been rapidly completed to erect a new theatre on a commodious if not elegant plan. The manager is to deliver tickets for two seasons for the amount of the respective subscriptions, and it is imagined that the money which will be received at the doors from non-subscribers will enable him to conduct the business without difficulty, and when the limited number of performances is completed the entire property is to be vested in him. The building is already in a state of forwardness, and the day of opening is anxiously expected.

to keep their promises.[1]  This was apparently the first time that scenery was expressly painted in London for America, the regular scene painter of the American Company being Jacob Snyder, whom Mr. Douglass found at Providence in 1762.  Snyder was esteemed a fair artist.  Charles Durang wrote that he remembered an excellent street-scene of Snyder's painting in the old Southwark Theatre, as well as other stock scenery that remained in it till the house was burnt, in 1821.  The set of scenes by Doll, for Annapolis, was an unusual luxury.  Another set painted by Richards, of London, was procured for the Annapolis theatre the following year.

The new theatre was built on ground leased from St. Anne's Parish, in West Street, on the site now occupied by Adams' Express Office.  "The structure," Eddis wrote, in November, 1771, "is not inelegant, but, in my opinion, on too narrow a scale for its length; the boxes are commodious and neatly decorated; the pit and gallery are calculated to hold a number of people without incommoding each other; the stage is well adapted for dramatic and pantomimical exhibitions; and several of the scenes reflect great credit on the painter."

[1] MR. DOUGLASS' APPEAL. — Mr. Douglass begs leave to acquaint the Gentlemen who have subscribed to the new Theatre in Annapolis that all the materials for the building are now purchased and workmen engaged to complete it by the first of September. He assures them that nothing will be wanting on his part nor on the parts of the gentlemen who have undertaken to superintend the work, to render it as commodious and elegant as any theatre in America.  He has sent to London to engage some performers, and expects them and a new set of scenes painted by Mr. Doll in a few weeks.  In short, the Public, whose favors he most gratefully acknowledges, will, he flatters himself, be convinced by the efforts he makes to entertain them, that he has a proper sense of their goodness, and an unremitting desire to make every return in his power for the obligations he is under to them.

He would esteem it a very great favor if the Gentlemen who have neglected to pay their subscription money will be good enough to send it as soon as possible, as the sum collected is by no means sufficient to answer the necessary demands that will very soon be made.

Annapolis, June 6th, 1771.

The building was of brick, with seating capacity for about six hundred persons. The new theatre was certainly in marked contrast with the old church. It is not surprising, therefore, to find in the columns of the *Maryland Gazette* a rhymed address from the old church to the inhabitants of Maryland's ancient capital complaining that,

> Here in Annapolis alone
> God has the meanest house in town,

and asking, at least, an equal share with the theatre in the indulgence and esteem of the people. This address, both in its temper and logic, is entirely different from everything relating to the theatre printed in America previous to the Revolution.

It is a singular fact that a claim for Annapolis, that it had the first theatre on this continent

### CHURCH AND THEATRE.

Of sunshine oft a casual ray
Breaks in upon a cloudy day
O'erwhelmed with woe; methinks I see
A ray of hope thus dart on me.
Close at my door, on my own land,
Placed, it seems, by your command,
I've seen, I own, with some surprise
A novel structure sudden rise.
There let the stranger stay, for me,
If virtue's friend, indeed, she be;
I would not if I could restrain
A moral stage; yet would I fain
Of your indulgence and esteem
At least an equal portion claim.
And decency, without my prayers,
Will surely whisper in your ears,—
"To pleasure if such care you show
A mite to duty, pray, bestow."
Say, does my rival boast the art
One solid comfort to impart,
Or heal, like me, the broken heart?
Does she, like me, pour forth the strain
Of peace on earth, good will to men?
Merit she has; but, let me say,
The highest merit of a play,
Tho' Shakspere wrote it, but to name
With mine were want of sense or shame.

built expressly for dramatic uses, should ever have been made in the face of such ample testimony to the contrary, or being made, should have been allowed. The only authority for it is the assertion of a single blunderer—the writer in the *Maryland Gazette* in 1828. His mistake, being accepted by Dunlap, has been repeated ever since without inquiry, even by the Annapolis historians, Ridgely and Riley, notwithstanding its contradiction stared them in the face in the Maryland

State Library. While Dunlap stands pre-eminent as a historical blunderer, Mr. Benson J. Lossing, who has been making mistakes in American history for fully half a century, is almost his equal. Lossing, in a note in the first number of the *American Historical Record*, of which he was the editor, not only repeats Dunlap's mistake, but in describing a sketch of Annapolis in water color by Chevalier Colbert who came to this country with the Count de Volney, in 1795, and returned with him in 1798, adds one of his own. "The most prominent building delineated," he says in describing the sketch, "is the old State House, yet standing. On its left is seen the tower of the old Episcopal church, and on its right a three-story building, the theatre in which Hallam performed, built on ground leased from the church." Not only had the State House in Colbert's sketch been long replaced by the present structure, but the three-story building "on its right" was the college, not the theatre. The theatre, if it is included in the sketch, must be the insignificant looking structure on the high ground near the church.

According to the *Maryland Gazette* "the new Theatre in West Street" was opened on the 9th of September with the "Roman Father" and the "Mayor of Garratt," "to a numerous and brilliant audience, who expressed the greatest satisfaction not only at the performance but with the house, which is thought to be as elegant and commodious for its size as any theatre in America." An occasional prologue was spoken previous to the performance by Mr. Douglass, and at its close Mrs. Henry spoke an occa-

PROLOGUE.
———
To call forth genius, bid fair science bloom,
Whilom enveloped in Cimmerian gloom;
The mind, by ignorance inthralled, to free
From the hard bonds of rude barbarity;
For this, at first was formed,—for this the stage
Still claims th' indulgence of a polished age.

sional epilogue. In the prologue such local allusions as that to the rising stadthouse show that the poet was either an American by birth or long association, while the pedantic allusions to Greece and Rome, to Thespis and Æschylus, were characteristic of Colonial scholarship. The reverence for Shakspere, too, was then, as now, more thoroughly American than English. This prologue seems to indicate that the house was not fully completed on the opening night. Indeed the epilogue as well as the prologue alludes to the unfinished state of the theatre, showing that the players had taken possession of the house before the carpenters departed.

In ancient Greece, in distant era, long
From some rude cart, his dramas Thespis sung;
And Athens saw revolve full many an age
Ere buskins, scenes and all the pomp o' the stage
Grave Æschylus taught; and with well-earned applause
Fast fixed the system of dramatic laws.
Long, too, had Rome, for arms and arts renowned,
Extended far her empire's narrow bound,
Ere she beheld her theatres arise
With towers and columns reaching to the skies.
Thus has true taste, like the revolving sun,
From East to West in even tenor run.
Now on these shores the goddess stands confest
And reigns supreme in every generous breast,
Nobly exerted by the thirst for fame,
To emulate the Greek and Roman name.
View yonder stadthouse, rising from the ground,
Whilst private buildings multiply around;
Sacred to Shakspere! this your structure, see,
For which each actor thanks you thus,—by me.
Here solemn tragedy, imperial queen,
In awful and majestic state is seen;
An unsheathed dagger in her zone she wears,
And in her hand her regal sceptre bears;
'Tis hers each manly feeling of the heart,
Each soft sensation, to awake by art;
To teach the lab'ring breast to heave the sigh
When lovers suffer, or when heroes die.
Here, too, behold with soft bewitching smiles,
Gay Comedy the yielding heart beguiles.
'Tis hers with gentle force and happy powers
To wing with joy your gayer, lighter hours;
Oh, may she often here these arts diffuse,
And you, receiving from a sportive Muse
Pleasing instruction, mixed with soft delight,
Retire improved on each successive night.
So shall ye chase that demon, Spleen, away
And all shall catch good humor at a play.
To you, our friends, raised by whose bounteous hands,
This rude and yet unpolished structure stands,
Great is the debt of gratitude we owe,—
Great are the bounties you may yet bestow.
This debt to pay shall be our constant aim,
Whilst future favors shall increase your claim;
The heart that truly feels a favor done,
Hastes not impatient to repay it soon.

Be ours the pleasing task each night to learn
The happy art your plaudits how to earn;
Be 't yours with candor—yes—it rests with you,
Not to withhold your praise,—should praise be due.

This haste was probably due to a desire to have the stage in working order before the week of the races—a gala-week at Annapolis—which began on the Monday following the opening of the theatre.

The epilogue was different in measure and in theme, but it was not so smooth in treatment as the prologue. The charm of the epilogue is the avowal of Mrs. Henry (Ann Storer) that she was born an actress. If, as has been assumed, the Storer sisters were the daughters of the once famous Covent Garden vocalists, each of these actresses might with truth have asserted, " i' faith, I was born one." Although this Miss Storer was recognized as Mrs. Henry at the time this epilogue was written, as Mrs. Hogg she was destined to be the mother of a family of sons, some of whom lived down to the present decade, avoiding,

EPILOGUE.

Well, now that 'tis over—the ice fairly broken,
The epilogue must be, by me, they say, spoken;
At a loss, I must own, I am for a beginning,
Which divines say the case is seldom in sinning;
And a sinner I am, for no woman e'er breathing
Turned actress but straight she was reckon'd a heathen.
And how then, in conscience, can I, a forlorn one
Be thought any other, for i' faith, I was born one.
'Twas but lately in France (the politest of nations
Where actresses all have the best educations)
Allowed that a Christian funeral's befitting
An actor, this great stage of life on his quitting;
To our sins (if they're such) we hope you will be kinder
And to the fair actress, if really you find her
Deserving of favor, give due commendation,
(The heaven she aspires to) instead of damnation.
    But to come to the point; suppose me just entered,
And excuse the digression on which I have ventured;
Yet before I say more—let me look on your faces—
And learn from your smiles, ye wits, critics and graces,
That you of your bounty have not yet repented,
And—with our endeavors to please you're contented.
For the unfinished state of ou  house make allowance,
Seeing we, of the time we've had, have not been truants.
    To correct what is wrong, to add what is deficient
In the house; and ourselves, if we can, more proficient
To render, in this our theatrical calling,
Is a determination united we're all in.
Of our obligations I know 'tis expected,
That I should say something—I have been directed
To tell you—as how—it shall be our endeavor
And ambition to merit your favor forever—

as far as was possible, all mention of their theatrical descent.

Considering the interest that attaches to

With more to that purpose—But lest I should tire ye
Excuse me till some other night I desire ye.
  For epilogue, so much,—yet ere I dismiss it,
You'd think me full proud, if I did not solicit,
Fair Ladies and Gentlemen, from you some token
That you're not displeased with what I have spoken
On behalf of us all.—Your applause must declare it,
Then grant it to me—and the others shall share it.

the opening of a new theatre, built as the Annapolis theatre was, it is possible to obtain only a very unsatisfactory account of the season

ANNAPOLIS PERFORMANCES.

1771.
Sept. 9—Roman Father . . . Whitehead
        Mayor of Garratt . . . . Foote
      20—Maid of the Mill . . . Bickerstaff
        Old Maid . . . . . . Murphy
Oct.  5—Jealous Wife . . . . . . Colman
        Midas . . . . . . . O'Hara
      7—Cymbeline . . . . . Shakspere

that followed from the columns of the *Maryland Gazette.* Only three of the performances were advertised in that journal, and besides these three bills the name of only one play presented during the season has come down to us.

This was Shakspere's "Cymbeline," and it is only mentioned because another of the local poets of Annapolis rushed into print with some more verse in praise of Miss Hallam as *Imogen.* These stanzas were signed " Paladour," and as they were dated Thursday, October 10th, it follows that the performance of " Cymbeline " must have occurred on the 7th. This poem, although it has no merit in itself, has some value, both in showing the esteem in which Miss Hallam con-

To MISS HALLAM
On seeing her last Monday night in the character
of *Imogen.*

Say, Hallam, to thy wondrous art
    What tribute shall I pay?
Say, wilt thou from a feeling heart
    Accept this votive lay?

A votive lay to thee belongs,
    For many a pleasing tear,
That fell for Imogen's foul wrongs
    On fair Fedele's bier.

Fair, fair Fedele! how thy charms
    The huntsmen's pity moved!
Artless as theirs, such soft alarms
    My melting bosom proved.

In nature's breast, superior joy
    The power of beauty wakes;

And the wild motion of her eye
  An easier prisoner takes.

From earliest youth, with raptures oft
  I've turned great Shakspere's page;
Pleased when he's gay, and soothed when soft,
  Or kindled at his rage.

Yet not till now, till taught by thee,
  Conceived I half his power!
I read, admiring now I see,
  I only not adore.

E'en now amid the laurel choir
  Of blissful bards on high,
Whom list'ning deities admire,
  The audience of the sky!

Methinks I see his smiling shade,
  And hear him thus proclaim,
" In Western worlds to this fair maid,
  I trust my spreading fame!

" Long have my scenes each British heart
  With warmest transports filled;
Now equal praise, by Hallam's art,
  America shall yield."

tinued to be held, and in fixing the date of one of the most important productions of the season at Annapolis. It will be remembered, besides, that the lines addressed to Peale on his portrait of the actress were dated just one month later. It is not improbable that Peale's lost picture was on exhibition at Annapolis at the time.

Only one cast of the Annapolis season of 1771 has come down to us, that of the " Roman Father " on the opening night. The only new name is that of Mr. Goodman, who probably made his *debut* in Philadelphia the previous season. Goodman was not only more than a substitute for Mr. Allyn, but, with the exception of Mr. Henry, he was the most capable recruit added to the American Company before the Revolution. He was a Philadelphian by residence and education and, probably, by birth. At the time he became "stage-struck" he was a student in the office of Mr. Ross, a lawyer. He accompanied the company on the Southern tour of 1771–2, and returned with it

ROMAN FATHER.

| | |
|---|---|
| Roman Father | Mr. Hallam |
| Tullus Hostilius | Mr. Douglass |
| Publius | Mr. Goodman |
| Valerius | Mr. Wall |
| First Citizen | Mr. Morris |
| Second Citizen | Mr. Woolls |
| Third Citizen | Mr. Parker |
| Fourth Citizen | Mr. Roberts |
| Soldier | Mr. Tomlinson |
| Valeria | Mrs. Henry |
| Horatia | Miss Hallam |

to Philadelphia in October, 1772, where, so far as the bills are a guide, he made his first appearance for the season of 1772–3 on the 11th of November as *Major Sturgeon* in the "Mayor of Garratt." From this it may be inferred that he played the same part in the afterpiece on the opening night at Annapolis.

At the close of the Annapolis season, about the beginning of February, 1772, the American Company went to Williamsburg, as appears from a preliminary notice printed in the *Virginia Gazette,* January 23d, 1772. It is impossible to give anything like a full list of the company's repertoire this season, but that Mr. Douglass' forces arrived on time and began a vigorous campaign is apparent from an announcement of the intended production of new plays,[1] which the *Gazette* afforded its readers simultaneously with its account of the meeting of General Assembly.

When "A Word to the Wise" was produced the *Virginia Gazette* [2]

PRELIMINARY NOTICE.

*⁎⁎* The American Company of Comedians intend for this place by the meeting of the General Assembly, and to perform till the end of the April Court. They then proceed to the Northward by engagement, where it is probable they will continue some years.

---

[1] NEW PLAYS.—We hear that a new comedy, called "The Brothers," written by Mr. Cumberland, author of the much approved "West Indian," is now in rehearsal and will soon make its appearance on our theatre; also that "False Delicacy" and a "Word to the Wise," the productions of the ingenious Mr. Hugh Kelly, whose spirited letter to the Lord Mayor (Beckford) has been read by most people, are in great forwardness.

[2] A WORD TO THE WISE. — Williamsburg, April 2d.—Mr. Kelly's new comedy of "A Word to the Wise" was performed at our theatre last Thursday for the first time, and repeated on Tuesday to a very crowded and splendid audience. It was received both nights with the warmest marks of approbation; the sentiments with which this excellent piece is replete were greatly and deservedly applauded, and the audience, while they did justice to the merit of the author, did no less honor to their own refined taste. If the comic writers would pursue Mr. Kelly's plan and present us only with moral plays the stage would become (what it ought to be) a school of politeness and virtue. Truth, indeed, obliges us to confess that for several years past most of the new plays that have come under our observation have had a moral tendency, but there is not enough of them to supply the theatre with a variety of exhibitions sufficient to engage the attention of the public, and the most desirable enjoyment by too frequent repetition becomes insipid.

criticised the comedy, not as was customary at that time, under the guise of correspondence, but as the opinion of the paper itself. This was not only one of the best of Mr. Kelly's comedies, but its success at Williamsburg is especially noteworthy, because it had failed at Drury Lane only two years before. The cause of the Drury Lane failure was purely political. Kelly, after the success of his first comedy, "False Delicacy," went into journalism and espoused the ministerial cause in his newspaper with great warmth. This made him many powerful enemies, who went deliberately to work to damn his next play, regardless of its merits. The plot succeeded and the piece was played only twice. In Virginia the comedy had a better fortune. As the virulence of English faction did not reach the Colonies it was judged solely upon its merits and approved. So unanimous was this approval that when "False Delicacy" was announced for production in the *Gazette*, on the 9th of April—one of the few formal advertisements of the season—it was thought worth while to declare that it was by the author of "A Word to the Wise." Even at that day, it will be observed, there was a newspaper demand for moral plays, and the desire for novelty combined with excellence was stronger in Virginia than it is now.

> FALSE DELICACY.
> ————
> On Tuesday Next, being the 14th Instant,
> A new COMEDY, called
> FALSE DELICACY.
> By the Author of A WORD TO THE WISE.
>
> ☞ It may not be improper to give notice that the Theatre in Williamsburg will be closed at the end of the April Court, the American Company's engagements calling them to the Northward, from whence, it is probable, they will not return for several years.

On the 22d of April the bill comprised the "Provoked Husband" and "Thomas and Sally," with Mrs. Stamper for the first time as *Dorcas* in the farce, and on the 28th "The Way to Keep Him" and the "Oracle" were the pieces. The last announcement of the season was dated May 7th. Whether either of Mr. Cumberland's comedies were actually produced is not proved, but the probabilities are that both the " Brothers " and the " Fashionable Lover " were seen at Williamsburg in 1772, because Mr. Douglass never made promises that he failed to keep. It may be assumed, therefore, that the " Fashionable Lover " closed the season, after which the company made its way Northward, stopping at Annapolis in September.

LAST ANNOUNCEMENT.

☞ We are authorized to inform the public that the new comedy of the " Fashionable Lover," now acting at the Theatres Royal, Drury Lane and Edinburgh with the utmost applause, will shortly appear on our theatre. Such is the industry of the American Company that although the piece has not been above ten days in the country it has been rehearsed more than once and is already, we hear, fit for representation.

Either during or at the close of this Southern tour the connection of Mr. and Mrs. Tomlinson with the American Company came to an end. The Tomlinsons had been under Mr. Douglass' management since 1758, a period of nearly fifteen years. It is probable their first appearances in this country were made in New York at the theatre on Cruger's Wharf. On the opening night of the theatre on Society Hill, near Philadelphia, on the 25th of June, 1759, Mr. Tomlinson played *Omar* in " Tamerlane." Mrs. Tomlinson was first seen at that house as *Myrtilla* in the " Provoked Husband," on the 6th of July. The lady seldom

MRS. TOMLINSON'S PARTS.

*Plays.*

| | |
|---|---|
| Beggars' Opera | { Mr. Slammekin<br>{ Mrs. Coaxer |
| Busybody | Mrs. Scentwell |
| Clandestine Marriage | Trusty |
| Committee | Mrs. Chat |
| Constant Couple | Lady Darling |
| Cymbeline | Helen |
| Lear | Aranthe |
| Macbeth | Witch |
| Mourning Bride | Attendant |
| Provoked Husband | { Myrtilla<br>{ Mrs. Motherly |
| Recruiting Officer | Lucy |
| Suspicious Husband | Lucetta |
| Tender Husband | Aunt |
| Theodosius | { Delia<br>{ Marina |

*Farces.*

| | |
|---|---|
| Citizen | Corunna |
| Devil to Pay | Lucy |
| Miller of Mansfield | Kate |

appeared, her list of parts comprising only twenty roles in fifteen years, but Mr. Tomlinson was seldom out of the bill. That he was not an actor of much force is apparent in the fact that as was his relative rank at the beginning so it was at the end of his career. But that he was useful and trustworthy is equally apparent in the fact that he held a position that was at least respectable for so many years. He began with such parts as *Kent* in " Lear," *Antonio* in the "Merchant of Venice," *Sciolto* in the " Fair Penitent," *John Moody* in the "Provoked Husband" and *Obadiah* in the " Committee," and ended with *Philip* in "Alexander the Great," *Pembroke* in " King John " and *Don Pedro* in the "Wonder." Allyn was in his way at the outset, Henry at a later period, and finally Goodman, toward the close of his career. In the activity of the last two years of the company's existence he took no part, and so missed many roles that would have been his in the new productions of that

MR. TOMLINSON'S PARTS.

*Plays.*

| | |
|---|---|
| A Bold Stroke for a Wife | Sacbut |
| Alexander the Great | Philip |
| All for Love | Serapion |
| Beaux' Stratagem | { Mr. Sullen<br>Boniface |
| Beggars' Opera | { Peachum<br>Lockit |
| Cato | Lucius |
| Clandestine Marriage | Sergeant Flower |
| Committee | Obadiah |
| Conscious Lovers | Humphrey |
| Constant Couple | Vizard |
| Country Lasses | { Vulture<br>Sir John English |
| Cymbeline | Caius Lucius |
| Distressed Mother | Phœnix |
| Don Quixote in England | Sir Thomas |
| Douglas | Officer |
| Drummer | Butler |
| Earl of Essex | Sir Walter Blunt |
| Fair Penitent | Sciolto |
| Gamester | { Jarvis<br>Bates |
| George Barnwell | Blunt |
| Hamlet | { Ghost<br>King<br>Lucianus<br>Gravedigger |
| Henry IV | Worcester |
| Inconstant | Petit |
| Jealous Wife | John |
| King John | Pembroke |
| Lear | Kent |
| Love for Love | Sir Sampson Legend |
| Love Makes a Man | Charius |
| Macbeth | Seyton |
| Merchant of Venice | Antonio |
| Miser | James |
| Mourning Bride | Hali |
| Orphan | Chaplain |
| Orphan of China | { Octar<br>Morat |
| Othello | Ludovico |

Prince of Parthia . . . . . . . . Vardanes
Provoked Husband . . . . . John Moody
Recruiting Officer . . . . . . . . Recruit
Richard III . . . . . . . { Catesby
                            Buckingham
Roman Father . . . . . . . . . Soldier
Romeo and Juliet . . . . . { Capulet
                             Montague
                             Paris
School for Lovers . . . . . . . . Steward
Suspicious Husband . . . . . . Tester
Tamerlane . . . . . . . . . . . . Omar
Theodosius . . . . . . . . . { Leontine
                               Atticus
Venice Preserved . . . . . . . . . Duke
Wonder . . . . . . . . . Don Pedro

*Farces.*

Apprentice . . . . . . . . . . Simon
Catherine and Petruchio . . . . . Baptisto
Citizen . . . . . . . . . . Sir Jasper
Cock-lane Ghost . . . Counsellor Prosequi
Contrivances . . . . . . . . . . Robin
Devil to Pay . . . . . . . . . Jobson
Harlequin Collector . . . . . { Doctor
                                Porter
                                Miller
Harlequin Restored . . . . . . . Pierot
High Life Below Stairs . . . . { Kingston
                                 Tom
Honest Yorkshireman . . . . . . Slango
Lethe . . . . . . . . . . { Charon
                            Bowman
Love a la Mode . . Sir Theodore Coodchild
Lying Valet . . . . . . . Justice Suttle
Mayor of Garratt . . . . . Sir Jacob Jollop
Miss in her Teens . . . . . Captain Loveit
Mock Doctor . . . . . . . { Hellebore
                            Harry
Neck or Nothing . . . . . Mr. Stockwell
Polly Honeycomb . . . . . . . . Ledger
Virgin Unmasked . . . . . . . . Quaver
Witches . . . . . . . . . . . . Pierot

period, beginning with the "Way to Keep Him" and ending with "She Stoops to Conquer." No public notice was taken of his retirement, and so it is impossible to say whether it was his own act or in consequence of his death. The latter supposition is the more probable, as it is known that Mrs. Tomlinson was living in New York during the British occupation, where she played with the military Thespians who opened the John Street Theatre in 1777, and was accorded a benefit at the close of the season of 1777–78. There was a Miss Tomlinson, but nothing is known of her beyond the fact that she made her *debut* as one of Antony's children in "All for Love." Of the actors on the American stage in 1758 only Hallam, Douglass and Morris were with the company when Tomlinson left it, in the beginning of 1772, and of these only Hallam was earlier as a pioneer of the drama in America. Tomlinson's parts comprise his biography.

# CHAPTER XXVII.

## ‚SOUTHWARK THEATRE, 1772-3.

ANOTHER BRILLIANT SEASON IN PHILADELPHIA—MORE NEW PIECES
PRODUCED — PRESENTATION OF THE SECOND AMERICAN PLAY,
THE "CONQUEST OF CANADA" — MRS. MORRIS, AN OLD-TIME
FAVORITE, MAKES HER DEBUT — CHANGES IN THE AMERICAN
COMPANY.

ON its way to the Northward from Williamsburg, as noted in
the preceding chapter, the American Company again stopped
at Annapolis, where "A Word to the Wise" was presented on the
first of September. A new set of scenes, painted by Mr. Richards, of
London, was provided for the comedy. After this, Dunlap informs
us, with his usual recklessness of statement, the "routine of playing
and traveling from the North American Colonies to the West Indies
and back again occupied the Thespians, without leaving any memorable trace until the year 1773, when, on the 14th of April, Douglass
opened the theatre in New York, giving notice that it would be
impossible to keep it open 'longer than the end of May.'" So far
were the Thespians from making a voyage to and from the West
Indies at that time, that after a brief season at Annapolis they returned
to Philadelphia, where they reopened the Southwark Theatre on the
28th of October, 1772, and kept it open until the last day of
March, 1773.

This was the fourth prolonged season of the American Company at the Southwark Theatre. It will be seen from the list of performances, which, full as it is, unfortunately is not complete, that thirty-two full pieces and twenty-two farces, some of them new, were produced in Philadelphia at the time Dunlap says the company was not " leaving any memorable trace." Among the pieces played for the first time before a Philadelphia audience were " A Word to the Wise," by Kelly, and the " West Indian " and the " Fashionable Lover," both by Cumberland, and all previously produced in Virginia; another comedy by Cumberland, played at Williamsburg as the "Brothers" but here presented as the " Shipwreck; " Bickerstaff's " Lionel and Clarissa," Foote's "Englishman in Paris," Garrick's "Cymon," Arthur Murphy's "Way to Keep Him," previously played in Virginia, and the " Conquest of Canada," an American drama never before acted. None of the farces

LIST OF PERFORMANCES.

1772.

Oct. 28—Word to the Wise . . . . Kelly
Padlock . . . . . . Bickerstaff
Nov. 2—Roman Father . . . . Whitehead
Midas . . . . . . . . O'Hara
4—Love in a Village . . Bickerstaff
Old Maid . . . . . . . Murphy
9—West Indian . . . . Cumberland
Miss in her Teens . . . . Garrick
11 Mourning Bride . . . Congreve
Mayor of Garratt . . . . . Foote
16—Hamlet . . . . . . . Shakspere
Miller of Mansfield . . . Dodsley
18—Shipwreck . . . . . Cumberland
Lethe . . . . . . . . . Garrick
23—Way to Keep Him . . . Murphy
Honest Yorkshireman . . Carey
25—Maid of the Mill . . . Bickerstaff
Lying Valet . . . . . . Garrick
30—Fashionable Lover . Cumberland
Guardian . . . . . . . Garrick
Dec. 2—George Barnwell . . . . . Lillo
Love a la Mode . . . . Macklin
7—Cymbeline . . . . . Shakspere
Upholsterer . . . . . . Murphy
9—West Indian.
Devil to Pay . . . . . . Coffey
14—Lionel and Clarissa . . Bickerstaff
High Life Below Stairs . Townley
16—Romeo and Juliet . . . Shakspere
Old Maid.
21—Romeo and Juliet.
Old Maid.
23—Suspicious Husband . . . Hoadly
Thomas and Sally . . Bickerstaff
28—Richard III . . . . . Shakspere
Musical Lady . . . . . Colman
30—School for Lovers . . Whitehead
Padlock.
1773.
Jan. 4—Lionel and Clarissa.
Love a la Mode.

Jan.  6—Tamerlane . . . . . . . Rowe
    Catherine and Petruchio Shakspere
  11—King Henry IV . . . Shakspere
    Devil to Pay.
  13—Love for Love . . . . Congreve
    High Life Below Stairs.
  18—Conscious Lovers . . . . Steele
    Love a la Mode.
  20—Shipwreck.
    Englishman in Paris . . . Foote
  25—False Delicacy . . . . . Kelly
    Lethe.
  27—Othello . . . . . . . . Shakspere
    Midas.
Feb.  1—Tempest . . . . . . Shakspere .
    Neptune and Amphitrite.
    Miss in her Teens.
  3—Tempest.
    Neptune and Amphitrite.
    High Life Below Stairs.
  8—Beggars' Opera . . . . . Gay
    Mayor of Garratt.
  10—Theodosius . . . . . . . Lee
    Honest Yorkshireman.
  15—Lionel and Clarissa.
    Edgar and EmmelineHawkesworth
  17—Conquest of Canada . . Cockings
  22—Conquest of Canada (last time.)
    Love a la Mode.
  24—Word to the Wise.
    Catherine and Petruchio.
March 3—Cymon . . . . . . . Garrick
  8—Fashionable Lover.
    Edgar and Emmeline.
  10—Merchant of Venice . . Shakspere
    Hob in the Well . . . . Cibber
  (Mr. and Mrs. Henry's benefit.)
  15—West Indian.
    Bucks Have at Ye All.
    Padlock.
    (Mr. Hallam's benefit.)
  17—Beaux' Stratagem . . . Farquhar
    Catherine and Petruchio.
  (Mr. and Mrs. Morris' benefit.)
  22—Earl of Essex . . . . . Jones
    Citizen . . . . . . . Murphy
  (Benefit of Woolls and Wall.)

played during the season were new to the American stage, except one, Joseph Reed's "Register Office." This list of productions, new and old, must be acknowledged as extraordinary. It included the best of the English dramatists, from Shakspere to Kelly and Cumberland. With the single exception of Shakspere the works of all these playwrights have been banished from the stage, and of the nine pieces of the master, played in Philadelphia in 1772–3, three, "Cymbeline," "Henry IV" and the "Tempest," have not been seen by this generation of play-goers. There is no living *Imogen* or *Falstaff.* Neither Cibber nor Farquhar, Congreve nor Rowe, Lee nor Whitehead, Steele nor Macklin, Foote nor Garrick, Murphy nor Colman, Bickerstaff nor O'Hara, Kelly nor Cumberland, has been accorded a revival since early in the century. Tragedies such as the "Mourning Bride" and the "Roman Father" have no modern representative. There is no actress on the English speaking stage capable of playing these high comedy roles. No living manager, except Augustin Daly, has sufficient knowledge of

Mar. 24—Recruiting Officer . . . Farquhar
　　Edgar and Emmeline.
　(Byerly, Parker and Johnson's benefit.)
　29—Wonder . . . . . . . Centlivre
　　Register Office . . . . . . Reed
　(Mr. and Mrs. Henry's benefit.)
　31—Tempest.
　　Neptune and Amphitrite.
　　Guardian.

stage-business to produce one of these masterpieces of the last century. If "A Word to the Wise" or the "Fashionable Lover" was to be played by any company except his, it would be so utterly lacking in the flavor of the old school that we should think our grandfathers were satisfied with very insipid stuff. And yet were it possible to realize, even in imagination, the performances of Mr. Douglass' company for a season, we should learn how completely the Nineteenth century has failed to realize the dramatic promise of the Eighteenth.

Kelly's "Word to the Wise," with which the season opened, was probably played in Philadelphia with the same cast as at Williamsburg and Annapolis. Although the comedy failed at Drury Lane through the opposition of a party formed to prevent its representation for political reasons, the author was consoled for his disappointment by a large subscription to its publication, at a crown, $1.25, for

WORD TO THE WISE.

Captain Dormer . . . . . . . Mr. Hallam
Sir George Hastings . . . . . Mr. Henry
Sir John Dormer . . . . . . Mr. Douglass
Villars . . . . . . . . . Mr. Goodman
Willoughby . . . . . . . . Mr. Morris
Mrs. Willoughby . . . . . . Mrs. Morris
　(Being her first appearance on that stage.)
Miss Willoughby . . . . . . Miss Storer
Lucy . . . . . . . . . Miss Richardson
Miss Montagu . . . . . . Miss Hallam

each copy. It is not improbable that Mr. Kelly also found consolation in the success that attended the successive productions of the comedy in America. At Williamsburg, as has been shown, it was highly praised by the *Virginia Gazette*, and in Philadelphia it was favorably noticed by a correspondent of the *Pennsylvania Chronicle*.[1]   The ladies in the cast are all warmly praised, but only Miss Hallam, as *Miss Montagu*, is specially mentioned.   This is to be regretted, as Mrs. Morris made her Philadelphia *debut* as *Mrs. Willoughby*.   In this critique Mr. Hallam's *Mungo* in the " Padlock," which was the afterpiece, was accorded higher praise than was ever before given to any part acted on the American stage, except Miss Hallam's *Imogen.*

While it is uncertain whether Mr. Cumberland's comedy, the " Brothers," was played at Williamsburg, where it was announced for production early in 1772, it is certain it was produced in Philadelphia as the "Shipwreck." When the " Brothers " was first played Woodward had the part of *Ironsides*, Yates that of *Sir Benjamin Dove* and Quick, then a young performer, was the *Skiff.* Smith, at whose suggestion the comedy was written, played *Young Belfield.* Mrs. Green was the *Lady Dove*, and Mrs. Yates the heroine, *Sophia.*

SHIPWRECK.

| | |
|---|---|
| Young Belfield | Mr. Hallam |
| Belfield | Mr. Henry |
| Captain Ironsides | Mr. Goodman |
| Sir Benjamin Dove | Mr. Morris |
| Patterson | Mr. Byerly |
| Skiff | Mr. Woolls |
| Old Goodwin | Mr. Douglass |
| Philip | Mr. Wall |
| Jonathan | Mr. Parker |
| Francis | Mr. Johnson |
| Lady Dove | Mrs. Morris |
| Violetta | Mrs. Henry |
| Lucy Waters | Miss Storer |
| Kitty | Mrs. Harman |
| Fanny | Miss Richardson |
| Sophia | Miss Hallam |

[1] PENNSYLVANIA CHRONICLE, Oct. 31st, 1772.—On Wednesday last the theatre in Southwark was opened by the American Company with Kelly's " Word to the Wise " and the "Padlock" to a most crowded and brilliant audience. The " Padlock " we have with pleasure seen many repetitions of the last season, and Mr. Hallam in *Mungo* was then supposed excellent, but we now, upon the judgment of gentlemen of undoubted knowledge and taste in theatrical performances, pronounce him to be the best *Mungo* upon the British stage; the other characters, except *Leander*, which we verily believe Mr. Wall does as well as he can, and therefore we must by no means censure him, are well supported. * * * The performers in the " Word to the Wise " are entitled to much praise for being so correct, spirited and characteristic. The ladies, besides their pleasing figures, were genteel, elegant and fashionable in their deportment. Miss Hallam, in the sprightly *Miss Montagu*, was as much a woman of fashion as we have seen on any stage.

Garrick was in the house on the first night of the comedy, and was surprised at hearing himself complimented in the epilogue to a new piece in the rival establishment. The epilogue was spoken by Mrs. Yates. The piece had a good run at Covent Garden, where it was originally produced in 1769, but neither in merit nor success did it compare with either of Mr. Cumberland's pieces, the "Fashionable Lover" or the "West Indian," played at the Southwark Theatre this season. When the former was originally produced at Drury Lane it was coldly received, but after its objectionable features were modified it met with a fair degree of success. The latter was not only one of the best comedies of its time, but it had a great and deserved success. The "West Indian" was first played in 1771, a year before the production of the "Fashionable Lover."

FASHIONABLE LOVER.

Mortimer . . . . Mr. Hallam
Aubrey . . . . . . Mr. Henry
Tyrrel . . . . . Mr. Goodman
Lord Abberville . . Mr. Byerly
Dr. Druid . . . . . Mr. Morris
Bridgemore . . . . Mr. Parker
Napthali . . . . . . Mr. Wall
Jarvis . . . . . . Mr. Woolls
Le Jeunesse . . . Mr. Roberts
Colin Macleod . Mr. Douglass
Lucinda . . . . . Mrs. Henry
Mrs. Bridgemore . Mrs. Douglass
Betty . . . . . . Miss Storer
Mrs. Mackintosh MissRichardson
Augusta Aubrey . Miss Hallam

WEST INDIAN.

Belcour . . . . . Mr. Henry
Major O'Flaherty . Mr. Goodman
Mr. Stockwell . . . Mr. Morris
Captain Dudley . Mr. Douglass
Charles Dudley . . . Mr. Wall
Fulmer . . . . . Mr. Byerly
Varland . . . . . Mr. Parker
Stukeley . . . . Mr. Johnson
Sailor . . . . . . Mr. Woolls
Lady Rusport . . Mrs. Douglass
Louisa Dudley . . Miss Storer
Mrs. Fulmer . . . Mrs. Henry
Lucy . . . . Miss Richardson
Charlotte Rusport Miss Hallam

King was the original *Belcour*, Moody the *O'Flaherty* and Mrs. Abington the *Charlotte Rusport*. In the "Fashionable Lover" *Lord Abberville* was originally acted by Dodd, *Aubrey* and his daughter *Augusta* by Mr. and Mrs. Barry, *Mortimer* by King, and *Dr. Druid* by Baddeley. Hallam generally played *Belcour*—as *O'Flaherty* Henry was admirable. Miss Hallam as *Augusta Aubrey* and *Charlotte Rusport* had no possible rival in the company except Mrs. Morris.

After the success that attended the production of Dryden's version of the "Tempest," in 1770, Mr. Douglass evinced a partiality for "show-pieces." Among these was "Cymon," a so-called "dramatic romance," by Garrick, a wretched production, devoid of wit, humor and poetry, which owed whatever success it obtained at Drury Lane to the vocal performers and the scene-painter. It was the story of Cymon and Iphigenia greatly extended, heightened by incantation, and rendered entertaining by fine scenery, splendid dresses, brisk music and lively dances. It made the judicious grieve but met with great success.

CYMON.

| | |
|---|---|
| Cymon . . . . . . . . . . . | Mr. Hallam |
| Merlin . . . . . . . . . . | Mr. Goodman |
| Linco / First Demon } . . . . . . . | Mr. Woolls |
| Dorus . . . . . . . . . . | Mr. Morris |
| Damon . . . . . . . . . . . | Mr. Wall |
| Dorilas . . . . . . . . . . | Mr. Byerly |
| Cupid / First Shepherdess } . . . . . | Miss Storer |
| Second Shepherdess / Dorcas } . . | Miss Richardson |
| Urganda . . . . . . . . . | Mrs. Morris |
| Fatima . . . . . . . . . . . | Mrs. Henry |
| Sylvia . . . . . . . . . . | Miss Hallam |

Another "show-piece" which was produced for the first time on any stage this season was a play called the "Conquest of Canada," which is interesting because of the elaborate way in which it was presented, as well as from the fact that it was supposed to have been of American origin and consequently the second American play ever performed on the stage. It was a tragedy based upon the conquest of Quebec and the death of Wolfe, but the author, George Cockings, was an Englishman who held a small place under the Gov-

CONQUEST OF CANADA.

By Authority.
By the American Company,
At the Theatre in Southwark This Evening will be presented a New Historical Tragedy, NEVER PERFORMED, called the
CONQUEST OF CANADA, or
The Siege of Quebec.

| | |
|---|---|
| General Wolfe . . . . . . . . | Mr. Hallam |
| Leonatus * . . . . . . . . | Mr. Douglass |
| Britannicus † . . . . . . . . | Mr. Henry |
| Montcalm . . . . . . . . | Mr. Goodman |
| Levi . . . . . . . . . . . | Mr. Morris |
| Bougainville . . . . . . . . . | Mr. Wall |
| Ochterlony . . . . . . . . . | Mr. Henry |
| Peyton . . . . . . . . . . . | Mr. Byerly |

* Mon–t–n.    † T–n–d.

ernment at Boston. His later life was spent in England, where for thirty years previous to his death, which occurred February 6th, 1802, he was register of the Society of Arts, Manufactures and Commerce. Mr. Cockings wrote a poem called "The American War," and at one time he read Milton by way of a lecture. His play was printed in London, in 1766. It was a wretched composition, neither prose nor verse. It is apparent from Mr. Douglass' advertisement that he had the earnest co-operation of the military then stationed in Philadelphia, but, notwithstanding the pageantry, the play failed. It was played only twice.

First Caledonian Chief by a Gentleman (Being his first appearance on any Stage.)
Second Caledonian Chief by Mr. Woolls.
Sea and Land officers by Messrs. Byerly, Johnson, Parker, Woolls, Roberts and a Young Gentleman (who never appeared on any Stage before).
Jemmy Chaunter (with a song in character) by Mr. Woolls.
Sailors by Messrs. Johnson, Roberts, &c., &c.

| | |
|---|---|
| Sophia | Miss Hallam |
| Abbess | Mrs. Morris |
| First Nun | Mrs. Henry |
| Second Nun | Miss Storer |
| Maid | Miss Richardson |
| Sophronia | Mrs. Douglass |

After the Play DANCING by MR. FRANCIS.

It will be taken as a favor if the Town for this night will dispense with a Farce, as the Stage will be much crowded with the ARTILLERY, BOATS, &c., necessary for the Representation of the Piece, and with the men from both Corps, whose assistance the Commanding Officers are good enough to indulge us with.

TICKETS, without which no Person can be admitted, are sold at the bar of the Coffee house.

Boxes, 7s. 6d.    Pit, 5s.    Gallery, 3s.

Bickerstaff's comic opera, "Lionel and Clarissa," which was originally produced at Covent Garden, in 1768, was presented for the

### LIONEL AND CLARISSA.

| | |
|---|---|
| Lionel | Mr. Woolls |
| Colonel Oldboy | Mr. Goodman |
| Sir John Flowerdale | Mr. Douglass |
| Mr. Jessamy | Mr. Wall |
| Harman | Mr. Henry |
| Jenkins | Mr. Parker |
| Clarissa | Miss Storer |
| Lady Mary Oldboy | Mrs. Harman |
| Jenny | Mrs. Henry |
| Diana Oldboy | Miss Hallam |

first time in America this season as the "School for Fathers," the name applied to it when it was revived at Drury Lane after its successful run at the rival house. Mr. Vernon was the original *Lionel*, and Mrs. Baddeley the first *Clarissa*.

Mrs. Wrighten, known in this country as Mrs. Pownall, was the Covent Garden *Diana*. The originality of this production has never been questioned, neither the characters nor incidents being borrowed from any other author.

Foote's two-act comedy, the " Englishman in Paris," although it was produced at Covent Garden for Macklin's benefit as early as 1753, was not played in the Colonies until this season, and then only as an afterpiece. Mr. Macklin was the original *Buck* and Miss Macklin the *Lucinda*. It was said of *Lucinda* that the part seemed written to give Miss Macklin an opportunity of displaying her varied qualifications of acting, singing and dancing, in all of which she obtained universal applause. Its production in this country was intended, no doubt, to give Miss Storer, who possessed like talents, a similar opportunity.

### ENGLISHMAN IN PARIS.

| | |
|---|---|
| Buck | Mr. Goodman |
| Sir John Buck | Mr. Morris |
| Mr. Subtle | Mr. Henry |
| Classic | Mr. Parker |
| Daupaine | Mr. Roberts |
| Solitaire | Mr. Wall |
| Gamut | Mr. Woolls |
| Roger | Mr. Johnson |
| Marquis | Mr. Byerly |
| Mrs. Subtle | Miss Richardson |
| Lucinda | Miss Storer |

The only new farce this season, unless Foote's "Englishman in Paris" is regarded as a farce rather than a comedy, was the "Register Office," at that time a popular afterpiece at Drury Lane. The object of this little piece was to expose the pernicious practices of intelligence offices or employment agencies, still called "register offices" in England. The provincial characters, the Scotch peddler, the Irish spalpeen and *Maria*, the

### REGISTER OFFICE.

| | |
|---|---|
| Captain Le Brush | Mr. Hallam |
| Lord Brilliant | Mr. Goodman |
| Scotchman | Mr. Douglass |
| Irishman | Mr. Henry |
| Frenchman | Mr. Roberts |
| Harwood | Mr. Wall |
| Tricket | Mr. Morris |
| Gulwell | Mr. Byerly |
| Frankly | Mr. Woolls |
| Williams | Mr. Johnson |
| Maria | Miss Storer |
| Margery Monfort | **Mrs. Henry** |

Yorkshire servant-maid, are particularly well drawn. In *Captain Le Brush* Mr. Hallam had the part of a slip-slop military man, whose ignorance constantly led him into the use of hard words, the meaning of which he did not understand, but his impudence was so great that he was never known to blush when his absurdities were detected. The farce never became a favorite afterpiece with American audiences, probably because the evils at which it was aimed did not exist in this country at that time.

While the company was in Virginia Arthur Murphy's comedy, the "Way to Keep Him," was played, probably with the same cast as at Philadelphia this season. The lesson of the comedy is to teach wives to preserve the affections of their husbands by practicing the same arts after as before marriage. Originally this piece was in only three acts, but it was extended to five by the deft introduction of *Sir Bashful* and *Lady Constant* into the comedy.

WAY TO KEEP HIM.

| | |
|---|---|
| Lovemore | Mr. Hallam |
| Sir Bashful Constant | Mr. Douglass |
| Sir Brilliant Fashion | Mr. Henry |
| William | Mr. Goodman |
| Sideboard | Mr. Morris |
| Richard | Mr. Parker |
| Thomas | Mr. Roberts |
| Mrs. Lovemore | Mrs. Henry |
| Lady Constant | Mrs. Morris |
| Muslin | Miss Storer |
| Mignionet | Miss Richardson |
| Furnish | Mrs. Harman |
| Widow Belmour | Miss Hallam |

The play was not without humor, but its great charm was in the fact that it was a series of pictures of domestic life. This comedy, it will be remembered, was first acted in this country by the New American Company at Annapolis, in 1769.

The first of Shakspere's plays presented at the Southwark Theatre this season was "Hamlet," last played at that house during the engagement of 1769-70. The masterpiece, which was presented on the 16th of November, 1772, was followed by "Cymbeline," on the 7th of December. The casts of these tragedies at this time not only show the changes that had been made in the company, but the rise or descent of the actors. In " Hamlet " Hallam, Douglass and Morris retained their former roles, but Henry, who before played *Horatio*, now succeeded Wall as *Laertes*, while Wall sank into the *Player King*, previously played by Allyn and Malone; Goodman was the successor of Tomlinson as the *Ghost*, Parker was *Horatio*, instead of Henry, Byerly had Platt's part of *Bernardo*, Miss Richardson was the *Player Queen*, instead of Mrs. Harman or Mrs. Henry (Miss Storer), and Miss Hallam succeeded Miss Cheer as *Ophelia*. In "Cymbeline" Douglass

#### HAMLET.

| | |
|---|---|
| Hamlet | Mr. Hallam |
| King | Mr. Douglass |
| Polonius | Mr. Morris |
| Laertes | Mr. Henry |
| Ghost | Mr. Goodman |
| Horatio | Mr. Parker |
| Marcellus | Mr. Woolls |
| Bernardo | Mr. Byerly |
| Player King | Mr. Wall |
| Lucianus | Mr. Roberts |
| Francisco | Mr. Johnson |
| Guildenstern | Mr. Woolls |
| Rosencranz | Mr. Byerly |
| Player Queen | Miss Richardson |
| Queen | Mrs. Douglass |
| Ophelia | Miss Hallam |

#### CYMBELINE.

| | |
|---|---|
| Posthumous | Mr. Hallam |
| Cymbeline | Mr. Douglass |
| Iachimo | Mr. Henry |
| Bellarius | Mr. Goodman |
| Cloten | Mr. Wall |
| Guiderius | Mr. Parker |
| Arviragus | Mr. Woolls |
| Caius Lucius | Mr. Byerly |
| Pisanio | Mr. Morris |
| Philario | Mr. Parker |
| Cornelius | Mr. Roberts |
| Frenchman | Mr. Woolls |
| Captain | Mr. Johnson |
| Queen | Mrs. Douglass |
| Helen | Miss Richardson |
| Imogen | Miss Hallam |

#### ROMEO AND JULIET.

| | |
|---|---|
| Romeo | Mr. Hallam |
| Mercutio | Mr. Douglass |
| Capulet | Mr. Henry |
| Friar Laurence | Mr. Morris |
| Escalus | Mr. Goodman |
| Paris | Mr. Woolls |
| Benvolio | Mr. Wall |
| Tybalt | Mr. Parker |
| Montagu | Mr. Byerly |
| Apothecary | Mr. Roberts |
| Lady Capulet | Mrs. Douglass |
| Nurse | Mrs. Harman |
| Juliet | Miss Hallam |

#### RICHARD III.

| | |
|---|---|
| Richard | Mr. Hallam |
| Edward V | Mr. Wall |
| Henry VI | Mr. Morris |
| Richmond | Mr. Henry |
| Buckingham | Mr. Douglass |
| York | Miss Richardson |
| Tressel | Mr. Henry |
| Catesby | Mr. Parker |
| Ratcliff | Mr. Woolls |
| Oxford | Mr. Johnson |
| Lady Anne | Mrs. Henry |
| Duch'ss of York | Mrs. Harman |
| Queen Elizabeth | Mrs. Morris |

now had the title-role, instead of Allyn; Henry, who had previously played *Bellarius*, was now *Iachimo*, instead of Douglass, Goodman was *Bellarius*, Parker *Guiderius*, instead of Greville, and *Philario*, instead of Morris; Byerly *Caius Lucius* instead of Tomlinson; Miss

Richardson *Helen,* instead of Mrs. Tomlinson, and Miss Hallam *Imogen,* in which she made a greater impression than her predecessor, Miss Cheer. The other Shakspere plays afford similar contrasts. In "Romeo and Juliet" Miss Hallam now played *Juliet* to Mr. Hallam's *Romeo.* Henry was *Capulet,* instead of Morris; Morris *Friar Laurence,* instead of Allyn or Greville; Goodman *Escalus,* instead of Broadbelt or Malone; Wall *Benvolio,* instead of Godwin, as at the John Street Theatre, New York, in 1767; Parker *Tybalt,* instead of Wall or Henry, and Byerly *Montagu,* instead of Tomlinson. Mr. and Mrs. Douglass and Mrs. Harman retained their previous roles. In "Richard III" Henry played *Richmond,* instead of Douglass, while Douglass was content with *Buckingham,* as in New York, in 1767. Miss Richardson was the

### KING HENRY IV.

| | |
|---|---|
| Hotspur | Mr. Hallam |
| King Henry | Mr. Morris |
| Prince of Wales | Mr. Henry |
| Sir Walter Blunt | Mr. Goodman |
| Worcester | Mr. Byerly |
| Vernon | Mr. Parker |
| Westmoreland | Mr. Wall |
| Northumberland | Mr. Woolls |
| Bardolph | Mr. Johnson |
| Francis | Mr. Roberts |
| Sir John Falstaff | Mr. Douglass |
| Poins | Mr. Byerly |
| Douglas | Mr. Woolls |
| Peto | Mr. Wall |
| First Carrier | Mr. Goodman |
| Second Carrier | Mr. Parker |
| Prince John | Mr. Roberts |
| Hostess Quickly | Mrs. Harman |
| Lady Percy | Mrs. Morris |

### TEMPEST.

| | |
|---|---|
| Prospero | Mr. Douglass |
| Ferdinand | Mr. Hallam |
| Alonzo | Mr. Byerly |
| Antonio | Mr. Parker |
| Hipolito | Mr. Wall |
| Gonzalo | Mr. Johnson |
| Stephano | Mr. Morris |
| Trinculo | Mr. Henry |
| Ventoso | Mr. Johnson |
| Mustachio | Mr. Woolls |
| Ariel | Miss Storer |
| Caliban | Mr. Goodman |
| Sycorax | Mr. Roberts |
| Miranda | Mrs. Henry |
| Dorinda | Miss Hallam |

### MERCHANT OF VENICE.

| | |
|---|---|
| Shylock | Mr. Henry |
| Antonio | Mr. Hallam |
| Bassanio | Mr. Douglass |
| Gratiano | Mr. Goodman |
| Lorenzo | Mr. Woolls |
| Duke | Mr. Byerly |
| Salanio | Mr. Wall |
| Salarino | Mr. Dermot |
| Tubal | Mr. Roberts |
| Gobbo | Mr. Byerly |
| Launcelot | Mr. Morris |
| Jessica | Miss Hallam |
| Nerissa | Miss Richardson |
| Portia | Mrs. Morris |

### OTHELLO.

| | |
|---|---|
| Othello | Mr. Hallam |
| Iago | Mr. Douglass |
| Cassio | Mr. Goodman |
| Roderigo | Mr. Wall |
| Ludovico | Mr. Henry |
| Brabantio | Mr. Morris |
| Duke | Mr. Byerly |
| Montana | Mr. Parker |
| Gratiano | Mr. Woolls |
| Officer | Mr. Johnson |
| Messenger | Mr. Roberts |
| Emilia | Mrs. Douglass |
| Desdemona | Mrs. Henry |

*Duke of York*, a part that had been played by Miss S. Dowthwaite, among others. Parker succeeded Tomlinson as *Catesby*, and Mrs. Morris was *Queen Elizabeth*, instead of Mrs. Douglass. Miss Cheer, in her time, had been the *Lady Anne*, now in possession of Mrs. Henry. In "King Henry IV" Mrs. Morris succeeded Miss Cheer as *Lady Percy*, Henry became the *Prince of Wales*, instead of Wall; Goodman *Sir Walter Blunt*, instead of Henry; Byerly *Worcester*, instead of Tomlinson, and *Poins*, instead of Malone; Parker *Vernon*, instead of Greville; Wall *Westmoreland*, instead of Raworth, and *Peto*, instead of Roberts, and Roberts *Francis*, instead of *Peto*, and *Prince John*, instead of Mrs. Wall. This is the first cast extant of the Shakspere-Dryden "Tempest." In "Othello" and the "Merchant of Venice" the only important changes were the assumption of *Desdemona* in the former by Mrs. Henry and of *Portia* in the latter by Mrs. Morris, in which Miss Hallam condescendingly consented to play *Nerissa*. These contrasts show that the company had four young actresses capable of playing leading roles, that Mr. Goodman was already a favorite with the public and the management, and that Mr. Henry was ascending slowly and Mr. Wall descending rapidly.

CATHERINE AND PETRUCHIO.

| | |
|---|---|
| Petruchio | Mr. Goodman |
| Grumio | Mr. Morris |
| Biondello | Mr. Wall |
| Hortensia | Mr. Parker |
| Baptista | Mr. Byerly |
| Tailor | Mr. Roberts |
| Curtis | Mrs. Harman |
| Bianca | Miss Richardson |
| Catherine | Mrs. Morris |

The "Conscious Lovers" was seen in Philadelphia for the first time in six years. In New York the comedy had not been played since 1768 when it was given for Mr. Morris' benefit. The only changes in the cast were Goodman as *Sir John Bevil*, Byerly as *Cymberton*, Parker as *Humphrey*, Roberts as *Daniel*, Miss Storer as *Phillis*,

Mrs. Harman as *Mrs. Sealand*, Miss Richardson as *Lucinda* and Mrs. Morris as *Isabella*.

The casts that are appended at the bottom of this and the following pages show the changes that had occurred in the representatives of familiar parts. Mr. and Mrs. Tomlinson had withdrawn, while Messrs. Goodman, Byerly and Johnson, and Mrs. Morris and Miss Richardson were recent acquisitions. It is not improbable that all these were seen at the Southwark Theatre before the Southern tour was undertaken—Miss Richardson certainly was. Little is known of this lady, who apparently was an actress of experience, beyond the fact that she played "walking ladies," such as *Fanny* in the "Shipwreck," in which she is first noticed, and afterward *Lucy Waters* in the same play; *Theodosia* in the "Maid of the Mill," and *Mrs. Trippet* in the "Lying Valet;" the *Lady* in "Love a la Mode;" *Lucy* in the "West Indian" and in the "Devil to Pay; "*Lucetta* in the "Suspicious Husband" and *Mrs. Subtle* in the "Englishman in Paris;" the *Player Queen* in "Hamlet," *Mysis* in "Midas" and *Lucy* in a "Word to the Wise." Her first appearance this season was in the part last named. More important than the acquisition of Miss Richardson was that of Mrs. Morris. She began with the little part of *Margery* in "Love in

NEW CASTS OF FAMILIAR PIECES.

| MOURNING BRIDE. | | TAMERLANE. | | THEODOSIUS. | |
|---|---|---|---|---|---|
| Osmyn | Mr. Hallam | Monesses | Mr. Goodman | Varanes | Mr. Hallam |
| King | Mr. Douglass | Axalla | Mr. Wall | Theodosius | Mr. Henry |
| Garcia | Mr. Henry | Omar | Mr. Henry | Leontine | Mr. Goodman |
| Gonzales | Mr. Morris | Dervise | Mr. Morris | Marcian | Mr. Douglass |
| Heli | Mr. Parker | Haly | Mr. Parker | Atticus | Mr. Woolls |
| Selim | Mr. Wall | Stratocles | Mr. Byerly | Lucius | Mr. Parker |
| Alonzo | Mr. Byerly | Tanais | Mr. Woolls | Aranthus | Mr. Wall |
| Perez | Mr. Woolls | Zama | Mr. Johnson | Pulcheria | Mrs. Morris |
| Zara | Mrs. Morris | Mirvan | Mr. Roberts | Marina | Miss Storer |
| Leonora | Miss Storer | Selima | Mrs. Henry | Flavella | Miss Richardson |
| Almeria | Miss Hallam | Arpasia | Mrs. Morris | Athenais | Miss Hallam |

a Village," but was seen a week later as *Zara* in the "Mourning Bride." When *Lady Dove* was introduced into the "Shipwreck." on its second representation, she played the part, and subsequently she appeared as *Millwood* in "George Barnwell," *Mrs. Sullen* in the "Conscious Lovers," *Lady Beverly* in the "School for Lovers," *Portia* in the "Merchant of Venice," *Lady Constant* in the "Way to Keep Him," *Catherine* in "Catherine and Petruchio" and *Queen Elizabeth* in "Richard III." Her first appearance was made as *Mrs. Willoughby* in a "Word to the Wise." This Mrs. Morris was the second wife of Owen Morris. She was described by Dunlap as a tall, elegant woman, and by William B. Wood as an imposing, well-formed person, with a

### NEW CASTS OF FAMILIAR PIECES.

#### GEORGE BARNWELL.

| | |
|---|---|
| George Barnwell | Mr. Hallam |
| Thorowgood | Mr. Douglass |
| Trueman | Mr. Parker |
| Uncle | Mr. Henry |
| Blunt | Mr. Morris |
| Maria | Miss Storer |
| Lucy | Mrs. Harman |
| Millwood | Mrs. Morris |

#### SUSPICIOUS HUSBAND.

| | |
|---|---|
| Ranger | Mr. Hallam |
| Mr. Strictland | Mr. Douglass |
| Frankly | Mr. Henry |
| Bellamy | Mr. Parker |
| Jack Meggot | Mr. Wall |
| Jester | Mr. Morris |
| Buckle | Mr. Woolls |
| Simon | Mr. Johnson |
| Mrs. Strictland | Mrs. Henry |
| Jacintha | Mrs. Morris |
| Lucetta | Miss Richardson |
| Milliner | Miss Storer |
| Landlady | Mrs. Harman |
| Maid | Mrs. Wall |
| Clarinda | Miss Hallam |

#### NEPTUNE AND AMPHITRITE.

| | |
|---|---|
| Neptune | Mr. Woolls |
| Amphitrite | Miss Storer |

#### SCHOOL FOR LOVERS.

| | |
|---|---|
| Modely | Mr. Hallam |
| Sir John Dorilant | Mr. Douglass |
| Bellmour | Mr. Wall |
| Steward | Mr. Morris |
| Lady Beverly | Mrs. Morris |
| Araminta | Mrs. Henry |
| Celia | Miss Hallam |

#### LOVE FOR LOVE.

| | |
|---|---|
| Valentine | Mr. Hallam |
| Sir Sampson Legend | Mr. Henry |
| Scandal | Mr. Douglass |
| Tattle | Mr. Wall |
| Foresight | Mr. Morris |
| Jeremy | Mr. Byerly |
| Frapland | Mr. Parker |
| Buckram | Mr. Woolls |
| Ben | Mr. Goodman |
| Angelica | Mrs. Henry |
| Miss Prue | Miss Storer |
| Mrs. Foresight | Miss Richardson |
| Nurse | Mrs. Harman |
| Mrs. Frail | Mrs. Morris |

#### THOMAS AND SALLY.

| | |
|---|---|
| The Squire | Mr. Woolls |
| The Sailor | Mr. Henry |
| Dorcas | Mrs. Harman |
| Sally | Miss Hallam |

#### EARL OF ESSEX.

| | |
|---|---|
| Essex | Mr. Hallam |
| Southampton | Mr. Henry |
| Lord Burleigh | Mr. Morris |
| Raleigh | Mr. Byerly |
| Lieutenant | Mr. Woolls |
| Queen Elizabeth | Mrs. Morris |
| C. of Nottingham | Mrs. Henry |
| Countess of Rutland | Miss Hallam |

#### BEAUX' STRATAGEM.

| | |
|---|---|
| Archer | Mr. Hallam |
| Aimwell | Mr. Douglass |
| Sullen | Mr. Henry |
| Foigard | Mr. Goodman |
| Freeman | Mr. Wall |
| Gibbet | Mr. Woolls |
| Boniface | Mr. Byerly |
| Bagshot | Mr. Dermot |
| Hounslow | Mr. Roberts |
| Scrub | Mr. Morris |
| Dorinda | Miss Richardson |
| Cherry | Mrs. Henry |
| Gipsy | Miss Storer |
| Mrs. Sullen | Mrs. Morris |

#### EDGAR AND EMMELINE.

| | |
|---|---|
| Edgar | Mr. Hallam |
| Emmeline | Miss Hallam |

very mysterious manner. Wood, however, did not know her until twenty years after this period. She was long considered the greatest attraction in the company, but Wood says she was greatly overvalued, as she was without education and her enunciation was wretchedly imperfect. Late in life she suffered from the want of a retentive memory, and Wood says that from his knowledge of her professional pride this must have been a natural defect. Mrs. Morris' portrait is included among the prints known as the Lopez and Wemyss collection. She continued in the Philadelphia theatre until late in life, and died in that city about 1825.

## NEW CASTS OF FAMILIAR PIECES.

### RECRUITING OFFICER.
Captain Plume . . . Mr. Hallam
Sergeant Kite . . . Mr. Douglass
Captain Brazen . . . Mr. Byerly
Justice Balance . . . Mr. Morris
Worthy . . . . . . . Mr. Woolls
Bullock . . . . . Mr. Goodman
Justice Scale . . . . Mr. Dermot
First Recruit . . . . . Mr. Wall
Second Recruit . . Mr. Roberts
Melinda . . . . . . Mrs. Henry
Rose . . . . . . . Miss Hallam
Lucy . . . . . Miss Richardson

### FALSE DELICACY.
Cecil . . . . . . . Mr. Hallam
Colonel Rivers . . Mr. Douglass
Lord Winworth . . . Mr. Henry
Sir Harry . . . . . . . Mr. Wall
Sidney . . . . . . . Mr. Byerly
Lady Betty . . . . Mrs. Morris
Miss Rivers . . . . Mrs. Henry
Miss Marchmont . . Miss Storer
Sally . . . . . Miss Richardson
Mrs. Harley . . . Mrs. Douglass

### LYING VALET.
Sharp . . . . . . . Mr. Morris
Gayless . . . . . . . . Mr. Wall
Guttle . . . . . Mr. Goodman
Trippet . . . . . . Mr. Byerly
Cook . . . . . . . Mr. Parker
Melissa . . . . . Mrs. Morris
Mrs. Gadabout . . Mrs. Harman
Mrs. Trippet . Miss Richardson
Kitty Pr . . . . Mrs. Henry

### BEGGARS' OPERA.
Macheath . . . . Mr. Hallam
Peachum . . . . . Mr. Douglass
Lockit . . . . . . Mr. Morris
Mat . . . . . . Mr. Goodman
Filch . . . . . . . . Mr. Wall
Nimming Ned . . . Mr. Byerly
Ben Budge . . . . Mr. Parker
Jemmy Twitcher . . Mr. Johnson
Lucy . . . . . . . Miss Storer
Mrs. Peachum . . . Mrs. Morris
Mrs. Coaxer . . . Mrs. Henry
Jenny Diver . Miss Richardson
Mrs. Slammekin . . . Mrs. Wall
Moll Brazen . . . . Mr. Roberts
Diana Trapes . Miss Richardson
Polly . . . . . . . Miss Hallam

### MAID OF THE MILL.
Aimworth . . . . Mr. Hallam
Sir Harry Sycamore Mr. Goodman
Fairfield . . . . Mr. Douglass
Farmer Giles . . . Mr. Woolls
Ralph . . . . . . . Mr. Wall
Mervin . . . . . Mr. Parker
Lady Sycamore . Mrs. Douglass
Theodosia . . . Miss Richardson
Fanny . . . . . . . Miss Storer
Patty . . . . . . Miss Hallam

### PADLOCK.
Mungo . . . . . . Mr. Hallam
Don Diego . . . . Mr. Woolls
Leander . . . . . Mr. Wall
Ursula . . . . . . Mrs. Morris
Leonora . . . . . Miss Hallam

### WONDER.
Don Felix . . . . . Mr. Hallam
Colonel Briton . . . . Mr. Henry
Don Pedro . . . . Mr. Goodman
Don Lopez . . . . . Mr. Byerly
Frederick . . . . . . Mr. Woolls
Lissardo . . . . . . Mr. Morris
Valguez . . . . . . Mr. Roberts
Gibby . . . . . . Mr. Douglass
Isabella . . . . . . Miss Storer
Flora . . . . . . . Mrs. Henry
Iris . . . . . Miss Richardson
Violante . . . . . Miss Hallam

### LOVE IN A VILLAGE.
Justice Woodcock . Mr. Douglass
Hawthorn . . . . Mr. Woolls
Young Meadows . . Mr. Henry
Sir William . . . . ..Mr. Morris
Eustace . . . . . . Mr. Byerly
Hodge . . . . . . Mr. Parker
Lucinda . . . . . Miss Storer
Mrs. Deborah . . Mrs. Douglass
Margery . . . . . Mrs. Morris
Rosetta . . . . . Miss Hallam

### LETHE.
Frenchman . . . . Mr. Hallam
Æsop . . . . . Mr. Douglass
Mercury . . . . Mr. Woolls
Old Man . . . . . Mr. Morris
Fine Gentleman . . . Mr. Byerly
Tattoo . . . . . Mr. Goodman
Charon . . . Mr. Johnson
Mrs. Tattoo . . . . Miss Hallam
Mrs. Riot . . . . . Miss Storer

"The mysterious manner alluded to in Mrs. Morris," Mr. Wood wrote, "was not confined to the stage, but the chariness of her exposure to the vulgar eye of day was very amusing. So inveterate was her dislike to being seen in daylight that Mr. Morris obtained from a near relative of mine permission to put up a little gate in his garden, by which Mrs. Morris could pass from her lodgings in Maiden Lane direct to the theatre, without a circuit of Broadway. On the few occasions of her showing off freely as a pedestrian, I can truly assert that much more curiosity and bustle were excited than latterly at a Fanny Ellsler or a Fanny Kemble. She seemed to realize the boast of Bolingbroke—

> "Being seldom seen,
> She could not stir, but like a comet
> She was wondered at.

### NEW CASTS OF FAMILIAR PIECES.

**HIGH LIFE BELOW STAIRS.**

| | |
|---|---|
| Lovel | Mr. Hallam |
| Freeman | Mr. Parker |
| Lord Duke | Mr. Wall |
| Sir Harry | Mr. Henry |
| Philip | Mr. Morris |
| Coachman | Mr. Woolls |
| Kingston | Mr. Byerly |
| Lady Bab | Miss Storer |
| Lady Charlotte | Miss Richardson |
| Cook | Mrs. Harman |
| Chloe | Mr. Roberts |
| Kitty | Mrs. Henry |

**MUSICAL LADY.**

| | |
|---|---|
| Old Mask | Mr. Morris |
| Mask | Mr. Wall |
| Freeman | Mr. Parker |
| Rosini | Mr. Roberts |
| Lady Scrape | Miss Storer |
| Laundress | Mrs. Harman |
| Sophy | Miss Hallam |

**OLD MAID.**

| | |
|---|---|
| Old Maid | Mrs. Harman |
| Captain Cape | Mr. Morris |
| Clerimont | Mr. Wall |
| Mr. Harlow | Mr. Byerly |
| Heartly | Mr. Parker |
| Mrs. Harlow | Mrs. Henry |

**MAYOR OF GARRATT.**

| | |
|---|---|
| Major Sturgeon | Mr. Goodman |
| Sir Jacob Jollop | Mr. Douglass |
| Sneak | Mr. Morris |
| Lint | Mr. Wall |
| Bruin | Mr. Byerly |
| Roger | Mr. Parker |
| Mrs. Bruin | Mrs. Harman |
| Mrs. Sneak | Mrs. Henry |

**MILLER OF MANSFIELD.**

| | |
|---|---|
| King | Mr. Henry |
| Miller | Mr. Morris |
| Richard | Mr. Byerly |
| Lord Lurewell | Mr. Wall |
| Joe | Mr. Woolls |
| Peggy | Miss Richardson |
| Kate | Miss Storer |
| Margery | Mrs. Harman |

**HOB IN THE WELL.**

| | |
|---|---|
| Hob | Mr. Hallam |
| Friendly | Mr. Woolls |
| Sir Thomas Testy | Mr. Morris |
| Old Hob | Mr. Byerly |
| Dick | Mr. Johnson |
| Hob's Mother | Miss Richardson |
| Betty | Mrs. Henry |
| Flora | Miss Storer |

**DEVIL TO PAY.**

| | |
|---|---|
| Sir John Loverule | Mr. Woolls |
| Jobson | Mr. Henry |
| Butler | Mr. Morris |
| Doctor | Mr. Byerly |
| Coachman | Mr. Johnson |
| Cook | Mr. Parker |
| Footman | Mr. Wall |
| Blind Fiddler | Mr. Roberts |
| Lady Loverule | Mrs. Harman |
| Lucy | Miss Richardson |
| Lettice | Mrs. Wall |
| Nell | Miss Storer |

**UPHOLSTERER.**

| | |
|---|---|
| Barber | Mr. Wall |
| Quidnunc | Mr. Byerly |
| Feeble | Mr. Morris |
| Bellmour | Mr. Parker |
| Rovewell | Mr. Woolls |
| Harriet | Miss Richardson |
| Termagant | Mrs. Henry |

**LOVE A LA MODE.**

| | |
|---|---|
| Callaghan O'Brallaghan | Mr. Henry |
| Archy MacSarcasm | Mr. Douglass |
| Squire Groom | Mr. Wall |
| Beau Mordecai | Mr. Morris |
| Sir Theodore | Mr. Parker |
| The Lady | Miss Richardson |

" The walk of half a dozen miles, which the less artificial actors of modern times sometimes bodily execute, between the rehearsal and dinner, would have puzzled Mrs. Morris not a little, from the fact of her indulging, among other peculiarities of dress, in a pair of heels of such dangerous altitude as required the utmost caution."

The season was almost without incidents, but a note appended to the announcement of the " Recruiting Officer" for the 24th of March, 1773, when Mrs. Morris played *Sylvia* for the joint benefit of Messrs. Byerly, Parker and Johnson, is curious in itself and indicative of the character of the actress.

Mr. Durang, in his "History of the Philadelphia Stage," published in the *Sunday Dispatch*, thinks the deprecatory manner of this announcement indicates a fear on the part of the actress that she would not be able to play *Sylvia* well. The probability is that Mrs.

MRS. MORRIS' CARD.

\*\*\* Mrs. Morris in Respect to those few Ladies and Gentlemen, who thro' kindness to her have advised her not to play the Part of Sylvia, begs leave to assure them, that she performs it now in compliance with the Request of many friends to the Theatre, and with a fixed Rule amongst the Performers, to lend each other every help they can in Time of Benefits.

### NEW CASTS OF FAMILIAR PIECES.

#### MISS IN HER TEENS.

| | |
|---|---|
| Captain Flash . . . . | Mr. Henry |
| Captain Loveit . . . | Mr. Johnson |
| Fribble . . . . . . . | Mr. Wall |
| Puff . . . . . . . . | Mr. Morris |
| Jasper . . . . . . . | Mr. Woolls |
| Tag . . . . . . . . | Mrs. Henry |
| Miss Biddy . . . . . | Miss Storer |

#### MIDAS.

| | |
|---|---|
| Midas . . . . . . | Mr. Goodman |
| Apollo . . . . . . . | Mr. Woolls |
| Jupiter . . . . . . . | Mr. Morris |
| Sileno . . . . . . . | Mr. Parker |
| Damætus . . . . . . . | Mr. Wall |
| Pan . . . . . . . . | Mr. Byerly |
| Juno . . . . . . . . | Mrs. Henry |
| Mysis . . . . . . | Mrs. Harman |
| Daphne . . . . . . | Mrs. Morris |
| Nysa . . . . . . . . | Miss Storer |

#### GUARDIAN.

| | |
|---|---|
| Guardian . . . . . . | Mr. Hallam |
| Sir Charles . . . . . | Mr. Morris |
| Young Clackit . . . . | Mr. Wall |
| Lucy . . . . . . . | Mrs. Henry |
| Miss Harriet . . . | Miss Hallam |

#### ROMAN FATHER.

| | |
|---|---|
| Roman Father . . . | Mr. Hallam |
| Tullus Hostilius . . | Mr. Douglass |
| Publius . . . . . | Mr. Goodman |
| Valerius . . . . . . | Mr. Wall |
| First Citizen . . . . | Mr. Morris |
| Second Citizen . . . | Mr. Byerly |
| Third Citizen . . . . | Mr. Woolls |
| Fourth Citizen . . | Mr. Johnson |
| Soldier . . . . . . | Mr. Parker |
| Valeria . . . . . . | Mrs. Henry |
| Horatia . . . . . . | Miss Hallam |

#### HONEST YORKSHIREMAN.

| | |
|---|---|
| Gaylove . . . . . . | Mr. Woolls |
| Sapscull . . . . . . | Mr. Wall |
| Muckworm . . . . . | Mr. Morris |
| Blunder . . . . . . | Mr. Parker |
| Slango . . . . . . | Mr. Byerly |
| Combrush . . . . . | Mrs. Morris |
| Arabella . . . . . | Miss Storer |

#### CITIZEN.

| | |
|---|---|
| Young Wilding . . . | Mr. Hallam |
| Young Philpot . . . . | Mr. Wall |
| Old Philpot . . . | Mr. Morris |
| Beaufort . . . . | Mr. Woolls |
| Sir Jasper . . . . . | Mr. Byerly |
| Quilldrive . . . . . | Mr. Roberts |
| Corunna . . . . | Miss Richardson |
| Maria . . . . . . | Miss Hallam |

Morris did not consider the part sufficiently stately for her grand style. Other incidents of the season were the occasional appearances, between the acts, of Mrs. Stamper, as a singer, and Mr. Francis, as a dancer. Mrs. Stamper was the lady who played *Dorcas* in "Thomas and Sally," at Williamsburg. She was now advertised as from the Theatre Royal, Edinburgh. Mr. Francis was announced as from the Theatre in Amsterdam. This dancer's real name was Francis Mentges, which he made illustrious as a Colonel in the Revolutionary army, while he afterward rendered his assumed name of William Francis distinguished as an actor. When General Washington came to Philadelphia, in 1787, as a member of the Constitutional Convention, Francis was among those who welcomed him and escorted him into the city. The old actor's features as *Sir George Thunder* have been preserved in an engraving in the series of prints known as the Lopez and Wemyss series. Nothing is known of the actors who were added to the company about this time beyond the parts played by them.

In the letter of " Philo-Theatricus," dated October 30th, 1772, and printed in the Pennsylvania *Chronicle*, from which the criticism of the acting in a "Word to the Wise" and the "Padlock," above quoted, was taken, complaint is made of a grievance that the writer said must be remedied. " Some ruffians in the gallery who so frequently interrupted the performance, and in the most interesting scenes," wrote "Philo-Theatricus" in his suggestive letter, "deserve the severest reprehension; they are too despicable to argue, otherwise they might be told that because they pay three shillings for their admittance into a public assembly they are not therefore entitled to commit frequent outrages upon that part of the audience who go there really to see the play and be instructed and entertained; or to interrupt the actors who are doing their best to entertain them. They might be informed that, though they have an undoubted right to every species of entertainment promised them in the bills, they have not the smallest title to anything else, and that if they call for a song or a prologue of which no notice is given in the bills, the actors have an equal demand upon them for an extraordinary price for a compliance with their request." The remedy suggested by "Philo-Theatricus" to the manager of the theatre was "to engage a number of constables and dispose them in different parts of the gallery, who, upon the smallest disturbance for the future, may be authorized by any magistrate—and there are always enough in the house—to apprehend and carry to the workhouse such rioters, by which means peace will be restored and a few examples deter others from the like outrages."

When the Philadelphia season closed the company went to New York to play its last engagement in that city prior to the Revolution.

# CHAPTER XXVIII.

---

## LEAVE-TAKINGS.

NOTWITHSTANDING Mr. Douglass announced when he opened the New York Theatre on the 14th of April, 1773, that it would be impossible to keep it open longer than the end of May the season was extended to August.

This season, which was destined to be the last in New York for many years, seems to have begun with a disposition among a part of the audience to annoy the actors. "The repeated insults," Mr. Douglass announced on the 3d of May, "which some mischievous persons in the gallery have given, not only to the stage and orchestra, but to the other parts of the house, call loudly for reprehension." He then says that unless these disorders are amended "the gallery for the future will be shut up." This threat seems to have had the desired effect. The season in New York opened with Murphy's comedy, the "Way to Keep Him," which was new to that city, and "Catherine and Petruchio," with Mrs. Morris for the first time there as the *Shrew*.

Mrs. Wall was *Curtis,* instead of Mrs. Harman. A comparison of the list of performances with that of the previous season at the Southwark Theatre will show that most of the pieces played there were reproduced at the John Street Theatre. The familiar pieces in this list not produced in Philadelphia during the season of 1772–3 were "King John," "Clandestine Marriage," "Gamester," "Constant Couple," "Jane Shore," "Damon and Phillida" and "Harlequin Collector." The works given for the first time in New York were Milton's "Comus," Garrick's "Irish Widow," O'Brien's "Cross Purposes" and Goldsmith's "She Stoops to Conquer." Garrick's "Irish Widow" was new in London as well as in New York. This little piece was taken from Molière's "Mariage Forcée" and was chiefly intended to introduce Mrs. Barry (Mrs. Crawford), to whom it was dedicated, to the public in a new light. In New York Mrs. Morris played the *Widow Brady.* But in spite of the addition of new

LIST OF PERFORMANCES.

1773.
April 14—Way to Keep Him . . . Murphy
Catherine and Petruchio Shakspere
19—Clandestine Marriage
Garrick and Colman
26—King John . . . . . . Shakspere
30—Earl of Essex . . . . . . Jones
Englishman in Paris . . . Foote
May 3—Beaux' Stratagem . . . Farquhar
Midas . . . . . . . . O'Hara
7—Love in a Village . . . Bickerstaff
Mayor of Garratt . . . . . Foote
11—Gamester . . . . . . . Moore
Padlock . . . . . . Bickerstaff
14—Mourning Bride . . . Congreve
Midas.
17—Maid of the Mill . . . Bickerstaff
21—Beggars' Opera . . . . . . Gay
Catherine and Petruchio.
24—Theodosius . . . . . . . . Lee
Lying Valet . . . . . . Garrick
28—Hamlet . . . . . . . Shakspere
Cross Purposes . . . . . O'Brien
June 1—Cymon . . . . . . . . Garrick
3—Tempest . . . . . . Shakspere
Neptune and Amphitrite.
Damon and Phillida . . . Cibber
7—Cymon.
Cross Purposes.
11—School for Lovers . . Whitehead
Lethe . . . . . . . . Garrick
14—Richard III . . . . . Shakspere
Midas.
(Mrs. Douglass' benefit.)
21—Comus . . . . . . . Milton
High Life Below Stairs . Townley
(Benefit of Miss Cheer and Mr. Woolls.)
24—West Indian . . . . Cumberland
Love a la Mode. . . . . Macklin
(Benefit of Mr. Henry and Mr. Wall.)

June 28—Tamerlane . . . . . . . Rowe
Irish Widow . . . . . . Garrick
(Mr. and Mrs. Morris' benefit.)
July     1—Constant Couple . . . Farquhar
Harlequin Collector.
(Benefit of Mr. Hallam and Mr.
Goodman.)
8—Recruiting Officer . . . Farquhar
Guardian . . . . . . . Garrick
(Benefit of Mr. Byerly and Mr.
Parker.)
12—Jane Shore . . . . . . . Rowe
(Benefit of Mr. Roberts and Miss
Richardson.)
19—Merchant of Venice . . Shakspere
Miller of Mansfield . . . Dodsley
(Benefit of Mr. Dermot and Mr.
Francis.)
26—George Barnwell . . . . . Lillo
Edgar and Emmeline Hawkesworth
(Benefit of the New York Hospital.)
Aug.   2—She Stoops to Conquer . Goldsmith
Musical Lady . . . . . Colman
5—She Stoops to Conquer.
Padlock.

comedy and farce from time to time the old masterpieces still held a prominent place in the repertoire of the company, and the names of Farquhar, Congreve, Cibber and Rowe occur as often as those of Garrick, Murphy, Bickerstaff, Cumberland and Goldsmith.

Milton's Masque, which was originally presented at Ludlow Castle, on Michaelmas Night, in 1634, has not often been given on the American stage. It would be interesting to know if Dr. Arne's music, which he composed specially for Dalton's version of "Comus," was sung on this occasion. It may be assumed that such was the case, for while the masque is truly poetical it is deficient in dramatic action, and it is not likely that Woolls would have given it on the occasion of his joint benefit with Miss Cheer without the music, even with the powerful assistance of that actress so long absent from the stage.

COMUS.
———

Comus . . . . . . . . . . . Mr. Henry
First Spirit . . . . . . . . Mr. Byerly
Second Spirit . . . . . . . Mr. Morris
Third Spirit . . . . . . . . Mr. Woolls
Elder Brother . . . . . . . Mr. Blackler
Younger Brother . . . . . . Mr. Goodman
Euphrosine . . . . . . . . Miss Storer
Sabina . . . . . . . . . . Miss Hallam
The Lady . . . . . . . . . Miss Cheer

The farce, "Cross Purposes," was by the celebrated Irish actor, William O'Brien. To judge from a "preliminary notice" in Rivington's *Gazette*,[1] on the 6th of June, it was probably through kindly personal remembrances that O'Brien's farce was brought out in New York. This piece had been acted at Covent Garden a year before, where it had considerable success.

It contains many happy touches of genuine humor and some admirable strokes of satire leveled at the follies of the times. Of the New York life of O'Brien and his high-born wife there are, unfortunately, few details.

CROSS PURPOSES.

| | |
|---|---|
| Mr. Grub | Mr. Goodman |
| Francis Bevil | Mr. Douglass |
| Harry Bevil | Mr. Henry |
| George Bevil | Mr. Hallam |
| Chapeau | Mr. Wall |
| Robin | Mr. Morris |
| Consol | Mr. Byerly |
| Emily | Miss Storer |
| Housemaid | Miss Richardson |
| Mrs. Grub | Mrs. Morris |

As it happened, the production of Goldsmith's masterpiece, "She Stoops to Conquer," was the farewell of the American Company at New York. It was played twice. This great comedy was originally acted at Covent Garden the same year it was first produced at New York. Mr. Gardner was the original *Sir Charles Marlow,* Mr. Lee Lewis *Young Marlow,* Mr. Quick *Tony Lumpkin,* Mr.

SHE STOOPS TO CONQUER.

| | |
|---|---|
| Hardcastle | Mr. Goodman |
| Sir Charles Marlow | Mr. Morris |
| Young Marlow | Mr. Henry |
| Hastings | Mr. Byerly |
| Tony Lumpkin | Mr. Hallam |
| Landlord | Mr. Woolls |
| Diggory | Mr. Hughes |
| Mrs. Hardcastle | Mrs. Morris |
| Miss Hardcastle | Miss Hallam |
| Miss Neville | Miss Storer |

Shuter *Hardcastle,* Mrs. Green *Mrs. Hardcastle* and Mrs. Buckley *Miss Hardcastle.* Mr. Du Bellamy, who came to America soon after the Revolution, but was known by another name, was the original *Hastings.* The only comment that needs to be made on this great

[1] NOTICE IN RIVINGTON'S GAZETTE.— The new farce of "Cross Purposes," to be performed to-morrow, was written by William O'Brien, Esq., formerly of Drury Lane Theatre: a gentleman who, with his amiable consort, Lady Susan, daughter of the Right Hon. the Earl of Ilchester, resided several years in this city.

production is that it is the one comedy produced by the Old American Company that still holds its place on the stage.

The only additional casts printed in the New York papers this season, apart from those of the new pieces, were two—of the "Constant Couple" and "Damon and Phillida." Whatever changes were made in the pieces that had been played

DAMON AND PHILLIDA.

| | |
|---|---|
| Damon . . . . . | Mr. Woolls |
| Arcas . . . . . | Mr. Byerly |
| Corydon . . . . | Mr. Morris |
| Mopsus . . . . | Mr. Parker |
| Cymon . . . . . | Mr. Wall |
| Phillida . . . . | Miss Storer |

CONSTANT COUPLE.

| | |
|---|---|
| Beau Clincher . | Mr. Goodman |
| Angelica . . . | Miss Hallam |
| Parly . . . | Miss Richardson |
| Lady Darling . | Mrs. Douglass |
| Lady Lurewell . | Mrs. Morris |

in Philadelphia a few months before were due, as a rule, to the changes in the company. These, however, were not important. Mr. Johnson had dropped out, and Messrs. Hughes and Blackler, neither of whom attained to eminence, were occasionally put down for small parts. Mr. Dermot, who was with the company in Philadelphia, succeeded Johnson as *Roger* in the "Englishman in Paris," Byerly succeeded him as *Jemmy Twitcher* in the "Beggars' Opera," and Parker as *Ventoso* in the "Tempest." The other minor changes were Mrs. Wall, instead of Mrs. Harman, in the "Way to Keep Him;" Dermot as *Nimming Ned* in the "Beggars' Opera," instead of Byerly; Wall as *Mat o' the Mint*, instead of Goodman; Woolls as *Varland* in the "West Indian," instead of Parker, and Henry as *Major O'Flaherty*, instead of Goodman. Miss Storer and Miss Richardson exchanged parts in "Theodosius." In the "Merchant of Venice" Hallam was *Shyloch* once more, although Henry had played the Jew that Shakspere drew upon at least one occasion in Philadelphia; Henry was *Antonio*, Dermot the *Duke*, instead of Byerly, Hughes *Salarino*, instead of Dermot, and Miss Storer *Jessica*, instead of Miss Hallam. Mr. Hallam still retained the lead, of course, but Miss Hallam divided the choice of the female parts with Mrs. Morris. Mrs. Douglass seldom appeared, but she played the *Queen* in " Hamlet," as usual. Miss Cheer emerged from her retirement to take a benefit in conjunction with Mr. Woolls. She played *Araminta* in the "School for Lovers," on the 11th of June, and for her own and Woolls' benefit the *Lady* in " Comus " and *Kitty* in " High Life Below Stairs." She also recited a Mason's epilogue to the " West Indian," on the 24th. Mrs. Harman was still with the company at the opening of the season, but she died on the 27th of May, 1773.

A notice of Mrs. Harman's death was printed in Rivington's *Gazette,* on the 3d of June. This brief tribute to the virtues of a worthy woman was the first obituary notice of an actress ever printed in an American newspaper. When Mrs. Morris, the first, was drowned in the Kill von Kull, in December, 1767, the papers reported the accident in the fewest possible words, adding, by way of description, that the victim was " of the play-house."

OBITUARY OF MRS. HARMAN.

On Thursday last, died, in the 43d year of her age, Mrs. Catherine Maria Harman, granddaughter to the celebrated Colley Cibber, Esq., poet-laureate. She was a just actress, possessed much merit in low comedy, and dressed all her characters with infinite propriety, but her figure prevented her from succeeding in tragedy and genteel comedy. In private life she was sensible, humane and benevolent. Her little fortune she has left to Miss Cheer, and her obsequies were on Saturday night attended by a very genteel procession to the cemetery of the old English Church.

Now, however, a number of interesting facts relating to the deceased actress were printed. Mrs. Harman's full name was given. This, in connection with the fact that she was a granddaughter of Colley Cibber, enables us to identify her as the daughter of Charlotte Charke. Dying in her forty-third

MRS. HARMAN'S PARTS.

*Plays.*

| | |
|---|---|
| Beaux' Stratagem | Lady Bountiful |
| Beggars' Opera | Mrs. Peachum / Diana Trapes |
| Busybody | Patch |
| Cato | Lucia |

| | |
|---|---|
| Conscious Lovers . . . . . | { Phillis<br>{ Mrs. Sealand |
| Constant Couple . . . . . . . | Mob's Wife |
| Cymbeline . . . . . . . . . . . | Pisanio |
| Distressed Mother . . . . . | Andromache |
| Douglas . . . . . . . . . . . . . | Anna |
| Drummer . . . . . . . . . . . | Abagail |
| Fair Penitent . . . . . . . . . | Calista |
| False Delicacy . . . . . . . . . | Sally |
| Gamester′. . . . . . . . . . . | Charlotte |
| George Barnwell . . . . . . . . | Lucy |
| Hamlet . . . . . . . . . | { Ophelia<br>{ Player Queen |
| Henry IV . . . . . . . | Hostess Quickly |
| Inconstant . . . . . . . . . . | Oriana |
| Jealous Wife . . . . . . . . . . | Toilet |
| King John . . . . . . . | Prince Henry |
| Lear . . . . . . . . . . . . . | Regan |
| Lionel and Clarissa . . | Lady Mary Oldboy |
| Love for Love . . . . . . . . . | Nurse |
| Love in a Village . . . . . . . | Margery |
| Macbeth . . . . . . . . . . . | { Hecate<br>{ Witch |
| Merchant of Venice . . . . . . | Nerissa |
| Midas . . . . . . . . . . . . | Mysis |
| Miser . . . . . . . . . . . . | Lappet |
| Orphan . . . . . . . . . . . | Florella |
| Othello . . . . . . . . . . | Emilia |
| Provoked Husband . . | { Lady Grace<br>{ Lady Wronghead |
| Recruiting Officer . . . . . . . | { Melinda |
| Richard III . . . . . | { Lady Anne<br>{ Duchess of York |
| Romeo and Juliet . . . . . . . . | Nurse |
| School for Lovers . . . . . | Lady Beverly |
| Shipwreck . . . . . . . . . . . | Kitty |
| Suspicious Husband . . . | { Mrs. Strictland<br>{ Landlady |
| Tamerlane . . . . . . . . . . | Selima |
| Tender Husband . . . . . . . | Fainlove |
| Theodosius . . . . . . . . . . | Pulcheria |
| Way to Keep Him . . . . . . | Furnish |
| Wonder . . . . . . . . . . . . | Iris |

*Farces.*

| | |
|---|---|
| Catherine and Petruchio . . . . . . | Curtis |
| Contrivances . . . . . . . . . . | Betty |

year, after being fifteen years in America, Mrs. Harman must have been in her twenty-eighth year when she crossed the Atlantic. We gather, besides, from this obituary a just estimate of her abilities as an actress and of the esteem in which she was held as a woman. Indeed, we even catch a glimpse of her figure and person in the intimation that her comeliness was not equal to her skill. In the bequest of her little fortune to Miss Cheer we see evidence that her husband had long ceased to occupy her thoughts, and that Miss Cheer, for whom she must have felt a peculiar friendship, had continued to reside in New York after her retirement. More than this, it is not improbable that Miss Cheer's benefit was part of the Harman legacy, and that her re-appearance was due to the death of that estimable actress.

Visitors to the New York of twenty years ago will remember the splendid structure in Broadway that was then the New York Hospital. It was as a contribution toward this noble charity that the performance of the 26th of July was given. The advertisement for this benefit contained a quaint reference to its object.[1] From this it will be seen that the assistance given by the players to the New York Hospital, at the close of Mr. Douglass' administration,

| | |
|---|---|
| Deuce is in Him | Mad. Florival |
| Devil to Pay | Lady Loverule |
| Harlequin Restored | Cook |
| High Life Below Stairs | Cook |
| Hob in the Well | Hob's Mother |
| Lethe | Mrs. Tattoo |
| Lying Valet | Melissa / Mrs. Gadabout |
| Mayor of Garratt | Mrs. Bruin |
| Miller of Mansfield | Margery |
| Musical Lady | Laundress |
| Old Maid | Old Maid |
| Polly Honeycomb | Mrs. Honeycomb |
| Spirit of Contradiction | Mrs. Partlet |
| Thomas and Sally | Dorcas |
| Upholsterer | Termagant |
| Witches | Cook |

was not characterized by the illiberality of sentiment displayed by the managers of the Pennsylvania Hospital in accepting a similar gift fourteen years before, when he was only beginning his career as a theatrical manager in the American Colonies. For the Hospital benefit the Rev. Dr. Myles Cooper, Provost of King's, now Columbia, College, wrote a prologue suited to the occasion, that was spoken by Mr. Hallam. This was the only time in the long history of the American stage before the Revolution when a clergyman in any way contributed

### DR. COOPER'S PROLOGUE.

With melting breast the wretch's pangs to feel,
His cares to soften, or his anguish heal;
Woe into peace by pity to beguile.
And make disease, and want, and sorrow smile;
Are deeds that nobly mark the gen'rous mind,
Which swells with liberal love to human kind,
And triumphs in each joy to others known
As blissful portions added to his own.

[1] EXTRACT FROM THE HOSPITAL ADVERTISEMENT. — *₊* It is hoped that all who are charitably disposed or wish well to so laudable and useful an undertaking will countenance this play with their presence, or otherwise contribute their mite to so good a work as providing a receptacle for the sick and needy. It is hoped by the friends of the hospital that the moral of the play to be acted will have some influence with those who are otherwise no friends to the theatre.

Small though our powers, we pant with honest heart,
In pity's cause to bear a humble part;
We gladly give this night to aid a plan
Whose object's charity and good to man.

Patrons of charity! While time endures,
Be every bliss of conscious virtue yours!
The hoary father snatched from want and pain,
Oft to his consort and his youthful train
Shall praise the hand that rais'd his drooping head,
When every hope, when every friend had fled,
That raised him, cold and naked, from the ground,
And pour'd the healing balsam in his wound.
With kindly art detain'd his parting breath,
And back repelled the threat'ning dart of death.
The plaintive widow, shedding tears of joy,
As fondly watching o'er her darling boy,
Her anxious eyes with keen discernment trace
The dawn of health relumining his face,
Shall clasp him to her breast with raptures new,
And pour the prayer of gratitude to you.
In you the long lost characters shall blend,
Of guardian, brother, father, husband, friend!
And sure if bliss in mortal heart can shine,
That purest bliss, humanity! is thine.

Let not mistaken avarice deplore
Each mite diminished from his useless store,
But tell the wretch—that liberal acts bestow
Delights which hearts like his can never know.
Tell—for you feel—that generous love receives
A double portion of the joy it gives,
Beams o'er the soul a radiance pure and even,
And antedates on earth the bliss of heaven.

This night to youth our moral scene displays
How false, how fatal are the wanton's ways;
Paints her alluring looks, fallacious wiles,
And the black ruin lurking in her smiles;
Bids us the first approach of vice to shun,
And claims a tear for innocence undone.

While scenes like this employ our humble stage
We fondly hope your favors to engage;
No ribald page shall here attendance claim,
Which decency or virtue brands with shame;
No artful hint that wounds the virgin's ear,

to the literature of the theatre or gave the drama any recognition, either direct or indirect. It will be observed that Dr. Cooper's prologue is by all odds the best written for our stage between 1752 and 1774. Dr. Cooper, who was a graduate of Oxford University, was an active Tory when the Revolution broke out, and was reported to be one of the authors, if not the author, of a tract, entitled "A Friendly Address to all Reasonable Americans," which was answered by Alexander Hamilton, then a student in the college, in a pamphlet of great ability. Cooper became very obnoxious to the Whigs, and on the 10th of May, 1776, he was driven from the college by a mob, led by "Sons of Liberty." He succeeded in reaching a British vessel and sailed for England. This event he commemorated in a poem,

No thought that modesty would blush to hear;
We ask no patronage—disclaim applause—
But while we act and speak in virtue's cause,
This is our aim, and while we this pursue
We ne'er can fail of patronage from you.

printed in the *Gentleman's Magazine,* describing the attack of the mob and his flight when

———— ———— the furious throng
An entrance forcing, poured along,
And filled my peaceful cell;
Where harmless jest, and modest mirth,
And cheerful laughter oft had birth,
And joy was wont to dwell.

Although Mr. Douglass was still the manager of the American Company Mr. Henry appears to have been taking an active part in the business, as is shown by an

ADVERTISEMENT.

All persons having any demands on the American Theatre are requested to send in their accounts to the subscriber, that they may be paid. JOHN HENRY.

advertisement in the New York papers on the 1st of July, just four days before the close of the season and the final leave-taking of the New York public.

From New York the Company went to Annapolis for the races.

A similar event to the final departure of these favorite performers from New York occurred in Philadelphia four months later. Before the Southwark Theatre opened, on the 1st of November, 1773, for the brief season that proved to be the last engagement of the company in Philadelphia before the Revolution, it was announced that the stay of Mr. Douglass' forces could be for a fortnight only. The limit was not exceeded, except by one night, when, in consequence of the vessel in which the company was to sail for Charleston being delayed, the "West Indian" was given, with Mrs. Douglass as *Lady Rusport.* The bills for five of the six nights of this short season have been preserved, and of these we have casts for three nights—the 3d, 10th and 15th of November. In the "Earl of Essex" no change was made since the play was last performed in Philadelphia, except the substitution of Miss Storer for Mrs. Henry as *Countess of Nottingham* and of Mr. Hughes for Mr. Byerly as *Sir Walter Raleigh*. In the farce Miss Wainwright appeared as *Maria*, the first time in six years. Hughes also succeeded Byerly as *Sir Jasper Wilding*, and Mr. Douglass was advertised as *Dapper*, Mr. Roberts as *Quilldrive* being dropped. The cast of the "Padlock" was identical with that previously printed, but for the "Clandestine Marriage" there was a new distribution of parts. As this was the last time the comedy was performed in Philadelphia by the old American Company, and on the last night but one of acting at the Southwark Theatre before the Revolution, it is worth reproduction here. It will be noted that Miss Wainwright was the *Chambermaid*. This, however, was not her last appearance on the stage, her farewell being made as *Lucy* in "Cross Purposes," which was the afterpiece to the "West Indian" on the 15th. In the "West Indian,"

LIST OF PERFORMANCES.

1773.
Nov.  1—Lionel and Clarissa . . Bickerstaff
       Love a la Mode . . . . Macklin
      3—Earl of Essex . . . . . . Jones
       Citizen . . . . . . . Murphy
      8—Hamlet . . . . . . . Shakspere
       Irish Widow . . . . . Garrick
     10—Clandestine Marriage
              Garrick and Colman
       Padlock . . . . . . Bickerstaff
     15—West Indian . . . . Cumberland
       Cross Purposes . . . . . O'Brien

CLANDESTINE MARRIAGE.

Lord Ogelby . . . . . . . . Mr. Hallam
Sir John Melville . . . . . . Mr. Douglass
Lovewell . . . . . . . . . . Mr. Henry
Sterling . . . . . . . . . . . Mr. Morris
Sergeant Flower . . . . . . Mr. Goodman
Canton . . . . . . . . . . Mr. Hughes
Brush . . . . . . . . . . . . Mr. Wall
Traverse . . . . . . . . . . Mr. Dermot
Truman . . . . . . . . . . Mr. Woolls
Miss Sterling . . . . . . . Miss Hallam
Miss Fanny . . . . . . . . . Miss Storer
Betty . . . . . . . . . Miss Richardson
Chambermaid . . . . . . Miss Wainwright
Housekeeper . . . . . . . . . Mrs. Wall
Mrs. Heidelberg . . . . . . Mrs. Douglass

on this occasion, Hallam played *Belcour*, Henry *O'Flaherty*, Woolls *Varland*, Hughes *Fulmer*, and a gentleman made his *debut* as *Charles Dudley*. The other parts were unchanged. In "Cross Purposes" Morris played *Mr. Grub*, instead of Goodman, Hughes *Robin*, instead of Morris, and Dermot *Consol*, instead of Byerly. When the curtain fell that night the doors of the theatre Mr. Douglass had built seven years before closed forever upon his management.

On the last night of the performance in Philadelphia Mr. Goodman spoke an epilogue, which, although not intended as such, proved a last farewell. No mention of it was made in the Philadelphia papers, but it was printed in the *Virginia Gazette* at Williamsburg, on the 13th of January, 1774. There is no hint as to the authorship, but its phraseology is so personal to the actor as to convey the impression that he was also the poet. The most interesting fact in connection with it

GOODMAN'S EPILOGUE.
—

To strike with magic touch the attentive ear;
To draw from pity's eye the generous tear;
To soothe the heart and feel another's woe;
To catch the uplifted sword and save the blow;
To wake with melody the breathing lyre;
To warm the soul and animate its fire:
Labors like these, in far sublimer lays,
Be crowned with laurels and unenvied bays.
    Should friendship move poor me to paint distress,
For I can feel, ye rich, but not redress;
Oh could each generous heart whose tears will flow
For others' griefs, but mitigate the woe!
Then would the world in happy concord join,
And warring nations feel the change divine;
Friendship and love erect their sacred throne,
And hail sweet peace an offspring of their own.
But I, alas, by fortune placed so low,
Must check my fond ideas as they flow.
What! cries the proud, shall paltry play'rs engage
To preach up reformation to the age?
Shall they, whose borrowed wit can scarcely raise
The sniggering leer, or vulgar shouts of praise,
Shall they by reason or by judgment shine,
Whose "ten low words oft creep in one dull line?"
Mere *strollers*, so our chronicles have shown,        [gone.
Like Hamlet's ghost—they're here—they're there—they're
    To these good gentlemen I'd speak one word—
A slave ere now gave counsel to his lord—

Tho' we inured to bear the public jeers
Of ambling authors, in their awkward geers,
Yet can we whip and cut the comic muse,
And beat, if virtue drives, whene'er we chuse;
Or, if with tragedy we're loaded deep
We mourn *Monimia*, and for virtue weep,
Praise virtue's cause in whatsoe'er we say,
For she's the heroine, whate'er the play.
   Thus *Belisarius*, seamed with many a fear,
The poor returns of long and fearful war,
Whose mind with virtue and with truth elate
Beyond the vassals of inglorious state,
'Twas thus she spoke aloud this firm decree,
"My sons, be virtuous and, my sons, be free."

      (*Taking leave*)

Ladies, the favors which your bounty show
Will raise my gratitude, where'er we go;
And now, kind gentlemen, with heart sincere,
I take my leave and thank your goodness here.

is that it should have been first printed in Virginia weeks after its delivery in Philadelphia and while the company was performing at Charleston. It is to be remembered, however, that the advertisements in the Philadelphia papers announced the Farewell Epilogue to be spoken by Mr. Hallam. This intention was probably changed to allow Mr. Goodman to speak his own production.

It may be well to add that down to the Revolution Philadelphia was the most important theatrical city in the Colonies.

# CHAPTER XXIX.

## THE CHARLESTON THEATRE.

OPENING OF THE FIRST THEATRE IN SOUTH CAROLINA—A COMPLETE
LIST OF THE PERFORMANCES—A BRILLIANT SEASON—CHARLES-
TON AUDIENCES IN 1773–4—A SLIGHT SPIRIT OF OPPOSITION
MANIFESTED.

IN Rivington's *Gazette*, under date of July 27th, 1773, it was
announced that a large subscription had been solicited and was
raising for building an elegant theatre in Charleston, S. C., in which
Mr. Douglass' American Company would perform during the winter.
Mr. Douglass evidently had gone to Charleston on this business before
the close of the New York season, leaving Mr. Henry in charge, as it
was announced he would sail thence for Philadelphia on the 30th of
August with Captain Blewer, "having secured the patronage of the
gentlemen of that city, which will enable him to build and open an
elegant theatre before Christmas." This indicates that the Charleston
Theatre was built upon a plan similar to that which enabled Mr.
Douglass to build the theatre at Annapolis, in 1771. The house was
not large, but it was more commodious than either the Southwark
Theatre at Philadelphia or the John Street Theatre in New York. It
was said of it that it was elegantly finished and well supplied with new
scenery. How long this theatre stood is uncertain, but it does not
seem to have been used as a play-house after the Revolutionary war.

Previous to the erection of this building entertainments such as the concerts of the St. Cecilia Society were given in a large, inelegant structure, situated, Josiah Quincy, Jr., says in his " Journal," down a yard.

The new Charleston Theatre was opened on the 22d of December, 1773, with " A Word to the Wise" ånd " High Life Below Stairs."

LIST OF PERFORMANCES.

1773.
Dec. 22—Word to the Wise . . . . Kelly
High Life Below Stairs . Townley
24—Hamlet . . . . . . . Shakspere
Cross Purposes . . . . . O'Brien
27—Suspicious Husband . . . Hoadly
Catherine and Petruchio. Shakspere
30—Clandestine Marriage
Garrick and Colman
Mayor of Garratt . . . . . Foote
1774.
Jan. 1—Earl of Essex . . . . . Jones
Irish Widow . . . . . . Garrick
3—Love in a Village . . Bickerstaff
Lethe . . . . . . . . Garrick
5—Gamester . . . . . . Moore
High Life Below Stairs.
8—Beaux' Stratagem . . . Farquhar
Miller of Mansfield . . . Dodsley
10—Constant Couple . . . Farquhar
Catherine and Petruchio.
13—Mourning Bride . . . Congreve
Lying Valet . . . . . Garrick
15—She Stoops to Conquer . Goldsmith
Irish Widow.
17—Jane Shore . . . . . . Rowe
Cross Purposes.
19—Busybody . . . . . Centlivre
Love a la Mode . . . . Macklin
24—Cymbeline . . . . . Shakspere
Honest Yorkshireman . . Carey
25—Beggars' Opera . . . . . Gay
Love a la Mode.
27—Romeo and Juliet . Shakspere
Miss in her Teens . . . Garrick

This was the beginning of a season of fifty-nine nights, during which as many as forty-eight distinct plays and twenty-nine farces were given. The season lasted until the 19th of May, 1774, a period of five months. When it closed a complete list of the performances, from the beginning, was printed in the *South Carolina Gazette.* As already mentioned, this is the only complete list of any season before the Revolution, except that for the Annapolis engagement of 1760. It is, however, in every way more interesting than the Annapolis repertoire. The good people of Charleston had not only an opportunity of witnessing the American Company's last performances before the Revolution and of seeing the performers at their best, but the list of performances presented for their approbation is almost bewildering in extent and variety. Nearly everything that then held the stage was produced at least once during the season. Nine of Shakspere's masterpieces were given, including " Julius Cæsar," for the first time in America. Dryden, Vanbrugh, Congreve, Farquhar, Colley Cibber, Whitehead, Otway and Addison were all represented. Eight of Garrick's productions were in the list. Bickerstaff's English operas, then in the height of their popularity, were sung, and the comedies of Kelly and Cumberland were in the bills from time to time. Goldsmith's masterpiece, " She Stoops to Conquer," was twice played, and Murphy's " Way to Keep Him " and " Apprentice " once each. There was, besides, an afterpiece, "Young America in London," the title of which seems to indicate that it was of local

Jan. 29—Merchant of Venice . . Shakspere
     Devil to Pay . . . . . . . Coffey
  31—Richard III . . . . . . Shakspere
     Thomas and Sally . . . Bickerstaff
Feb.  2—Tempest . . . . . . . . Dryden
   4—Love in a Village.
     Love a la Mode.
   7—Wonder . . . . . . . Centlivre
     Midas . . . . . . . . . O'Hara
  10—Alexander the Great . . . . Lee
     Miller of Mansfield.
  12—Tempest.
     Guardian . . . . . . . Garrick
  14—George Barnwell . . . . . Lillo
     Edgar and Emmeline Hawkesworth
  17—King Henry IV . . . Shakspere
     Thomas and Sally.
  19—Theodosius . . . . . . . . Lee
     Citizen . . . . . . . . Murphy
  21—Bold Stroke for a Wife . Centlivre
     Mayor of Garratt.
  24—Othello . . . . . . . Shakspere
     Damon and Phillida . . . Cibber
  26—She Stoops to Conquer.
     Edgar and Emmeline.
  28—Jealous Wife . . . . . . Colman
     Citizen.
Mar.  2—Shipwreck . . . . . Cumberland
     Catherine and Petruchio.
   4—Lionel and Clarissa . . Bickerstaff
     Lethe.
   7—Fashionable Lover . Cumberland
     Padlock . . . . . . Bickerstaff
  10—Maid of the Mill . . . Bickerstaff
     High Life Below Stairs.
  13—Lear . . . . . . . . Shakspere
     Irish Widow.
  14—Tempest.
     Padlock.
  16—Cymon . . . . . . . . Garrick
     Miss in her Teens.
  18—Recruiting Officer . . . Farquhar
     Oracle . . . . . . . Mrs. Cibber
  21—West Indian . . . . Cumberland
     Devil to Pay.

Mar. 25—Provoked Husband . . Vanbrugh
       Lying Valet.
    26—Romeo and Juliet.
       Hob in the Well . . . . Cibber
April 4—Lionel and Clarissa.
       Englishman in Paris . . . Foote
    6—English Merchant . . . Colman
       Contrivances . . . . . . Carey
    8—Fair Penitent . . . . . . Rowe
       Cross Purposes.
   11—Roman Father . . . . Whitehead
       Irish Widow.
   13—Way to Keep Him . . . Murphy
       Contrivances.
   15—Constant Couple.
       Lying Valet.
   18—False Delicacy . . . . . . Kelly
       Witches.
   20—Julius Cæsar . . . . . Shakspere
       Register Office . . . . . . Reed
   22—Macbeth . . . . . . Shakspere
       Young America in London.
   25—West Indian.
       Midas.
   27—Tamerlane . . . . . . Rowe
       Catherine and Petruchio.
   29—Cymbeline.
       Love a la Mode.
May  2—Bold Stroke for a Wife.
       Neck or Nothing . . . . Garrick
    4—Orphan . . . . . . . Otway
       Miss in her Teens.
    7—Clandestine Marriage.
       Apprentice . . . . . . Murphy

OPENING OF THE CHARLESTON THEATRE.
—On Wednesday last the new theatre in this town was opened with Mr. Kelly's "Word to the Wise" and " High Life Below Stairs," with an occasional prologue and epilogue spoken by Mr. Hallam and Mrs. Douglass. The performance gave universal satisfaction. Mr. Hallam in particular in *Captain Dormer* displayed his extraordinary theatrical talents in a most splendid manner. Indeed, all the performers did great justice to their characters;

origin. If this assumption is correct it was the first farce by an American author that found its way to the stage.

The records of this season, doubly interesting because it was the first and last campaign before the Revolution, are exceedingly meagre. All the Charleston papers printed just before and immediately after the opening of the new theatre are lost. Fortunately Rivington's New York *Gazette*, which was the best newspaper of that period in the modern sense, contained an account of the opening that almost compensates the loss of the South Carolina reports. Indeed, it is not improbable that the account printed in Rivington's *Gazette*[1] was copied from the *South*

but that gentleman's superior abilities were so remarkably striking that we could not pass them over unnoticed. The house is elegantly finished and supposed for the size to be the most commodious on the continent. The scenes, which are new and well designed, the dresses, the music and what had a very pleasing effect, the disposition of the lights, all contributed to the satisfaction of the audience, who expressed the highest approbation of their entertainment.

*Carolina Gazette.* From this it will be seen that Mrs. Douglass spoke the epilogue on this occasion, thus proving beyond all question that a report of her death,

May 11—Cato . . . . . . . . . Addison
Reprisal . . . . . . . Smollett
(A Masonic benefit.)
16—Douglas . . . . . . . . Home
Devil to Pay.
19—King John . . . . . Shakspere
Guardian.

printed in many newspapers the previous September, was a mistake. In the *South Carolina Gazette* [1] of the 30th of May there was, however, a very satisfactory report of the close of the season. From this account it will be noted that Mr. Douglass had laid out a very elaborate programme for the future, extending over a period of three years. This programme, fortunately for the country but unfortunately for the theatre, was not destined to be carried out, for on the 24th of October, 1774, the Continental Congress passed a resolution recommending a suspension of all public amusements. Information of this resolution was conveyed to Mr. Douglass in a letter from Peyton Randolph, the President of Congress, and with its receipt was closed the history of the American theatre before the Revolution.

[1] CLOSE OF THE CHARLESTON SEASON.—On Friday last the theatre which opened here the 22d of December was closed. Warmly countenanced and supported by the public the manager and his company were excited to the most strenuous efforts to render their entertainments worthy of so respectable a patronage. It was considered how late it was in the season before the house could be opened, the variety of scenery and decorations necessary to a regular theatre, the number of plays represented and that almost every piece required particular preparations, it must be confessed that the exertions of the American Company have been uncommon and justly entitles them to those marks of public favor that have for so many years stampt a merit in their performances. The choice of plays hath been allowed to be very judicious, the director having selected from the most approved English poets such pieces as possess in the highest degree the *utile dulce*, and while they entertain improve the mind by conveying the most useful lessons of industry and virtue. The company have separated until the winter, when the New York Theatre will be opened. Mr. Hallam being embarked for England to engage some recruits for that service. The year after they will perform at Philadelphia, and in the winter following we may expect them here with a theatrical force hitherto unknown in America.

Scratch me, countryman!—and I'll scratch thee.

Only one advertisement printed this season, that was in any way complete, has come down to us through the existing files of the Charleston papers. This is an announcement of a Masonic benefit, contained in the *South Carolina and Country Gazette Journal* of the 10th of May, 1774. It affords us full casts of the play and farce, the only ones we have of the Charleston season of 1773-4. The only new name is that of Mr. Davis, who played *Hearty* in the farce. These casts indicate that no important changes had been made in the company, only the name of Mr. Wall being missing among those of the older members. It may be assumed, therefore, that with slight modifications, owing to these unimportant changes, the pieces presented at Charleston were played substantially as they had previously been cast at New York and Philadelphia.

The first theatrical season in Charleston was evidently a great event in the history of that city. It is not surprising that the players

ADVERTISEMENT.

The last time but ONE of performing this season
By Permission of
His Honor the Lieutenant-Governor
For the BENEFIT of the Charity Fund of the Union Kilminning Lodge, appropriated to the Relief of all Members of the Society of Freemasons, their Wives, Widows, Children and Orphans when in distress
At the New THEATRE
On Wednesday, May 11th, 1774
By the American Company
Will be presented the Tragedy of
CATO.
Never Performed There.

Cato . . . . . . . . . . . Mr. Douglass
Sempronius . . . . . . . . . Mr. Hallam
Portius . . . . . . . . . . . Mr. Henry
Marcus . . . . . . . . . . Mr. Goodman
Juba . . . . . . . . . . . Mr. Hughes
Syphax . . . . . . . . . . . Mr. Morris
Lucius . . . . . . . . . . . Mr. Dermot
Decius . . . . . . . . . . . Mr. Woolls
Lucia . . . . . . . . . . . Miss Storer
Marcia . . . . . . . . . . . Mrs. Morris

An occasional PROLOGUE to be spoken by Mr. Hallam.
An EULOGIUM on Masonry to be spoken as an Epilogue by Mr. Goodman.
The Masonic Anthem by Mr. Woolls.
To which will be added
A Comedy of Two Acts called
THE REPRISAL,
or The Tars of Old England.
Never Performed There.

Lieut. O'Clabber, with a song . . Mr. Henry
Ensign Maclaymore . . . . . Mr. Douglass
Lieut. Lyon . . . . . . . . Mr. Goodman
Capt. Champignon . . . . . . Mr. Roberts
Black, a drunken sailor . . . . Mr. Hallam

met with a warm reception at the hands of the Charleston play-goers. In Philadelphia and New York those who arrogated to themselves a finer clay than the ordinary mortal is made of disdained the drama as interpreted by the strolling players of the American Company. Ladies who held

Hearty . . . . . . . . Mr. Davis
Brush . . . . . . . . Mr. Hughes
Halyard, with "Hearts of Oak " Mr. Woolls
Harriet . . . . . . . . . . . Miss Storer
(With a song in Character.)
To conclude with Rule Britannia.
At the end of Act I a new Mason's song, with a Chorus.
Boxes, 35s.   Pit, 25s.   Gallery, 20s.
No money will be taken at the doors, nor any person admitted without tickets.
The doors will be opened at Five and the PLAY begin precisely at a Quarter past Six o'clock.

themselves aloof from their commoner sisters seldom went to entertainments of any kind and never to the play.   In Charleston the best society was fond of amusement—it was the fashion for the fine lady to be seen in public.   Early in 1773 Josiah Quincy, Jr., of Boston, attended a concert of the St. Cecilia Society, and was astonished to find as many as two hundred and fifty ladies present, this, he was assured, being an unusually small number.   In richness of dress he found the Charleston ladies to surpass their sisters of the North, and their superiors in manners—as he quaintly put it, " in taciturnity during the performance greatly before our ladies."   The gentlemen, too, dressed with richness and elegance, and many wore their swords. Mr. Douglass' audiences throughout the season were always large, and in the matter of attire the most brilliant the American Company had ever played before.   Still there was opposition to profane stage-plays, even in Charleston.   "From the bad opinion I begin to entertain of the play-house now building," a lady signing herself "Cleopatra" wrote in the *South Carolina Gazette*, on the first of November, 1773, "and the evils it might probably produce, I considered it as no other than the D——'s Synagogue, and resolved never to set foot on the inside of it." "Cleopatra," however, seems to have changed her mind, for she added that she had actually adopted a plan of life quite contrary to that which she was so foolish as to think a more laudable way of spending her time and money. Later, "at a time when the theatre is crowded and the Church neglected," a " Friend of the Clergy" recommended for their imitation, through the *South Carolina and Country Gazette Journal*, a specimen of the pulpit eloquence aimed at the stage by the Rev. Mr. Toplady. The opposition, however, does not seem to have become virulent, and the season closed as brilliantly as it had opened.

# CHAPTER XXX.

## GENERAL SUMMARY.

CLOSE OF THE EPOCH — DEATH OF MRS. DOUGLASS — REVIEW OF MR. HALLAM'S CAREER—MR. DOUGLASS, MR. HENRY, MR. MORRIS AND MR. WOOLLS—MISS HALLAM—THE STORER FAMILY—THE SECOND MRS. MORRIS—MR. GOODMAN—MISS RICHARDSON—THE MINOR MEMBERS OF THE COMPANY.

ALTHOUGH the season at Charleston was the last work performed by the American Company before the Revolution, the last performances by professional players took place at the Southwark Theatre, on the 19th and 23d of September, 1774. These were called "An Attic Evening's Entertainment," and were given by Mr. Goodman, of the American Company, and Mr. Allen, of the Theatre Royal, Edinburgh. This is the first mention of Allen, who remained in America during the War for Independence, and was a manager and actor afterward. He was the father of Andrew Jackson Allen, a noted theatrical character of the first half of the present century. Goodman and Allen's entertainments consisted of " specimens of elocution taken from the writings of the most approved English authors," together with an Introductory Address to the Town, spoken by Mr. Goodman, a humorous and satirical oration delivered by Mr. Allen, the " Lecture on Heads," by Goodman and Allen, and " Bucks Have at Ye All," after

(337)

the manner of Mr. King, of the Theatre Royal, Drury Lane, by Mr. Allen. A month later, on the 24th of October, Congress passed a resolution recommending a suspension of all amusements, and thus closed the first epoch in American theatrical history.

In parting with the actors and actresses who made the theatrical epoch previous to the Revolution the first place must of course be accorded to Mrs. Douglass. According to Dunlap she died in Philadelphia in 1773. This is apparently based on a report of her death, published in Rivington's *Gazette*, September 23d, 1773. The announcement was copied into the *Pennsylvania Chronicle* of the 27th, but as the company was

REPORT OF MRS. DOUGLASS' DEATH.

———

Last week died at Philadelphia Mrs. Douglass, wife of Mr. Douglass, manager of the American Company of Comedians, mother of Mr. Lewis Hallam and of Mrs. Mattocks, of Covent Garden Theatre, and aunt of Miss Hallam; a lady who, by her excellent performances upon the stage and her irreproachable manners in private life, had recommended herself to the friendship and affeçtion of many of the principal families on the Continent and in the West Indies.

not at the Southwark Theatre at the time Annapolis was substituted for Philadelphia. The report, however, was a mistake, for Mrs. Douglass played *Mrs. Heidelberg* in the "Clandestine Marriage," on the 10th, and *Lady Rusport* in the "West Indian," on the 15th of November, at the Southwark Theatre, and then accompanied her husband and the company to Charleston, where she delivered the epilogue on the opening night of the new theatre. Her death, therefore, must have occurred in

MRS. DOUGLASS' PARTS.

———

*Plays.*

| | |
|---|---|
| A Bold Stroke for a Wife . . . | Mrs. Lovely |
| Albion Queens . . . . . | Mary of Scotland |
| Alexander the Great . . . . . | Lysigambis |
| All for Love . . . . . . . . . | Octavia |
| Beaux' Stratagem . . . . . . | Mrs. Sullen |
| Beggars' Opera . . . . . . . | Mrs. Coaxer |
| Careless Husband . . . . . . | Lady Betty |
| Cato . . . . . . . . . . . . . | Marcia |
| Clandestine Marriage . . . | Mrs. Heidelberg |
| Committee . . . . . . . . . | { Ruth<br>{ Mrs. Day |
| Conquest of Canada . . . . . . | Sophronia |
| Conscious Lovers . . . . . . . | { Isabella<br>{ Indiana |

1774. According to the recollections of John North, who was the janitor or care-taker of the Southwark Theatre for many years, both before and after the Revolution, Mrs. Douglass died at a large frame house that then stood at Fifth and South Streets, nearly opposite the theatre. She had been complaining for a long time of a hurt she received in the theatre, and the inference is that it was this that finally led to her death. Mrs. Douglass was highly respected in Philadelphia, and Mr. North said all the ladies in the neighborhood of the theatre attended her funeral. She was buried in the grounds of the Second Presbyterian Church, at Third and Arch Streets. This burial-ground unfortunately has been dug up and the ashes of the dead scattered, so that it is impossible to identify the spot where her remains reposed. The house in which Mrs. Douglass died was a tavern, and was afterward known

| | |
|---|---|
| Constant Couple | { Lady Lurewell / Lady Darling |
| Cymbeline | Queen |
| Distressed Mother | Andromache |
| Douglas | Lady Randolph |
| Drummer | Lady Truman |
| Earl of Essex | Countess of Rutland |
| Fair Penitent | { Calista / Lavinia |
| False Delicacy | Mrs. Harley |
| Fashionable Lover | Mrs. Bridgemore |
| Gamester | Mrs. Beverly |
| George Barnwell | Millwood |
| Hamlet | Queen |
| Inconstant | Bissarre |
| Jane Shore | Jane Shore |
| Jealous Wife | Lady Freelove |
| King John | Queen Eleanor |
| Lear | Cordelia |
| Love for Love | { Angelica / Mrs. Frail |
| Love in a Village | Mrs. Deborah |
| Love Makes a Man | Louisa |
| Macbeth | { Lady Macbeth / Lady Macduff |
| Maid of the Mill | Lady Sycamore |
| Merchant of Venice | Portia |
| Miser | Mrs. Wisely |
| Mourning Bride | Zara |
| Orphan of China | Mandare |
| Othello | { Emilia / Desdemona |
| Prince of Parthia | Thermusa |
| Provoked Husband | { Lady Townly / Lady Grace |
| Recruiting Officer | Sylvia |
| Richard III | Queen Elizabeth |
| Roman Father | Valeria |
| Romeo and Juliet | { Juliet / Lady Capulet |
| Suspicious Husband | Clarinda |
| Tamerlane | Arpasia |
| Theodosius | Athenais |
| Tunbridge Walks | Hillaria |
| Twin Rivals | Constance |
| Venice Preserved | Belvidera |
| West Indian | Lady Rusport |
| Woman is a Riddle | Lady Outside |

*Farces.*

| | |
|---|---|
| Anatomist . . . . . . . . . . . | Beatrice |
| Harlequin Collector . . . . . . | Columbine |
| Lethe . . . . . . . . . . . | { Fine Lady<br>{ Mrs. Riot |
| Neck or Nothing . . . . . | Mrs. Stockwell |
| Oracle . . . . . . . . . | Fairy Queen |
| Tom Thumb . . . . . . | Queen Dollalolla |

as the "Convention of 1787." For a sign it had a painting representing the Federal Convention, beneath which were inscribed the following lines:

These thirty-eight men have signed a powerful deed
That better times to us shall very soon succeed.

Besides his mother, Mrs. Douglass, Mr. Hallam was the only member of the American Company who began with it at its beginning and remained with it without interruption from 1752 to 1774. Mr. Hallam enjoyed the distinction among his contemporaries of being an excellent general actor, both in tragedy and comedy. High comedy, however, was his forte. In parts like *Ranger*, *Marplot* and *Capt. Dormer* he was very clever. But his style of acting, like the costumes of the period, was formal, stiff and prim. One of his most noteworthy low comedy roles was *Tony Lumpkin* in "She Stoops to Conquer," of which he was the original in America. As a pantomimist Hallam was a great favorite, his *Harlequin* being especially remarkable

MR. HALLAM'S PARTS.

*Plays.*

| | |
|---|---|
| A Bold Stroke for a Wife . | { Freeman<br>{ Col. Feignwell |
| Albion Queens . . . . . . . . . | Page |
| Alexander the Great . . . . . . | Alexander |
| All for Love . . . . . . . . | Marc Antony |
| Beaux' Stratagem . . . . . . . | Archer |
| Beggars' Opera . . . . . . . | Macheath |
| Busybody . . . . . . . . . . | Marplot |
| Cato . . . . . . . . . . . | Sempronius |
| Clandestine Marriage . . . . | Lord Ogleby |
| Committee . . . . . . . | Colonel Blunt |
| Conquest of Canada . . . . | General Wolfe |
| Conscious Lovers . . . . . | { Daniel<br>{ Young Bevil |
| Constant Couple . . . | { Dicky<br>{ Sir Harry Wildair |
| Country Lasses . . . . . . . . | Modely |
| Cymbeline . . . . . . . . | Posthumous |
| Cymon . . . . . . . . . . | Cymon |
| Distressed Mother . . . . . . . | Orestes |
| Don Quixote in England . . . | Don Quixote |
| Douglas . . . . . . . . . . | Norval |
| Drummer . . . . . . . . . . | Tinsel |
| Earl of Essex . . . . . . . . | Essex |
| Englishman in Paris . . . . . . | Buck |
| Fair Penitent . . . . . . . | { Servant<br>{ Horatio<br>{ Lothario<br>{ Altamon |

for activity and grace. It was also said of him that he was very piquant in the delivery of prologues and epilogues, which were then indispensable to the play. His list of parts shows a wonderful range, and he seems to have been equally admired whether he appeared in tragedy, comedy, farce or pantomime. But previous to the Revolution he had practically no rival. There was no actor with whom to compare him, and he took care that there should be no opportunity for comparisons. For nearly a quarter of a century the stage of the New World was his own. He was an absolute sovereign of the theatre. Not only did he have the choice of parts, but of plays. He was at once the star and the stage-manager. Even Henry was not allowed to aspire to many important roles until after the Revolution, when he became Hallam's partner. According to John Durang, Hallam was accustomed to say of Henry after the

| | |
|---|---|
| False Delicacy | Cecil |
| Fashionable Lover | Mortimer |
| Gamester | Beverly |
| George Barnwell | George |
| Hamlet | Hamlet |
| Henry IV | Hotspur |
| Inconstant | Mirabel |
| Jane Shore | Hastings |
| Jealous Wife | Oakley / Lord Trinket |
| King John | Falconbridge |
| Lear | Edgar / Lear |
| Love for Love | Ben / Valentine |
| Love in a Village | Hodge |
| Love Makes a Man | Clodio |
| Macbeth | Macbeth |
| Maid of the Mill | Aimworth |
| Merchant of Venice | Portia's Servant / Antonio / Shylock |
| Miser | Ramillie / Lovegold |
| Mourning Bride | Osmyn |
| Orphan | Chamont |
| Orphan of China | Zapheniri |
| Othello | Cassio / Iago / Othello |
| Prince of Parthia | Arsaces |
| Provoked Husband | Manly / Lord Townly |
| Recruiting Officer | Capt. Plume |
| Richard III | Prince of Wales / Tressel / Richmond / Richard |
| Roman Father | Roman Father |
| Romeo and Juliet | Balthazar / Romeo |
| School for Lovers | Modely |
| She Stoops to Conquer | Tony Lumpkin |
| Shipwreck | Young Belfield |
| Suspicious Husband | Ranger / Tester |
| Tamerlane | Bejazet / Haly |
| Tender Husband | Humphrey Gubbin |

| | |
|---|---|
| Theodosius . . . . . . . . . | { Marcian<br>{ Varanes |
| Twin Rivals . . . . . . . . . | . Frizure |
| Venice Preserved . . . . . . . | . . Pierre |
| Way to Keep Him . . . . . . | Lovemore |
| West Indian . . . . . . . . . | . Belcour |
| Wonder . . . . . . . . . . . | Don Felix |
| Word to the Wise . . . . | Captain Dormer |
| Zara . . . . . . . . . . . . . | . . Ozman |

*Farces.*

| | |
|---|---|
| Brave Irishman . . . . . . . | Dr. Clyster |
| Catherine and Petruchio . . . . | Petruchio |
| Citizen . . . . . . . . . | Young Wilding |
| Cross Purposes . . . . . . . | George Bevil |
| Damon and Phillida . . . . . . . | Mopsus |
| Deuce is in Him . . . . . | Colonel Tamper |
| Edgar and Emmeline . . . . . . . | Edgar |
| Guardian . . . . . . . . . . . | Guardian |
| Harlequin Collector . . . . . . | Harlequin |
| High Life Below Stairs . . . . . | Lovel |
| Hob in the Well . . . . . . . | { Dick<br>{ Hob |
| Honest Yorkshireman . . . . . | Gaylove |
| Lethe . . . . . . . . | { Fine Gentleman<br>{ Drunken Man |
| Love a la Mode . . . . . . | Squire Groom |
| Lying Valet . . . . . . . . . | . Sharp |
| Mayor of Garratt . . . . | { Matthew Mug<br>{ Major Sturgeon |
| Miller of Mansfield . . . . . . . | Miller |
| Miss in her Teens . . . . . . . | . Flash |
| Neck or Nothing . . . . . . . . | . Slip |
| Old Maid . . . . . . . . . | Clerimont |
| Padlock . . . . . . . . . . | Mungo |
| Register Office . . . . . | Captain Le Brush |
| Reprisal . . . . . . . . . . . | . Block |
| Upholsterer . . . . . . . . . | Pamphlet |
| Witches . . . . . . . . . . | Harlequin |

latter's death that he was a splendid amateur actor. It would, perhaps, not be unjust to Hallam should he be placed in the same category. Hallam was a graceful dancer and a skillful fencer. In learning the latter accomplishment, it was said, he received a hurt in one of his eyes, which gave, in some points of view, an odd expression to his face. This was scarcely perceptible, however, and generally his countenance was well adapted to the business of the stage, especially in comedy. In person he was above the medium height, thin, straight and wiry. This is all we know of the personal appearance of the first actor whose training and career entitles him to be called American. The description we owe to Dunlap. It is at least not so much of a caricature as the drawing Dunlap made of him for the frontispiece to Major Tyler's comedy, the "Contrast."

After Mr. Hallam the oldest members of the company of continuous service were Messrs. Douglass, Morris, Woolls and Henry. Among these the name of Mr. Douglass stood first, both as actor and manager, throughout the entire period. Whatever may have been his qualifications for the stage, and they certainly were respectable,

### THE LEADING MEN—THEIR PARTS.

| PLAYS. | Douglass. | Henry. | Morris. | Woolls. |
|---|---|---|---|---|
| A Bold Stroke for a Wife . . . . . . | Colonel Feignwell . Sir Philip . . . . . | Tradelove . . . . . | Periwinkle . . . . . Tradelove . . . . . | Simon Pure . . . . |
| Alexander the Great | Clytus . . . . . . | Lysimachus . . . . | Cassander . . . . . | Thessalus . . . . . |
| All for Love . . . . | Ventidius . . . . . | | Alexas . . . . . . | Myris . . . . . . . |
| Beaux' Stratagem . | Boniface . . . . . . Aimwell . . . . . . | Aimwell . . . . . Sullen . . . . . . . | Scrub . . . . . . . | Gibbet . . . . . . |
| Beggars' Opera . . | Peachum . . . . . Moll Brazen . . . . | . . . . . . . . . . | Lockit . . . . . . Beggar . . . . . . | Macheath . . . . . |
| Busybody . . . . . | Sir Jealous Traffic . | Sir George Airy . . | Sir Francis Gripe . | . . . . . . . . . . |
| Cato . . . . . . . | Cato . . . . . . . | Portius . . . . . . | Syphax . . . . . . | Decius . . . . . . |
| Clandestine Marriage | Sir John Melville . | Lovewell . . . . . | Sterling . . . . . | Truman . . . . . . |
| Committee . . . . . | Colonel Careless . . | Teague . . . . . . | Mr. Day . . . . . | Abel . . . . . . . |
| Conquest of Canada | Leonatus . . . . . | Ochterlony . . . . Britannicus . . . . | Levi . . . . . . . . | 2d Caledonian Chief Jemmy Chaunter . |
| Conscious Lovers . | Sealand . . . . . . | Sir John Bevil . . . | Tom . . . . . . . | |
| Constant Couple . . | Colonel Standard . | Beau Clincher . . . | Alderman Smuggler | Dickey . . . . . . |
| Country Lasses . . | Heartwell . . . . . | Carbuncle . . . . . | Freehold . . . . . | Sneak . . . . . . |
| Cymbeline . . . . | Cymbeline . . . . . Iachimo . . . . . . | Iachimo . . . . . . Bellarius . . . . . | Bellarius . . . . . Pisanio . . . . . . | Arviragus . . . . Frenchman . . . . |
| Cymon . . . . . . | . . . . . . . . . . | . . . . . . . . . . | Dorus . . . . . . | Linco . . . . . . First Demon . . . . |
| Distressed Mother . | Pyrrhus . . . . . . | | Pylades . . . . . . | |
| Don Quixote in England . . . . . . . | Grizzel . . . . . . | | Sancha Panza . . . | Cook . . . . . . . |
| Douglas . . . . .:. | Lord Randolph . . | | Norval . . . . . . | . . . . . . . . . . |
| Drummer . . . . . | Coachman . . . . . Sir George Truman | . . . . . . . . . | Fantome . . . . . Gardener . . . . . | . . . . . . . . . |
| Earl of Essex . . . | Southampton . . . | Southampton . . . | Burleigh . . . . . | Lieutenant . . . . |
| Englishman in Paris | . . . . . . . . . . | Mr. Subtle . . . . . | Sir John Buck . . . | Gamut . . . . . . |
| Fair Penitent . . . | Lothario . . . . . Horatio . . . . . . | Sciolto . . . . . . | Rossano . . . . . . | . . . . . . . . . . |
| False Delicacy . . . | Colonel Rivers . . . | Lord Winworth . . | . . . . . . . . . . | . . . . . . . . . . |
| Fashionable Lover . | Colin Macleod . . . | Aubrey . . . . . . | Dr. Druid . . . . . | Jarvis . . . . . . . |
| Gamester . . . . . | Stukely . . . . . . | . . . . . . . . . . | James . . . . . . . Bates . . . . . . . | |
| George Barnwell . . | Thorowgood . . . . | Uncle . . . . . . . | Trueman . . . . . Blunt . . . . . . . | . . . . . . . . . . |
| Hamlet . . . . . . | Ghost . . . . . . . King . . . . . . . | Horatio . . . . . . Laertes . . . . . . | Horatio . . . . . . Polonius . . . . . | Guildenstern . . . . Rosencranz . . . . Marcellus . . . . . |
| Henry IV . . . . . | Sir John Falstaff . . | Prince of Wales . . Sir Walter Blunt . . | King Henry . . . | Northumberland . . Douglas . . . . . . |
| Inconstant . . . . . | . . . . . . . . . . | . . . . . . . . . . | Old Mirabel . . . . | Third Bravo . . . . |
| Jane Shore . . . . | . . . . . . . . . . | | Gloster . . . . . . | Belmour . . . . . . |
| Jealous Wife . . . | Major Oakley . . . | Charles . . . . . . | Russet . . . . . . | Tom . . . . . . . . |
| King John . . . . . | King John . . . . . | Hubert . . . . . . | Pandulph . . . . . | Melun . . . . . . . |
| Lear . . . . . . . | Edgar . . . . . . . | Edmund . . . . . . | Kent . . . . . . . Gloster . . . . . . Albany . . . . . . | . . . . . . . . . . |
| Lionel and Clarissa | Sir John Flowerdale | Harman . . . . . . | | Lionel . . . . . . . |
| Love for Love . . . | Valentine . . . . . Scandal . . . . . . | Sir Sampson Legend | Foresight . . . . . | Buckram . . . . . . |

his ability as a business man is unquestionable.    The fact that he
maintained the American Company intact for the long period of fifteen

THE LEADING MEN—THEIR PARTS.

| PLAYS. | *Douglass.* | *Henry.* | *Morris.* | *Woolls.* |
|---|---|---|---|---|
| Love in a Village    . | Justice Woodcock · | Eustace . . . . .<br>Young Meadows . . | Sir William Meadows | Hawthorn . . . . . |
| Love Makes a Man | Carlos . . . . . . . | . . . . . . . . . . | Don Lewis    . . . . | Priest . . . . . . . |
| Macbeth . . . . . | Macduff . . . . . . | Malcolm    . . . . | Banquo . . . . . .<br>Lenox . . . . . . . | Hecate  . . . . . . . |
| Maid of the Mill . | Fairfield . . . . . . | . . . . . . . . . . . | . . . . . . . . . . . | Farmer Giles    . . . |
| Merchant of Venice | Bassanio    . . . . | Tubal . . . . . . .<br>Shylock . . . . . | Launcelot . . . . . | Lorenzo . . . . . . . |
| Midas . . . . . . . | . . . . . . . . . . . | . . . . . . . . . . . | Jupiter . . . . . . | Apollo    . . . . . . |
| Miser . . . . . . | Frederick . . . . . | List . . . . . . . . | Ramillie . . . . . .<br>Decoy . . . . . . . | Sparkle . . . . . . . |
| Mourning Bride  . . | King  . . . . . . . | Garcia . . . . . . | Gonzales    . . . | Mute . . . . . . .<br>Perez . . . . . . . |
| Orphan . . . . . | . . . . . . . . . . . | Castalio . . . . . | Acasto    . . . . . | . . . . . . . . . . . |
| Orphan of China . . | Zaniti . . . . . . . | Timurkan . . . . . | Mirvan . . . . . . | Zimventi . . . . . |
| Othello . . . . . | Othello . . . . . .<br>Iago . . . . . . . | Cassio . . . . . . .<br>Ludovico . . . . . | Brabantio . . . . . | Gratiano . . . . . |
| Prince of Parthia . | Artabanes . . . . . | . . . . . . . . . . . | Bethas    . . . . . | . . . . . . . . . . . |
| Provoked Husband | Manly . . . . . . .<br>Lord Townly . . . | . . . . . . . . . | Sir Francis    . . . .<br>Squire Richard  . . | Squire Richard  . . |
| Recruiting Officer  . | Sergeant Kite . . . | Captain Brazen  . . | Worthy . . . . .<br>Justice Balance  . . | Worthy . . . . . . |
| Richard III  . . . . | Buckingham . . . .<br>King Henry . . . .<br>Richmond . . . . .<br>Richard . . . . . . | Richmond . . . . .<br>Tressel . . . . | Stanly . . . . . .<br>King Henry . . . . | Ratcliff . . . . . . |
| Roman Father . . . | Tullius Hostilius . .<br>Publius Horatius . | Publius Horatius . . | First Citizen . . . . | Third Citizen  . . . |
| Romeo and Juliet  . | Mercutio  . . . . .<br>Montagu . . . . . | Tybalt  . . . . . .<br>Capulet . . . . . | Friar Laurence   . . | Paris . . . . . . . |
| School for Lovers . | Sir John Dorilant  . | . . . . . . . . . . | Steward . . . . . . | . . . . . . . . . . . |
| She Stoops to Conquer | . . . . . . . . . . | Young Marlow  . . | Sir Charles Marlow | Landlord . . . . . |
| Shipwreck . . . . . | Old Godwin . . . . | Belfield . . . . . . | Sir Benjamin Dove | Skiff . . . . . . |
| Suspicious Husband | Strictland . . . . .<br>Frankly . . . . . | Frankly . . . . . . | Tester . . . . . . .<br>Bellamy . . . . . . | Buckle . . . . . . |
| Tamerlane . . . . . | Tamerlane . . . .<br>Monesses . . . . . | Monesses . . . . .<br>Omar . . . . . . | Dervise  . . . . . | Mirvan . . . . . .<br>Tanais . . . . . . |
| Tempest  . . . . . | Prospero . . . . . | Trinculo . . . . . . | Stephano . . . . . | Mustachio . . . . . |
| Tender Husband  . | Sir Harry Gubbin  . | Mr. Clerimont . . . | Mr. Tipkin . . . . | . . . . . . . . . . . |
| Theodosius . . . . | Lucius . . . . . . .<br>Marcian . . . . . | Theodosius  . . . . | Aranthes . . . . .<br>Theodosius . . . . | Atticus . . . . . . |
| Venice Preserved . | Priuli . . . . . . . | Jaffier . . . . . . | . . . . . . . . . . . | . . . . . . . . . . . |
| Way to Keep Him . | Sir Bashful Constant | Sir Brilliant Fashion | Sideboard . . . . . | . . . . . . . . . . . |
| West Indian . . . . | Captain Dudley  . . | Belcour . . . . . .<br>O'Flaherty  . . . . | Mr. Stockwell . . . | Sailor . . . . . . |
| Wonder . . . . . . | Gibby . . . . . . . | Colonel Briton . . . | Lissardo . . . . . .<br>Don Lopez . . . . | Frederick . . . . . |
| Word to the Wise . | Sir John Dormer . . | Sir George Hastings | Willoughby . . . . | . . . . . . . . . . . |
| Zara  . . . . . . . | Lusignan . . . . . | . . . . . . . . . . | . . . . . . . . . . . | . . . . . . . . . . . |
| FARCES. | | | | |
| Apprentice  . . . . | . . . . . . . . . . . | Gargle  . . . . . . | Wingate . . . . . . | President . . . . . |
| Brave Irishman  . . | Dr. Gallipot . . . . | Capt. O'Blunder . . | Tradewell . . . . . | . . . . . . . . . . . |
| Catherine and Pe-<br>truchio  . . . . . | Hortentio . . . . . | Tailor . . . . . . . | Grumio . . . . . . | Peter . . . . . . . |

years is in itself a proof of his managerial skill. His list of parts shows that he played many important roles in his time. He was especially fond of Scotchmen. In the Shaksperean drama he was the original *King John* and *Sir John Falstaff* on the American stage. Mr. Douglass' services in the establishment and development of the drama on this

## THE LEADING MEN—THEIR PARTS.

| FARCES. | Douglass. | Henry. | Morris. | Woolls. |
|---|---|---|---|---|
| Chaplet | | | | Damon |
| Citizen | Old Philpot | Young Wilding | Old Philpot | Beaufort |
| Cock-lane Ghost | Irish Sergeant | | Shadrach Bodkin | |
| Comus | | Comus | Second Spirit | Third Spirit |
| Contrivances | | | Argus | Rovewell |
| Cross Purposes | Francis Bevil | Harry Bevil | Robin | |
| Damon and Phillida | | | Corydon | Damon |
| Deuce is in Him | Major Belfort | | | |
| Devil to Pay | Doctor | Jobson | Butler | Sir John Loverule |
| Guardian | | | Sir Charles | |
| Harlequin Collector | Anatomist / Clown / Doctor | | Clown / Anatomist | Magician |
| High Life Below Stairs | Freeman | Sir Harry | Philip | Coachman |
| Hob in the Well | | | Sir Thomas Testy | Friendly |
| Honest Yorkshireman | | | Muckworm | Gaylove |
| Lethe | Æsop | | Old Man | Mercury |
| Love a la Mode | Sir Archy | Sir Callaghan | Beau Mordecai | |
| Lying Valet | | | Cook / Sharp | |
| Mayor of Garratt | Sir Jacob Jollop / Bruin | Crispin Heeltap | Crispin / Sneak | First Mob |
| Miller of Mansfield | | King | Dick / Miller | Joe |
| Miss in her Teens | | Capt. Flash | Puff | Jasper |
| Mock Doctor | Gregory | | Sir Jasper | Leander |
| Musical Lady | | | Old Mask | |
| Neck or Nothing | | Sir William | Martin | |
| Neptune and Amphitrite | | | | Neptune |
| Old Maid | Captain Cape | | Capt. Cape / Heartly | |
| Padlock | | | | Don Diego |
| Polly Honeycomb | | | Mr. Honeycomb | |
| Register Office | Scotchman | | Tricket | |
| Reprisal | Ensign MacClaymore | Lieut. O'Clabber | Lieut. O'Clabber | Halyard |
| Spirit of Contradiction | Steer | | Mr. Parlett | |
| Thomas and Sally | | Sailor | | Squire |
| Upholsterer | Upholsterer | Bellman | Feeble | Rovewell |
| Virgin Unmasked | | | Goodwill | |
| Witches | Statuary | | Pantaloon | Mercury / Necromancer |

continent have never been fully appreciated, his achievements being robbed of their significance by the fictions relating to the Hallams with which Dunlap began his so-called " History of the American Theatre."

Although Mr. Henry was kept in the background by Hallam during this period of his service on the American stage he had managed to impress the public with his general excellence, while in Irish parts it was universally recognized that he was inimitable.

Owen Morris—"Old Mr. Morris," as he was afterward known— was held to be an excellent actor in the serious fathers, and he was especially clever in humorous and eccentric old men, as *Sir Francis Gripe, Alderman Smuggler, Old Mirabel* and *Beau Mordecai.* His Shaksperean roles, as *Polonius, Brabantio, King Henry* and *Friar Laurence* were highly esteemed. Mr. Morris lived to be a very old man, his latter years being spent in retirement in Philadelphia.

Stephen Woolls was a fair singer, but as an actor it is fair to assume his merits were not great. It was said that he sang the music of *Hecate* very effectively, and he was above all things else an honest man. Both Morris and Woolls were sharers in the American Company down to the Revolution. They resumed their places in the company under Hallam and Henry after the War for Independence, Mr. Douglass being the only one of the quintette whose career on the American stage ended with the epoch.

As the leading lady of the old American Company at the time of its dissolution Miss Hallam asserts her right to consideration. That she was the niece of Mrs. Douglass and the cousin of Mr. Hallam may be accepted as established. It is not likely that a journalist as well informed as James Rivington would have made the mistake of calling Mrs. Douglass her aunt instead of her mother, especially as he mentions Mrs. Mattocks as Mr. Hallam's sister. Her list of parts shows her to have been first in everything, from *Statira* and *Juliet* to *Polly* in the " Beggars' Opera,"— in tragedy, comedy and farce. In her day her admirers sang her praises with a fervor and passion that her predecessor, Miss Cheer, had never been able to command. Even allowing for poetic license and enthusiasm she must have had a fair share of personal beauty, else the Maryland poet would scarcely have dared to exclaim in his impassioned, pedantic way :—

> Ye Gods ! 'Tis Cytherea's face !

The poem accords Miss Hallam theatrical talents of the most versatile order, making her one of the few actresses who have had the ability to catch Shakspere's glowing ray ; investing her comedy with the power to compel laughter to hold his sides and make the pit resound with ios of enjoyment, and matching her elo-

MISS HALLAM'S PARTS.

| Plays. | |
| --- | --- |
| Alexander the Great | Statira |
| Beaux' Stratagem | Dorinda |
| Beggars' Opera | Polly |
| Busybody | Isabinda |
| Cato | Lucia |
| Clandestine Marriage | Miss Sterling |
| Committee | Isabella |
| Conquest of Canada | Sophia |
| Conscious Lovers | Lucinda |
| Constant Couple | Angelica |
| Cymbeline | Imogen |
| Cymon | Sylvia |
| Distressed Mother | Cleone |
| Earl of Essex | { Countess of Nottingham / Countess of Rutland |
| False Delicacy | Miss Marchmont |
| Fashionable Lover | Augusta Aubrey |
| George Barnwell | Maria |
| Hamlet | Ophelia |
| Jealous Wife | Harriet |
| King John | Blanche |
| Lionel and Clarissa | Diana Oldboy |
| Love for Love | Angelica |
| Love in a Village | { Lucinda / Rosetta |
| Maid of the Mill | Patty |
| Merchant of Venice | Jessica |
| Miser | Harriet |
| Mourning Bride | { Attendant / Almeria |
| Provoked Husband | Miss Jenny |
| Recruiting Officer | Rose |
| Roman Father | Horatia |
| Romeo and Juliet | Juliet |
| School for Lovers | Celia |
| She Stoops to Conquer | Miss Hardcastle |
| Shipwreck | Sophia |
| Suspicious Husband | Clarinda |
| Tamerlane | Arpasia |
| Tender Husband | Niece |

| | |
|---|---|
| Theodosius . . . . . . . . . | { Mirina<br>{ Athenais |
| Way to Keep Him . . . . | Widow Belmour |
| West Indian . . . . . . | Charlotte Rusport |
| Wonder . . . . . . . . . . | { Violante<br>{ Isabella |
| Word to the Wise . . . . . | Miss Montagu |

*Farces.*

| | |
|---|---|
| Brave Irishman . . . . . . . . . . | Lucy |
| Citizen . . . . . . . . . . . . | Maria |
| Comus . . . . . . . . . . . . | Sabina |
| Deuce is in Him . . . . . . . . | Emily |
| Edgar and Emmeline . . . . . | Emmeline |
| Guardian . . . . . . . . | Miss Harriet |
| Harlequin Collector . . . . . . | Haymaker |
| High Life Below Stairs . . . . . | Lady Bab |
| Hob in the Well . . . . . . . . | Flora |
| Honest Yorkshireman . . . . . . | Arabella |
| Lethe . . . . . . . . . . | Mrs. Tattoo |
| Love a la Mode . . . . . . . | Charlotte |
| Miss in her Teens . . . . . . | Miss Biddy |
| Musical Lady . . . . . . . . . | Sophy |
| Neck or Nothing . . . . . . . | Miss Nancy |
| Oracle . . . . . . . . . . . | Cynthia |
| Padlock . . . . . . . . . . . | Leonora |
| Reprisal . . . . . . . . . | Miss Harriet |
| Thomas and Sally . . . . . . . . | Sally |

cution only with the notes of her singing voice when her looks inform the strings. Of Miss Hallam after her return to England there is no information. After being sung of by the poets and painted by Peale she was destined to be ignored, if not entirely forgotten by the dramatic historians. She has always been confounded with her cousin, the Miss Hallam of 1752–4, and her merit as an actress denied, while her parts show that she occupied a more important position on the American stage than had ever been filled by her aunt, Mrs. Douglass.

Of the three Storer sisters who came to the Southwark Theatre at the same time with Mr. Henry, in 1767, Ann was the eldest, and until shortly before the Revolution, when she was known as Mrs. Henry, the most prominent actress. Her list of parts shows her in a favorable light as an actress from the very beginning of her career. It is true she did not occupy the front rank, especially in tragedy, at any time, *Desdemona* being her

ANN STORER'S PARTS.

*Plays.*

| | |
|---|---|
| Alexander the Great . . . . . . | Parisates |
| All for Love . . . . . . . . . . | Octavia |
| Beaux' Stratagem . . . . . . . | Cherry |
| Beggars' Opera . . . . . . . | Mrs. Coaxer |
| Clandestine Marriage . . . . . . | Betty |
| Conquest of Canada . . . . . . | First Nun |
| Conscious Lovers . . . . . . . . | Isabella |
| Cymon . . . . . . . . . . . . . | Fatima |
| Distressed Mother . . . . . . . | Cephisa |
| Earl of Essex . . . Countess of Nottingham |
| False Delicacy . . . . . . . Miss Rivers |

best role in the Shakesperean drama, but all her parts were responsible, and some of them excellent. She suddenly dropped out of the bills altogether, Miss Richardson taking her part of *Betty* in the " Clandestine Marriage," when it was last played in Philadelphia, in 1773, and her sister succeeding her in the " Earl of Essex," as already noted. It does not follow that she did not remain with the company until the end, although it is more probable that she separated from Mr. Henry in the winter of 1772–3 and retired. She died in New York, in 1816. Her son, the late George Hogg Biddle, used to tell of meeting the celebrated Mrs. Wheatley in the street as a boy,

| | |
|---|---|
| Fashionable Lover | . . . . . . . Lucinda |
| Hamlet . | . . . . . . . . . . Player Queen |
| King John | . . . . . . Lady Falconbridge |
| Lear . | . . . . . . . . . . . . . . Regan |
| Lionel and Clarissa | . . . . . . . . Jenny |
| Love for Love | . . . . . . . . . Angelica |
| Midas . | . . . . . . . . . . . . Juno |
| Orphan . | . . . . . . . . . . . . Serina |
| Othello | . . . . . . . . . Desdemona |
| Recruiting Officer | . . . . . . . . Melinda |
| Richard III . | . . . . . . . . Lady Anne |
| Roman Father | . . . . . . . . . Valeria |
| Romeo and Juliet | . . . . . Lady Capulet |
| School for Lovers | . . . . . . Araminta |
| Shipwreck . | . . . . . . . . . Violetta |
| Suspicious Husband | . . . . Mrs. Strictland |
| Tamerlane . | . . . . . . . . . . Selima |
| Tempest . | . . . . . . . . . . Miranda |
| Way to Keep Him | . . . . Mrs. Lovemore |
| West Indian | . . . . . . . . Miss Fulmer |
| Wonder . | . . . . . . . . . . . . Flora |

*Farces.*

| | |
|---|---|
| Catherine and Petruchio | . . . . . Bianca |
| Guardian | . . . . . . . . . . . . Lucy |
| High Life Below Stairs | . . . . . . . Kitty |
| Hob in the Well | . . . . . . . . Betty |
| Lying Valet . | . . . . . . . . . Kitty Pry |
| Mayor of Garratt | . . . . . . . Mrs. Sneak |
| Miss in her Teens | . . . . . { Miss Biddy / Tag |
| Neck or Nothing | . . . . . . . . . Jenny |
| Register Office | . . . . . Margery Monfort |
| Upholsterer | . . . . . . . . Termagant |

who recognized him because of his resemblance to his mother.

Fanny Storer, the second of the sisters, who became Mrs. Mechler, was on the stage with the old American Company for only a brief period. Dunlap is authority for the statement that she became Mrs. Mechler, but he seems to fix the date of her marriage after Mr.

FANNY STORER'S PARTS.

*Plays.*

| | |
|---|---|
| Constant Couple | . . . . . . . . . Parly |
| Fair Penitent | . . . . . . . . . Lucilla |
| Suspicious Husband | . . . . . . Jacintha |

*Farces.*
High Life Below Stairs   . . Lady Charlotte
Miss in her Teens . . . . . . . . . Flash

Henry's death, while Mr. Ireland confounds her with her younger sister, Maria. Her list of parts shows her in only three plays and two farces. Her last appearance was in New York, in 1768, when she played *Flash*, and her sister, Maria, *Fribble* in " Miss in her Teens." As Maria was called Miss Storer in the bills, when Ann became Mrs. Henry, it is probable that Fanny's marriage occurred about this time.

Maria Storer became more of a favorite than either of her elder sisters. Growing from childhood into womanhood under Mr. Henry's eye their subsequent relationship is peculiar—perhaps reprehensible. It is sad to reflect that her girlish beauty and great gifts should have led him into wishing to make her the successor of her sister, or that she should have been willing to occupy her sister's place. Dunlap sees in Henry's successive relationships to the Storer family " a glimpse at the state of manners and morals among these teachers of virtue and morality," and declares that " it is unjust to fix a stigma on a profession which appertains to an unworthy individual," but he does not point out the unworthy individual. On the contrary, his ambiguity and dul-

MARIA STORER'S PARTS.

*Plays.*

| | |
|---|---|
| Beaux' Stratagem | Gipsy |
| Beggars' Opera | Lucy |
| Cato | Lucia |
| Clandestine Marriage | Miss Fanny |
| Comus | Euphrosine |
| Conquest of Canada | Second Nun |
| Cymon | { Cupid / First Shepherdess |
| Earl of Essex | Countess of Nottingham |
| Englishman in Paris | Lucinda |
| False Delicay | Miss Marchmont |
| Fashionable Lover | Betty |
| George Barnwell | Maria |
| King John | Prince Arthur |
| Lionel and Clarissa | Clarissa |
| Love for Love | Miss Prue |
| Love in a Village | Lucinda |
| Macbeth | Fleance |
| Maid of the Mill | Fanny |
| Midas | Nysa |
| Mourning Bride | Leonora |
| Orphan | Page |
| She Stoops to Conquer | Miss Neville |
| Shipwreck | Lucy Waters |
| Suspicious Husband | Milliner |
| Tempest | Ariel |
| Theodosius | Marina |
| Way to Keep Him | Muslin |

ness have left the stigma on Ann Storer's name. To her it certainly did not belong, whether there was or was not a marriage ceremony at the time Henry first recognized her as his wife. Whether he afterward actually married Maria Storer is equally problematical. It seems certain, however, that his fondness for the younger sister caused his separation from the elder, because the younger had supplanted the elder before the public long before she took the name

West Indian . . . . . . . . Louisa Dudley
Wonder . . . . . . . . . . . . . Isabella
Word to the Wise . . . . Miss Willoughby

*Farces.*

Cross Purposes . . . . . . . . . . Emily
Damon and Phillida . . . . . . . Phillida
Devil to Pay . . . . . . . . . . Nell
High Life Below Stairs . . . . . Lady Bab
Hob in the Well . . . . . . . . . Flora
Honest Yorkshireman . . . . . . Arabella
Lethe . . . . . . . . . .· . . . Mrs. Riot
Miller of Mansfield . . . . . . . Kate
Miss in her Teens . . . . . . . . Fribble
Musical Lady . . . . . . . Lady Scrape
Neptune and Amphitrite . . . . Amphitrite
Register Office . . . . . . . . . Maria

AN ODE
INSCRIBED TO MISS STORER.

Genius of Harmony, descend,
  In all thy smiles appear,
And pleased, thy Storer's voice attend ;
  For her thou lov'st to hear.
Bid every ruder sound remove,
  Bid care, bid sorrow fly,

For now thy Storer wakes the lay
  And, mistress of the heart,
Does with our yielding passions play,
  Submissive to her art.
'Tis hers to lead the mind along,
  With love's own ardor warm ;
Hers all the various powers of song,
  And music's magic charm.

'Tis portion of th' ethereal flame,
  This high-wrought charm is given
To those alone of finer frame,
  The favorites of heaven.
For sure, it asks celestial art,
  And all the Seraph's skill,
To rule th' emotions of the heart,
  Or fix the wavering will.

Mrs. Henry. As an actress and singer Maria Storer was held in high esteem, even before she reached womanhood. The Maryland poets invoked Peale to paint her as *Ariel,* when singing his praises for painting Miss Hallam as *Imogen,* and an Ode, signed " Philomelos," inscribed to her and printed in the *Maryland Gazette,* October 14th, 1773, was as fulsome as the verses addressed to Miss Hallam in previous years. Dunlap pronounces her the best public singer America had known previous to the year 1792, and

As on the banks of Nile's famed stream,
　Old Memnon's lyre renown'd,
Touch'd by the sun's enliv'ning beam,
　Return'd a tuneful sound.
So warm'd by some diviner ray,
　Some emanation bright
Of harmony, fair Storer's lay
　Thus pains us with delight.

While now she wakes the living lay,
　And fills the enraptured soul,
I feel my beating heart obey,
　And own her soft control.
Sweet Harmonist! prolong the strain,
　The melody of Heaven;
And soothe with songs the tender pain,
　Thy tender songs have given.

adds that she played tragedy and comedy with spirit and propriety, although her figure was rather *petite* for the former or for the heroines of Congreve and Cibber. Wood calls her "a prodigious favorite," but alludes to her silly and capricious conduct, which frequently led to a change in the performance through some captious objection to a character, a slender box-sheet, or a stinted proportion of applause. Charles Durang on the other hand, apparently on the authority of his father, John Durang, tells us that "opinions differed widely as to her merits as an actress." The testimony of none of them has much value. Wood, if he knew her at all, could have known her only as a boy, and his knowledge of her was so slight that he says she had previously been well esteemed at Bath as a principal singer. Durang calls her "Miss Storer of the London theatres," who, "soon after her arrival, became the wife of Mr. Henry." As has been shown, her training, both as a singer and an actress, was entirely American. Maria Storer died soon after Henry's death, in a house he had built back of the Southwark Theatre, heart-broken, demented and very poor.

No greater contrast is possible than between Maria Storer and the second Mrs. Morris. The one was slight, girlish, blue-eyed—the other tall, stately, imposing. The one was the ideal *Ariel* of our early drama—the other the *Portia*. Which was the greater favorite even Wood does not undertake to decide. Their line of parts was so distinctly opposite that there was in reality no opportunity for rivalry. No such queenly *Elizabeth* had ever been seen in America in the "Earl of Essex," when Mrs. Morris essayed the role; no such stately *Shrew* had been presented by her predecessors in "Catherine and Petruchio." In such parts as *Marcia, Arpasia* and *Pulcheria* she was superb. Tradition speaks without reserve of her excellence in the elegant comedy introduced by Kelly and Cumberland—*Lady Betty Lambton, Lady Dove, Lady Constant* and *Mrs. Willoughby.* She was the original *Mrs. Hardcastle* in "She Stoops to Conquer" in this country. An ideal English dame of the period she must have been, for it is recorded of her in her latter years that she was herself a fine specimen of the polished old lady of fantastic

MRS. MORRIS' PARTS.

*Plays.*

| | |
|---|---|
| Beaux' Stratagem | Mrs. Sullen |
| Beggars' Opera | Mrs. Peachum |
| Cato | Marcia |
| Conquest of Canada | Abbess |
| Constant Couple | Lady Lurewell |
| Earl of Essex | Queen Elizabeth |
| False Delicacy | Lady Betty Lambton |
| George Barnwell | Millwood |
| Henry IV | Lady Percy |
| Love for Love | Mrs. Frail |
| Love in a Village | Margery |
| Merchant of Venice | Portia |
| Midas | Daphne |
| Mourning Bride | Zara |
| Richard III | Queen Elizabeth |
| School for Lovers | Lady Beverly |
| She Stoops to Conquer | Mrs. Hardcastle |
| Shipwreck | Lady Dove |
| Tamerlane | Arpasia |
| Theodosius | Pulcheria |
| Way to Keep Him | Lady Constant |
| Word to the Wise | Mrs. Willoughby |

*Farces.*

| | |
|---|---|
| Catherine and Petruchio | Catherine |
| Cross Purposes | Mrs. Grub |
| Honest Yorkshireman | Combrush |
| Irish Widow | Mrs. Brady |
| Lying Valet | Melissa |
| Padlock | Ursula |

etiquette. At the close of the first quarter of the present century she still affected the styles of the beginning of the last quarter of the eighteenth—white cravat for the neck, short waist, long train gown and full head-dress. Mrs. Morris died in Philadelphia in 1829, having survived all the actors and actresses who were on the American stage before the Revolution.

Miss Richardson was an actress who came unheralded to the American Company and left it without a biographer. No Maryland poet sang her praises in halting verse, and Charles Wilson Peale was not implored to paint her portrait. Her history is only a name, and her fame is comprised in the modest line of parts in which she appeared. But even as a name a certain interest attaches to her, for like her predecessors in the same walk of the drama, Nancy George, Miss Palmer and Miss Wainwright, the only wonder is that she should ever have found herself in it, only to sink out of sight with such apparent indifference. Whether she accompanied the company to Charleston is uncertain, her last known appearance being during the farewell engagement in Philadelphia. There is a tradition that Lady Susan O'Brien played for two years with the American Company. The only actress with whom it would be possible to identify her is Miss Richardson, but the O'Briens seem to have returned to England before Miss Richardson's *debut*.

### Miss Richardson's Parts.

#### Plays.

|  |  |
|---|---|
| Beaux' Stratagem | Dorinda |
| Beggars' Opera | Jenny Diver |
| Clandestine Marriage | Betty |
| Conquest of Canada | Maid |
| Cymbeline | Helen |
| Cymon | Dorcas / Second Shepherdess |
| Englishman in Paris | Mrs. Subtle |
| False Delicacy | Sally |
| Fashionable Lover | Mrs. Mackintosh |
| Hamlet | Player Queen |
| Love for Love | Mrs. Foresight |
| Maid of the Mill | Theodosia |
| Merchant of Venice | Nerissa |
| Recruiting Officer | Lucy |
| Richard III | Duke of York |
| Shipwreck | Fanny |
| Tender Husband | Jenny |
| Theodosius | Flavella |
| Suspicious Husband | Lucetta |
| Way to Keep Him | Mignionet |
| West Indian | Lucy |
| Wonder | Iris |
| Word to the Wise | Lucy |

#### Farces.

|  |  |
|---|---|
| Catherine and Petruchio | Bianca |
| Citizen | Corunna |
| Cross Purposes | Housemaid |
| Devil to Pay | Lucy |
| High Life Below Stairs | Lady Charlotte |
| Hob in the Well | Hob's Mother |
| Love a la Mode | Lady |
| Lying Valet | Mrs. Trippet |
| Miller of Mansfield | Peggy |
| Upholsterer | Harriet |

All that is known of Mr. Goodman has already been told in this volume, but his list of parts is so interesting for a young man who went from a lawyer's office to the stage, at that early period of American dramatic history, that it is sure to command attention. From the very outset he was allowed as high a rank as was accorded to Mr. Henry, after ten years' service. It has long been the habit to accord the honor of being the first actor of American birth to John Martin, but Goodman seems to be entitled to that distinction. At the same time it ought to be remembered that the old American Company was almost wholly of American training, Hallam, Douglass, Henry, Morris, Woolls, Miss Hallam and Maria Storer having gained their theatrical experience in the Colonies. With the close of the Charleston season Mr. Goodman's name disappears from our dramatic annals. He deserves especially to be remembered as the original *Hardcastle* in the only

MR. GOODMAN'S PARTS.

*Plays.*

| | |
|---|---|
| Beaux' Stratagem | Foigard |
| Beggars' Opera | Mat o' the Mint |
| Cato | Marcus |
| Conquest of Canada | Montcalm |
| Constant Couple | Beau Clincher |
| Cymbeline | Bellarius |
| Cymon | Merlin |
| Englishman in Paris | Buck |
| Fashionable Lover | Tyrrel |
| Hamlet | Ghost |
| Henry IV | Sir Walter Blunt |
| Lionel and Clarissa | Colonel Oldboy |
| Love for Love | Ben |
| Maid of the Mill | Sir Harry Sycamore |
| Merchant of Venice | Gratiano |
| Midas | Midas |
| Othello | Cassio |
| Recruiting Officer | Bullock |
| Richard III | Buckingham |
| Roman Father | Publius |
| Romeo and Juliet | Escalus |
| She Stoops to Conquer | Hardcastle |
| Shipwreck | Captain Ironsides |
| Tamerlane | Monesses |
| Tempest | Caliban |
| Theodosius | Leontine |
| Way to Keep Him | William |
| West Indian | Major O'Flaherty |
| Wonder | Don Pedro |
| Word to the Wise | Villars |

*Farces.*

| | |
|---|---|
| Catherine and Petruchio | Petruchio |
| Comus | Younger Brother |
| Cross Purposes | Mr. Grub |
| Lethe | Tattoo |
| Lying Valet | Guttle |
| Mayor of Garratt | Major Sturgeon |
| Register Office | Lord Brilliant |
| Reprisal | Lieut. Lyon |

play of the period that has survived, " She Stoops to Conquer." It is to be regretted that as the first American actor our knowledge of Goodman is so incomplete.

Mr. Wall's service with the American Company was much longer than that of Mr. Goodman, but in spite of his experience he was completely eclipsed by the younger actor. Wall made his first appearance on the opening night of the Southwark Theatre, in 1766, as *Glenalvon* in " Douglas " and *Biondello* in " Catherine and Petruchio." His roles during his first season were generally those in which youth and good looks are important, as *Laertes* in "Hamlet," *Belmour* in the "School for Lovers," *Sullen* in the " Beaux' Stratagem" and *Young Clincher* in the " Constant Couple." Somehow he has left behind him the impression that he was the dandy of the company, both on and off the stage. Durang left a note to the effect that the early players were always fashionably attired, some of them dressing in the extreme of the foppish costume of the period. First among these

MR. WALL'S PARTS.

*Plays.*

| | |
|---|---|
| A Bold Stroke for a Wife . . . . | Freeman |
| Alexander the Great . . . . . | Hephestion |
| All for Love . . . . . . . . | Dolabella |
| Beaux' Stratagem . . . . . . | { Mr. Sullen / Scrub / Freeman } |
| Beggars' Opera . . . . . . . . . | Filch |
| Busybody . . . . . . . . . . | Charles |
| Cato . . . . . . . . . . . | Juba |
| Clandestine Marriage . . . . . . | Brush |
| Conquest of Canada . . . . . | Bougainville |
| Conscious Lovers . . . . . . . | Myrtle |
| Constant Couple . . . . . | Young Clincher |
| Country Lasses . . . . . . . . | Lurcher |
| Cymbeline . . . . . . . . . . | Cloten |
| Cymon . . . . . . . . . . . | Damon |
| Don Quixote in England . . | Squire Badger |
| Douglas . . . . . . . . . . | Glenalvon |
| Drummer . . . . . . . . . . | Butler |
| Englishman in Paris . . . . . . | Solitaire |
| False Delicacy . . . . | Sir Harry Newburg |
| Fashionable Lover . . . . . . | Napthali |
| Gamester . . . . . . . . . . | Lewson |
| Hamlet . . . . . . . . | { Player King / Laertes } |
| Henry IV . . . . . . | { Westmoreland / Peto / Prince of Wales } |
| Inconstant . . . . . . . . . | Dugard |
| Jane Shore . . . . . . . . . . | Dumont |
| Jealous Wife . . . . . . . . . | Charles |
| King John . . . . . . . . . | Dauphin |
| Lear . . . . . . . . . . . | { Edmund / Usher } |
| Lionel and Clarissa . . . . . | Mr. Jessamy |
| Love for Love . . . . . . . . . | Tattle |

theatrical fops I am irresistibly led to place Wall. A number of circumstances, each unimportant in itself, suggests this portrait. Once in Philadelphia he advertised the loss of his chest, indicating the value that the owner placed upon the wearing apparel it contained. In New York, at a later period, he bewailed the evil reports put in circulation in regard to him by some malicious person, showing in his wail the vanity of the coxcomb. In Baltimore, where he lived during the Revolution, he kept a horse for his own pleasure, until he became so hard pressed for money that he was compelled to advertise the animal for sale. As an actor Wall's ambition was certainly greater than his merit. In spite of his opportunities he gradually sank in the favor of his manager and the public, until he found himself allowed only the most insignificant roles, *Lint*, instead of *Jerry Sneak*, in the "Mayor of Garratt," and the *Usher*, instead

Love in a Village . . . . Young Meadows
Love Makes a Man . . . . . . Don Duart
Macbeth . . . . . . . . . . . Lenox
Maid of the Mill . . . . . . . . Ralph
Merchant of Venice . . . . . . Salanio
Midas . . . . . . . . . . . Damætas
Miser . . . . . . . . . . . Clerimont
Mourning Bride . . . . . . . { Selim / Garcia
Orphan . . . . . . . . . . . Polydore
Orphan of China . . . . . . . .
Othello . . . . . . . . . . Roderigo
Prince of Parthia . . . . . . . Gotarzes
Provoked Husband . . . . . Count Basset
Recruiting Officer . . . . . { Bullock / First Recruit
Richard III . . . . . . . { Buckingham / Edward V
Roman Father . . . . . . . . Valerius
Romeo and Juliet . . . . . . . { Tybalt / Benvolio
School for Lovers . . . . . . Belmour
Shipwreck . . . . . . . . . . Philip
Suspicious Husband . . . . { Frankly / Jack Meggot
Tamerlane . . . . . . . . { Axalla / Haly
Tempest . . . . . . . . . . Hipolito
Tender Husband . . . . . . Mr. Prince
Theodosius . . . . . . . . . Aranthes
Venice Preserved . . . . . . . Bedamar
West Indian . . . . . . Charles Dudley
Wonder . . . . . . . . . Colonel Blinker

*Farces.*

Apprentice . . . . . . . . . . . Dick
Brave Irishman . . . . . . . . Cheatwell
Catherine and Petruchio . . . . Biondello
Chaplet . . . . . . . . . . . Palemon
Citizen . . . . . . . . . . Young Philpot
Cock-lane Ghost . . . . { Peter Paragraph / Orator
Damon and Phillida . . . . . . . Cymon
Deuce is in Him . . . . . . . . Prattle
Devil to Pay . . . . . . . . . Footman
Guardian . . . . . . . . . Young Clackit
Harlequin Collector . . . . . . . Baboon
Harlequin Restored . . . . . . . Valet
High Life Below Stairs . . . . Lord Duke

Honest Yorkshireman . . . . . . Sapscull
Lethe . . . . . . . . . Fine Gentleman
Love a la Mode . . . . . . Squire Groom
Lying Valet . . . . . . . . . . Gayless
Mayor of Garratt . . . . . . { Jerry Sneak
                             { Lint
Miller of Mansfield . . . . Lord Lovewell
Miss in her Teens . . . . . . . . Fribble
Mock Doctor . . . . . . Squire Robert
Musical Lady . . . . . . . . '. . Mask
Neck or Nothing . . . . . . . . Belford
Old Maid . . . . . . . . . . Clerimont
Oracle . . . . . . . . . . . . Observer
Padlock . . . . . . . . . . . . Leander
Polly Honeycomb . . . . . . . . Scribble
Register Office . . . . . . . Harwood
Reprisal . . . . . . . . . . . . Brush
Spirit of Contradiction . . . . Lovewell
Thomas and Sally . . . . . . . . Sailor
Upholsterer . . . . . . . . . . Barber
Witches . . . . . . . . . . . . Valet

of the *Bastard*, in " King Lear."
He was pronounced unequal to
*Leander* in the " Padlock." He
seems to have dropped out alto-'
gether after the season at Annapolis, in 1773, where he remained
behind to give a " Lecture on
Heads" after the company had
departed for Philadelphia. In retirement, however, he was ill at
ease, and even before the close of
the War for Independence he organized a company at Baltimore,

where he built and opened the first theatre there, in the beginning
of 1782. Mrs. Wall, who occasionally played small parts, was
probably not an actress, but being
the wife of a member of the company was sometimes utilized by
the management. The slight experience thus gained enabled her
to shine for a very brief period as
the leading lady of the Baltimore
Company under her husband's
management, where their daughter, Miss Wall, was also brought
before the public. What became
of them afterward is unknown.
Wall was the cause of the Hallam

MRS. WALL'S PARTS.

*Plays.*

A Bold Stroke for a Wife . . Masked Lady
All for Love . . . . . . . . . . . Iras
Beaux' Stratagem . . . . . . . . Gipsy
Beggars' Opera . . . . . Mrs. Slammekin
Clandestine Marriage . . . . Housekeeper
Henry IV . . . . . . . . . Prince John
Love for Love . . . . . . Mrs. Foresight
Love Makes a Man . . . . . . . Honoria
Miser . . . . . . . . . . . . . Wheedle
Mourning Bride . . . . . . . Attendant
Suspicious Husband . . . . . . . Maid
Theodosius . . . . . . . . . . . Julia

*Farces.*

Catherine and Petruchio . . . . . { Bianca
                                  { Curtis
Devil to Pay . . . . . . . . . Lettice
Miller of Mansfield . . . . . . . Peggy
Mock Doctor . . . . . . . . Charlotte
Upholsterer . . . . . . . . . . Maria

and Henry company being officially called the Old American Company after the Revolution, as he adopted the name of the American Company for his Baltimore corps.

Whether there were two Parkers on the American stage at the same time, one, together with his wife, with the Virginia Company at Williamsburg, in 1768, and the New American Company at Annapolis, in 1769, and one without a wife, at least on the stage, with the American Company, from 1768 to 1774, is a question that existing records fail to settle. Mr. and Mrs. Parker made their first appearance at the Southwark Theatre, June 4th, 1767. While they were with the Virginia Company, from April to June, 1768, there was no person of the name with the American Company in New York. Mr. Parker first joined Mr. Douglass' forces at the Southwark Theatre in the season of 1768-9. As the Philadelphia season closed January 2d, 1769, there was ample time for him to join the New American Company at Annapolis, in February. While a Parker was at Annapolis from February to

MR. PARKER'S PARTS.

*Plays.*

| | |
|---|---|
| Alexander the Great | Polyperchon |
| Beggars' Opera | { Ben Budge / *Lockit* / *Beggar* } |
| Conscious Lovers | Humphrey |
| Constant Couple | Alderman Smuggler |
| Cymbeline | { Guiderius / Philario } |
| Douglas | Old Norval |
| Earl of Essex | Lieutenant |
| Englishman in Paris | Classic |
| Fashionable Lover | Bridgemore |
| George Barnwell | Truman |
| Hamlet | Horatio |
| Henry IV | { Vernon / Second Carrier } |
| King John | Salisbury |
| Lionel and Clarissa | Jenkins |
| Love for Love | Frapland |
| Love in a Village | Hodge |
| Midas | Sileno |
| Miser | { *James* / *Decoy* } |
| Mourning Bride | Heli |
| Orphan | *Polydore* |
| Othello | Montano |
| Richard III | Catesby |
| Roman Father | { Third Citizen / Soldier } |
| Romeo and Juliet | Tybalt |
| Shipwreck | Jonathan |
| Suspicious Husband | Bellamy |
| Tamerlane | { Axalla / Haly } |
| Tempest | Antonio |
| Theodosius | Lucius |

Venice Preserved . . . . . . . . *Renault*
Way to Keep Him . . . . . . { *William* / Richard
West Indian . . . . . . . . . . Varland

*Farces.*

Catherine and Petruchio . . . { Hortentio / *Grumio*
Damon and Phillida . . . . . . { Mopsus / *Cymon*
Devil to Pay . . . . . . . . . . Cook
Farmer's Return from London . . *Farmer*
Harlequin Skeleton . . . . . . . *Clown*
High Life Below Stairs . . . . . Freeman
Honest Yorkshireman . . . . . { *Sapscull* / Blunder
Love a la Mode . . Sir Theodore Goodchild
Lying Valet . . . . . . . . . . . Cook
Mayor of Garratt . . . . . . . . Roger
Miller of Mansfield . . . . . . . *Miller*
Miss in her Teens . . . . . Captain Loveit
Musical Lady . . . . . . . . . Freeman
Old Maid . . . . . . . . . . Heartly
Upholsterer . . . . . . . . . Belmour

June the American Company was playing in New York, but as there are no casts extant for this period it is impossible to say whether he and the Parker who was at Philadelphia a few months before are identical. I have placed the parts played by Mr. Parker in Maryland and Virginia in Italics. It will be observed that they are not of a character to disprove identity. If Parker left the American Company and rejoined it after playing a season with the opposition, it was the only case of the kind that occurred before the Revolution.

When the American Company closed its first season at the Southwark Theatre, in 1767, Messrs. Matthews and Platt retired, their places being filled by Malone and Roberts. Malone's career has been summed up in the chapter devoted to the New American Company. Roberts remained under Mr. Douglass' management until the old American Company disbanded. A later acquisition was Mr. Darby,

MR. BYERLY'S PARTS.

*Plays.*

Alexander the Great . Perdiccus
Beaux' Stratagem . . Boniface
Beggars' Opera . Nimming Ned
Comus . . . . . First Spirit
Conquest of Canada . . ! Peyton
Conscious Lovers . Cymberton
Cymbeline . . . Caius Lucius
Cymon . . . . . . . Dorilas
Earl of Essex . Sir Walter Raleigh
Englishman in Paris . Marquis
False Delicacy . . . . Sidney

MR. ROBERTS' PARTS.

*Plays.*

Alexander the Great . Eumenes
Beaux' Stratagem . . Hounslow
Conscious Lovers . . . Daniel
Country Lasses . Shacklefigure
Cymbeline . . . . . Cornelius
Englishman in Paris . Daupaine
Fashionable Lover . Le Jeunesse
Hamlet . . . . . { Lucianus / Osric
Henry IV . . . { Francis / Peto / Prince John

Fashionable Lover . Abberville

Hamlet . . . . { Bernardo / Rosencranz

Henry IV . . . . { Worcester / Poins

King John . . . . King Philip

Love for Love . . . . Jeremy

Love in a Village . . Eustace

Merchant of Venice . { Duke / Gobbo

Midas . . . . . . . . . Pan

Mourning Bride . . . Alonzo

Othello . . . . . . . Duke

Recruiting Officer . Capt. Brazen

Roman Father . Second Citizen

Romeo and Juliet . . Montagu

She Stoops to Conquer . Hastings

Shipwreck . . . . . Patterson

Tamerlane . . . . . Stratocles

Tempest . . . . . . . Alonzo

TenderHusband .Capt.Clerimont

West Indian . . . . . Fulmer

Wonder . . . . . Don Lopez

*Farces.*

Catherine and Petruchio. Baptista

Citizen . . . . . . Sir Jasper

Cross Purposes . . . . Consol

Damon and Phillida . . Arcas

Devil to Pay . . . . . Doctor

High Life Below Stairs. Kingston

Hob in the Well . . Old Hob

Honest Yorkshireman . Slango

Lethe . . . . Fine Gentleman

Lying Valet . . . . . Trippet

Mayor of Garratt . . . . Bruin

Miller of Mansfield . . Richard

Old Maid . . . . Mr. Harlow

Register Office . . . . Gulwell

Upholsterer . . . . Quidnunc

who joined it with Parker and Byerly in 1768, and left it with Godwin and Malone after only one season. Darby's parts with the American Company are in Roman letters—with the New American Company in Italics. The summary of his parts

King John . Robert Falconbridge

Merchant of Venice . . Tubal

Miser . . . . . . . . Charles

Othello . . . . . . Messenger

Recruiting Officer Second Recruit

Roman Father . Fourth Citizen

Romeo and Juliet . { Apothecary / Friar John

Tamerlane . . . . . . Mirvan

Tempest . . . . . Sycorax

Venice Preserved . . . Durand

Way to Keep Him . . Thomas

Wonder . . . . . . Valques

*Farces.*

Brave Irishman . . . Marquis

Catherine and Petruchio . Tailor

Citizen . . . . . Quilldrive

Devil to Pay . . Blind Fiddler

Harlequin Collector . . Porter

High Life Below Stairs . . Cloe

Mayor of Garratt . . . Snuffle

Musical Lady . . . . . Rosini

Register Office . . Frenchman

Reprisal . . Capt. Champignon

Witches . . . . . Monsieur

has been reserved for this place to show how unappreciated genius was sometimes able to assert itself even at that early period in the history of the Am-

MR. DARBY'S PARTS.

*Plays.*

Alexander the Great . Aristander

Beggars' Opera . . . *Peachum*

Earl of Essex . . *Southampton*

King John . . . . . Austria

Miser . . . . . . . *Ramillie*

Tamerlane . . . . . Tanais

Way to Keep Him . *Sir Bashful*

*Farces.*

Anatomist . . . . . . *Crispin*

Chaplet . . . . . . *Palemon*

Mock Doctor . . . . *Gregory*

erican stage, while unassuming usefulness, as in the case of Roberts, and modest talent, as in that of Byerly, went plodding on without recognition or reward. With Mr. Darby in such roles as *Sir Bashful Constant* and the *Mock*

*Doctor* there may have been reason for the judicious to grieve over the performances of the New American Company at Annapolis. Darby was, perhaps, the first actor on the American stage who left one company to seek promotion in another.

The remaining names that occur in the casts of the American Company during the last two years of its existence are Johnson, Dermot, Hughes, Blackler and Davis. Of these Mr. Johnson had the greater number of small parts that fell to the rank and file under Mr. Douglass' management. Johnson joined the company at the Southwark Theatre in the season of 1772–3, but remained with it for only a short time. Mr. Dermot also became a member of the company that season, but he went with it to New York for the farewell engagement there. In New York Hughes and Blackler were added to the company. Hughes accompanied Mr. Douglass' forces to Charleston, where Davis is named in the existing bills as playing *Hearty* in the

MR. DERMOT'S PARTS.

*Plays.*
Beaux' Stratagem . . Bagshot
Cato . . . . . . . . . Lucius
Clandestine Marriage . Traverse
Merchant of Venice . . Salarino
Recruiting Officer . Justice Scale

*Farce.*
Cross Purposes . . . . Consol

MR. HUGHES' PARTS.
*Plays.*
Cato . . . . . . . . . Juba
Clandestine Marriage . Canton
Earl of Essex . Sir Walter Raleigh
She Stoops to Conquer . Diggory
West Indian . . . . . Fulmer

*Farces.*
Cross Purposes . . . . Robin
Reprisal . . . . . . . Brush

MR. BLACKLER'S PART.
Comus . . . . . Elder Brother

MR. DAVIS' PART.
Reprisal . . . . . . . Hearty

MR. JOHNSON'S PARTS.

*Plays.*
Beggars' Opera . Jemmy Twitcher
Cymbeline . . . . . Captain
Englishman in Paris . . Roger
Hamlet . . . . . . Francisco
Henry IV . . . . . Bardolph
Othello . . . . . . . Officer
Richard III . . . . . Oxford
Roman Father . Fourth Citizen
Shipwreck . . . . . . Francis
Suspicious Husband . . Simon
Tamerlane . . . . . . Zama
Tempest . . . . . { Gonzalo / Ventoso
West Indian . . . . . Stukely

*Farces.*
Devil to Pay . . . . Coachman
Hob in the Well . . . . Dick
Lethe . . . . . . . Charon
Miss in her Teens . Capt. Loveit
Register Office . . . Williams

" Reprisal." Oddly enough Dunlap ignores Hughes and says the only new name added to the *dramatis personæ* during the last New York engagement was that of Blackler.

Every preparation had been made for a vigorous campaign during the winter of 1774–5; Mr. Hallam, who had gone from Charleston to London, having sent out his cousin, Thomas Wignell, as his own substitute. Wignell, who afterward became an important figure on the American stage, especially in Philadelphia, where he was the first manager of the Chestnut Street Theatre, arrived in New York only a day before the news that Congress had passed a resolution recommending that all public amusements should be suspended reached that city. He was sitting under his hairdresser's hands, Dunlap says, when he learned that all the theatres on the Continent were virtually closed by this recommendation. Wignell hearing the news in the barber's chair was the last incident in the History of the American Theatre before the Revolution.

END OF THE EPOCH.

# INDEX.